Praise for *Billionaires' Row*

"*Billionaires' Row* is a necessary book about how *not* to build a city. Katherine Clarke has the rare ability to make you understand both the personalities and the numbers behind our modern Towers of Babel along 57th Street; the result is a coolly devastating portrait of the game of greed and ego that's permanently scarred the skyline—and the psyche—of New York."

—Thomas Dyja, author of *New York, New York, New York*

"Rich, highly readable . . . *[Billionaires' Row]* colorfully relates the human, financial and political dramas behind the creation of super-luxury apartment edifices."

—*New York Post*

"*Billionaires' Row* takes the reader on an in-depth journey into the machinations that built the Manhattan skyline and the colorful characters whose ego and daring has redefined twenty-first century New York. In her deeply researched account, Katherine Clarke expertly traces several key developers as they—through cajoling, manipulation, and lavish spending—meticulously amass large swaths of Midtown to construct towers that have come to symbolize unprecedented feats of human engineering, as well as the hubris and chutzpah of real estate men. Part investigation, part biography, this book is a study of how wealth and ambition trumps all when it comes to the Big Apple."

—Julie Satow, author of *The Plaza: The Secret Life of America's Most Famous Hotel*

"Some years hence, anthropologists or aliens will look to a half-dozen spindly towers that rise improbably high above the southern edge of New York's Central Park when trying to understand this particular age of hyper-wealth. In the meantime, the rest of us can consult *Billionaires' Row*, Katherine Clarke's thrilling chronicle of those towers and the people who built them."

—*Financial Times*

"Katherine Clarke knows the world of real estate down to the ground—indeed, down to the bedrock! But she carries that knowledge lightly as she describes the swashbuckling egos, the daredevil deals, and the tsunami of wealth that are imposing skyline-shaping changes in one of the world's most iconic cities. *Billionaires' Row* is deeply informative, delightfully entertaining, and addictively readable. I loved it!"

—**Diana B. Henriques,** *New York Times* **bestselling author of**
The Wizard of Lies **and** *A First-Class Catastrophe*

"An immersive crash course in high-end real estate, Kathy Clarke's *Billionaires' Row* turns the latest New York City skyscrapers—known as supertalls—into symbols of the unchecked ambitions, egomania, and greed of both those who build them and those who can afford to live above it all. To rewrite Oscar Wilde, Even up as high as the stars, you're barely out of the gutter."

—**Michael Gross,** *New York Times* **bestselling author of**
740 Park **and** *House of Outrageous Fortune*

"*Billionaires' Row* lifts the curtain on the opaque world of ultra-luxury real estate and New York's new generation of supertall skyscrapers. As entertaining as it is educational, this book offers a captivating portrait of the powerful mix of ego, money and competition that—a century after the Empire State and Chrysler Buildings—continues to transform the city's skyline."

—**Kate Ascher, professor of urban development, Columbia
University, and author of** *The Heights: Anatomy of a Skyscraper*

"A gimlet-eyed look at the mega-skyscrapers that have been rising along New York's Central Park . . . [and] a revealing work of financial reporting in a time of staggering inequality."

—*Kirkus Reviews*

"Kathy Clarke has aced the luxury real estate beat at the *Wall Street Journal* with stories that pry open the lives of the rich and powerful. In *Billionaires' Row,* she has accomplished a far greater feat with a deeply reported, remarkable tale of the financial bubble that remade the New York skyline. She chronicles a race to the sky among ego-rich developers, one that resulted in a street of super-luxury slim towers, dashed dreams, and meager profits. This book is thrilling, incisive, and a lot of fun to read."

—**Eliot Brown,** *Wall Street Journal* **bestselling
coauthor of** *The Cult of We*

Billionaires' Row

Billionaires' Row

TYCOONS, HIGH ROLLERS,
and the EPIC RACE TO BUILD the World's
Most EXCLUSIVE SKYSCRAPERS

Katherine Clarke

CURRENCY
NEW YORK

2024 Crown Currency Trade Paperback Edition

Copyright © 2023 by Katherine Clarke
Map copyright © 2023 by Jeffrey L. Ward, Inc.

Published in the United States by Crown Currency,
an imprint of the Crown Publishing Group, a division of
Penguin Random House LLC, New York.

CROWN is a registered trademark and CROWN CURRENCY
and colophon are trademarks of Penguin Random House LLC.

Originally published in hardcover in the United States
by Crown Currency, an imprint of the Crown Publishing Group,
a division of Penguin Random House LLC, in 2023.

Illustrations by Alan Witschonke copyright © Alan Witschonke.
Used by permission of Alan Witschonke.

Library of Congress Cataloging-in-Publication Data
Names: Clarke, Katherine (Journalist), author.
Title: Billionaires' row / Katherine Clarke.
Description: First edition. | New York: Currency, [2023] |
Includes bibliographical references and index.
Identifiers: LCCN 2022056930 (print) | LCCN 2022056931 (ebook) |
ISBN 9780593240069 (hardcover; alk. paper) |
ISBN 9780593240076 (ebook)
Subjects: LCSH: Real estate development—New York State—New York. |
Manhattan (New York, N.Y.) | Billionaires—New York State—New York.
Classification: LCC HD268.N5 C63 2023 (print) |
LCC HD268.N5 (ebook) | DDC 333.33/8097471—dc23/eng/20230221
LC record available at lccn.loc.gov/2022056930
LC ebook record available at lccn.loc.gov/2022056931

Paperback ISBN 978-0-593-24008-3
Ebook ISBN 978-0-593-24007-6

Printed in the United States of America on acid-free paper

currencybooks.com

2 4 6 8 9 7 5 3 1

Map by Jeffrey L. Ward

To Mum, Dad, & John

Come, let us build ourselves a city, with a tower that reaches to the heavens, so that we may make a name for ourselves.

GENESIS 11:4

Contents

AUTHOR'S NOTE   xi

PROLOGUE: THE PINNACLE   xxvii

PART I: Dreaming of Sky

CHAPTER 1:   Saving Harry Macklowe   3

CHAPTER 2:   The Original Palace Corners   15

CHAPTER 3:   The Rabbi, the Jeweler, and the Developer   33

CHAPTER 4:   The Chess Master   47

CHAPTER 5:   California Dreaming   66

CHAPTER 6:   Hitting the Jackpot   82

CHAPTER 7:   Inventing an Icon   104

CHAPTER 8:   Make Way for the Billionaires   121

CHAPTER 9:   Throwing Shade   138

PART II: Turbulence

CHAPTER 10: "Too Much Money"   159

CHAPTER 11: New Kids on the Block   167

CHAPTER 12: The "Prince"   183

CHAPTER 13: Supply and Demand   188

CHAPTER 14: The Best Building in New York   198

CHAPTER 15: Starting Wars   212

CHAPTER 16: Disdain in Paradise   226

CHAPTER 17: Selling Billionaires' Row   232

PART III: Falling Back to Earth

CHAPTER 18: Shadowy Figures   247

CHAPTER 19: The Music Stops   259

CHAPTER 20: "Gone to Zero"   273

CHAPTER 21: Knives Out   282

CHAPTER 22: Casualties of War   292

CHAPTER 23: Not a Good Look   302

CHAPTER 24: New York on Pause   311

CHAPTER 25: Tower of Hell   319

CHAPTER 26: See You in Court   328

CHAPTER 27: Seeds of Recovery   334

CHAPTER 28: Resentment   341

EPILOGUE: A LASTING LEGACY   345

ACKNOWLEDGMENTS   351

NOTES   353

INDEX   361

Author's Note

To gaze south from New York City's Central Park these days is to look upon a physical manifestation of tens of billions of dollars in global wealth. A series of supertall, ultra-thin condominium towers bear down on the southern end of the park, casting long shadows.

Though these buildings have dramatically reshaped the city's iconic skyline, the average New Yorker will likely never set foot in any of them. No tourist will peer through a telescope from observation decks as they might at the Empire State Building or cut a rug on a revolving dance floor as they might have at 30 Rockefeller Center's Rainbow Room. Unlike the skyscrapers of yesteryear, there are almost no public areas within these towers. This group of "supertalls," which collectively have come to be known as Billionaires' Row, was built with a single constituency in mind: the richest people on earth. They are gilded, gated communities in the sky. To enter these buildings, one must be explicitly invited.

Beginning with the groundbreaking of the residential apartment tower One57 around 2010, the skyscrapers of Billionaires' Row have shot up at a rapid clip, each promising to be taller, thinner, pricier, and more luxurious than the last, transforming what was once a run-down strip filled with schlocky souvenir shops, fur emporia, and diners into the most expensive real estate on earth. The buildings, and the dollars spent in order to gain access to them, have become objects of global fascination, spawning untold numbers of newspaper articles, YouTube videos, and Instagram pictures. A group of young "Outlaw Instagrammers" was even arrested for illegally scaling the superstructure of one of the buildings, 432 Park Avenue, in pursuit of pictures that might go viral. In a world awash with the cheap and disposable, they offer, in addition to their obvious height, a feeling of permanence, a look at something that might outlive us all.

The sudden emergence of these towers, which seemed to transform the Midtown skyline virtually overnight, belied the fact that relatively few major residential skyscrapers had been built in the United States in recent decades. New York had been losing ground to cities like Dubai and Shanghai.

Now, gazing up at these "supertalls," one can't help but fantasize about what goes on within their walls. Are oligarchs in there counting their money? Are supermodels bathing in diamond-filled bathtubs? Are American hedge fund billionaires facing off against Saudi sheikhs for the best views? Are they all up there looking down on us?

While most of us wonder such things, I'm fortunate to be able to ask questions like this for a living. I first began reporting on Billionaires' Row when I started on the real estate beat in 2011. At the time, the press was focused on just one building, the under-construction One57, which they called the Billionaire Building. Backed by Saudi financiers and quickly racking up deals in the tens of millions of dollars with moneyed buyers from all over the world, the building rapidly became an object of international intrigue. In the subsequent years, as more copycat supertalls started to rise along the same corridor, each vying for the same small pool of billionaire purchasers, it became clear that this was a much bigger story. It was a story about the enormous rise in global wealth and the people who work to capture a piece of it for themselves. It was a story about hubris, sophisticated financial engineering, architectural daring, shady money, and one-upmanship. I was hooked.

IN THE COURSE of the reporting for this book, I spoke with a source who invoked the work of Michel Foucault, a French philosopher whose writings about power and social control I had studied only briefly as an undergraduate. In his book *Discipline and Punish: The Birth of the Prison,* first published in 1975, Foucault focused his attention on the panopticon, a type of institutional building, or prison, designed in the eighteenth century by the English philosopher Jeremy Bentham. The concept of the panopticon was interesting to Foucault because its very design acted as a system of control. A single ring-shaped building would be divided into separate cells visible from a watchtower in the center. While the occupants of the cells would be visible to the occupant of the watchtower, shutters on the watchtower ensured that its occupant would never be visible to the occupants of the cells. The design allowed a single security guard to observe all of a prison's inmates without the inmates' being able to tell whether they were being watched. The principle of the panopticon was that power should be always visible but never verifiable.

I thought of the panopticon recently when I made a return visit to 432 Park Avenue. If you have ever walked past the entrance to the dramatic condominium building on East 56th Street hoping to catch a glimpse of one of its well-heeled occupants, you will know how slim is your likelihood of success. That's because the lobby of the tower, designed by the late Uruguayan architect Rafael Viñoly, was conceived specifically to avoid prying eyes.

Obsessed with the idea of privacy, the developers of 432 Park tasked Viñoly with radically reducing the time between exiting a car and disappearing into the sanctuary of the building. To that end, builders installed sliding wooden pocket doors separating the front desk area, which was visible to outsiders, from the elevator banks where residents would momentarily linger as they waited to go upstairs. The pocket doors would quickly conceal the residents. The design had the effect of creating an inner sanctum for the building, capitalism's answer to transcending the temporal realm. As you step behind those doors, you become part of an anointed class. Shielded from onlookers, residents would then board an Hermès-leather-lined elevator cab shooting them as much as 1,396 feet upward to their apartments.

I find the analogy of the panopticon useful in thinking about Billionaires' Row and the architecture of power that it represents. As the real estate entrepreneur Myers Mermel put it to me, these buildings are "class made manifest in glass, steel, and stone," a physical reminder every day of the global social hierarchy.

The story of Billionaires' Row is a story about money: who has it and how they spend it.

These slender towers bring together celebrities, financiers, and, yes, Russian oligarchs and Saudi princes. They offer panoramic views of the city from enormous heights, and amenities—to use the jargon of the real estate industry—that include private clubs and restaurants, pools, juice bars, fitness centers, basketball courts, and golf simulators.

They're also largely empty. A study by the residential brokerage firm Serhant recently found that as of 2020, roughly 44 percent of the new luxury units along Billionaires' Row remained vacant, either unsold or unoccupied. They are homes, but they are also investment vehicles for the global super-rich. Some of the owners have never set foot in their own apartments, viewing them instead as one might a stock or bond or an artwork from a great master—a vessel in which to store wealth.

As a journalist, I come at this subject not to score any particular political point, but with the goal of understanding the story of these towers and what it reveals about the way power and influence work in twenty-first-century New York—and thus the world. To cover these towers and the incredible story behind them, however, necessarily involved unpacking the complicated relationship between these buildings and their developers, and the ordinary people who look up at them. Some lionize the men—and they are all men—behind these towers as visionaries, pioneers, and personifications of the American dream. Others paint them as evil, greedy villains who put profits before people and who've turned lying, cheating, stealing, and satisfying the whims of their own egos into a business model.

In these pages, I will attempt to show that the true stories behind the rise of these towers and the people that built them are far from black-and-white. They are messy and filled with moments of ingenuity, fuzzy math, hubris, triumph, and despair. And beneath the gleaming façades of these skyscrapers is an unseen underbelly of complicated financial engineering, litigation, and sabotage.

One thing I can tell you for sure: The world of ultra-luxury real estate development is not for the faint of heart. It's a blood sport. The risks involved in assembling a well-located site, lining up financiers and overseeing construction at more than a thousand feet—never mind then finding billionaire buyers to fill up the new towers—are almost unimaginable to a person unfamiliar with this world.

Some of the men behind these towers are gifted showmen, others are numbers guys. Some fancy themselves architectural visionaries, while others thrive at the strategic art of negotiation and land assemblage. Some live relatively modest lives outside the professional limelight, while others live as lavishly as the people who buy their condos.

But for all their differences and peccadilloes, all of these men share a few important traits. They are all risk takers and swashbucklers, seemingly immune to the incredible pressures that would crush most of us. Many are proficient litigators, with a tendency to believe that the rules don't apply to them.

That the real estate industry isn't heavily regulated makes it fundamentally different from the worlds of corporate finance or banking. These developers most often head privately held firms, driven by their personalities and free of the constraining influence of public investors or an entourage of corporate flacks. They typically don't do earnings calls or file documents with the SEC. They win and lose fortunes, and they never have to tell you about it.

This world feels like the Wild West. That may be why it attracts its fair share of cowboys.

To some extent, this book is a cautionary tale about timing the market. It shows that the developers who persisted with their projects through the global financial crisis of 2008 reaped the rewards when they were able to release their product to the world amid the recovery, while those who waited until it was safe to get back in the water often missed the wave.

My hope is that readers will also gain insight into the forces that have shaped how architects and designers have imagined a new built environment for the twenty-first century. Ultimately, the phenomenon of Billionaires' Row may prove reflective of a unique moment in time, one in which the forces of land scarcity and global wealth creation collided to create the perfect storm for developers. It is unlikely to be repeated anytime soon.

A word on methodology: For the purposes of this book, I've chosen to define the Billionaires' Row corridor as a series of specific supertall towers rather than by any strict geographic parameters. Roughly speaking, it stretches along the southern edge of Central Park from about 56th to 59th streets, spanning from about Eighth Avenue to Park Avenue, past the opulent Plaza hotel and the horse-drawn carriages that carry tourists around Central Park. It sits between the bustling Midtown business district that includes Times Square and the more historically gilded East and West Side corridors of Central Park. This story focuses predominantly on the five buildings that I believe best illustrate the themes of the Billionaires' Row story—from east to west, 432 Park Avenue, 111 West 57th Street, One57 at 157 West 57th Street, Central Park Tower at 217 West 57th Street, and 220 Central Park South.

This portrait of the rise of Billionaires' Row draws on more than a hundred interviews with people who have shared with me their experiences in building, financing, designing, and living in these towers. Some spoke on the condition that I would not reveal their identity as sources, with some citing nondisclosure agreements, ongoing litigation, or professional relationships they didn't wish to jeopardize. Where their recollections of events varied, I have done my best to present the version of events around which there is the most consensus and to note the dissenting views.

Most of the interviews for this book were conducted in 2021 and 2022, though I also drew on my experience in writing about these projects, and visiting all of them in various stages of construction over my years as a reporter. I've been fortunate enough through the course of my career, first at *The Real Deal,* then at the New York *Daily News,* and finally at *The Wall Street Journal,* to have had access to most of these characters through various interviews over the years. Many of my sources sat down with me multiple times in the course of my reporting for this book, allowing me hours of their time. The contents of the book have been subjected to fact-checking, and all the people who played a material role in the story have been given an opportunity to comment on or clarify the revelations herein.

Part of my motivation for writing this book was that as a reporter, I can't help but observe that the colorful characters who've made the New York real estate world so dynamic are increasingly few and far between, much like other rough-and-tumble elements of the city, as more publicly traded behemoths and institutional investors enter the fray. In some ways, this book memorializes that dying breed of New York real estate kingpins who took big swings and risked losing it all.

The Tycoons

Gary Barnett (né Gershon Swiatycki) A numbers whiz and the king of the Manhattan property assemblage game, Barnett, now in his midsixties, was a pioneer on Billionaires' Row, moving ahead with the development of his tower One57 during the depths of the global financial crisis of 2008. He then gambled that he could pull off the same feat twice with the construction of his second Billionaires' Row building, Central Park Tower. Some consider his two projects as bookends to the real estate cycle, the first making the market and the second proving the market had faltered. More turtleneck than Tom Ford, and an observant Othodox Jew, he lives modestly with his family in Monsey, New York.

Harry Macklowe One of New York real estate's best known personalities, Harry Macklowe has ridden the roller coaster of the Manhattan market for decades. Now in his mideighties, he's known to play close to the edge when it comes to leverage, and has won and lost his property empire more than once. He is obsessed with the architectural and artistic legacy of his own Billionaires' Row tower, 432 Park Avenue, and what it says about him as a tastemaker. With the looks of an aging Robert De Niro, he is a prominent art collector and is known to live a life almost as flashy as the billionaires for whom he builds. He's likely to be spotted in designer scarves and velvet loafers.

Steve Roth The bare-knuckle fighter of the bunch, Steve Roth, now in his early eighties, is better known as an office mega-landlord than as a builder of luxury condominiums. For him, building and designing his Billionaires' Row tower at 220 Central Park South was more a personal passion project than a typical investment. The chief executive of a publicly traded company, he projects the image of a buttoned-up Wall Street type, but, unlike the heads of many public companies, he rarely hesitates to speak his mind.

Michael Stern The new kid on the block. Seeming to emerge from nowhere as the Billionaires' Row boom got underway, the stubby young upstart, now in his early forties, moved quickly from small projects to massive ones. However, no one seemed to know much about his backstory or how he pulled it off. His building, 111 West 57th Street, quickly became embroiled in litigation and besieged by infighting.

The Towers

One57 The first tower to debut on Billionaires' Row, One57 set a new standard for condominium pricing across the city. Since its construction began in 2010, people have called it "the Billionaire building," and sure enough, major buyers included Michael Dell and Bill Ackman. The 1,004-foot-tall property, developed by Gary Barnett, is known for its divisive design by the French architect Christian de Portzamparc, which comprises a blueish façade made to look like a waterfall.

432 Park Visible even from Long Island, the 1,396-foot, Rafael Viñoly–designed 432 Park has a strikingly minimalist, gridlike design. Starting construction in 2011 and spearheaded by Harry Macklowe, the property battled successfully with One57 for the earliest Billionaires' Row buyers, though its reputation was later sullied by allegations of construction defects.

220 Central Park South

A classic limestone tower by architect Robert A. M. Stern, Steve Roth's 220 Central Park South rises to just 952 feet. Starting construction in 2013, the tower quickly logged some of Billionaires' Row's biggest-ticket deals, including the sale of a nearly $240 million apartment to billionaire hedge funder Ken Griffin.

111 West 57th Street

Designed by SHoP Architects to weave through a historic Steinway piano showroom, 111 West 57th Street stands 1,428 feet tall, with an ornamented façade of terra-cotta and brass filigree and a featherlike tapering spire. Starting construction in 2015, it is the brainchild of Michael Stern and his partners.

Central Park Tower

Central Park Tower, designed by Adrian Smith + Gordon Gill Architecture, is the tallest primarily residential building in the world at 1,550 feet. Starting construction in 2014, the glassy tower represented Gary Barnett's second crack at the Billionaires' Row apple.

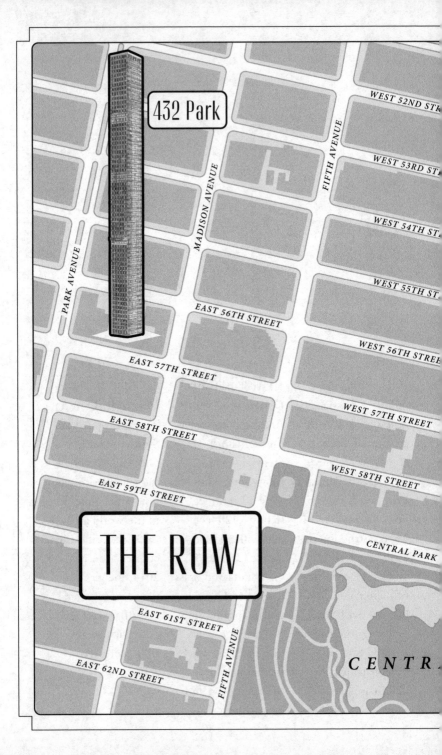

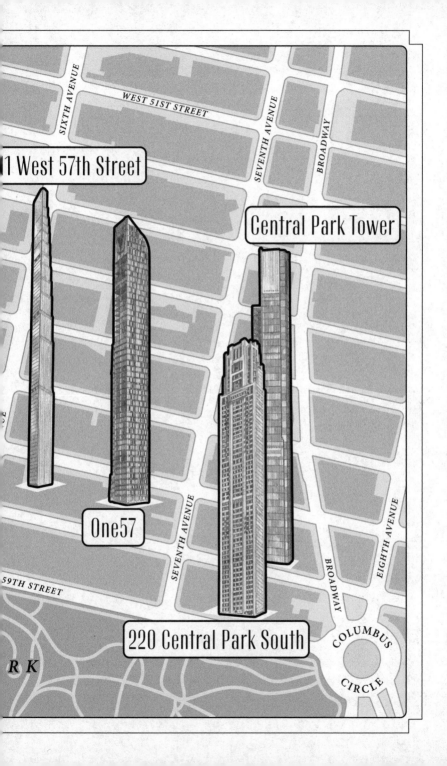

Billionaires' Row

The Pinnacle

New York City, Circa 1945

Harry Macklowe and his older brother, Lloyd, piled into the backseat of their father's Buick. The boys could hardly contain their excitement at the adventure that awaited them.

Their father, Mack, was taking them to see one of the world's great man-made wonders. For children growing up in the suburb of New Rochelle in Westchester County, twenty miles north of Manhattan, it was a rite of passage to visit the observation deck atop the Empire State Building, which, completed about fourteen years earlier in the midst of the Great Depression, would soon come to symbolize the city's postwar economic boom.

The journey took more than an hour. As the trio left Westchester and passed through the Bronx and into Manhattan, Macklowe, who was about eight years old, and his eleven-year-old brother peered out the windows as the streets seemed to get ever more crowded block by block.

The city buzzed with excitement. The hardships and angst of World War II were almost over and the streets were typically packed, with men in wool coats and fedoras weaving a path through the traffic and women in silk stockings and shoulder pads walking arm in arm. Street peddlers sold fish, bread, and fresh ears of corn, while classic coupes and delivery trucks jostled for right of way.

Mack was no stranger to these streets. Born in Brooklyn, he was one of nine children born to a pair of Polish émigrés who moved to the United States in the late 1800s speaking only Yiddish. Like many New Yorkers, he and his wife had migrated to the commuter suburbs in the 1930s toward the end of the Great Depression. They bought a Tudor-style home on a quiet, leafy street named Alpine Road. Mack made a good living running a company that bought fabric from a mill, then designed and finished it before reselling it to manufacturers of clothing and housecoats. Trips with the children to the city took place with some regularity. Harry would later recall attending the original productions of shows like *Oklahoma!*, which debuted in 1943 at the St. James Theater, and *South Pacific*, which debuted in 1949 at the Majestic. He loved performers like Ezio Pinza, Mary Martin, and Ethel Merman.

To little Harry Macklowe, who was outfitted for the trip to the Empire State Building in shorts, a newsboy cap, and a cowhide jacket, the city seemed enormous, but even its tallest buildings looked minuscule compared to the behemoth office tower. A veritable city within a city and towering roughly 1,250 feet, the building had already been immortalized by the movie *King Kong,* which had opened to rave reviews at Radio City Music Hall a decade earlier.

As they approached the building from Fifth Avenue, Harry gazed up, overwhelmed by the building's enormous height. The Macklowes boarded one of the building's sleek high-speed elevators to the observation deck nestled beneath the building's distinctive mast. The elevators were the fastest in the world at that time, moving at 800 feet per minute up and down seven miles of elevator shafts. They were so fast, in fact, that local regulations had to be amended to allow for them to travel at such speed. For the most part, they shuttled visitors up and down without incident. However, that same year, when a B-25 Mitchell bomber crashed into the building's 79th floor and lodged in one of the elevator shafts, the elevator went into free fall. Thankfully, the sole occupant, the twenty-year-old female operator, survived unscathed.

From the vantage point of the observation deck, the vast panorama of the city unfolded beneath the Macklowes. They could see Central Park, the Bronx, and all the way to Connecticut.

The vista left an indelible impression on the young Harry Macklowe.

THE CONSTRUCTION OF the Empire State Building that began about fifteen years earlier had marked the pinnacle of a skyscraper boom that had permanently changed the New York skyline. Exemplified by the construction of landmarks both uptown and downtown, most notably the Chrysler building at 42nd Street and Lexington Avenue, 40 Wall Street in the Financial District, and of course the Empire State Building, the boom had taken the form of a veritable race to the sky as wealthy titans of industry vied to build a succession of towers, each taller than the last. The race was set against a backdrop of the postwar monetary and cultural excesses of the Roaring Twenties, a period of great economic expansion made possible by advancements in technology and one that gave rise to a stock market frenzy.

That battle for the skies pitted the architect William Van Alen against his former business partner turned archrival, H. Craig Severance, to build the world's tallest building. Van Alen was responsible for the Chrysler building, that Art Deco tower with its angular metal cladding and ornate gargoyles, while Severance spearheaded the design of the Bank of Manhattan Trust Building on Wall Street, now owned by the Trump Organization. Severance famously thought he had won out over Van Alen after making plans to enhance the height of his tower to 927 feet at the last minute. That illusion was shattered, however, when Van Alen unveiled a surprise 185-foot spire for the top of his tower, which he had secretly built inside the superstructure to be hoisted into place later, bringing his building's final height to 1,046 feet. Even after the two buildings were completed, the men continued to argue over whose was taller. Ultimately, it didn't matter. A year later in 1931, the Empire State Building bested both.

Little did a young Harry Macklowe know, as he stood on the observation deck that day, that he too would one day be swept up in a race to the sky, one that would make an equally significant impact on the New York skyline. His, however, would be a race defined less by the bravado of American industrialists and more by an influx of wealth from around the world.

Years later, in his eighties, Macklowe could still recall that day in vivid detail.

"The one disappointment in my life," he told me, "is that my parents are not alive to see that their son built a building that is as tall as the Empire State Building."

PART I

Dreaming of Sky

CHAPTER 1

Saving Harry Macklowe

"Maybe we should take a walk?"

It was 2008, the depths of the global financial crisis, and Harry Macklowe had been stuck for hours at the Lower Manhattan offices of his law firm when his broker, a real estate power player named Darcy Stacom, suggested the septuagenarian might want to step outside and clear his head.

As Macklowe and Stacom headed for the doors, a team of lawyers and brokers stayed behind as they continued to hammer out the final terms of a deal Macklowe desperately didn't want to make: the sale of the iconic General Motors Building on New York's Fifth Avenue.

The General Motors Building, a gleaming marble-clad tower anchoring the southeast corner of Central Park, was the crown jewel of Macklowe's real estate portfolio, which at one point included at least ten trophy office buildings in and around Midtown. Built in the 1960s by the architects Edward Durell Stone & Associates with Emery Roth & Sons, the building was a defining example of the International Style, characterized by clean rectilinear forms, and it appealed to Macklowe's taste for what he deemed "architectural purity." The firm he founded, Macklowe Properties, had beaten out at least a dozen other developers to buy it in 2003 for a record-breaking $1.4 billion, the most ever paid for a skyscraper in the United States, putting down a nonrefundable $50 million deposit in a highly leveraged deal. He had then taken great pleasure in restoring its tasteful, stripped-down aesthetic by removing the big gold letters on its marble exterior that spelled out T-R-U-M-P, one of the former owners.

Initially, the real estate community had scoffed at the high price Macklowe paid for the tower, but he had proved them wrong when he unveiled a new glass cube at its base that would serve as the striking entrance for Apple's latest New York retail store, which would attract around fifty thousand visitors per week in its first year. It was a feat of ingenuity that would double the value of the building but, more than that, would mark Macklowe's entry into the New York real estate establishment. Each time he told the tale of the cube, Macklowe, a gifted raconteur, played an increasingly outsized role in its creation, alongside Apple founder Steve Jobs.

The coup at the GM Building had stroked Macklowe's ego as an architect, visionary, and taste maker. A slight man with a passing resemblance to Robert De Niro, Macklowe was used to living the high life, racing yachts in regattas off the coast of Sardinia and rubbing shoulders with the city's elite in the Hamptons in his designer loafers and polka-dot scarves.

Following the unveiling of the Apple cube, he had made a celebratory splurge, paying $60 million for seven apartments at the famed Plaza hotel across the street from the GM tower with an eye toward combining them into one sprawling private residence where he could wake up each morning and admire his handiwork. The modernist architect Charles Gwathmey, known for designing homes for celebrities like David Geffen and Steven Spielberg, was tapped to design it. It would ultimately look more like an art gallery than a home.

It was when he was riding high on his success at the GM Building, however, that he made another deal that would land him in the dire financial straits he now found himself in.

In 2007, the developer had completed a record-breaking, highly leveraged $7.25 billion transaction to buy eight trophy office buildings from the private equity giant Blackstone. It made the GM Building price tag look like chump change. The deal, completed in just ten days at the height of what now appeared to have been a dizzyingly overheated pre-financial-crisis market, had dazzled the industry and cemented his reputation for having nerves of steel. Though some branded the deal as reckless, others saw it as the move of a visionary who, as in the case of the Apple cube, recognized opportunity where others did not. With the single deal, Macklowe had more than doubled the size of his real estate portfolio.

However, as the subprime mortgage crisis spilled over into the commercial real estate world, Macklowe struggled to lock down a lender willing to refinance a short-term, high-interest, multibillion-dollar bridge loan he had secured from his lenders, Fortress Investment Group and Deutsche Bank, to buy the Blackstone portfolio. And, to make matters worse, he had pledged the General Motors Building, among other properties, as collateral for more than $7 billion in debt used for the deal. Suddenly, Macklowe was being crushed by the weight of his debt and had no choice but to sell the GM Building to get out from under it. His real estate empire was being torn apart, and with it his relationship with his wife, Linda, and his only son, Billy, whom he had appointed president of Macklowe Properties. Both resented the financial missteps that had led to this moment.

With his fortunes turned, along with those of most of the finance and real estate industries, an ashen-faced Macklowe had been forced to sit in a conference room with Linda and Billy as advisers shuttled back and forth between them and the bidders for the building. His son later described him as looking like "a deer in the headlights."

Agreeing to clear his head, Macklowe strode outside with Stacom into a warm May evening, the kind that gets New Yorkers out on the street in droves after a brutally long winter. It was late, but

tourists were strolling around Battery Park in search of a view of the
Statue of Liberty, and commuters, some tipsy from after-work
drinks on nearby Stone Street, were headed to their subway stops
and ferries. He and Stacom, a tall blonde with a notoriously sharp
tongue, strolled southward until Macklowe paused outside the
Staten Island Ferry Terminal, looking up at the sleek, simple glass-
walled building on the southern tip of the island of Manhattan.

Eager to change the subject from the matter at hand, Macklowe
launched into an impromptu lecture on the building's architecture.
It was typical of Macklowe, who was always more interested in the
romance of art and architecture than in the cold realities of the
market. Stacom stopped him in his tracks. Enough was enough, she
told him. By clinging to the General Motors Building, he was de-
stroying his family and his reputation. It was time for him to stop,
accept the loss, and rebuild.

Macklowe looked at the broker, his eyes moist with tears. "Is it
really that bad?" he asked her.

"Harry," she said, "it's worse."

THE BOY FROM New Rochelle had hardly been an overnight success. Macklowe had clawed his way into the real estate ranks over
the course of decades.

He started as a college dropout. Confident and in a hurry to
make his mark in the world of business, he had attended just one
semester of college in Alabama in the mid-1950s. He had wanted
to go to Yale but hadn't been accepted there—or to any of the
other "really good schools" he had applied to on the East Coast, he
said. So he followed a school pal to Alabama. Just a few months
later, he headed back to the city, chalking up his brief moment in
the South as a life experience. "It was an entirely different culture.
It wasn't something that satisfied me, and I thought that I could do
much better," Macklowe said later. He did admit that there was one
upside: It was in the South that he had discovered Dr Pepper.

Back in New York, he took a job as a trainee in a Madison Avenue advertising firm called Kudner, making $35 a week. It was a big firm, and Macklowe was the lowest on the totem pole. As a messenger traversing the city each day from the advertising agency headquarters at 575 Madison Avenue, he frequently whizzed past the art galleries that lined 56th and 57th streets. There were the galleries of Sidney Janis, Pierre Matisse, and others, and they provided as comprehensive a view of twentieth-century art as could be found almost anywhere in the world.

Harry first met his future wife, Linda, a diminutive brunette, shortly after, at a summer party on Long Island. Several days later, they ran into each other again in the lobby of a publishing company office, where she was working as a receptionist and he in advertising sales. "Didn't I meet you the other night?" he asked, peering down the front of her sweater. The pair married shortly thereafter in 1959 at a synagogue in New Rochelle, hosting a wider celebration later with some 150 friends and family at the Savoy-Plaza Hotel on Central Park. He was just twenty-one years old. She was twenty. Neither had much money. Linda continued to work until the couple's older child, their daughter, Elizabeth, came along in 1960, and then, eight years later, their son, Billy.

Even then, Macklowe was never short on vision and ideas. His mother, Charlotte, was something of an artist, painting in pastels and watercolor, and Macklowe said he inherited her interest in art and design. In high school, he had a penchant for mechanical drawing. Once he got into advertising, he became interested in typefaces, reproduction, and illustration. He said he bought his first piece of art at age twenty-one, a graphic by the Spanish artist Joan Miró that depicted a frog. It was called *Denizens of the Deep*. He couldn't afford to buy the piece outright—it was priced at $125— so the gallery owner allowed him to pay it off over several months.

Trying to work his way up the corporate ladder in advertising, Macklowe began to feel stymied. He was too young and inexperienced to make it into the most important meetings, but he was too impatient to wait years for a seat at the table. Reckoning that he needed a career in which he could be the architect of his own destiny, he turned to real estate.

At the suggestion of a friend, he interviewed at a handful of commercial real estate brokerage firms, including the real estate firm of Julien Studley, which specialized in advocating for tenants in lease negotiations. He would later say that he received offers from all the companies but opted to go with Studley because it offered a higher share of commissions—around 50 percent—in lieu of salary and therefore had a much higher ceiling in terms of potential earnings.

It took Macklowe a year before he started routinely doing deals, but he seemed blessed with an innate confidence that belied his lack of experience. He initially leaned on his ties to the advertising sector to lease office spaces to agencies and photographers. He checked *The New York Times* each morning for which agency, whether it was McCann Erickson or Benton & Bowles or someone else, had scored the biggest contracts that week, using it as a cheat sheet for which companies might be looking to expand their footprint.

As Macklowe's book of business grew, he struck out on his own a few years later, starting a competing brokerage with his mentor, the realtor Mel Wolf. Soon he was rolling the profits into his own real estate investments. With limited capital, he started small, upgrading loft buildings and brownstones, but with each year, he set his sights higher. It was only a matter of time before he began building rental housing, hotels, and for-sale apartments. By the 1980s, just a couple of decades after returning from Alabama, he was one of the most active builders in Manhattan.

In time, the cash flowing from Harry's real estate portfolio began to afford him and Linda a more luxurious lifestyle. The couple invested significantly in art—with no need to pay for their purchases in installments—and spent weekends frequenting galleries and meeting with artists and collectors. Unlike many of their contemporaries, they eschewed stocks, bonds, and other investments in favor of accumulating a collection of internationally renowned modern and contemporary artworks.

Linda had been interested in art since childhood. She went to Music & Art, the specialized high school in Harlem that's now part of the LaGuardia High School of Music & Arts, and had frequented MoMA and all the city's museums as a teenager. After the couple's first child, Elizabeth, was born, Linda went to Hunter College and the New School to continue her study of painting, she said. In the 1970s, she worked with the city on the conception of a sculpture garden at One Dag Hammarskjold Plaza, just north of the United Nations on the south side of 47th Street between First and Second avenues, where Harry owned an office building. Later in the marriage, she worked for years as a curator at Wave Hill, a cultural center in the Bronx, and would personally curate the art for the lobbies and public spaces at Harry's buildings.

"Harry built buildings, I built the art collection," she said.

Over time, Macklowe acquired an image as a gambler and a showman—and someone unafraid of flouting the rules. His early reputation was marred—or made, depending how you look at it—by a stunt he pulled in 1985 in which he ordered the late-night demolition, without a permit, of four buildings in Times Square. The dead-of-night move came on the eve of an order from the city, scheduled to take effect just hours later, that would ban the demolition of single-room-occupancy properties (SROs), affordable hotels for New Yorkers who might otherwise be homeless. Macklowe was never criminally indicted for the illegal demolition, because the state was unable to establish criminal intent, but he agreed to pay $2 million to settle a civil suit brought against him by the city. According to Macklowe, the city repaid him after the New York Court of Appeals held that the ban on SRO demolitions was constitutionally invalid. Nevertheless, to his chagrin, the stench of the incident followed him for years afterward, sullying his credibility.

By the 1980s, Macklowe's most prestigious projects included

Metropolitan Tower, a sixty-eight-story condominium just east of Carnegie Hall, completed in 1987, and the Hotel Macklowe, the fifty-two-story hotel built on the former site of the SROs. Macklowe envisioned Metropolitan Tower, a striking triangular tower wrapped in black glass, as his first major foray into constructing architecturally significant buildings, but it never quite got the recognition he expected. Some likened the dark and imposing edifice to Darth Vader, the *Star Wars* villain. "I never got the compliments for it," he later moaned in *The New York Times.* "I thought it was outstanding."

To those around him, Macklowe's philosophy as a developer was clear. He believed in being wedded to a singular vision for a project and had a complete commitment to his own instincts. It was about finding a path to creating value in a building, then having the determination and capacity to stay with it despite outside forces. That was how wealth was made, he said.

He would listen to advice from attorneys and advisers but often ignore it. He believed the big decisions had to be made by himself and himself alone. There were no bad deals, only good deals that could go bad because of timing or forces beyond his control.

As a former broker, he excelled at the marketing side of the business more than the numbers side. He was charming and had a gift for selling lenders and prospective partners on a lofty vision. He always played a little too close to the edge. He would eventually lose the Macklowe hotel and at least two other properties in the real estate bust of the early 1990s, when the United States went through an eight-month recession.

Indeed, there was perhaps no figure who personified the highs and lows of the rough-and-tumble Manhattan real estate market quite like Harry Macklowe—except maybe Donald Trump. The tumultuous career of Harry Macklowe, once described by a *New York Times* reporter as real estate's answer to Icarus, had the markers of a classic Greek tragedy.

His son, Billy, joined the company in 1993, and in time the younger Macklowe helped transform his father's company from a

simple collection of assets into a more serious, disciplined operation, instituting procedures and best practices, regular meetings and
reporting. While Billy shared his father's features, albeit with more
piercing blue eyes, he was Harry's opposite in more ways than not.
While Harry was always considered a risk taker, Billy was more
conservative and encouraged his father to share equity risk—that is,
to bring in outside investors—and keep debt to more moderate
levels. "I was always trying to protect us," Billy said later.

Harry hadn't heeded those calls when it mattered most.

In early 2007, Macklowe had been on top of the world. The
deal for the Blackstone portfolio and the General Motors Building
had marked his comeback. Now, in just twelve months, he had lost
almost everything, yet again.

AS THE PAIR gazed out over New York harbor from Battery Park,
Macklowe realized Stacom was right. It was time to rebuild.

As the night crept into the early morning, around two o'clock,
the Macklowes signed the contract. The General Motors Building
would be sold, along with three other Manhattan skyscrapers, to
Boston Properties, a real estate giant headed by the New York *Daily
News* publisher, Mort Zuckerman. "He'll live to fight another day,"
Jonathan Mechanic, Harry Macklowe's attorney, told *The Wall
Street Journal* that morning.

But the stress of the collapse put pressure on Macklowe's relationship with Billy, who blamed him for the financial miscalcula-
tions that had forced them to sell their most prized asset and had left
him putting out the fires of what had amounted to a financial in-
ferno. As the assembled parties gathered in the lobby of the lawyers'
office building to bid farewell late that evening, Billy refused a hug
from his father, he said. This was not a celebration.

In fact, Billy would soon move to wrest the reins of the company from his father's grasp, having negotiated directly with their
lenders and partners to help get the family out of a very tight spot.

The consensus was that Macklowe had overpaid for the Black-stone buildings, pushing ahead despite the obviously high degree of risk. The $7.25 billion price he paid was based on the expectation that Macklowe could attract new tenants at significantly higher rents, but in this changed economic environment, that had seemed unlikely to would-be lenders. While his vision for adding value to the buildings may have been sound when he purchased the portfolio, the turn in the capital markets had made it a pipe dream.

His wife, Linda, was furious, and their relationship too had turned openly hostile. In the 1990s, Harry had had to turn over some of his business properties to his lenders because of an investment backed by a personal guarantee, and, as Linda later asserted in court proceedings, he had sworn to her that he would never again personally guarantee a loan. But in 2007, when he personally guaranteed the financing for the Blackstone portfolio, he had broken that promise. Now they were all paying the price. (Harry claimed he made no such promise.)

"He never told her about the personal guarantee," Billy said later of the Blackstone buildings. "She found out when she read an article in *The Wall Street Journal*."

On May 27, 2008, just days after the announcement on the sale of the GM Building, Billy, then forty, told the *Journal* that he would take the helm of the Macklowe family enterprise from there on in, and Harry was stepping down as chairman. "There's a different way of business going forward," he told the paper.

Behind the scenes, he said the move was spurred at least in part by the fact that his father, who had once been a golden boy with the banks following his early success with the GM Building, had become unpopular among lenders. "After all that transpired, we were advised that Harry wasn't financeable," he said. "Once the [Blackstone] deal blew up, Harry's halo was gone and nobody wanted to touch him."

Billy, once a keen mountaineer, would later describe his father as a "peak bagger." In mountaineering speak, that's someone who wants to get to the top of the mountain—in Harry's case, buying the building—but never worries about how they'll get back down. "They think summiting is the end of the climb when it's really the halfway mark," he said.

THOUGH THE PAST year had been shambolic, Harry Macklowe still had one ace up his sleeve.

A few years prior, he had purchased the famed Drake Hotel on 57th Street.

The city's most renowned brokers agreed that the Drake was one of the best development sites in New York. Its location on Park Avenue and 56th Street, one block over from the Four Seasons Hotel, was unparalleled in cachet. With the right assemblage of properties, its developer would be able to build a supertall tower unlike any ever built in the city, without any additional city approvals. Fueling Macklowe's ambitions was the fact that he knew the block better than almost anyone else. These were the same buildings that housed the galleries he had biked past as a messenger.

The aging Drake had opened in the golden age of the 1920s. By the 1960s, it was known largely for being home to Shepheards, a disco hotspot where young people could be spotted doing the latest dance craze, whether it was the Jerk, the Monkey, or the Watusi. Revelers stood in line, even in freezing temperatures, to get into the club, Egyptian-themed with two large gold sphinxes flanking the entrance.

The hotel itself had been a draw, including as a New York base for a host of A-list rock stars, including Jimi Hendrix and members of Led Zeppelin and the Who. Hendrix recorded a string of thirty-six demos there.

The hotel's arguably most infamous incident occurred in 1973 when Richard Cole, the road manager for Led Zeppelin, staying at the Drake for the band's Madison Square Garden gig, discovered that nearly $200,000 was missing from the band's safety deposit box at the hotel. Police soon descended on the luxury hotel, questioning employees, band members, and groupies; Cole voluntarily took a lie detector test, which he passed. There were no indications that the box had been physically broken into, and the cops speculated that perhaps someone had stolen Cole's key and then later returned it without him noticing. The mystery was never solved.

By 2006, when Macklowe bought the hotel for $418 million, the Drake was well past its heyday—and no longer associated with a rock star or celebrity clientele—but was still operational and in fine condition, a reliable spot for tourists and business travelers in search of affordable nightly rates in Midtown.

With the hotel in hand, Macklowe set his sights on the neighbors, buying up a handful of the adjacent townhouses to maximize the potential of the site and carve out a dramatic wall of retail at the base of the tower. He planned to build an architecturally daring new condominium tower that would serve as his legacy, a permanent mark on the Manhattan skyline. He dreamed of creating a structure taller than the Empire State Building.

If Macklowe's troubles had become a symbol of the sting that overextended investors had experienced as the market turned from boom to bust, the Drake project was a shot at redemption.

In 2007, prior to the collapse of the Blackstone deal, the project had been moving full steam ahead. Macklowe had obtained a letter of intent from the department store Nordstrom to enter into negotiations to acquire roughly 250,000 square feet of space at the base of the new Drake site skyscraper, which would provide much-needed funds for the tower's construction. While the letter of intent was in no way binding, it represented a vote of confidence in the project that he could tout around town.

Upon his return from meeting with Nordstrom in Seattle, Macklowe had been pleased to get an email from his banker at Deutsche Bank, Jon Vaccaro. "Congrats!" Vaccaro wrote. "Good momentum."

Now, just a year later, with his standing in the industry on uneven footing, Macklowe just needed to stall his antsy creditors long enough to find the money to actually build the tower.

CHAPTER 2

The Original Palace Corners

The origins of the 57th Street corridor as a mecca for the ultra-wealthy date to the 1860s, when Mary Mason Jones, a great-aunt of the famed high society writer Edith Wharton and the widow of onetime Chemical Bank president Isaac Jones, built Marble Row, a series of houses between 57th and 58th streets on Fifth Avenue, on land she had inherited from her father.

A grande dame of high society, Jones was the inspiration for Mrs. Manson Mingott, the imposing matriarch in Wharton's 1920 novel *The Age of Innocence,* and Marble Row the inspiration for Mingott's gilded home.

Jones's move to the area raised eyebrows among New York's moneyed class. Despite the allure of nearby Central Park, opened in 1858, 57th Street was still considered a no-man's-land—too far uptown to be fashionable and still surrounded by farmland—in contrast with the tony enclaves around Washington Square and 34th Street.

However, Jones knew how to make a statement. Designed in the style of a French château, the homes she commissioned broke with tradition in their use of glistening white marble on the exterior as opposed to the usual brown sandstone of the city's row houses. She lived in one and rented the others to wealthy friends.

"It was her habit," Wharton wrote of Mingott, "to sit in a window of her sitting-room on the ground floor, as if watching calmly for life and fashion to flow northward to her solitary doors. She seemed in no hurry to have them come, for her patience was equalled by her confidence. She was sure that presently the hoardings, the quarries, the one-story saloons, the wooden green-houses in ragged gardens, and the rocks from which goats surveyed the scene, would vanish before the advance of residences as stately as her own—perhaps (for she was an impartial woman) even statelier."

Society eventually did, as Jones predicted, come to her. Within a decade, the surrounding streets would draw some of New York's wealthiest families, such as the Vanderbilts and the Whitneys. In the early 1880s, Cornelius Vanderbilt II began building what would eventually, after several extensions, be considered the largest private home ever built in the United States. The red brick and limestone palace on the corner of 57th Street and Fifth Avenue was modeled after the Château de Blois in France, with turrets and dormers, arched windows, and ornate chimneys. It reportedly had about 130 rooms, including a 65-by-50-foot ballroom with a ceiling frescoe that took the French artist Édouard Toudouze almost a year to paint, and a grand porte cochere designed to welcome the carriages of the social elite. By the end of the 1800s, *The New York Times* had dubbed the intersection of 57th and Fifth "the palace corners."

However, the intersection's status as the new nexus of New York's residential elite was not to last. Starting around the turn of the twentieth century, the area just south of Central Park began to morph from residential to commercial. This trend was hastened with the arrival of Carnegie Hall, the landmark concert hall built around 1890 for the American industrialist Andrew Carnegie at the corner of 57th Street and Seventh Avenue. It was followed in 1907 by the grand opening of the Plaza. The iconic hotel's inaugural guest was the millionaire Alfred Gwynne Vanderbilt, cementing its status as the most fashionable lodging in town. The expansion of the city's elevated railway up Central Park West around the turn of the century only quickened the area's transformation. By the 1930s, 57th Street, then the only two-way street north of 14th, was filled with art galleries, designers, and musical showrooms. A *New York Times* reporter writing in 1938 compared the thoroughfare to the Rue de la Paix, the famed shopping street in Paris.

With the neighborhood no longer a bucolic residential oasis amid the din of Midtown traffic, some of New York's most well-heeled residents decided it was time to migrate still farther north, onto some of the quieter blocks surrounding the park. The east and west side corridors of Central Park soon became known for their gracious cooperative buildings. On the west side of the park emerged a collection of storied cooperatives known for drawing the artists and wealthy bohemians of the day, such as the renowned Dakota building, which dates to the 1880s and is perhaps best known today as the location of John Lennon's murder in 1980.

On the east side, a stodgier set of buildings emerged, including 740 Park Avenue, often recognized as New York City's most illustrious cooperative, built by James T. Lee, Jacqueline Bouvier Kennedy's grandfather, around 1930.

The further uptown migration of the wealthy paved the way for the slow decline of the 57th Street corridor into the schlocky patchwork that it became by the late twentieth century.

JONATHAN MILLER HAD seen thousands of apartments during his burgeoning career as a New York City property appraiser, including everything from basement studios with feces-stained walls to sprawling Versailles-like Gilded Age townhomes. But he had never seen anything quite like this.

In the early 1990s, he got the call to appraise a Fifth Avenue penthouse owned by Adnan Khashoggi, the high-flying Saudi Arabian arms dealer known for his dramatic displays of wealth and playboy reputation. The Middle Eastern financier had recently been acquitted of federal charges in connection with what prosecutors alleged was his role in helping the former Filipino president Ferdinand Marcos and his wife, Imelda, hide money and property they had stolen when they fled their country several years earlier. Now Khashoggi was looking to sell his enormous 18,000-square-foot apartment in Olympic Tower, a glass skyscraper at the corner of West 52nd Street that had been developed by a partnership that included the Greek shipping magnate Aristotle Onassis.

As Miller walked into the duplex spread, which overlooked the spires of St. Patrick's Cathedral, the realities of Khashoggi's extravagant lifestyle came into plain view. One of the world's richest men, Khashoggi had filled the apartment with masterpieces by artists like Degas and Miró. There were valuable trinkets in every direction, in bronze, silver, and ivory. There was a ballroom, a sauna, a caterer's kitchen that could serve as many as three hundred guests and, perhaps most notably, an indoor lap pool, a rarity in even the most affluent Manhattan circles. Khashoggi had created the spread in the 1970s by combining sixteen individual units. The total price tag: $1.45 million.

Miller, a self-described numbers guy more easily wowed by a well-maintained spreadsheet than by the lavish trappings of wealth, was uncharacteristically awed. "I remember thinking that this was not normal," he said later. "There were Ming vases and Monets everywhere. The master suite had his and hers double king beds, one with a mink bedspread and one with a sable bedspread." Walking through the vast unit, Miller recalled as a kid reading a news report about a wealthy Manhattanite who had had to rent a crane to lift his massive quartz dining room table into his apartment. This was that same apartment, he realized.

Completed in the mid-1970s, as New York City slid into a fiscal crisis, the newly constructed Olympic Tower had represented a different breed of residential building, a far cry from the prime Fifth Avenue and Park Avenue cooperatives that had previously been the gold standard for luxury apartment living in the city. For starters, it was a condominium. The condominium concept was still novel to a New York audience more accustomed to townhouses and cooperatives. The city's first ever condominium, the St. Tropez on East 64th Street, had been built less than a decade earlier, in 1965.

Compared to the city's elite cooperatives, Olympic Tower had tighter, less generous layouts. The floor plans didn't have the grand entertaining spaces, lavish entry galleries, or servants' quarters of the co-op world. For buyers looking for larger apartments, the only option would be to combine several units into one. Instead, convenience was prioritized over space, with residents trading in individual square footage for hotel-like amenities. For example, many came with a team of multilingual concierges who could cater to residents' every whim, whether booking them into the best restaurants or arranging for a limousine to pick them up at the airport.

The condo concept was different from cooperatives in other important ways that appealed to a certain set of buyers. For one thing, purchasers could actually own their apartments and then, separately, pay common charges for the upkeep of their building's common space. By contrast, residents of a cooperative were individual shareholders in a corporation, with their own boards and bylaws. Technically, residents did not own their apartments; rather, they owned shares in the corporation and had the right to occupy their apartments via what's known as a proprietary lease. Common charges, a significant factor for pied-à-terre buyers, were also lower in a condo, since the building itself does not have a mortgage.

Many of the city's most prestigious co-ops wouldn't allow financing, or capped it at 50 percent of what the buyer had paid for their shares. Buyers were also required to make significant personal financial disclosures, offering up multiple years of tax returns, bank statements, proof of cash reserves, and letters from employers.

They operated like selective private clubs that could exclude anyone for any reason, without any legal or regulatory disclosure requirements. The newly rich, as well as the Jewish, Black, or foreign, were often unwelcome. Co-op boards were, and still are, albeit to a lesser extent, known to rule with an iron fist, banning sublets, mortgages, and, in what's occasionally become explosive tabloid fodder, celebrities. Megastars like Madonna, Mariah Carey,

Billy Joel, and Cher have all reportedly been rejected by New York
co-op boards. Foreigners were also frowned upon. In the mid-
2000s, for instance, the billionaire Len Blavatnik was reportedly
turned away from two prominent co-op buildings—927 Fifth Avenue and the San Remo—despite being an American citizen and
one of the world's wealthiest people. He eventually managed to buy
New York Jets owner Woody Johnson's penthouse at 834 Fifth Avenue for $77.5 million.

The closed-door system, a vestige of Edith Wharton's New
York, allowed co-op boards to deny even the most financially able
applicants for any reason with complete impunity. A simple "not
our kind" whispered to a neighbor would suffice. Co-ops could
pick and choose with whom they wanted to mingle, and the Russian oligarchs and Arab sheikhs that would later flock to Billionaires' Row were almost certainly verboten.

Co-op boards also frowned upon, or sometimes outright
banned, corporate ownership, meaning buyers could not shield
their identities with the use of limited liability companies or trusts.
For foreign buyers, therein lay a key advantage of condos. In addition to the potential tax benefits of buying through a corporation,
buyers from overseas often wished to use such a structure in order
to purchase discreetly and avoid attracting attention from their government at home. And condos were also theoretically more liquid
assets, since a move to sell them was entirely at the owner's discretion and did not require approval by the building's board.

Aristotle Onassis and his partners in Olympic Tower realized
that by gearing the building to an international audience, they
could open up a whole world of potential buyers with deeper
pockets than even the wealthiest New Yorkers. While many of
New York's upper crust viewed such towers as gaudy, and balked at
their busy Midtown location, the buildings held appeal for the international jet set. Close to 80 percent of the buyers at Olympic
Tower were initially from overseas, and nearly a quarter hailed from
Mexico or Venezuela, where rising crime had the wealthy looking
for safer pastures.

It was the beginnings of a profound transformation in the Manhattan new development business. The city was becoming more international and cosmopolitan and the building became a haven for visiting sheikhs and wealthy foreign dignitaries who wanted to be close to the hustle and bustle of Fifth Avenue, Central Park, and Carnegie Hall. For the first time, the New York real estate market was geared not to the well-bred of the upper echelons of New York's social elite, but rather to members of the newly mobile international jet set class seeking a pied-à-terre in Manhattan.

Builders had started thinking less about appealing to those with breeding and more about appealing to those with money.

BEYOND FOREIGNERS, THE new condominium buildings of the 1970s and 1980s also drew a class of wealthy New Yorkers who had grown tired of the draconian restrictions their co-op boards imposed.

The Galleria, a glassy fifty-seven-story apartment tower with a quirky pre-deconstructivist top and a dramatic glass atrium lobby, located at 117 East 57th Street between Lexington and Park avenues, was one such building. The project, which debuted in 1975, was initially bankrolled in part by a prominent billionaire of the period, Stewart R. Mott. Mott was an eccentric philanthropist and an heir to the General Motors fortune. His father, Charles Stewart Mott, had sold a company to GM in the early 1900s and had been named a director of the auto giant and one of its largest shareholders. For his part, the younger Mott seemed to take joy in thumbing his nose at the company that made his family so wealthy. A self-described beatnik, he drove around in a run-down Volkswagen and openly criticized GM for not taking a public stance against the Vietnam War.

One of Mott's interests was farming—and he did it right in Manhattan. At 800 Park Avenue, the tony white-glove co-op on the Upper East Side where he had lived for decades in the penthouse, his neighbors took him to court over this unusual hobby.

Mott, then in his late thirties, had been cultivating a farm on the rooftop, complete with a chicken coop, rabbits, a compost pile, and an array of fruits and vegetables that included New Zealand spinach, Persian limes, and hot Portuguese peppers. His pride and joy was his collection of seventeen varieties of radishes. Neighbors complained that one of his many flowerpots might fall from the roof and injure a passing pedestrian or that the weight of his machinery, lumber, and soil—he'd reportedly moved more than 40 tons of soil to the roof to create the minifarm—might result in structural damage to the building.

With his neighbors up in arms at the co-op, Mott began envisioning owning a sprawling penthouse that could accommodate his lifestyle. He scoured the city for possibilities, but at many of the most exclusive cooperatives, he found himself unwelcome, his reputation having preceded him.

A solution soon presented itself. Mott entered into a deal with a local real estate development firm to prepurchase a massive quadruplex penthouse at a new condo building the company was building at 117 East 57th Street. Mott would put down an early deposit, and in return the developer would build him the penthouse of his dreams with the strength to support the multiple feet of soil he needed to grow his produce. A full ten thousand square feet of outdoor space, spread across multiple levels, would be reserved for the farm, with a solarium on either side. Meanwhile, the penthouse's top level would be home to just a single master suite, from which Mott could lie in bed and look over Central Park. It would be his "country home in the middle of the city," he told *The New York Times.*

Despite endless months of detailed discussions between Mott and the building's architect, David Kenneth Specter, the plans didn't bear out. Within a year or two, the developer claimed that the costs of accommodating Mott's ambitious agricultural pursuits had spiraled out of control, increasing the cost of the apartment from $1.3 million to about $3.5 million. The builder argued that if Mott didn't pay it, he would find someone else who could. Mott, who died in 2008, walked away, telling *The Times,* "They can sell it to an Arab for $5 million and make a tidy profit." (Today, Mott's would-be dream penthouse is owned by the magician David Copperfield.)

In some ways, Mott represented a new kind of ultra-wealthy homebuyer for New York, one who existed outside the established caste system and didn't play by its rules. His story was a harbinger of a new era in New York's high-end real estate market.

AMONG THOSE TAKING inspiration from the success of Olympic Tower, and furthering the evolution of the New York City condo tower, was a then up-and-coming developer named Donald Trump.

With Trump Tower, the then thirtysomething Queens-born real estate scion looked to raise his profile and carve out a place for himself in the ranks of legendary Manhattan developers. It was just his second project since leaving his father Fred Trump's real estate company, which focused mostly on middle-class housing in the outer boroughs.

Opening in 1983 on Fifth Avenue between 56th and 57th streets, Trump Tower was a beacon of extravagance, excess, and fervent optimism, with its peach marble and polished brass atrium and bronze reflective glass façade. Doormen wore scarlet Beefeater-type uniforms, and brass flower planters spelled out the initials D.T. Prices for the building's condos started at around $1 million.

Like Olympic Tower, Trump Tower was the product of a special zoning district that had been established in 1971 by the city's planning commission to help maintain Fifth Avenue's status as a prominent shopping corridor. The zoning provided for shopping on the ground floors, offices in the middle levels, and condos up top. The stores on the lobby level included super-luxury brands like Asprey's of London and the jewelers Cartier, Harry Winston, and Buccellati.

The tower was an immediate commercial success, drawing surprisingly positive reviews from the architecture critic at *The New York Times* and hordes of buyers who quickly snapped up the pricey units, among them Johnny Carson, Steven Spielberg, and Sophia Loren, as well as a string of international purchasers.

When Trump's book, *The Art of the Deal,* was published a few years later, the developer threw a black-tie bash in the lobby, and guests were served slices of a giant cake replica of the building, wheeled in by what was described by the *New Yorker* writer Jane Meyer as "a parade of women waving red sparklers."

"Trump Tower is a building the critics were skeptical about before it was built, but which the public obviously liked," wrote Trump in the book. "I'm not talking about the sort of person who inherited money 175 years ago and lives on 84th Street and Park Avenue. I'm talking about the wealthy Italian with the beautiful wife and the red Ferrari. Those people—the audience I was after—came to Trump Tower in droves."

By the late-1980s, thanks to the success of Olympic Tower and Trump Tower, a cluster of new copycat high-rise condo towers was going up in the area. In some ways, those buildings would serve as a precursor to Billionaires' Row. Clustered together by 57th Street and Seventh Avenue, they inspired similar debates around city planning and architecture, not to mention taste. There was Macklowe's "Darth Vader"–style Metropolitan tower, one of a trio of towers that shot up amid a boom in foreign investment into real estate, along with César Pelli's Carnegie Hall Tower, a sixty-story building with a multitone stepped masonry façade, and CitySpire, a giant concrete slab designed by Helmut Jahn in postmodern style with a Moorish-inspired dome and angled terraces.

With Metropolitan Tower, Macklowe pushed the bar for amenity-rich luxury even higher. His was the first building in New York to have a chauffeur's waiting lounge and complete catering facilities for the residents. The Club Metropolitan, designed in a nautical theme with parquet floors and wood paneling, offered full meals and beverage service from breakfast to late evening seven days a week—a dormitory cafeteria for the global rich.

The building also had a 50-foot indoor swimming pool, steam

rooms, a sauna, and squash courts as well as a temperature- and humidity-controlled wine cellar where residents could store their favorite vintages. Another innovation was Metropolitan Tower's marketing program, which included a ten-minute promotional film and a lifestyle brochure with a foldout that showed panoramic views of the building featuring exterior lighting that created a dynamic effect on the skyline even before construction was complete.

For the building's four model units, Macklowe tapped a series of internationally recognized architecture and design firms, including Juan Pablo Molyneux, a sought-after Chilean architect, and Andrée Putman, a Parisian who had recently overseen the design of Ian Schrager's new Morgan's Hotel in Murray Hill.

Competition among the three new towers was stiff. Metropolitan Tower was the most modern of the bunch. Designed by Schuman, Lichtenstein, Claman & Efron, whose partners went on to have a role designing for many of New York's best-known developers through their company SLCE, it was a shard of pointy dark glass in the middle of an area filled with more traditional midsized buildings.

The architectural and city planning debate inspired by these three buildings would foreshadow the even more heated debates to come with the emergence of the plans for the Billionaires' Row supertalls two decades later. Metropolitan and Carnegie Hall towers, for instance, were separated only by a slender brownstone that housed the Russian Tea Room. Both developers had tried but failed to buy the site to expand their tower; some critics argued that the resulting hodgepodge of high- and low-rise buildings added to the feeling of incongruity on the block. "When plans for these three skyscrapers were announced in 1985 and 1986, at the peak of the real-estate boom that has now ended with a thud, they seemed like the height of absurdity," the architecture critic Paul Goldberger— the same one who had praised the Trump Tower—wrote in the *Times* in 1990. "What kind of city planning was going on in New York if it was possible to put up 60- and 70-story towers cheek-byjowl in midtown Manhattan? What rhyme or reason was there to the city if these skyscrapers were so different that they looked as if they had been put there to defy each other?"

THE CORE OF what would become Billionaires' Row—the 57th Street thoroughfare from Park Avenue to Eighth Avenue—spans only a mile. Walking from one end to the other, one can still see vestiges of the past 100 years of development and architectural evolution. As developers brought new towers to 57th Street in the late 1980s and early 1990s, one challenge they had to contend with was more emotional than logistical: the corridor's shoddy reputation with wealthy New Yorkers.

To most moneyed Manhattanites, 57th Street didn't scream luxury so much as schlock. Since its origins as a once far-flung building site for Manhattan mansions, the area around 57th Street, particularly from Sixth Avenue to Broadway, had evolved from an elegant shopping corridor to a mecca for kitschy themed restaurants selling branded T-shirts and baby back ribs. One catalyst for the corridor's down-market trend was the arrival of the Hard Rock Cafe at 221 West 57th Street in 1984, with its 60-foot-long bar designed to look like a Fender Stratocaster guitar.

By the 1990s, there was a plentitude of Vegas-like establishments to choose from. Among them were Planet Hollywood, backed by Sylvester Stallone, Bruce Willis, Demi Moore, and Arnold Schwarzenegger and replete with display cases of Hollywood props and costumes; the Motown Cafe, based in a former automat, where the hostesses danced like the Supremes and the menu was modeled after a two-record Motown album jacket; the Jekyll & Hyde Club, a spooky horror-themed supper club with animatronic props, skeletons, and special effects; and the Harley-Davidson Cafe, with its motorcycle memorabilia and macho decor.

Some bemoaned the so-called "theme-parking of 57th Street" as a loss for the city. "This quintessentially Manhattan thoroughfare looks to be on the verge of seceding from New York and linking

up with Anaheim, Calif., and Orlando, Fla., in a confederacy of
kitsch," wrote the architecture critic Herbert Muschamp. Others
didn't seem to mind. The opening of the Harley restaurant in 1993
drew members of the glitterati, including a teenage Ivanka Trump,
clad in an all-denim ensemble and sporting braces on her teeth. She
posed for photos alongside her father. Nancy Sinatra, dressed in a
Playboy T-shirt, sunglasses, and leather biker boots, straddled a
tiger-themed motorcycle. The prizefighter Joe Frazier larked
around in a pair of novelty chicken overalls alongside O. J. Simpson
and Nicole Brown Simpson.

As the new millennium approached, however, the glitzy show
seemed to be nearing its curtain call. Its moment had been short-
lived. As the novelty of these themed restaurants wore thin, and
with the resurgence of Times Square several blocks farther south,
many of the new establishments called it quits. The Motown Cafe
closed its doors permanently, while the Hard Rock Cafe ultimately
moved to the site of the former Paramount Theater at 43rd Street
and Broadway.

Themed restaurants weren't the only dying business on the 57th
Street corridor. In the early twentieth century, the corner of Broadway and 57th Street had been the heart of a thriving commercial
district known as Automobile Row. Plush car showrooms were
once ubiquitous along the strip; in the industry's early years, having
a glitzy showroom along Broadway, then considered the main street
of the world, was a way for the car companies to show that the
automobile was here to stay. The car showrooms began to pop up
along the corridor in the first decade of the twentieth century, as
horse-drawn carriages were beginning to be replaced with cars, or
what were then known as "horseless carriages."

Shortly after the turn of the century, a series of prominent new
structures, often designed by leading American architects on behalf
of the major car corporations, were erected along Broadway. "I
think more cars were sold here than anyplace, especially during
World War II, and especially used cars," one car dealer told the
Times in 2011. "The GIs were leaving to go overseas, and the

wholesalers would go knocking on doors: 'Do you want to sell your car?'"

By the 2000s, Automobile Row was no more. The showrooms had been driven out of the area by high rents and the escalating value of land. Many had migrated to the Far West Side in search of more affordable spaces. Only fragments of its history remained. Among them, on the corner of 57th Street and Broadway, stood a pair of buildings at 1780 Broadway and 225 West 57th Street, once owned by the B. F. Goodrich Company, a leading American manufacturer of automobile tires and other rubber products. The two mid-rise buildings once shared an automotive freight elevator. At 1780 Broadway, there had once been a tire showroom on the ground floor.

A hulking convention center at the southwest corner of Central Park, known as the New York Coliseum, was also ready to take its final bow. Dating to around 1956, the sprawling convention center had originally been envisioned by the New York planning czar Robert Moses, the chairman of the Triborough Bridge and Tunnel Authority, who used federal slum clearance funds to make way for its construction by tearing down old theaters and shops. Designed by the architects Leon and Lionel Levy, it was large enough to host several major conventions at a time, including the International Flower Show and the New York International Auto Show, and consisted of a massive windowless exhibition building and an attached twenty-three-story office tower. When it opened, it was seen as a major boon to the local economy—Mayor Robert F. Wagner had called it "one of the wonders of the modern world"—though it was hardly an architectural showpiece. "It's a great utilitarian achievement, but architecture is something else again," the unimpressed architect Frank Lloyd Wright once said of the structure, saying that the building was "all right for New York" but that he hoped the style wouldn't spread to other parts of the country.

By the approach of the new millennium, however, the convention center was run-down and dated and had stopped hosting conventions. The opening of the Jacob K. Javits Convention Center on

Manhattan's Far West Side in 1986 effectively put it out of business. Soon it gained a new reputation. According to some press reports, women and children would frequently be seen waiting outside the center for charter buses that would take them to upstate prisons to visit incarcerated friends and family. Homeless encampments also appeared.

Just like that, the West 57th Street corridor had become a transient neighborhood. Office workers trudged through it on their way to the subway. Young women who had moved to New York from the Midwest with big dreams and little money streetwalked along the corridor and holed up at greasy Midtown hotels. A steady stream of tourists walking between Central Park and Times Square discarded litter, which would be trodden into the ground by other fanny-pack-wearing visitors behind them.

Miller, the appraiser, lived in a building on West 60th Street right behind the convention center in the 1980s. "The signs of urban decay were just intense," he said. "I remember looking over it and thinking, 'How, in such a beautiful city, can you have such a dilapidated structure to welcome so many people who are visiting Central Park?' It just seemed out of place."

Efforts to sell the Coliseum by Metropolitan Transportation Authority (which took over from the Triborough Bridge and Tunnel Authority) started in the mid-1980s under Mayor Ed Koch and bled into Mayor Rudy Giuliani's administration. Plans submitted by developers drew lawsuits and community opposition. Multiple deals were made and then botched, while the facility sat empty, a hole at the center of a neighborhood teetering toward decline.

BY 2008, WHEN Macklowe was searching for the cash to build his skyscraper at the site of the Drake Hotel, the 57th Street corridor remained home to a confused mixture of ultra-luxury stores, cheesy souvenir shops, antiquaries, galleries, dressmakers, and historic apartment houses, spliced between modern glass office and residential buildings.

At the corner of Fifth Avenue stood the jewelry giant Tiffany & Co.'s flagship store, in operation since 1940 and housed within a sedate Art Moderne–style structure designed by the architecture firm Cross & Cross, complete with the famed Tiffany Atlas clock above the door. On the opposite corner, Van Cleef & Arpels, the onetime jeweler to Grace Kelly, Elizabeth Taylor, and Eva Peron, occupied the ground floor of the department store Bergdorf Goodman.

As you made your way west, you would pass the Solow Building, a glass office tower built by the developer Sheldon Solow with such a sweeping, curved façade that you might have been tempted to try to slide down it, and the famous Rizzoli bookstore, a favorite of New York's literary scene for its grand architectural feel, with an elaborately decorated ceiling, chandeliers, and a second-floor balcony with wrought iron railings.

Then there was the Steinway building, the landmark piano showroom that had operated at the location since the 1920s, housed in a classic Warren & Wetmore building clad in limestone. It had a base decorated with medallion portraits of classical composers like Brahms and Bach as well as sculptural embellishments by the Italian American sculptor Leo Lentelli, which depicted the Muse of Music placing a wreath on the head of Apollo, the Greek god of music. The building was a throwback to the heyday of the strip's musical past, when piano showrooms, music schools, and record labels followed Carnegie Hall to the area.

As one approached Seventh Avenue, there was the Russian Tea Room. The Art Deco–style tea room opened in the 1920s as a meeting place for Russian expatriates by onetime members of the Russian Imperial Ballet.

Then came Carnegie Hall, the iconic landmark concert hall. While Lincoln Center had stolen away some of its sheen, the building, designed by William Burnet Tuthill in Italian Renaissance Revival style with a reddish-brown Roman brick façade, was still one of the most prominent concert halls in the world.

On the opposite corner stood the Osborne, one of the city's

first major high-rise apartment towers, made possible by the adoption of steel construction and the invention of the elevator. Constructed in the mid-1880s and impressively clad in heavy rusticated stone, it had been the home of Leonard Bernstein, who was said to have written *West Side Story* there.

Moving farther west toward Broadway, one encountered the Art Students League, a landmark 1892 French Renaissance building housing works by some of the most prominent artists who had studied there, including Georgia O'Keeffe, as well as Lee's Art Shop, a famous family-run art store housed in a French Renaissance Revival–style building with ornamentation elaborately carved from Indiana limestone, which had originally been developed for the American Society of Civil Engineers and Architects in the late 1800s.

In short, the street had little cohesion. A few recent changes to the area around the corridor, however, served as a harbinger of what was to come.

The Coliseum was no more. A new roughly $1.7 billion, 2.8-million-square-foot real estate project spearheaded by the Related Companies had taken its place in 2003 and had transformed the corner of 59th Street and Central Park West. The project comprised a Mandarin Oriental hotel, offices, a jazz club, a luxury shopping mall, a Whole Foods Market, restaurants by Thomas Keller and Jean-Georges Vongerichten, and high-end condominiums spread across a pair of twin 750-foot towers that *The New York Times* described as exclamation points on the West Side skyline. Though there had been speculation during the time of its construction about whether buyers would want to live in twin high-rises so soon after 9/11, the project, known as the AOL Time Warner Center, was succeeding in drawing ultra-wealthy condo buyers from around the world.

And then there was 15 Central Park West, a new limestone tower near the corner of Central Park and next door to the Trump International Hotel. Developed by the Zeckendorf brothers, William and Arthur, scions of an iconic New York real estate family, the building, on the corner of 61st Street and Central Park West, was the pinnacle of luxury real estate in the city at the time, with apartments trading at never-before-seen prices to celebrities and financiers. Opening its doors around 2008, it quickly became one of the world's most powerful addresses, with residents including Sting, Alex Rodriguez, and Goldman Sachs CEO Lloyd Blankfein. Bloggers at the real estate gossip site *Curbed* dubbed it "the limestone Jesus."

More than a decade later, real estate insiders would point to the redevelopment of the Coliseum and the construction of 15 Central Park West as markers of the sea change that was about to take place on the 57th Street corridor.

CHAPTER 3

The Rabbi, the Jeweler, and the Developer

arry Macklowe wove his way through a crowded room full of men wearing dark robes and black hats and into a windowless, dimly lit conference room with Formica laminate floors. It was around 2008, and, holding court in the back room of the Jewish learning center near the base of the Queensboro Bridge, sat a man with a long grizzled beard and little oval glasses.

He was Rabbi Yoshiyahu Pinto, a kabbalah-espousing mystic, who looked distinctly older than his thirtysomething years. The great-grandson of a famed Moroccan-born mystic known as the Baba Sali, Pinto had an aura that had attracted acquaintances ranging from LeBron James to Congressman Anthony Weiner, as well as business magnates like Jay Schottenstein of American Eagle and the real estate tycoon Charles Kushner, the father of Jared Kushner. Some of the rabbi's devotees considered him as much a business adviser as a spiritual one—seeking him out to bless deals, dispense advice, and even curse their enemies. They stood in line to kiss his hand and begged his close circle for private audiences. Israel's former defense minister claimed the rabbi had helped him wake up from a coma, while others claimed he had saved them from questionable business deals.

Pinto's fame had come to mean fortune as well. His charitable organization, Mosdot Shuva Israel, was attracting media attention for renting a mansion on Lily Pond Lane, one of the most exclusive and expensive enclaves in the Hamptons. *The Jewish Daily Forward* reported that Pinto's charity spent $77,000 to rent the house for three weeks in August 2008. The charity was also known for spending heavily on luxury travel and pricey jewelry. Pinto reportedly flew first class and had footed a $75,000 bill for a monthlong stay at a luxury hotel in Buenos Aires, Argentina.

Though he was Jewish himself, Macklowe was not overtly religious and was hardly a follower of Rabbi Pinto. He had come to the Jewish learning center purely on a matter of business—one that had taken a turn for the worse. Weeks earlier, Macklowe thought he had struck a deal with one of Pinto's devotees, a man who many referred to as "the Godfather of Bling," to purchase a townhouse adjacent to the Drake Hotel on East 57th Street. It was part of his plan to assemble a dramatic wall of retail at the base of his new tower. Now it looked as though the agreement was already falling apart.

The Pinto devotee was Jacob Arabo, né Yakov Arabov, better known to his clientele as Jacob the Jeweler. Arabo, who had made a name providing diamond-encrusted baubles to athletes and musicians, had connections to hip-hop going back to the legendary Brooklyn rapper Notorious B.I.G. and a client list that included everyone from Mariah Carey, Madonna, Jay-Z, and Sean "Diddy" Combs to athletes like David Beckham, Derek Jeter, and Shaquille O'Neal. The Uzbek American jeweler looked the part, wearing three-piece suits, sporting slicked-back jet-black hair, and traveling around the city in a Maybach Mercedes. In "Touch the Sky," Kanye West raps "I went to Jacob an hour after I got my advance," and in Drake's music video for the song "When to Say When & Chicago Freestyle," the rapper and his crew are seen picking out watches and chains in Arabo's office.

Arabo would bedazzle anything, from hubcaps to video game

controllers. The townhouse, at 48 East 57th Street, was home to his company's showroom, a gleaming monochromatic retail space with VIP suites on the upper floors for private appointments.

The jeweler was just one of a motley array of mysterious international business people and cranky, prideful New Yorkers standing between the Macklowes and their wall of retail. Macklowe and his son, Billy, however, were determined to pick them off one by one. In real estate, the process is known as "assemblage."

To put together their assemblage, they used every negotiation tool in their arsenal, digging deep in their pockets to offer above-market prices, calling in favors, and even promising to find the owners better locations for their businesses, then footing the bill for their move. Macklowe was relentless. At one point, after about fourteen months of negotiations, he and his son paid close to $20 million to get the luxury watch company Audemars Piguet to move across the street to free up one of the brownstones.

With each deal, he plowed more and more of his own money into the project, but he reasoned that it would be worth the investment. By 2008, the Macklowes had most of the pieces they wanted for their new tower, with a few notable exceptions, including the Jacob & Co. building, a holdout tenant in another building they had purchased from the late king of Morocco, and a townhouse owned by Turnbull & Asser, the British-made bespoke clothing company owned by Ali Fayed, the younger brother of former Harrods boss Mohamed Al-Fayed. Al-Fayed in particular seemed immune to the Macklowes' overtures. ("It's really hard to compel people with money with money," Billy Macklowe said later of Al-Fayed.)

The deal with Arabo in particular had gotten under Harry Macklowe's skin. Weeks earlier, the elder Macklowe and Arabo had met in one of the VIP sales suites of Arabo's townhouse and agreed on the terms of a sale: Macklowe would buy the property, which Arabo had acquired for about $12 million in 2004, for $50 million, a number he told the jeweler was more than twice what it would be worth to any buyer but him. The men had scribbled the terms of the deal on a scrap of paper and both written their initials on it. The formal contract would be forthcoming.

Two weeks later, when Macklowe still hadn't received the promised contract from Arabo, he called him. The jeweler said he had upped his price to $100 million.

"I said, 'Jacob, how could you do that? We shook hands,'" Macklowe later recalled.

Arabo's answer: "My rabbi told me I should charge $100 million."

Macklowe was incensed. He would have to meet this rabbi and set him straight. He quickly arranged a meeting with the pair at the Jewish learning center.

The meeting would not go as Macklowe had hoped. As the trio settled into the dimly lit back room, there was immediate confusion. The rabbi didn't speak English, while Macklowe spoke barely a word of Yiddish or Hebrew. The three men sat there in a circle holding hands as Macklowe made his case to the rabbi and Arabo—hardly an impartial observer—translated. The bottom line, Macklowe told the pair, was that he could pay only $50 million.

It didn't play well. Rabbi Pinto bounced up from his chair and jumped up and down in rebuke, Macklowe said. Even if Macklowe couldn't understand his words, it was clear that the rabbi was saying, in no uncertain terms, that the deal would not be happening at that price.

Arabo would later serve almost two years in prison after pleading guilty to falsifying records and giving false statements to investigators looking into a multistate drug ring. Authorities had accused the jeweler of conspiring to launder drug profits for the Detroit-based ring, known as the "Black Mafia Family." Rabbi Pinto later served time in an Israeli prison after being convicted of bribing a senior police official.

As for Macklowe, he never did get his hands on the townhouse.

BY EARLY 2008, the wind was firmly out of Harry Macklowe's sails. Owing to the costly acquisition of some of the adjoining brownstones, his Drake project had ballooned to at least three quarters of a billion dollars even before there was a shovel in the ground. He and Billy had been looking for months for an equity partner to help bankroll the project, but Deutsche Bank, which had lent the company more than $500 million to acquire the hotel, was growing increasingly impatient.

It wasn't hard to see why. By 2008, Deutsche Bank was mired in its own recession-related mess. In their eagerness to grow their U.S. footprint, they had unwittingly carved out a niche financing big-name New York developers who would go on to hit the skids, including Donald Trump, Harry Macklowe, and Ian Bruce Eichner. Around the same time, Eichner was handing Deutsche the keys to the Cosmopolitan Resort Casino in Las Vegas, a $3.9 billion casino-hotel that the bank had helped finance, following an epic default on payments.

With its books under strain, Deutsche Bank had asked Macklowe to put more equity into the Drake deal. He had complied, paying off $156.3 million in loans on the Drake to shore up his position and raising his stake in the project to $250 million. Now, in order to move the deal forward and avoid a foreclosure, he desperately needed to find an equity partner to inject some fresh capital. However, with the market on life support and his own reputation in jeopardy, it was a nearly impossible task. And for those rare players out there looking to do deals, Harry Macklowe wasn't exactly number one on their list.

He hung on to shreds of optimism despite the headwinds. "The New York investment community at that period of time was so cynical, so burnt, that they couldn't see the real potential for the development site," he would later say.

The Macklowes had burned through their rolodex looking for potential partners. They talked to Leonard Litwin, a prominent political donor and the founder of Glenwood Management, who expressed interest in forming a partnership only if the building would include rental apartments and could take advantage of the 421-A tax abatement program. The program would grant the developers a significant tax break in return for incorporating some low-income housing into the project. Harry dismissed the notion out of hand. "I thought, what a heresy that would be to have subsidized housing on Park Avenue and 56th Street," he said.

They also talked to Dubai's Emaar Properties, former New York governor Eliot Spitzer, and even the casino magnate Steve Wynn, who envisioned bringing a hotel to the site. None of the discussions were panning out.

Sitting that spring in his office on the 21st floor of the GM Building, which he continued to lease following the sale of the building, Macklowe argued with his longtime friend Arthur Cohen about the future of the project. Cohen, too, was a New York real estate institution, a developer of Olympic Tower alongside Aristotle Onassis. At one point, it was estimated by *The New York Times* that he was involved in one of every seven commercial real estate deals that took place in Manhattan. If there was a deal to be made for the Drake, Cohen would know how to get it done.

The crux of the debate: Macklowe didn't want to cede complete control of the project to any financier. It was his project and he should lead it. Cohen told him that was unrealistic. Given the amount of money needed to jump-start the Drake, and in light of Macklowe's recent financial follies, a financier would want to steer the project.

Cohen had his own designs on the property. The prior year, he had teamed up with a couple of unlikely partners to buy up distressed New York City real estate. Among them was the Washington lobbyist Paul Manafort, a longtime Republican campaign consultant who had worked with Presidents Reagan and Bush senior and would later become a notorious figure during the investigations into the Russian interference in the 2016 U.S. presidential election.

The other was Brad Zackson, a former consigliere to President

Trump's father, Fred Trump, starting in the 1980s. Zackson had served almost five years in prison stemming from an incident in which he and his brother Stephen and a friend allegedly attempted to shoot a nightclub bouncer, and he had then overseen leasing at many of the senior Trump's rental buildings in Brooklyn and Queens. He had been trying to make his name as a developer in his own right for years. Like his longtime employers the Trumps, Zackson had an uncanny knack for self-promotion. He once dated *Footloose* star Lori Singer, and in his office, he displayed pictures of himself with politicians such as Mario Cuomo, Bill Clinton, and Fidel Castro. He had once held a $1,000-a-plate fundraiser for then governor Mario Cuomo and hired airplanes to fly over New York on Election Day trailing banners reading GIULIANI + CUOMO: DON'T BREAK UP THE TEAM. And he dressed the part of a master dealmaker, often in pin-striped suits and snazzy waistcoats. One developer recalled Zackson's arriving to a meeting in a green Bentley, clad in a three-piece suit and carrying a silver walking cane topped with a lion. (Zackson said the Bentley was green and the cane was an exaggeration.)

This peculiar trio formed a partnership, CMZ Ventures, named for their initials: Cohen Manafort Zackson. The "bizarre" partnership of "mismatched heavies," as the *Observer* would call them, had looked at buying and redeveloping several high-profile properties, including the Helmsley Park Lane Hotel on Central Park South and two private islands in the Bahamas. The Drake, as a first project, would be a bold statement for the new entity—not to mention a Hail Mary rescue for Macklowe. In July 2008, the trio signed a letter of intent to purchase the Drake site for $850 million, planning to develop it along with Macklowe.

While they had little money of their own, the partnership had deep connections. They recruited Frank Orenstein, a hotel guru who was working with Kazakh investors, to attract some big names to hang their logo on the project. The trio talked to the casino giant MGM, which expressed interest in opening a hotel and loft concept at the location, and to the Italian luxury goods brand Bulgari. They convinced Bulgari that the location would be perfect for a branded hotel and condos. Prepared by the prominent SLCE Architects, the Bulgari plans called for a more than 700,000-square-foot mixed-use tower with a five-level luxury retail mall topped by fourteen stories of commercial office space, eleven stories of an ultra-luxury six-star hotel, and thirty-three stories of apartments, according to an appraisal done for CMZ by the commercial real estate firm Grubb & Ellis. The retail site would include themed holographic displays and Bulgari-branded spa facilities.

On the basis of Bulgari's commitment to the project, the partnership was able to attract yet another equity partner. The French asset management firm Inovalis was willing to buy into the deal for about $850 million, pending due diligence, and would take a 50 percent stake in the project. CMZ would take 25 percent and Orenstein's company Alatau would take the remaining 25 percent. Under the terms, Macklowe could also elect to buy into the deal and would be listed as a co-developer of the project.

Cohen encouraged his friend to take the deal, but Macklowe resisted. Despite his financial challenges, Macklowe still held a key piece of leverage: the nearby brownstones he had acquired to expand the site assemblage. Macklowe had financed them independently of the main hotel site, and Deutsche Bank didn't have a claim on all of them. Without those separate pieces, any buyer of the Drake would never get the density they needed for the tower, and the resulting property would have no physical retail frontage on 57th Street. It was a shrewd play by Macklowe and one that everyone speculated was intentional. "Harry doesn't do anything by accident," one real estate broker said.

Representatives for Inovalis would later claim that Zackson and Cohen had assured them that while the properties would not be included in an executed letter of intent to buy the property, Macklowe would ultimately include them in the sale at no additional cost. Now, becoming concerned, they negotiated a reduction in their share of the pre-due-diligence deposit required to secure the deal, reducing their $5 million contribution to just $500,000.

By late summer, with signs of cold feet increasing, Inovalis asked for an extension to the deal's due diligence period. An appraisal had come in lower than the company had expected, and its representatives came to understand that Macklowe would not easily give up the brownstones. In court documents relating to a dispute over the deposit several years later, the French company's lawyers would say they suspected that CMZ, Alatau, and perhaps Macklowe were attempting to divert its investment for their own gain. "It became clear to Inovalis that the longer it took to secure the additional properties, the more leverage Harry Macklowe would have to command an exorbitant price to include these properties," the company's lawyers wrote.

That September, unsurprisingly, Inovalis pulled out. CMZ needed a new equity partner.

MACKLOWE'S QUEST TO find money for the Drake project in unconventional places was in some ways an early reflection of how the market for commercial real estate financing was evolving.

A century ago, financing a major skyscraper was, if not exactly easy, then at least a far less byzantine undertaking. During the skyscraper boom of the late 1920s and early '30s, for instance, the standard sources of financing tended to be savings banks, insurance companies, and bond houses. The most popular source of cash came via selling bonds to the public at a rate of return of around 6 percent, then charging the building's developer a fee on that sum. Sometimes it was even simpler than that. In the 1920s, Walter Chrysler eschewed corporate funds and personally financed the construction of the Chrysler Building, so that his sons would have something to be responsible for.

In recent decades, however, as the real estate market has gone through boom and bust cycles, government oversight aimed at preventing the excessive risk taking that led to the financial crisis transformed the financing landscape and made it significantly more complex. The introduction of regulatory schemes like President

Barack Obama's 2010 Dodd–Frank financial overhaul and Basel III, a regulatory accord that requires banks to maintain certain leverage ratios and keep certain levels of reserve capital on hand, forced domestic banks to tighten their purse strings and reduce their risk profiles. Consequently, they started lending at a significantly lower loan-to-value ratio than they had in the past.

By the end of the aughts, traditional commercial banks like Wells Fargo, J.P. Morgan Chase, and Citi, which had typically financed the construction of major New York buildings, were licking their wounds from a series of underwriting misfires during the housing bubble. As the fallout from the financial crisis became clear, they were levied with billion-dollar fines and forced into a largely defensive position in the market.

As a result, a shadow lending market developed in which unorthodox and less regulated lenders made up the financing shortfall when traditional banks were tapped out. These included everything from private equity and hedge funds to sovereign wealth funds and ultra-high-net-worth individuals. This new breed of lender, hungry for high returns and more willing to dispense with banks' strict underwriting requirements, was sometimes willing to "loan-to-own," an industry term for a company's acquiring debt on a property and eventually foreclosing, taking ownership of the property itself. That was something that traditional banks and insurance companies typically desperately wanted to avoid.

In the new reality that developers like Macklowe faced, which contended with regulations imposed following the 2008 financial crisis, their task was piecing together a patchwork of financiers and lenders to make up for the void left by the big banks. It would be a complicated world in which loans and positions were "sliced, diced, pledged and repledged," sometimes without the knowledge of the original developers, wrote the New York real estate attorneys Joshua Stein and Richard Fries in a 2019 paper on the subject. The Frankenstein's-monster-like financing arrangements grew to incorporate "often cumbersome and impractical concepts and multifaceted relationships among an expanding collection of parties," the attorneys wrote.

Another way of looking at it was that many lenders were wet behind the ears. "It was the first time that many of them had played in real estate," said the appraiser Jonathan Miller. "In my mind, that made them less appreciative of the risk."

LATER IN THE summer of 2008, Brad Zackson, the flamboyant *Z* of CMZ Ventures, found himself in a nondescript conference room of an upmarket hotel on the Côte d'Azur in the south of France.

Across the table was a silver-haired Ukrainian billionaire named Dmytro Firtash. Firtash had made his fortune serving as a middleman in natural gas deals between a Ukrainian state-owned gas company and Gazprom, the Kremlin-backed Russian gas company. U.S. authorities would later claim that Firtash also had ties to Russian organized crime. He also was acquainted with Paul Manafort, the *M* of CMZ. They reportedly met in the early 2000s while doing political consulting for the eventual Ukrainian president, Viktor Yanukovych. Now Firtash was eyeing real estate investments in the United States, and Manafort was his man on the ground.

With the deal with Inovalis for the Drake site on the ropes, Zackson and Manafort had flown to Europe to meet with Firtash, hoping the oligarch might solve their financing problems at the Drake. Zackson was immediately struck by Firtash's appearance, especially his mouth. How, he thought to himself, could a man with so much money and likely access to some of the best medical care in the world have such bad teeth? "They were crooked and ugly. They looked like they were rotting out of his mouth," Zackson said.

Zackson tried to ignore the Eastern European oil mogul's distracting dental state as the Ukrainian, through translators, made jokes about the U.S. financial crisis. Billionaires, he laughed, were becoming millionaires overnight. Zackson found the remarks a little uncouth, he said later. After all, Zackson was barely a million-aire himself.

Firtash had already expressed interest in the Drake site, but now Zackson and Manafort were looking for a firm commitment, and Firtash seemed willing to give it. The Americans left the meeting on a high, with promises of a multi-million-dollar deposit for the Drake.

Zackson emailed Macklowe with good news. "Returned from our investor meeting in Monte Carlo and want you to know it could not have gone better," he wrote. Firtash had agreed to provide $112 million in equity for the project and would wire a $25 million deposit in the coming weeks.

A deal couldn't come quickly enough for Macklowe, who was running out of time. As Labor Day approached, Deutsche Bank filed suit against the developer over the unpaid loan balance of $482.98 million it said his company owed. The loan had matured less than a year earlier, on November 30, 2007, the bank said, and had not been repaid.

Macklowe was furious. In court papers he filed in response to the lawsuit, his lawyers made it clear that Macklowe took person-ally the bank's move to foreclose. Macklowe's response cited the more than $250 million of his own cash equity in the Drake site and accused Deutsche Bank of fraudulently inducing him to infuse over $190 million since the real estate and credit markets "began their precipitous slide in the middle of 2007" with repeated prom-ises that the bank would refinance the loans on which it was now filing to foreclose.

In a filing that contained claims that *The New York Times* com-pared to the cries of a "jilted lover," Macklowe's lawyers argued that Deutsche Bank, a lender but also Macklowe's trusted financial adviser, had "betrayed that trust" by "making false promises it never intended to keep" in order to induce him to pay off, from his own personal assets, nearly $150 million in mezzanine loans relat-ing to the Drake properties and to make roughly $40 million in additional cash infusions into the project. Much of the debt he had paid off had been nonrecourse debt held directly by Deutsche Bank.

The bank had strung him along, they suggested, until it got what it wanted, then refused to honor its commitments. If it "goes forward under the present, virtually unprecedented market conditions—and there is no sign of improvements in the near term—Macklowe's cash investments, including those induced by Deutsche Bank's fraud, will almost certainly be a total loss," they said in court filings.

As the summer came to an end, Macklowe, despite the fighting spirit of his court statements, could see the walls were closing in. His son, Billy, was furious at the family firm's predicament, and his wife, Linda, too, had lost patience. Zackson recalled that Macklowe's driver would knock on the door if the group worked late into the evening. "He would say, 'Your wife wants you home now.'" In meetings, Zackson recalled, Harry "was screaming at Billy," to the consternation of everyone in the room.

And yet no amount of screaming at his son could secure the capital that Macklowe needed.

ULTIMATELY, THE FIRTASH deal would not materialize. Zackson would later say that he believed Firtash was simply anxious not to be seen putting money in the United States at a time of such political upheaval at home in Ukraine.

However, in a civil case filed in the United States District Court in 2011, the former Ukrainian prime minister, Yulia Tymoshenko, would claim that Firtash was in cahoots with Semion Yudkovich Mogilevich, a Ukrainian-born Russian organized crime boss who was on the FBI's most wanted list, and that Firtash and his associates had used phony deals with companies like CMZ to funnel money through the United States under the guise of investing in real estate projects like the Drake. Tymoshenko's attorneys alleged that Firtash used the premise of the projects to launder money, then withdrew the funding prior to closing.

They alleged that the real estate deals "gave the impression" that Firtash was investing in legitimate business ventures when in fact he only wanted to keep them out of the jurisdiction of Ukrainian courts and conceal illegal kickbacks being paid to Ukrainian government officials, then funnel the money back to Ukraine to fund the suppression of political opposition efforts there. (The suit was ultimately thrown out for lack of evidence.)

The botched deal would later come under scrutiny from Robert Mueller, the special counsel overseeing an investigation into allegations of Russian interference in the 2016 U.S. presidential election, which examined Manafort's dealings with the Ukrainian oligarch.

It was revealed, thanks to a 2008 memo written by Manafort's associate Rick Gates, that Manafort planned to fund his interest in the Drake deal through his company Pericles, a private equity fund he had established in the Cayman Islands along with another oligarch, the billionaire Russian industrialist Oleg Deripaska, in 2007. Both Manafort and Gates would ultimately serve time in prison as a result of the Mueller probe.

Following the collapse of the deal, CMZ folded. With Firtash out of the picture, Manafort, too, was out, and Cohen didn't want to continue to fund the overhead. The company's phones and internet service were cut off and the New York State Department of Labor opened an investigation into the company for failing to fully pay employees and misclassifying them as "independent contractors" to avoid paying them worker's compensation and unemployment benefits. Zackson faded back into oblivion.

Meanwhile, as another summer came and went, the vacant Drake site, enclosed in fencing, became overgrown with weeds.

CHAPTER 4

The Chess Master

New York City had long been considered the home of the sky-scraper. However, by the turn of the twenty-first century, the city was losing ground to Asia and the Middle East in the race to build the world's first megatall buildings.

Though it has been hotly contested, the title of New York's first skyscraper is widely thought to belong to Lower Manhattan's Tower Building, a since-demolished eleven-story structure completed in 1889 and designed by the architect Bradford Lee Gilbert. While a far cry from our modern notion of supertall buildings, the property is said to have been the first in the city supported not by its exterior masonry walls but by an interior frame of steel columns and beams, stronger and lighter than iron.

The steel frame construction techniques that made it possible quickly caught on, leading to a flurry of new high-rise towers around the turn of the twentieth century—and the very first race to the sky. Those new buildings were typically affiliated with the city's biggest banks and corporations, which saw architecture as powerful social currency and wanted to make a concrete statement about their status in the burgeoning metropolis.

The first building to crest above the spire of Trinity Church was the twelve-story New York World Building, constructed down-town for the publishing magnate Joseph Pulitzer as the headquar-ters of the newspaper by the same name in 1890. For years, New York churchgoers had tried to resist the capitalist impulse to build taller than houses of worship, citing a moral obligation, but to no avail. Soon after Pulitzer's building came the forty-story Singer Building, designed at the turn of the century for the then president of the Singer sewing machine corporation.

Both structures were eclipsed in 1909 by the completion of the Metropolitan Life Insurance Company Tower on Madison Square Park, the design of which, with its bells and clock faces, was in-spired by St. Mark's Campanile in Venice. In 1913, the construc-tion of the Woolworth Building on Broadway cemented the advent of the skyscraper era.

Some of these buildings proved short-lived, as dramatic ad-vances in technology quickly made them obsolete. The New York World Building was demolished in 1955 to make way for a larger entrance to the Brooklyn Bridge, while the others, with the excep-tion of the landmarked Woolworth Building, were replaced with yet taller towers.

By the time the Empire State Building debuted in the 1930s, Manhattan had been divided into two separate skyscraper business districts, the high peaks of downtown and Midtown separated by a valley of low-rise buildings in between. With New York as its trophy cabinet, North America led the world in skyscraper construction. By 1930, ninety-nine of the world's hundred tallest buildings were located in North America. The Manhattan skyline, the product of a series of high-rise construction booms, was the envy of the world.

However, while New York was synonymous with its skyscraper-dominated skyline in the twentieth century, the pace and ambition of its skyscraper construction wasn't keeping up with what was happening in Asia and the Middle East a century later. Labor costs had made New York City one of the most expensive cities to build in, and land was scarce. Strict zoning regulations also meant that building a tower of more than a thousand feet in most parts of the city would involve facing off with community boards and planning officials. The barriers to entry were high.

Developers in New York also had less interest in building megatalls. For the most part, the demand for the space simply hadn't been great enough to justify the enormous cost of construction. By contrast, in Asia and the Middle East, the push to build tall emerged from less of a practical concern—to facilitate population growth and avoid urban sprawl—and more of a mission of symbolism and status. "Vanity height" took precedence over usability. Some supertalls were even paid for by governments rather than private developers.

We can see this play out in the shifting global supertall ranking. The United States held the record for the world's tallest building until 1998, when the Sears Tower in Chicago was eclipsed by the Petronas Towers in Kuala Lumpur. The title was then snagged in 2004 by Taipei 101 in Taiwan, which held it until 2009, when Dubai's famous Burj Khalifa was completed. It was followed by a series of other residential towers in Dubai, including the 1,356-foot tall Princess Tower, completed in 2012.

Why Dubai? As the capital city of the United Arab Emirates became a global financial capital starting in the early 2000s, new projects had risen to meet an increase in population and prestige, as well as to draw tourists from around the world. In contrast to more mature markets in the West, planning governance over building heights was more relaxed, allowing developers to shoot higher and higher.

At 2,717 feet tall, the Burj Khalifa is the tallest building in the world, though much of its span is purely for appearances. The top third of the building is unusable.

IT WAS EARLY 2009, and Gary Barnett was sitting in the living room of a private suite at a posh London hotel, meeting with a man who hailed from the world's new locus of skyscraper ambition.

In his midfifties at the time, Barnett had thinning hair with flecks of gray that poked out from his head at unruly angles, his slightly disheveled appearance more suggestive of a college professor than one of the city's most ambitious hotshot developers. While his occasional rival back in New York, Harry Macklowe, traversed Manhattan in designer loafers and silk pocket squares, Barnett was more likely to be seen in a comfortable pair of black sneakers, a boxy suit, and a novelty tie. While Macklowe sailed off the coast of Croatia, Barnett holed up in the Poconos, a decidedly middlebrow vacation destination in rural Pennsylvania once known for its honeymoon motels with heart-shaped beds. And while Macklowe seemed at ease with his iPhone, Barnett, a Luddite, clung to his old-school flip phone, instructing staff to print out any emails directed to him and sending written responses in what some described as "serial killer scrawl." It was hard to imagine him as an arbiter of taste and sophistication.

Though he and Macklowe were very different kinds of developers, they were both facing a similar problem: a shortage of funds. Barnett had gone to London to meet with Khadem al-Qubaisi, a top executive of two major Abu Dhabi government investment funds, Aabar Investments and Tasameem.

Al-Qubaisi had been named the managing director of the International Petroleum Investment Company (IPIC), the UAE's sovereign wealth fund, two years prior and was known as the trusted confidant and dealmaker of Sheikh Mansour bin Zayed al Nahyan, the United Arab Emirates' deputy prime minister and a member of the royal family. The lines between the kingdom's investments and al-Qubaisi's own personal investments, as well as those of Sheikh Mansour, were sometimes unclear even to those in his orbit. While Tasameem was sometimes identified in the press as a government fund, other reports have speculated that it was a vehicle for al-Qubaisi's personal investments.

With his slicked-back black hair and honed physique, al-Qubaisi was simultaneously a man of the East and of the West. At home, he reportedly wore traditional Emirati garb and kept a family household for his wife and children. Overseas, he lived a flashier life, throwing parties attended by models at his villa in the south of France, driving Ferraris and Bugattis, and switching out his robes for tight-fitting graphic T-shirts.

With al-Qubaisi at the helm, IPIC and one of its subsidiaries, Aabar Investments, had been on a spending spree. The young Arab had personally helped negotiate the bailout of Barclays Bank alongside Qatar in 2008 and had gobbled up stakes in major corporations such as Daimler-Benz, the parent company of the German luxury car brand Mercedes-Benz, and Virgin Galactic, the British billionaire Richard Branson's commercial spaceline. Now he was turning his attentions to luxury real estate.

Barnett had been introduced to executives at Aabar via a mutual friend, a private medical doctor whom he had met in New York and who had treated high-net-worth individuals from the Middle East. He had struck a deal before the financial crisis with one of al-Qubaisi's predecessors to finance a $1.4 billion condo project he was erecting on Manhattan's West 57th Street, just across from Carnegie Hall. Barnett had envisioned a ninety-story tower, a combination hotel and condo that would rise to more than a thousand feet. Unlike Macklowe's building, which would be set off to the east, this project, his most ambitious ever, would have dead-center views of Central Park.

Now Barnett was coming to al-Qubaisi, the new chief of Aabar, with a problem. He had dug a deep hole in the ground at the site, laying the foundations for his tower, but even with Aabar's prior commitment to put in $400 million, he didn't have enough equity in the project to get a construction loan. Times had changed, and the banks were requiring developers to have more skin in the game. His own pockets were empty, and with the stock markets churning and the economic outlook desperately uncertain, it was tough to find another equity partner to back him.

Mothballing the project, as Barnett feared al-Qubaisi might suggest, would mean years of shouldering expensive carrying costs while keeping creditors at bay. If they started now, they could be the first on the market when the tide turned. "I needed every dollar I could get my hands on," Barnett would say later, summing up his predicament.

Barnett had picked an odd time to erect what he told al-Qubaisi would be one of the world's most luxurious buildings, with pent-houses asking up to $100 million. Not only had the city never seen prices this high, but the Manhattan real estate market had hit hard times in 2009. Prices had collapsed by close to 20 percent, and some buyers of luxury condos became so unnerved by the free fall that they forfeited six-figure deposits rather than closing on deals they had made. In the first quarter of 2009, sales of co-ops and condominiums in Manhattan plunged nearly 60 percent compared with the first quarter of 2008.

Meanwhile, the U.S. economy remained sluggish. By the end of the year, real gross domestic product had fallen 4.3 percent from its peak in 2007, the largest decline in the postwar era, and the unemployment rate, which was 5 percent in December 2007, had reached 10 percent by October 2009. And compared to the free-wheeling days that precipitated the subprime mortgage crisis at the root of the financial crisis, home purchasing had gotten harder. The foreclosure crisis had precipitated broad changes across the nation's housing markets and significantly altered underwriting standards for mortgages. Banks required larger down payments, had stricter income and asset tests, and applied far greater scrutiny to borrowers. Loan officers complained that banks wanted to see everything but a buyer's shoe size. Foreign buyers—those without green cards or U.S. citizenship—faced particularly high levels of scrutiny.

It is hardly surprising, then, that there was little appetite for a project with the risk profile of Barnett's.

Going forward with the tower, which Barnett dubbed One57, "was completely tone-deaf to the economic situation that the world, not just the country, found itself in," said the appraiser Jonathan Miller of Barnett's decision to forge ahead while the market was in the doldrums. "At that point, we were talking about a global thermonuclear breakdown of the economy."

Barnett, however, took a different view of the market, believing the situation could play right into his hands. He had eyed the success, in the years immediately preceding the financial crisis, of the nearby condominium at 15 Central Park West with great interest. As prices went up and up at that building, he began reconsidering what prices might be achievable at his own. "We start thinking, 'You know, we have a way better view than those guys,'" he said of his 57th Street building, which he had been working to assemble since the late 1990s. It would be known as One57.

He believed the buyers for his new building wouldn't be the types of people who financed their deals. Rather, they were part of a new wealthy superclass circling the globe in search of safe places to park their capital. New billionaires were being minted every day in countries like China, Russia, Brazil, and India. Many of them looked to America as somewhere they could secure their capital when things were dicey at home. Following the lessons of the financial crisis, they would be wary of any investment that required financial engineering. Real estate transactions may have caused the world's financial meltdown, but real estate itself was still the ultimate "hard asset" in contrast to the fickle performance of fluid markets like stocks and bonds.

Barnett would thus build the world's most expensive safety deposit boxes, where investors could stash their money whether they intended to actually live in them or not. New York, he believed, would be the perfect place for the rich to park their capital. With billionaire Michael Bloomberg as the city's "CEO-mayor," the global elite saw the city as a beacon of stability. Bloomberg's New York projected an open-for-business image that had pulled the city out of the shadow of 9/11.

Perhaps most importantly to developers like Barnett, Bloomberg had also paved the way for the redevelopment of large swaths of the city, including the Brooklyn waterfront, which transformed from near-abandoned wasteland into scores of luxury residential buildings and landscaped park land on his watch. Roughly forty thousand new buildings were constructed while he was in office, and almost a third of the city was rezoned, making way for new development. Even as some New Yorkers began to speak out against wealth inequality—punctuated by the subsequent Occupy Wall Street protests and "occupation" of a downtown park—New York's mayor saw billionaires as a welcome addition to his city. "If we can find a bunch of billionaires around the world to move here, that would be a godsend. Because that's where the revenue comes to take care of everybody else," he once said.

Sitting that day in the upscale London hotel suite with al-Qubaisi, Barnett was channeling a similar energy as his city's mayor. People had a lot of confidence in New York and in America, and they were prepared to invest and store their wealth there, he said. It all but guaranteed a sharp increase in prices.

AL-QUBAISI TOOK LITTLE convincing about moving ahead with Barnett's plans. If Barnett was proposing a new species of skyscraper for New York, he was all in. The circles in which he moved internationally were filled with ultra-high-net-worth individuals to whom he knew the pitch would appeal.

Al-Qubaisi reassured Barnett. "It's the best site in New York City. Of course we're moving ahead with it," he said.

Barnett left the meeting with his coffers replenished. Aabar Investments and Tasameem would up their investment in the building to around $650 million, on top of the $50 million Extell was putting up.

Aabar would also help Barnett negotiate $700 million in loans from a syndicate led by Bank of America and Banco Santander. It was one of the largest construction loans made since the downturn.

"There will be buyers," al-Qubaisi told him, according to a report in *The Wall Street Journal*.

GETTING THE MONEY to build a skyscraper is an uphill battle, one that at times can verge on madness. Even more daunting than financing, though, was assembling the property to build, as Harry Macklowe was finding out the hard way at the Drake Hotel site.

But if assemblage was a game of chess, Gary Barnett was its undisputed grand master.

Born Gershon Swiatycki in 1955, Barnett grew up in far more modest surroundings than Macklowe. A member of a cloistered Orthodox Jewish enclave on New York's Lower East Side, as a child Barnett had lived tightly packed with his nine siblings on the top floor of a low-rise rent-controlled building on Pike Street near the base of the Manhattan Bridge. It was not an unusual arrangement for the neighborhood, which had become a hub of Jewish immigrants from Germany, Poland, and beyond, many of whom lived in crowded tenement buildings that often lacked indoor plumbing and were susceptible to fires.

Barnett's father, Chaim Swiatycki, was born in Poland and moved to the United States from Tel Aviv in 1938 as a student of theology. In New York, he taught at Mesivtha Tifereth Jerusalem, a nearby yeshiva founded in 1907, and became a respected rabbi and Talmudic scholar. Later he moved his growing family to Monsey, an enclave about an hour north of the city with a large Orthodox Jewish population.

As a child, Barnett dreamed of being a basketball player—he said he was actually pretty good for a short white boy—but it wasn't to be. More gifted with numbers than hoops, he studied math at Queens College and went on to earn an economics degree from Hunter College.

He had gotten into the real estate business incidentally. In 1980, while vacationing in Florida, Barnett met and eventually fell in love with Evelyn Muller, whose father, Shulim Muller, had founded the Belgian diamond company S. Muller & Sons, based in Antwerp. The company specialized in rough diamond sorting and trading and acted as a "sightholder" for the diamond mining colossus De Beers, meaning it was one of a small number of designated diamond-cutting centers authorized to purchase stones from the company, providing a crucial link from De Beers to the universe of brokers, cutters, and wholesalers who sell its stones. After they married, Muller invited Barnett to join the family business. He accepted a post in Antwerp, where he traded stones for more than a decade.

Later, when the Mullers decided to deploy some of their profits into the real estate business in the United States, Barnett, with no expertise to speak of, headed the effort, buying up office properties in Wichita, Kansas, and Louisville, Kentucky, and managing the business through late night phone calls. In 1995, he and Evelyn moved back to the States to expand the family's real estate efforts.

When Evelyn died in 1998 from cancer, Barnett became the single father of their five children. He threw himself into his work, continuing to collaborate with his late wife's family on real estate projects in New York. He would go on to remarry in 2001 to a woman named Ayala Braun, with whom he would eventually share ten children and a modest two-story house in Richmond Hill, Queens.

Having originally named his firm Diamond Heritage Properties, Barnett changed the company's name to Intell Management and Investment Company in 1998. Then, after he was sued by the tech company Intel, he changed it to Extell. In time, the company focused more on doing business in New York. Barnett's first major purchase was a graceful century-old apartment complex known as the Belnord on the Upper West Side. When it opened in 1909, the Belnord was thought to be the largest apartment complex in the United States. Its previous owner had been locked in a decades-long standoff with the building's rent-regulated and rent-stabilized tenants, and Barnett got more than he bargained for in trying to convert the apartments to market rate. He fell behind on his mortgage payments after a New York State court ruled that landlords could not raise rents on buildings with certain tax abatements. It was a taste of the complications and expenses that came with operating in the country's most populous city. Still, he would ultimately come out on top. In 2015, he sold the complex to his former partner Ziel Feldman for $575 million; he had bought it for just $15 million in 1994. Then, in 1998, he built a sleek modern tower in Times Square that would be the home of the W Hotel.

A few years later, Barnett made headlines for publicly sparring with the real estate magnate Bruce Ratner over the future site of the Renzo Piano–designed New York Times tower. Barnett owned a small parking garage, one of about eleven buildings slated to be condemned to make way for the tower, and he tried to band together with the other owners to hold the site hostage so that he could either develop it himself or extract a greater payment from Ratner. The gambit failed and he was forced to sell the site through eminent domain, whereby the government can force the sale of the property for state or public use.

His even greater brush with local fame came in 2005 when, for $1.76 billion, a consortium of Hong Kong investors sold him a 77-acre parcel on Riverside South that had been first optioned by Donald Trump and in which the future president still owned a 30 percent stake. The deal infuriated Trump, who said he believed the property was worth much more. He sued the Asian investors in federal district court, saying they had breached their fiduciary duty to sell the parcel to the highest bidder and accusing them of accepting a lowball offer from Barnett in exchange for kickbacks as part of a larger tax avoidance scheme. The suit was eventually dismissed on appeal, and Barnett proceeded to develop portions of the site into high-rise condos.

By the time One57 came around, Barnett had earned a reputation as a developer with big ambitions, one who was unafraid to go up against the long-standing giants of the New York real estate scene.

DESPITE THEIR PROFESSIONAL accomplishments and long ties to the city, neither Macklowe nor Barnett was born a New York real estate insider. By New York standards, they were both non-natives. Until relatively recently, the New York real estate industry was predominantly controlled by just a handful of very powerful families, whose development activity spanned generations and had helped shape the evolution of the city: the Rudins, Dursts, Roses, Fishers, and Tishmans. These families were known not just for their buildings, but also for their civic engagement. The Rudin Center for Transportation Policy and Management was named for the Rudins at New York University, while the majestic Rose Main Reading Room at the New York Public Library on Bryant Park was named for the Roses. *The New York Times* once described these clans as "to New York what the oil barons are to Houston or the steel bosses were to Pittsburgh." When one generation expired, the mantle was passed down to the next.

By the early 2000s, these real estate dynasties still controlled vast swaths of Manhattan real estate and held significant political influence. Still, they were beginning to lose some ground to publicly traded real estate investment trusts like SL Green and Vornado Realty Trust, whose hefty balance sheets and deep cash reserves meant they could get cheaper financing. The families had changed gears, focusing not so much on getting rich as on staying rich.

And then there was the new money: the likes of Barnett and Macklowe.

FOR DEVELOPERS, THE problem with New York is that there's not much room to build.

The most desirable Manhattan neighborhoods are full, every consecutive block jammed with buildings big and small, from low-rise townhomes to skyscraping towers. It's rare to find an undeveloped parcel of land, and even if a developer does stumble upon one, such parcels are usually too narrow to support the construction of a high-rise building.

To compensate, the city's most successful developers have become accomplished assemblers of land, buying up several buildings or parcels of land on a single block with the goal of combining them into a single plot. If Manhattan is like a *Monopoly* board, composed predominantly of 25-by-100-foot lots, it is the developer's mission to collect the most prized lots and combine them to build something bigger. As in *Monopoly,* structures can be built only when all the spaces in the area are owned by the same player.

New York City authorities began regulating the construction of high-rise buildings in 1916, when they passed the city's first zoning law mandating that towers of a certain height have setbacks so as to allow sunlight to reach the street and avoid shadows. A subsequent overhaul of the regulations in 1961, designed to prevent massive new buildings from blocking light and air from reaching the streets, completely changed the game, introducing a new formula to regulate building height known as FAR, or floor area ratio. According to the new regulations, each city lot would be granted a maximum developable floor space based on where it was located. Working out what they could build would be a simple calculation. If a property owner with a ten-thousand-square-foot site was granted a FAR of 3, for instance, they would simply multiply the numbers, for a maximum buildable floor area of thirty thousand square feet.

The new regulations meant that outside highly regulated historic districts, developers could essentially build whatever they wanted—completely avoiding any kind of public design-review process—provided that they followed the prescribed rules for their lot.

The rules also contained another provision that resulted in developers seeking out more than just the neighboring properties to their sites. They would often acquire what's known in New York as "air rights," the empty space above an existing building, from neighboring owners. If zoning laws allowed for the construction of a larger building than currently exists on a site, an owner could sell that buildable air to a developer so that they might enlarge their nearby project. Under the new rules, FAR could be used only once, so if an owner sold their unused rights to a neighbor, that owner would no longer have the right to develop a larger property on their own site.

Experts say that air rights in New York used to be seen as a standard commodity, trading at a singular price per square foot across the board. These days, the price of an air right or an easement can be higher than for the land itself, depending on how vital they are to a developer's ability to proceed with a project. In the eyes of Manhattan's most successful developers, the air is just invisible land that no one has built on yet.

The assemblage process requires massive amounts of patience, persuasion, and money, as well as an in-depth understanding of Manhattan's complex zoning code. Not only must developers persuade each individual owner to part with their property at a reasonable price and within a practical time frame, they then have to merge the sites and conceive of a building that can take advantage of the parcel they were dealt. Barnett knew how to use New York City's famously complicated zoning code to his advantage better than anyone else.

In some ways, 57th Street was perfectly primed as a playground for developers like him. It had the highest FAR in the city, and yet few were making use of it. Until the 2000s, the area was still largely populated by low-rise and landmark buildings with heaps of unused FAR that could potentially be sold to developers. Those low-rise buildings included religious institutions like churches and synagogues or nonprofits that had owned their buildings for decades. Some faced financial struggles and dwindling congregations and were glad for the opportunity for outside revenue from the sale of their air rights. On the flip side, however, their leaders were often unsophisticated when it came to real estate and negotiations. In other words, there was an unbelievable amount of low-hanging fruit.

Sophisticated developers like Barnett have long employed various tricks and strategies to maximize their FAR. Since the lower floors of their buildings have the worst views and are therefore the least valuable, they sometimes set their towers back from the street on narrower floorplates, thereby allowing them to use their FAR to add height to the building. Since FAR is measured by floor area and not by height, they go even taller by raising ceiling heights to increase the distance between floors. Going taller means maximizing the number of units that have compelling views of the park and thereby maximizing potential profits. The taller they build, the more value they squeeze out of a plot of land.

For Barnett, assemblage was a balancing act. The developer must rack up all the pieces of the puzzle by all means necessary, but without overextending his or her finances so much that the project becomes unviable. Sometimes he would disguise his purchases by purchasing through purpose-created corporate entities so as to avoid tipping off the neighbors to the grander plan, which would let them know they had leverage to negotiate a higher price for the sale of their own building or air rights.

A developer, he said, must be unafraid to walk away if a seller is overplaying their hand. He did exactly that at his W Hotel in Times Square, pushing forward with a smaller hotel development than a larger assemblage would have allowed after the seller declined to budge. "A lot of times people miscalculate. They go for too much and they wind up getting nothing," he said. "They came back to us when we were already in the foundations," he said of the Times Square project. "And we said, 'Sorry, too late.' We were already under construction and the financing was tied up."

The economics of assemblage can be unpredictable and punishing when the pieces don't fall into place, making such speculative projects more risky than many developers can stomach. In their early stages, these projects are also less appealing to the public markets and traditional lenders like banks, since their success is tied so closely with a given developer's ability to sew up the pieces.

Because developers often pay above-market prices for key pieces of an assemblage, they are left more vulnerable to shifts in the larger market. If an assemblage fails, it can be difficult to off-load the early pieces at any kind of financial gain, especially if the market tides have changed.

"This is not for the faint of heart," Barnett said.

STARTING IN THE late 1990s, Barnett spent more than a decade and hundreds of millions of dollars to secure the parcels of land and air rights he needed to put the One57 puzzle together. The journey involved negotiations with at least eighteen separate property sellers and at least twenty-two arm's-length transactions involving him or his affiliates.

The process began in March 1998, when Barnett's onetime partner, Ziel Feldman, inked a ground lease deal with the two elderly owners of an antiquated office building at 157 East 57th, which housed businesses like record labels and comedy promoters. The seller was Forrell & Thomas, a small music label that produced jingles for companies like Ballantine's Beer ("You get a smile every time with a Ballantine") and the New York World's Fair ("Part of the fun of the World's Fair is the subway special that takes you there"). The company had previously had its offices on the site and was one of a long line of music-related businesses that populated the strip of 57th Street between Sixth and Seventh avenues. Initially, when Barnett took over the lease from Feldman, he just sat on the property, thinking that at one point it might form part of a wider assemblage for a residential building. At the time, he didn't imagine just how large that assemblage might become.

He followed that deal in 2001 with a $7 million deal for a small building at 161 West 57th Street that was home to Uncle Sam Umbrellas and Canes, a storied New York City institution that had been in business for 134 years and was thought to be the last of its kind. (The umbrella store had drawn an elite clientele, from Sarah Delano Roosevelt to Charlie Chaplin. It sold high-end umbrellas with cigarette lighters concealed in their handles as well as more affordable models like their popular GustBuster, which was designed to withstand strong winds without popping inside out.)

Over the next few years, Barnett quietly expanded the site, adding an adjacent parking structure and courting the residents of nearby co-op buildings, such as Alwyn Court, an ornate century-old terra-cotta building at the corner of Seventh Avenue, and Joyce

Manor, a midblock red brick building dating to the 1930s, to sell their air rights. The co-op owners were suitably compensated for the rights, to the tune of about $5 million in the case of Joyce Manor. The owners of the Nippon Club, a Japanese gentleman's club at 145 West 57th Street, also agreed to part with their development rights.

Barnett continued assembling the site throughout the late 1900s and early aughts without a clear idea where he was headed or how far he might get. By the mid-aughts, he reviewed his progress. "We thought originally we might wind up with 250,000 or 300,000 square feet, but as we kept going on we would end up with over 550,000 square feet of FAR. All of a sudden, we realized we have a tall building. A really tall building."

By 2006, however, Barnett had reached an impasse. He had slowly been merging properties and development rights on both the western and eastern sides of the block into two large zoning lots, but now he needed to be able to combine the two. If he did that, he could finally unlock the full potential of the site, a tower with unprecedented views of Central Park and one that would top Trump International Hotel & Tower as the city's tallest residential spire. Without finding a way to combine the two lots, Extell would have to settle for a much more modest building—and all of Barnett's machinations would have been for limited reward.

Critical to unlocking the site was the Calvary Baptist Church, the more than century-old evangelical church at 123 West 57th Street formed by abolitionists and known for its weekly live radio broadcast, *The Calvary Hour,* which was at one point piped into the rooms of the neighboring Salisbury Hotel, also owned by the church. It had drawn high-profile worshippers like Presidents Richard Nixon and Bill Clinton; the Reverend Billy Graham even preached there. Its senior pastor, the Reverend David Epstein, the brother of the television host Kathy Lee Gifford, had started out in a small Black Methodist church in Virginia. For several years, Barnett had been sending letters and making calls to the church's top brass, but he had received no response. He had almost given up.

"I was getting nowhere, literally for years, and I was kind of pulling my hair out," Barnett recalled. "But as I kept on bidding the price up, I guess, at some point, they got smart. They got the right lawyers, the right advisers, and they figured out how to hold me up."

BRENT LEWIS WAS standing in the nave of the main sanctuary of the church on West 57th Street. Behind a dramatic Gothic Tudor entryway, the sanctuary was a sprawling space filled with towering ceilings, a large pipe organ, blood-red carpets, and row upon row of wooden pews.

It was an evening in February 2009, and Lewis, an investment banker who served as the church's treasurer, looked out over a sea of faces. The church was packed that day with hundreds of congregants, a diverse group that seemed to straddle every age group and ethnicity, from elderly retirees to young Wall Street types and young children who played among the pews.

Lewis's task was to walk the assembled congregation through a proposal made by Barnett to buy the church's "air rights," or the undeveloped land above its building. He had prepared a Power-Point presentation to explain the complicated mechanics of the deal.

The responses to Lewis's presentations were mixed.

Some among the congregation had reservations. Why shouldn't Calvary hold out and develop the property itself? Why let the developer reap the rewards? What would they even do with all the money that a sale would produce? Was it wise to sell the rights in the middle of one of the worst recessions the country had ever seen? An elderly, decades-long member of the congregation piped up: Shouldn't Calvary also be concerned about doing business with a developer whose partners were in the Middle East?

Lewis made the case to the congregation that Barnett's proposal would result in the highest value for the rights. Since the developer had already assembled a huge number of sites on the block, a deal with Calvary would mean adding square footage to his building at its highest point. Those floors would be the most valuable, and Extell would probably pay more than any other prospective buyer to make this work.

A few months later, extremely late in the acquisition process, Barnett finally cracked the keystone site. He convinced Calvary to accept $28.6 million for 45,000 square feet of air rights. The Calvary deal, which priced out to around $913 per buildable foot, was by far the most crucial, and therefore the most expensive, piece of the puzzle. With the certainty that the development would be realized once the deal closed, and with it the potentially stratospheric sales price from the resulting condos, Barnett was willing to reach deeper into his pockets. As part of the deal, Calvary negotiated that if it ever wanted to do a redesign of the church, it would receive free design and engineering services from Extell.

The deal valued the air rights at a significantly higher sum than any other piece of the assemblage. Despite the pricey final push, though, the incremental nature of the One57 assemblage allowed Barnett to secure the site for his tower at a relatively low cost, estimated to be just over $200 million. Ultimately, seven buildings would be demolished to make way for the tower.

"Gary Barnett was the right guy at the right time in a very scary market," said the luxury real estate agent Nikki Field. "He was the only one who kept his shovel in the ground and kept building. Everybody else pulled back because they were terrified of that mortgage crisis, and what it was going to do to real estate as a whole and New York in particular. But this guy really had the balls to keep going."

CHAPTER 5

California Dreaming

I n the fall of 2009, the commercial real estate broker Woody Heller got a call in his office at 399 Park Avenue. An attorney he knew needed an introduction to Harry Macklowe.

The attorney was calling on behalf of a Los Angeles–based private equity fund, which had made an offer to buy three residential rental buildings from Macklowe but for days had failed to get a response. The attorney knew that Woody, as the broker was known across the industry, was close to Harry and could get his attention.

Heller worked for the Manhattan brokerage then known as Studley, the same firm where Macklowe had gotten his start. He had a reputation as a cool-as-a-cucumber dealmaker who could navigate hairy transactions. With an undergraduate degree from Stanford, the tall, slender Heller, who was around fifty at the time, was a rare breed in the rough-and-tumble world of real estate. Articulate and thoughtful, Heller had considered a career as a composer before stumbling into a career in real estate, where he had quickly made a name for himself with deals for iconic properties like the Chrysler Building.

By this point in 2009, Macklowe's financial woes were widely known throughout the industry. Heller thought the developer might indeed agree to sell—Macklowe had even asked the broker's opinion about the value of the buildings weeks earlier. After hanging up with the attorney representing the private equity fund, Heller quickly rattled off an email to Macklowe, but days passed again with no response. Behind the scenes, Heller began to suspect Macklowe had other plans. Rumors were rampant that the developer planned to roll up the three buildings, which included a luxury rental on West 53rd Street called River Tower, and float an initial public offering—an unusual move for a relatively small private firm like Macklowe's—in a bid to raise some badly needed funds. He recognized that Macklowe was in a complex financial situation and that any decision he would make about the buildings would involve a lot of moving pieces.

A week later, Heller found himself huddled with his phone on the floor of a hallway in a hulking convention center in San Francisco, where he was attending a conference hosted by the Urban Land Institute. After days of silence, Macklowe had emerged—and suddenly had lots of questions about the mysterious private equity fund, which had zero footprint in New York. Who were they? Were they serious about the deal? Heller told the developer that he knew almost nothing about the company, but he offered to fly down to Los Angeles in a few days to meet with the principals. "Can you go tomorrow?" Macklowe asked.

No, Heller said. He would go two days later because he had promised his longtime girlfriend, Beth, who was flying in from New York that night, that the pair would spend the following day with a friend who lived in San Francisco. They had made reservations to eat at renowned chef Gary Danko's restaurant in Russian Hill.

"Okay, then," Macklowe said softly, dejected.

Hearing Macklowe's tone, Heller knew his fancy dinner plans would have to wait. There was a lot of money to be made on a potential commission for the sale of the rental buildings and it hadn't exactly been a booming twelve months. Things had gotten so tight that Heller, somewhat dramatically, had even been considering returning his extra cable boxes to save money on his television bill. If Macklowe wanted him in Los Angeles tomorrow, he would be there.

Then Macklowe asked a question that threw him further for a loop. "Do you think they'd be interested in being my partner on the Drake?" Macklowe wondered aloud, a hopeful tone in his voice. He desperately needed to find a partner to develop the Drake site. Without one, he would soon be handing the keys back to Deutsche Bank and iStar Financial, an investment manager that had purchased some of the debt.

Heller said he believed that CIM, the private equity firm, was a real estate investment trust that bought only established, stabilized buildings with reliable incomes from rents. "It's the complete opposite profile of an equity partner on a development site. How on earth could they do that?"

But he promised he would ask.

The following day, Heller found himself whisked from LAX to the CIM offices, a nondescript office complex on Wilshire Boulevard. Inside, Heller was directed into a conference room where Shaul Kuba, one of CIM's founders, was waiting for him. Though he had never met Kuba before, Heller was struck by the investor's focused, intense bearing, and the pair fell into an easy rapport.

CIM had been founded in 1994 by Kuba and his friend Avi Shemesh, both former Israeli paratroopers, and Richard Ressler, a former investment banker at Drexel Burnham Lambert, the firm famously forced into bankruptcy thanks to illegal dealings by the billionaire junk bond king Michael Milken. Ressler moved in extremely affluent and well-connected circles. His brother Tony had founded the private equity giant Apollo Global Management, which had quickly become one of the finance industry's most influential dealmakers, and their sister Debra had married Apollo's other co-founder, Leon Black. Richard Ressler was a shareholder in Brooke International, through which he had dabbled in the manufacture and sale of cigarettes in Russia and which was also making its mark in real estate, building a large office complex in Moscow.

Kuba and Shemesh had grown up together in a small town outside Tel Aviv, and their bond deepened during their three-year stint serving together as paratroopers in the Israel Defense Forces. After their service, the duo had immigrated to the United States and launched a series of business ventures, including a landscaping company. One of their clients was Ressler.

Kuba and Shemesh were investing the proceeds from their landscaping business in commercial real estate in West Hollywood. Impressed, Ressler suggested the pair go into business with him, and the group began by acquiring properties in Los Angeles, starting in Santa Monica and creeping toward Hollywood, where they bought a portfolio of buildings that included the former Kodak Theater, the storied location of the Academy Award ceremonies. They targeted distressed or undervalued properties in the urban core and courted influential politicians with major donations.

In time, CIM became a darling of institutional investors including city and state pension funds. By the end of 2011, it would have about $10.9 billion under management, including a hefty $1.7 billion investment from the California Public Employees' Retirement System (CalPERS), the nation's largest public pension fund.

It wasn't hard to see why. Between 2006 and 2011, the company would post an annual return of 7.4 percent, compared with a 20 percent annual decline for a batch of similar high-risk, high-return funds with a similar profile that CalPERS was tracking, *The Wall Street Journal* reported. Unlike some of its competitors, CIM had cleverly slowed its investing from 2006 to 2008 as it saw the market overheat, leaving it with deep pockets to enjoy the spoils of the downturn later.

Its reputation was not without blemish. In 2009, the *Los Angeles Times* reported that CIM had paid former Los Angeles deputy mayor Alfred J. R. Villalobos nearly $16 million in fees for securing investments from CalPERS and the California State Teachers' Retirement System. While CIM was not accused of any wrongdoing, and had parted ways with Villalobos prior to CalPERS's making a commitment to CIM, the news report cast an unwelcome spotlight on the company.

Undeterred, CIM now had a new target in mind: New York City. It had been evaluating investments in the city for more than a decade and now planned to enter with a splash. Impressed with the fund's ambitions, Heller advised Kuba to get on a plane two days later to meet Macklowe and his son at their offices. He knew the deal for the rental buildings would have to happen quickly. Kuba, keen to get the ball rolling, agreed.

"I know this is a ridiculous question, but I promised Harry I would ask," Heller said as the meeting came to a close. "Would you guys have any interest in partnering with him on his development projects?"

To Heller's surprise, Kuba did not dismiss the idea out of hand. The company managed other pools of money, including what's known as "opportunity funds," which were geared toward riskier investments exactly along the lines of the Drake project, he said. They could discuss it when they got to New York.

FOR ALL THE skill that developers like Harry Macklowe and Gary Barnett have at identifying potential building sites, assemblage is just the beginning. The dreams of constructing grand buildings on prime properties often run headlong into the nightmare of how to pay for them. And the unprecedented scale of the buildings that would become known as Billionaires' Row would entail years of financial wrangling—and the involvement of lenders who ranged from some of the world's biggest investment banks, private equity funds, and hedge funds to more untested sources, like sovereign wealth funds, ultra-high-net-worth individuals, and overseas con-glomerates.

The underlying financial structure of a proposed skyscraper is known as the project's "capital stack." The capital stack includes all the debt and equity used to build the tower and determines who gets paid, the order in which they will be paid, and how much risk each party will assume. It also determines which party has the right to foreclose—and when, and how—if the equity holders don't meet their stated obligations.

The stack is often compared to a cake with different layers, with each injection of money stacked above the last, each with its own sets of rights and obligations. The capital at the bottom of the stack typically gets paid out first, while the capital at the highest risk, on the top, gets paid out last.

The stack is put together piece by piece. Once a developer or "sponsor" has secured a site, he or she will typically team up with one or more partners with the goal of putting together enough equity for the project to entice a lender to write a construction loan. That's where figures like CIM and Khadem al-Qubaisi come in.

The money the sponsors and their investors inject into the deal—the top layer of the cake—is typically referred to as "common equity." It's the developer's "skin in the game." Common equity has the highest risk profile of any layer of the capital stack but potentially the greatest reward if a project succeeds. While their capital is the first in, the developer typically doesn't see any significant return until the majority of a building's units are sold. The last 15 percent of units typically determine the profitability of the whole enterprise. If the earlier units are sold at a significant discount, the profits from the project could be wiped out before sales ever reach that threshold.

The money provided by the construction lenders, typically large banks, and often a consortium of multiple banks, is usually positioned at the bottom of the capital stack, giving it the highest priority for repayment. These loans charge interest, much like the mortgage on a home, and the property secures the loan, giving the banks the highest claim on the asset. If the sponsor defaults on the loan, the banks can foreclose on the project and sell it to recover their funds. Depending on a borrower's risk profile, and the project's degree of leverage, interest rates for such "senior loans" run from 2 percent to around 10 percent.

If the project is still short on funds, or runs over budget during the construction, other types of financing can come into play, such as "mezzanine financing" and "preferred equity." Mezzanine lenders are typically brought in to plug a hole in the capital stack between debt and equity. Their priority is second to the senior lender, but consequently they charge higher interest rates, mostly in the range of 10 to 15 percent a year. The mezzanine loan is generally not secured by the property, unlike the mortgage, but instead by the sponsor's equity in the project.

Alternatively, the sponsors can raise more equity to plug the hole. Preferred equity investors typically enter a project late in the process and are positioned to get their money out before the developer and many other investors. Those preferred equity investors sometimes negotiate controlling rights in the project that see them take control over management decisions.

The layered cake, while the easiest way to conceptualize the financing structure, is also sometimes an oversimplification. The most complicated projects often pay out the different "layers" via what's called a waterfall—a complex formula that determines who gets paid what under what circumstances. The structure comes from private equity and structured-finance transactions and has increasingly been used by real estate developers who take on complex, large-scale projects with tremendous risk. As such projects have become behemoth undertakings, so too have the disputes over who pays what, or gets paid, when things go wrong.

The "sponsors," sometimes referred to as the developers or general partners of these projects, the Gary Barnetts and Harry Macklowes, are generally the ones making the pitch for financing at all of these stages. Sponsors are compensated in several ways—the development fee, paid out by the partnership in return for overseeing the entirety of the process, and sometimes a construction fee, if the sponsors have their own construction arm—but the most high-stakes piece of compensation comes from the potential return on their own equity investment as well as the sponsor's share of what's known in the industry as the "promote," that is, the profits from the final sales of the condo units. Those profits are typically doled out among the equity holders after the debt attached to the project has been paid off.

A sponsor's share of the promote is their lottery ticket, their chance to win big on a project. If units sell out fast and at high prices, they could make multiples of what they make from fees alone. If the project fails, they risk losing any initial investment they made personally—and, of course, their reputation—but it's primarily their investors' and lenders' capital that's at risk.

For many developers, the fees alone are enough of an incentive to build. If they make money on the lottery ticket, it's a bonus. One developer put it this way: "If I make no money on the equity, yes that's going to suck, but I'll take a tax loss and I'll carry that forward for the next deal that makes money. There's always a way to monetize the loss."

Sponsors are "more like Barnum & Bailey than they are like John Glenn," said Myers Mermel, a broker, of the role that the original developers play in a tower's journey. "They all want to make it seem as if they've boarded the Friendship 7, it's a risky ride and they're not sure they'll ever make it back to earth. In reality, it's more like they're putting on a show."

THE WEEKS FOLLOWING his trip to California were some of the busiest of Heller's career. Kuba and his partners at CIM had, as promised, flown promptly to New York to meet with the Macklowes. After two days of meetings and a tour of the rental buildings in question, Kuba had headed back to L.A. The Macklowes had also pitched him their plans for the Drake, and Kuba was impressed. Both eager to make a deal, the parties were engaged in near constant negotiations.

Suddenly finding themselves in the thick of what could be a

career-defining deal, Heller and his team at Studley began madly assembling each building's financials, working late into the night for days on end. Heller and the Macklowes went back and forth with iStar, a real estate investment trust that had purchased some of the project's debt from Deutsche Bank, and its chief executive, Jay Sugarman, over the sale of the loans. Sugarman agreed to give them more time to put the deal together. He was willing to sell the debt to CIM at a significant discount, or accept a significantly discounted payoff, in order to avoid a long and messy foreclosure. As negotiations continued, Ressler flew to New York to meet the Macklowes.

For the principals at CIM, the partnership with Macklowe represented a significant degree of risk. Even with their relationships, they knew they could face difficulty in securing a construction loan to actually build the tower. The ability to obtain financing had completely dried up with the onset of the global financial crisis, and no one was lending for speculative projects such as this one, which promised the tallest residential building in New York City. "That meant that they would have had to be prepared to put up all the money themselves. It was an unbelievably bold decision," Heller said later.

There was also the issue of the Macklowes themselves, who still pushed to keep as much control over the project as possible. Used to working alone with very few limited partners, Harry Macklowe had a particular vision for the tower and was likely to be uncompromising. The dynamic between father and son was also problematic. Harry viewed deals through a lens of blind optimism, while Billy was more cautious and pragmatic. "It wasn't a question of whether Harry was the right person for the job," Heller said. "The question was how to be Harry's partner, when he wasn't housetrained on having a partner."

Again, the brownstones became a point of contention. CIM didn't want to move ahead with a deal until the assemblage was locked down. "They were not really accustomed to New York development and the tectonic pace at which assemblages move," Billy Macklowe said later. "They said, 'We need it all now, or there's no deal.' They wanted everything neatly packaged with a red bow on it."

With CIM growing impatient, the Macklowes began furiously negotiating with Turnbull & Asser, the clothing company owned by the Harrods scion Ali Fayed, to lock down its townhouse, eventually striking a deal for a building swap that would give the company a new building the Macklowes had already purchased on the edge of the Drake site in return for one that was standing in the way of the project. Jacob & Co. and Turnbull would each have locations on the eastern edge of the new tower. Without the full wall of retail they had wanted, the Nordstrom deal fell apart, but the project could still go ahead.

Since the brownstones the Macklowes had already secured were not all part of the core loan collateral, the lenders arguably had no claim to them, and CIM needed them to carry out the plans. They would ultimately be Macklowe's saving grace, giving him the leverage he needed to hold on to a piece of the deal. While his equity in the project would be entirely wiped out, he would be left with a developer's fee and what is sometimes described as a "hope certificate," a percentage of the eventual profits from the project, potentially as high as 5 percent.

It had taken considerable trade-offs, but as the year drew to an end, it seemed Harry Macklowe was getting his deal despite the near-impossible market.

THE DEAL WAS slated to close just a few days before Christmas, and Heller could hardly wait. He and Beth planned to spend the week in celebration mode, skiing with her children in Aspen. In the meantime, the couple were scheduled to attend a wedding in Florida, where Heller, fearful of being overheard by the real estate people who were in attendance, spent the majority of the weekend sequestered in the hotel room juggling phone calls from Macklowe and CIM. Unlike most deals he had worked on, there was no broker on the other side of the deal. In fact, it was never completely clear who exactly Heller was representing or who would cut him a check at the finish line. This was a one-man-operated negotiation.

The hotel room had a spotty cell phone signal and the hotel room's landline didn't have conference calling, so Heller requested that an additional phone be delivered to his room. The two phones were located on opposite sides of the room, with their cords barely stretching far enough to reach his ears. He would turn the volume up so that both sides could hear each other on separate lines. He spent the weekend with a crick in his neck.

As he boarded the plane back to New York that Monday morning, expecting to hop on a connecting flight to Aspen upon arrival, Heller made one final call to the principals. Was CIM ready to go? Check. Was Harry ready to go? Check. He breathed a sigh of relief.

By the time he landed at JFK, however, there was a problem. "I think it would be better if you were here," Macklowe told him. It was that same wounded tone he had used to rope Heller into rushing to Los Angeles a few months prior.

Making his apologies to Beth and the kids once again, Heller rushed into Manhattan with his suitcase full of ski gear, determined to keep the deal from falling apart. He spent the rest of the week in Macklowe's offices at the General Motors Building trying to get the two sides back on the same page. Each night, he and the Macklowes would work late into the evening. Then, despite the advancing hour, Macklowe would leave the office with a huge canvas beach bag filled with papers. It was more material than most people could get through in a week. Macklowe was as stressed as his staff had ever seen him. By Christmas week, Heller believed he had put the deal back together.

But then, on the night when the Macklowes and Heller were expecting CIM to call and confirm that the deal was a go, Kuba called with bad news. The deal was off. (Heller said he couldn't remember exactly the reason Kuba had given, but he recalled being unsatisfied with the explanation.) "The three of us are sitting in a room and you could see in Harry's eyes this horrible vision that he wasn't going to be able to build his life's dream," Heller said. "He got extremely animated. It was the most upset I've ever seen him be." They packed up and left the office around midnight. No one said much as they filed out into the cold night.

For his part, Macklowe later blamed his son, Billy, for the deal's demise. According to Macklowe, Billy had been too uncompromising. "I had entrusted my son to negotiate. He was pushing very hard, and had no sense at all," he said later. "He was just being a ballbreaker. And I was embarrassed."

For Billy, the negotiations with CIM were just the latest showcase of his and his father's dysfunctional professional relationship. While Billy drilled down on the provisions of the deal, Macklowe was just happy to sign on the dotted line. When Billy had opposed one particular line in the contract that allowed CIM to turf Macklowe from the project entirely under certain circumstances, his father plowed ahead behind his back, he said. "He gave up a lot of protections," Billy said later. "He never read documents. And that is why he got in trouble throughout his whole career over and over."

After all the work and late nights he'd put in, all the personal sacrifices he'd made, Heller wasn't willing to let the deal go. When he got home that night, he dialed Kuba one more time and told him he wanted to know the real reason CIM was walking away. Without the Macklowes on the line this time, he got it. CIM, Kuba said, was not confident that it could pull off a successful partnership with the Macklowes. Heller, sensing that the door was still ajar, quickly went into dealmaker mode. Over the course of several hours, he convinced CIM that the partnership could work. He would collaborate with CIM and the Macklowes to figure out the terms under which they could work together.

By New Year's Eve, just a few days later, the deal was back on. The company agreed to pay off Macklowe's creditors, albeit at drastically discounted rates. In all, CIM acquired the property from the creditor group for about $305 million, less than half what CMZ, the outfit that included Brad Zackson, had planned to pay, then invested another $30 million from its own fund. As part of the deal,

CIM and Macklowe agreed that CIM would have the option to choose the developer for the project, and after interviewing several, they decided to stick with him.

The deal wiped out Macklowe's equity position in the project completely, and diminished his role in spearheading the tower's development. While he still had his "hope certificate," or potential share of the eventual profits, if there were any, and would still be the public face of 432 Park, CIM would have the final say on everything. (When asked by reporters exactly how much of a stake, if any, he had retained in the project, Macklowe would always indicate that it was plenty but decline to talk specifics.)

For CIM, the Drake would be the first in a string of major transactions as they entered the New York market. Later that year, they would buy up the discounted debt on the troubled Trump SoHo, a forty-six-story condo-hotel downtown that had posted lackluster sales amid the downturn, then partner with Trump's son-in-law Jared Kushner to buy a building in SoHo for about $50 million. They also added 11 Madison Avenue, the iconic Art Deco home of Credit Suisse's U.S. headquarters and the famed restaurant Eleven Madison, to their portfolio.

For Billy, on the other hand, the experience with his father negotiating the CIM deal marked the last straw. He was leaving Macklowe Properties and planned to start his own firm, the William Macklowe Company. "I'd had enough," he said.

Asked later to characterize what exactly had gone wrong, Billy said Harry was never his advocate. While he saw the children in other real estate dynasties being mentored by their fathers, his father was "a narcissist," according to Billy. "Harry liked the idea of having a son because it was the idea of real estate continuing along its dynastic path," he said. "He just never liked me. He was always competitive with me and, for his own reasons, saw me as a threat."

Meanwhile, with the Drake deal completed and his check (which eventually came from CIM) on the way, Heller, finally in a celebratory mood, headed to the jewelry store to buy a gift for Beth.

WITH CIM IN the driver's seat at last, the project was on stronger footing, but there was still the matter of finding a bank that would finance the construction of the tower and the project's other expenses. Once again it seemed that the private equity firm had the magic touch, lining up a series of transactions that would lower the project's leverage and catapult the value of its investment.

In a bid to limit its risk, CIM turned to Citigroup Inc.'s private bank, and an international roadshow, a series of investment presentations to investors across the world, to raise more than $400 million through a sale of part of its equity stake in the project. In other words, once the deal was done, CIM looked to off-load some of its investment on others—and for a far greater price than they themselves had paid—in order to help fund the construction. By the sheer fact that a financing deal had been signed, the project's appeal to other investors had grown.

Citi's private bank worked with a third of the world's billionaires, including many in China. They specialized in helping high-net-worth clients build bespoke private equity and real estate portfolios through what's known as "club deals," by which investors pool their money to grab stakes in prominent projects. In the course of a three-week period in June 2012, Citi managed to raise the full $400 million from its clients, who could invest as little as $250,000 at a basis or break-even number of about $2,000 per square foot, well below the asking prices for units at the building. The deal, which amounted to a sophisticated version of crowdfunding, effectively limited CIM's risk by off-loading some of its equity, and it doubled the value of its own stake overnight. With its own initial investment and the funds from Citigroup, CIM had close to two-thirds of the money it needed to build Macklowe's tower. Now it needed a construction lender to fund the rest.

WITH BANKS FACING greater scrutiny and enhanced liquidity requirements in the wake of the financial crisis, it was tough to find a traditional player to finance the remaining cost of the building's construction. Such loans were seen as too risky for the big banks. On major projects they did choose to fund, they would often syndicate or partner with other lenders.

So CIM sought an alternative lender to secure the funds, talking to hedge funds and private equity firms, which had stepped up to fill the void.

Ultimately, the company found its match in the form of a particularly unusual bedfellow: the Children's Investment Fund, started by London-based hedge fund manager Christopher Hohn. Hohn, who had grown up as the son of a Jamaican car mechanic in Addlestone, Surrey, before attending Harvard Business School, had a reputation as a take-no-prisoners activist investor capable of ousting high-profile CEOs. (A family New Year's card sent by Hohn in 2006 described his "exceptionally exciting year overthrowing German CEOs," *The Wall Street Journal* reported. One such chief executive, former Deutsche Börse boss Werner Seifert, was so enraged by Hohn's role in his ouster that he recounted the tale in a book aptly titled *The Invasion of Locusts.*)

Hohn founded his firm in 2004, while his wife, Jamie Cooper-Hohn, founded a parallel charity, the Children's Investment Fund Foundation, which received a $4 billion endowment, including funds from Hohn's firm. In other words, he would focus on making bucketloads of cash and she would focus on giving it away.

Now the Children's Investment Fund had seemingly come out of nowhere to fill the gap left by industry stalwarts like Bank of America and J.P. Morgan Chase in the construction financing game. It wrote huge checks quickly and without syndication, though it charged slightly higher interest rates than traditional banks for the privilege of dealing with a single lender as opposed to the bureaucracy associated with a consortium of banks.

Through its Irish subsidiary, Talos Capital, the foundation agreed to lend $400 million to CIM to build the tower.

WITH FINANCING SECURED, it looked as though the building would soon rise into the New York skyline. Macklowe had been envisioning a slender tower that would rise roughly 1,400 feet at a cost of roughly $1.2 billion. Seeing his vision to fruition would mean dramatically altering the Manhattan skyline and successfully building the tallest residential building in the history of the city, to be known as 432 Park.

However, there was a new problem. Macklowe and his new partners were behind the eight ball.

By the time they filed plans for their tower with the city's building department in 2012, construction crews would already be working around the clock to complete the superstructure for Gary Barnett's One57 a few blocks over. It would compete directly with 432 Park for the same billionaire buyers. As the market began to reemerge from the downturn, it would be One57, not 432 Park, that was first to the party.

CHAPTER 6

Hitting the Jackpot

Gary Barnett could see the future, and it included a real estate gold rush.

This was the message Barnett had been delivering in meeting after meeting, despite the market conditions. He was swimming against the tide, trying to convince skeptics that despite the still sluggish economy, there would be buyers for the 94 units he envisioned for One57.

With the financing in place, thanks to his Saudi partner, and talks under way for a nearly billion-dollar construction loan, Barnett was charging ahead with the planning and design for his tower. In some cases, the calls Barnett was making in late 2009 to ultra-high-end vendors, such as designers and fixture manufacturers, would be the first new business requests they had received in many months. The interior architect Thomas Juul-Hansen, a designer for big names like the restaurateur Jean-Georges Vongerichten and the rap mogul Damon Dash, couldn't believe his ears when he heard Barnett's plans. The market was completely stalled and this crazy guy wanted to build the most opulent building New York had ever seen. "People were standing on window ledges, figuring out which car to land on," Juul-Hansen would say later, describing the atmosphere when Barnett came calling.

If Barnett succeeded in his plans for the tower, One57 would be the first of a new era of skyscrapers for New York, a supertall, pencil-like tower with sweeping bird's-eye views over Central Park that promised to make you feel you were hovering in a helicopter over the city. Barnett would beat Macklowe to the punch on construction by close to two years, with One57's superstructure beginning to rise out of the ground by the summer of 2010. In addition to in-house amenities such as a 65-foot pool with Central Park views, a library, a theater, and a gym, buyers of the units would also have a Park Hyatt hotel on the lower floors offering residents hotel services on an à la carte basis. They could call on hotel management for room service or in-apartment spa services.

Despite his lofty rhetoric and grand vision, Barnett's own firm hadn't been immune to the fallout of the financial crisis, of course. During the depths of the downturn, Barnett had been forced to drop about 10 percent of Extell's staff as the economy tanked, he said. Those remaining were working harder than before. One day, as they toiled late into the evening on the relentless planning for One57, Extell's head of design, Roy Kim, turned to Barnett.

"This seems crazy," he said.

Barnett held his employee's gaze for a moment. "Either I'll look like an idiot or a genius," he said.

The 1,004-foot tower would be designed by Christian de Portzamparc, a Pritzker Prize–winning French architect best known in New York for having designed the nearby New York headquarters of luxury goods giant LVMH. Inspired by the idea of a waterfall and the work of the Austrian symbolist painter Gustav Klimt, the façade of One57 would comprise thousands of glass panels in various shades of blue designed to look like fluid ribbons cascading toward the street. At the base, curving setbacks around the entrance would give the illusion of moving water.

For Kim, Barnett's urbane head of design, the right look for
One57 would have to appeal to both New York buyers and buyers
from overseas. That meant balancing the need for understated elegance with moments of "bling" for the international buyers, who
were more turned on by lavish displays of wealth. For some of these
buyers, Kim sensed, the money in their wallets had little value unless they were able to advertise it.

Barnett, as a veteran of the diamond trade, knew his bling. At
his boss's behest, Kim spent months globe-trotting across China,
Italy, Korea, and Turkey sourcing materials for One57, quickly developing a reputation among purveyors as one of the most difficult
clients in the world. At one stone quarry in China, Kim was so
concerned about potential imperfections in the onyx he was purchasing for the lobby of the Park Hyatt portion of the tower that he
insisted that they lay out each individual slab on the floor of a huge
warehouse so he could inspect them. One quarry owner told him
the only pickier company was the tech giant Apple.

They sourced the marble from the world's most expensive quarry.
Carrara marble, a white or bluish-gray stone quarried in the north-
ernmost tip of Tuscany, was used to build some of the best-known
ancient Roman landmarks, such as the Pantheon, as well as in world-
famous sculptures like Michelangelo's *David*. Kim bartered with the
quarry's owner to get marble with the perfect veining and pattern he
thought would appeal to Barnett's diamond-trained eye. The full
marble slabs were then shipped to the United States before being
carved into single-slab bathtubs. One $130,000 slab of marble would
make just two tubs.

For the interiors of the building's apartments, Juul-Hansen put
together a veritable menu of options for finishes, design, and layout
packages—perfect for buyers who liked to make decisions but
didn't want to start from scratch. A buyer might opt for the rift-
sawn white oak for flooring or perhaps the rich rosewood in a
French herringbone pattern. In the kitchen, they could choose between a kitchen with hand-painted white cabinetry or one in stripy
Macassar ebony with a lacquer finish. Prices for the apartments

would start at around $6 million and stretch to around $100 million for a duplex penthouse.

Barnett took inspiration from London developers the Candy brothers, whose Knightsbridge condominium project One Hyde Park had established a track record in drawing the world's wealthiest buyers and was arguably, at that moment, the most exclusive address in the world. The project launched in 2007, prior to the financial crisis, and had nearly sold out by 2010 despite the downturn.

Kim and a friend were sent to London to pose as prospective buyers at the building, which was financed in part by Hamad bin Jassim bin Jaber al-Thani, the prime minister and minister of foreign affairs of Qatar. There, Kim found high design meets high security, with features like panic rooms, bulletproof glass, and guards trained by the British Special Forces, perhaps geared to appeal to Russian plutocrats and security-conscious buyers from the Middle East. The parking spaces in the underground garage were designed to be large enough to accommodate a Maybach.

In some ways, London was the harbinger of what was about to happen in New York. Foreign investors had been streaming into the British capital since the fall of the Soviet Union in the late 1980s, with Russians drawn to London's glamour and fancy private schools, not to mention its favorable tax laws. Later, as investors from China began piling into the market, the falling value of the British pound against numerous other currencies in the late 2000s made London all the more attractive.

The rush of capital into London had been dramatic. Between 2010 and 2011, roughly 53 percent of prime Central London properties that sold for £2 million or more went to foreign buyers, the *Guardian* reported. Many of the purchases were made not for owner occupancy but as investments. Projects like One Hyde Park were built to capitalize on those trends. One British banker told *Vanity Fair* that the project was "a symbol of the times, a symbol of the disconnect" between regular Londoners and the new foreign ruling class. "There is almost a sense of 'the Martians have landed.' Who are they? Where are they from? What are they doing?" he said.

New York had, of course, attracted its own share of foreign investment, but nothing like the Candys were seeing in London. Barnett aimed to change that.

IN LATE 2011, as Barnett geared up to launch sales at One57—a process that for a high-rise tower starts well before, sometimes years before, the completion of construction—a deal closed around the corner at 15 Central Park West, the building *Curbed* had dubbed "the limestone Jesus," that would completely change the game and lend credence to his forecasts for the market. He could feel the ground shifting in his favor.

That fall, Dmitry Rybolovlev, a Russian who had made a multibillion-dollar fortune from the privatization of a potash fertilizer producer and exporter named Uralkali, paid $88 million for a penthouse at the Zeckendorf building, which had been completed in 2008, just ahead of the financial crisis. The deal set a new record for a New York City home.

Rybolovlev had the kind of money Barnett wanted to capture at One57. A Russian whose lifestyle was straight out of a James Bond movie, Rybolovlev traveled around the world on private jets flanked by a handful of bodyguards and was president of Monaco's football club, AS Monaco. He had a mysterious past that had once found him on the wrong side of the law: In 1996, Rybolovlev spent eleven months in a Russian prison on charges of ordering the assassination of a business partner, but he was later acquitted.

A major art aficionado, with pieces by Leonardo da Vinci, Mark Rothko, and Pablo Picasso in his personal gallery, Rybolovlev was a New York real estate broker's dream, collecting trophy homes around the world. La Belle Époque, his penthouse residence in Monaco—famously the scene of the murder of the Lebanese Brazilian banker Edmond Safra—was valued at more than $300 million, and he owned other homes in Paris, Dubai, Geneva, and Gstaad, Switzerland. In 2008, he paid $95 million to buy the sprawling Palm Beach estate known as Maison de l'Amitié, or

House of Friendship, from Donald Trump. (Years later, the deal would become the subject of scrutiny amid investigations into President Trump's ties to Russia.)

The purchase of the penthouse at 15 Central Park West was made via a trust tied to his daughter, Ekaterina Rybolovlev. It was reported that Ekaterina had plans to make the apartment into a de facto high-end dorm room, staying there on and off while finishing her degree at Harvard University Extension School.

The sellers of the penthouse were the financier Sanford I. Weill, the former chairman of Citigroup, and his wife, Joan. Weill, who built a Wall Street empire over the course of two decades, had stepped down from his role at Citi roughly five years earlier and was now looking to spend more time at his 12,000-square-foot estate in the Sonoma, California, wine country. When the Weills put the property on the market for $88 million that November, the real estate community scoffed at the asking price. After all, the couple had paid less than half of that amount, just $43.7 million, for the apartment in 2007, and the market was only beginning to show signs of life again. But by November 22, within days of going on the market, the unit was in contract for the full asking price. (Weill said he planned to donate the proceeds from the sale to charity, but he never disclosed publicly exactly which charities benefited from the sale.)

The ten-room apartment, measuring roughly 6,700 square feet, had 12.5-foot ceilings, sculpted moldings, fireplaces, and nineteen glass floors that opened onto a park-facing terrace. It also had an unusual oval master bedroom; Weill had requested that the original rectangular bedroom be redesigned by the architect Robert A. M. Stern so that both he and his wife would have an unobstructed view of the sun rising over Central Park in the morning. Weill, who served as the chairman of the board of Carnegie Hall, had held many parties in the 33-foot-wide living room. At least once, the concert pianist Lang Lang had performed there for guests.

Weill had tapped Kyle Blackmon, a young rising star at the brokerage Brown Harris Stevens, to market the penthouse. It happened that Blackmon's mother, Sandra Feagan Stern, had worked under Weill as founder and managing director of Home Advisory & Concierge Services for Citigroup's Citi Private Bank, advising the bank's most elite clientele, but Blackmon would later say that nepotism had no role in his connection with the Weills. Rather, he said, he had met Weill's daughter, Jessica Bibliowicz, and her husband, Natan Bibliowicz, at a gala for the Alvin Ailey American Dance Theater and she had introduced them.

A native of Charlottesville, Virginia, Blackmon had been carving out a niche for himself in selling apartments at 15 Central Park West. Sensing that the building would be a phenomenon, the young agent persuaded his family to lend him $400,000 to put down a deposit on one of the building's smallest apartments for himself. "I came up with this theory that if I had the privilege to buy in such a world-class building, it would increase my probabilities of advising ultra-high-net-worth clients in that building," he said.

Following the purchase, he began memorizing every floor plan in the development, every price point, the number of wine cellars and staff suites. Then he started making calls. "I was cold calling into hedge funds. I was cold calling into private equity. Anyone that would listen to me I was talking to them about 15 Central Park West," he recalled.

In some ways, the deal with Rybolovlev was a master class in the art of negotiation. Together, Blackmon and Brown Harris Stevens president Hall Willkie devised a strategy to make prospective buyers salivate over the apartment. They would announce the listing in that Friday's edition of *The Wall Street Journal,* then deny all would-be buyers the chance to see it for nearly a week afterward. By making them wait to get in the door, the agents could line up multiple showings in a single day. When buyers arrived to view the apartment, others would arrive in the lobby after them with their own appointments, giving the impression that the unit was in high demand. Rybolovlev was promised the first appointment, nine o'clock on the first day of showings, and fell for the scheme hook, line, and sinker. He asked Blackmon and Willkie to cancel all sub-sequent showings for the week. He wanted the apartment and would pay the full asking price.

While the agents declined to cancel the remaining appoint-ments that day—the buyers were already on their way—they pledged that as long as a contract was signed within five business days at the full price, the seller would not accept an even higher offer.

Later, Rybolovlev's top consiglieres would ask the agents to jus-tify the enormous price tag. They pointed to the price Weill had paid for the unit, plus the enormous cost of a subsequent renova-tion. The remainder, they said, was justified by the presence of the other buyers in the lobby that afternoon.

Rybolovlev's purchase sent shock waves through the real estate industry. While the Russians had been buying in New York for years already, the deal signaled that a new breed of international buyers had even deeper pockets. Between 2009 and 2012, the number of Russian billionaires more than tripled, to 104, according to *Forbes*. Others had become rich overnight when the oil, gas, and mining industries in Russia had been privatized fifteen years before. "By the mid-1990s, we started seeing the ascension of all the money that was made in the former Soviet Union," said Edward Mermel-stein, a Ukrainian-born Manhattan attorney who specializes in dealings with foreign buyers. "It was so quick and so large. A lot of people just didn't understand what was even happening. And one day they wake up and they're billionaires."

Some of these oligarchs would later find themselves in the cross-hairs of President Vladimir Putin, who was looking to exercise greater control over the oligarch class. The answer, for many, was to stash their cash beyond Putin's reach. Some wealthy Russians looked to relocate to the United States through the EB-5 visa pro-gram, which allowed them to swap government-approved invest-ments in the United States for green cards.

Against that backdrop, the hopes of New York developers like Barnett were emboldened by a series of major transactions by ultra-

rich Russians. The Rybolovlev deal was the latest in a string by
Russian purchasers who agents said often gravitated toward prestigious addresses on Fifth Avenue or Central Park with flashy interiors rather than toward pricey downtown lofts or storied uptown
co-ops. They were particularly drawn to a trio of buildings clustered around the southern end of the park—15 Central Park West,
the Time Warner Center, and the Plaza. There was Andrei Vavilov,
a Russian former deputy finance minister and board member of the
Russian energy firm Gazprom, who sued the developers of the
nearby Plaza condos in 2008, alleging shoddy renovations on a
$53.5 million penthouse he had bought before purchasing a
$37 million apartment at the nearby Time Warner Center, just
a few blocks away. And there was Igor Krutoy, a prominent Russian
composer and media magnate, who purchased a $40 million apart-
ment at the Plaza after failed bids on apartments at the Time Warner Center and on the 15 Central Park West unit that ultimately
went to Rybolovlev.

Dealing with the new wave of Russian buyers could at times be
a far cry from brokers' more traditional clients. One agent said he
represented a Russian oligarch who was particularly worried about
his family's security and turned up to a showing flanked by two
bodyguards, each with their fingers on the trigger of concealed
weapons tucked into holsters around their bellies. Even on a high
level on the skyscraper, the oligarch had concerns about being at-
tacked by a passing helicopter and requested that the windows be
retrofitted with bulletproof glass.

"They were all scared of their own government. That's really
what it comes down to," said Ed Mermelstein, the Ukraine-born
attorney.

While developers cooed over the Rybolovlev deal, speculation
was rife across the industry that the Rybolovlev deal was not all that
it seemed. Some wondered whether that price might have been
inflated beyond what was reasonable because Rybolovlev, in the
midst of a multi-billion-dollar divorce battle, was trying to stash assets from his wife, Elena Rybolovleva. The mystique of the transac-

tion was only enhanced by Blackmon's refusal to discuss it in the press. "It seems suspicious that the purchase should come in the middle of Rybolovlev's knock-down, drag-out divorce war in Geneva," a columnist at *The New York Observer* speculated. "Could buying the apartment in his daughter's name assuage the financial pressure on Rybolovlev, whose wife is demanding $6 billion in the proceedings?"

Still, aboveboard or not, the repercussions of the Rybolovlev deal were almost instantaneous. Before it was even closed, word of the contract had begun circulating among real estate agents. For his part, Barnett quickly filed plans with the New York attorney general's office, which regulates the sale of condominiums, to raise prices across the board at One57. The building's glass-walled penthouse was almost immediately repriced to $110 million, 12 percent more than its initially scheduled asking price and a record ask for a Manhattan condominium. An even larger condo on the building's 75th and 76th floors with a two-story 51-foot-wide glass-enclosed "winter garden" was also repriced at $105 million. "I don't think one building makes the market, but it is a very good headline number. It has a good psychological effect on the market," Barnett told *The Wall Street Journal*. "I like it."

WHEN ONE57 QUIETLY launched sales in December 2011, it became clear that Barnett had timed the market exactly right.

The massive pullback on constructing and financing new projects during the recession meant that, as the market began to surge back stronger than anyone could remember, his tower was the only game in town. While Macklowe was still gearing up to start construction at 432 Park Avenue, the world was talking about One57.

The sales launch party in February 2012 was a black-tie affair with nontransferable invitations and strictly no guests. Invitees, who included architect Christian de Portzamparc and a who's who of the city's most influential brokers, had to show their invitations at the entrance. Once inside, they sipped champagne and nibbled on kosher sushi in a black box entryway before being led into the bright white sales gallery complete with a scale model of the building. "It was a magical real estate evening," said Kelly Kennedy Mack, whose Corcoran Sunshine group was heading the sales. "It was coming out of the recession and there was so much excitement among the community and that something big and transformational was really happening."

With the building now under construction but still far from complete, the One57 sales office and site of the opening party was the historic Fuller Building, a landmarked Art Deco tower near the project. The office was the most luxurious the brokerage community had ever seen, built at a cost of roughly $2 million. There, buyers could see floor plans projected on an IMAX-like giant screen, pull up photos, taken by drone, of the exact views from any floor of the building, and walk through a replica of the building's library complete with a 24-foot-long aquarium. A three-minute video explained de Portzamparc's inspiration for the design, a cloud turning into a waterfall reminiscent of the building's blue-tinged façade. Buyers could walk through replicas of the building's kitchens and bathrooms, inspecting the finishes. They would learn about the 20-ton "Rolls-Royce of window washing systems" that would be installed atop the tower with a fully rotating telescopic crane that could lower a basket down the thousand-foot wall of glass, enabling a cleaning crew to wash each window and guarantee crystal-clear views.

Real estate reporters from the country's largest newspapers and a new generation of real estate bloggers clamored to see the sales office, penning sensational tales about how life inside One57 might look, picking up on details like the building's $200,000 storage bins, or 54-square-foot subterranean storage lockers.

Buyers, too, were gushing. In its first year of sales, 2012, One57 lodged an unprecedented run of contract signings, with fifty deals signed totaling in excess of $1 billion. Money flooded in from all corners of the earth, each buyer seemingly even wealthier than the last.

Among them was a group of executives from the giant Chinese

conglomerate HNA Group Co. who bought four separate apartments, through four different limited liability companies, for roughly $154 million altogether. The apartments were tied to Guoqing Chen, a founder, along with his brother, Chen Feng, of HNA's Hainan Airlines.

Then came the Canadian investor Lawrence Stroll and the Hong Kong tycoon Silas Chou, the duo of fashion entrepreneurs known for directing the rise of brands like Tommy Hilfiger and Michael Kors. Michael Kors had just gone public, making the controlling stake the duo's company had bought for just $85 million in 2003 worth an estimated $1.86 billion. The deal had made Stroll, a racing enthusiast with a collection of Ferraris and McLarens, a billionaire for the first time. (Chou was already a member of the billionaire set. His father, Chao Kuang Piu, was a Hong Kong textile magnate and the co-founder of Dragonair, an airline subsequently acquired by Cathay Pacific.) Stroll paid $55.559 million for his unit, which spanned the building's entire 85th floor. Two months later, Chou paid $56.079 million for a unit three floors down, a sign that prices in the tower were rising fast. After sending a representative to scope out the building, Chou flew to New York on his private jet for a single day to see the building's sales presentation in person.

One Chinese buyer at the tower made headlines when she told a broker that she was buying a $6.5 million apartment for her daughter, who, she declared, was going to attend Columbia, NYU, or Harvard. Asked how old her daughter was at the time, the Chinese buyer responded that the child was two years old.

For the international jet set, money didn't seem to be an obstacle. "It was the first time new money—not just blue blood New York old money—bought into the idea of building as a brand," said the real estate agent Ryan Serhant, who sold multiple units in the building. "They wanted the ability to go anywhere in the world and say, 'I live in New York City. I'm at One57.' You don't even have to say the full address."

FOR THE SALES team, who stood to make millions in commissions, it was a gold rush. As such, positions were highly coveted.

Barnett selected a trio of top agents from Corcoran Sunshine to head up sales at the building, starting with Dan Tubb, a native Texan with a background in musical theater (he once had a stint as the understudy for every male part in a production of Stephen Schwartz's *Godspell*), and Jeannie Woodbrey, a boisterous veteran of the business who had headed sales at the Time Warner Center and Trump International Hotel and Tower. Both of them helped Barnett with the presales stage of the process, advising on floor plans and finishes. The pair were joined later in 2011 by Emily Sertic, a tall, elegant Canadian who had cut her teeth reselling expensive units for private clients at 15 Central Park West and the posh Upper East Side condominium One Beacon Court. A former model, she had been Miss Teen Canada and had posed for designers in Milan and Paris before getting into real estate.

Soon, Tubb, Woodbrey, and Sertic were packed shoulder to shoulder into a room no bigger than a walk-in closet at the back of the $2 million sales office with an air shaft for a window, fielding calls from would-be buyers and their brokers. In daily sales meetings, Barnett would spit out numbers like a computer and expect the team to match him in intensity.

In such close quarters, the cutthroat nature of the business was amplified. Sertic said there was "direct competition" between the on-site brokers for the best appointments with the buyers who seemed most likely to purchase. More delicate and softly spoken, she bristled at Woodbrey's rowdy nature. The tension between the pair was exacerbated when Sertic began dating one of Extell's on-staff architects. "The nature of our beast at that level is that it's very competitive. Everybody wants to do well and sell well and look good in front of the developer," Sertic said later.

Once, after dental surgery, Sertic came back to the office with a frozen mouth and a lisp only to find that, despite her objections, the others had scheduled her to lead a tour with Barnett and one of the project's equity partners that day. She could barely enunciate some of the presentation, never mind impress the boss. "To me, that was potentially complete sabotage," she said.

Under normal circumstances, such tactics might have resulted in Sertic's leaving the project, but the promise of One57 was too good to walk away from.

WHEN IT CAME to the selling, it felt as if the team could do no wrong. Buyers would watch the promotional movie in the sales office and become visibly emotional, Sertic said. The long view of the park, the "money shot" as they called it, was the true selling point.

Big names came through the sales office almost every day, each with their own set of unique requirements. For Steve Wynn, the casino magnate, who suffers from a rare eye condition, the team had to recalibrate the dim lighting in the sales office. A senior United Nations representative got halfway up in the construction hoist elevator before beginning to shake uncontrollably from a newly discovered fear of heights and had to be shuttled back to the ground.

From the back office, the team would quickly google the cultural norms overseas, particularly in the Middle East and China, to determine how they should address prospective buyers. Your Excellency, Your Highness, Your Eminence? Should they shake hands or bow? Should they openly discuss financials or be more subtle, writing figures on a piece of paper and passing it to the buyer? It was a steep learning curve.

Once, when a Saudi royal came for a tour, a project assistant wearing a short skirt was asked by the royal's entourage to step away from her role in serving refreshments to the guests for fear that her bare legs would offend. Sertic, who had worn a pantsuit that day, served the refreshments instead while Tubb gave the tour.

Thanks to the high level of demand, the appointment schedule was back to back, so the biggest challenge was keeping clients separate. If a broker arrived late with a client, the team risked one billionaire running into another, infringing on their privacy. Sometimes Sertic would have to stall an ultra-high-net-worth client in one room while Woodbrey or Tubb steered an even wealthier one through a different part of the presentation in another. At this price point, each client needed to feel that they had the sales team's undivided attention.

Many of the visitors to the office were people the sales team had never heard of, but they had built enormous amounts of wealth in unglamorous family businesses like manufacturing, or by inventing and patenting some new process or tool that was widely used in such diverse industries as farming or ophthalmology. Some were more demanding than others.

In one instance, a wealthy buyer said he was particularly sensitive to noise and wanted to understand how much street noise, or sounds from neighboring apartments, he would be able to hear from the unit he was considering. He persuaded the sales team to allow him to conduct an elaborate sound test, installing a machine with speakers and decibel meters in the unfinished unit and then measuring the levels of sounds his associates would make from above and below, playing music and stamping their feet. The tests were complicated by the fact that the building was not yet fully enclosed with glass. The same buyer also requested a last-minute impromptu tour of the construction site on the coldest day of the year, dragging his own broker and Tubb up in the thousand-foot construction hoist in windy and icy conditions. Once again, on the high floor he was considering, there were no windows yet, and they were completely exposed to the elements. "This guy is taking his time walking around the floorplate. His broker and I were standing in the corner thinking we were going to freeze to death," Tubb recalled.

It seemed that everyone in New York was desperate to see the building. Over time, the team developed a long list of bad actors who should under no circumstances be permitted to enter the sales gallery. From phony Middle Eastern princesses to full-fledged jailbirds, numerous repeat callers did not pass the smell test. After weeks of polite phone calls, the team would eventually be forced to ask for everyone's financials, and some would never be able to provide them.

In fact, Barnett's building was so popular that he felt comfortable turning some legitimate buyers away. Negotiations with Nick Candy, the developer of One Hyde Park, over the prospective purchase of a unit at One57 broke down after Barnett denied Candy the right to resell his unit before construction at the building was completed. Candy wanted to take advantage of a rising market, but Barnett didn't want to risk having his own units compete with resales in the tower.

He also turned away the high-rolling telecom mogul Michael Hirtenstein after the entrepreneur paid a construction worker to film a video of the views from an apartment he was eyeing on the building's 47th floor, then complained that his views would be partially obstructed by a sign at the neighboring Essex House hotel. "I can't tell you I would be so principled if I was having a hard time selling," Barnett told *The New York Times*. "We are not desperate to sell at all costs."

The building's two most expensive apartments were spoken for within the first eight months of sales. One went to the hedge fund billionaire Bill Ackman, who had been introduced to the building by his go-to interior designer, Anthony Ingrao, who had insisted that Ackman visit the sales office and see the property's model unit. The silver-haired head of Pershing Square Capital Management was curious about real estate, so he had obliged, even though he was not in the market for another New York apartment.

Ackman was impressed by the presentation, but fixated on one unit in particular. It was One57's so-called Winter Garden. The unit was only the building's second most expensive, but, as a self-confessed floor plan wonk, Ackman believed it was the best.

The apartment spanned 14,000 feet across two levels with more than 140 feet of frontage dead in the center point on Central Park and a curved glass atrium large enough to house a garden or a pool.

It was big, but not so big that it felt silly. It was high up—the equivalent of the top of 30 Rock—but not so high up as to get lost in the clouds on a murky day. Its position at the top of the building's L shape also meant that the floorplate was relatively uninterrupted by the building's structural core, giving it more usable square footage.

There was just one problem, the sales team told Ackman: The unit was already spoken for.

Ackman was not a man used to hearing the word no. He promptly dialed Barnett, whom he had known for years. In the 1990s, Ackman had even considered investing in the developer's plans for the W Hotel in Times Square, and they had remained on friendly terms. Barnett promised his old pal that, should the deal fall through for the Winter Garden, he would call Ackman right away. And he did exactly that a month or so later.

Ackman had just one hurdle to overcome. He and his then wife, Karen Herskovitz, shared an apartment at the Beresford, a storied Upper West Side cooperative, and she had no intention of leaving it for a sleek modern high-rise. In the end, he finally convinced her that he could buy the apartment as an investment and she would never have to live there. The hedge funder's plan was simple: Instead of living there, he would turn the apartment into a haven for a super-rich foreign buyer and flip it to one for $500 million.

He gave Ingrao, his interior designer, free rein to remake the unit to be as flashy and masculine as possible, with metal, concrete, and stone. He installed a 58-foot infinity pool where the water would fall into a slot in the floor. It would be heated, so that the buyer could host hot tub parties. A cube of glass and stone, it was the highest private swimming pool in the world. Ackman also persuaded Barnett to make the atrium's windows operable, so that he could open a 26-foot-tall wall of glass by pushing a button.

Ackman and some investor pals signed a contract to pay $91.5 million for the unit in June 2012. At the time, it looked as though that would be the most ever paid for a New York City apartment, but upstairs an even bigger deal was waiting to close.

In the early months of 2012, Barnett had shuttered the sales office and sent much of the staff home for a few hours. A premier
buyer had arrived to visit the penthouse, and his privacy was paramount. The circle must be kept small. It would be just Barnett, the
buyer and his wife, and their real estate agent, Leighton Candler,
and Corcoran chief executive Pam Liebman. Even the building's
in-house agents would not be permitted inside.

The buyer was ultimately revealed to be the Texas technology magnate Michael Dell, who had amassed his fortune from
the sale of personal computers. He quickly made a deal buying the
10,923-square-foot six-bedroom duplex apartment for $100.47 mil-
lion. It was the first deal in New York history to crack nine figures.
It was his deal, not Ackman's, that would hold the New York City
price record.

SOON THE MARKET was reaching new peaks—and everyone wanted
in on it. It was the beginning of a trend that the appraiser Jonathan
Miller describes as "aspirational pricing." Old-timers who had lived
along the 57th Street corridor for years saw the big-ticket asking
prices at neighboring new towers and tapped real estate agents to
market their older units for similarly outrageous sums, whether the
quality or location of the real estate warranted it or not.

In July 2012, a Long Island real estate developer named Steven
Klar listed his longtime Manhattan home, an octagonal penthouse
at the aging CitySpire tower on West 56th Street, for $100 million,
making it the highest-priced listing in the city at the time. The listing generated headlines around the world and prompted cries from
the brokerage community that the property was vastly overpriced
and would set unrealistic expectations for the market.

Klar justified the price by comparing the six-bedroom property
to a pricey painting or sculpture. "It's like a piece of art," he said.
"It's unique, it's special."

It was the beginning of a common refrain designed to combat
the sticker shock these asking prices elicited. Sellers and their agents

encouraged would-be buyers to think outside a fixed pricing para-
digm that relied on assigning intrinsic value to real estate based on
comparable sales and supply and demand dynamics and step instead
into the murky world of imagined valuations that characterize the
art market. If you looked at real estate the way you would a Leonardo da Vinci or an Amedeo Modigliani, who's to say what it
might be worth?

AS ONE57 LOGGED sale after sale, one source of prospective buyers
stood out from the rest: China.

As the number of Chinese people entering the ultra-high-net-
worth investor class ballooned as a result of the country's rapid economic growth, brokers across the city reported a rush of Chinese
capital into New York, to both high-end residential and trophy
commercial properties.

Plunging property prices in China, the result of restrictions put
in place by the government in a bid to deflate the country's housing
bubble, left well-heeled investors in search of a safe harbor for their
capital overseas, and as the yuan gained strength against the dollar,
the United States seemed like the perfect target.

As the market bounced back in 2012, some U.S. brokers estimated that Chinese investors accounted for as much as a third of
luxury sales, with Chinese investment in Manhattan more than
doubling in three years.

Real estate agents and developers scrambled to take advantage
of this new frontier, designing buildings that would appeal to Chinese sensibilities, flying representatives to Asia, arranging seminars
to educate prequalified Chinese buyers, and hiring Mandarin-
speaking staff. At a party for a new tower at one New York condo
tower, developers served Asia-inspired hors d'oeuvres like Matcha
green tea marshmallows and crispy chicken skin and hosted a presentation by a feng shui master. At Extell, marketers arranged to
have many of One57's most expensive apartments on the 80th

through 88th floors, to take advantage of the Chinese belief that eight is a lucky number.

The real estate agent Nikki Field was behind some of the priciest early deals with Chinese buyers at the building. While she knew that the busy 57th Street corridor wouldn't appeal to her Upper East Side clientele, she suspected it would be a hit with the Chinese who, like the Russians, often wanted to be at the center of the action. "Gary was smart enough to know that these weren't going to be local buyers or anyone from within two thousand miles of New York, so I immediately started offering it to our international clients," she said.

Sold on the promise of the building but not on the prestige of the location, Field developed a strategy for showing to foreign clients. She would make sure that no matter what direction they were coming from, her driver would take a detour so that prospective foreign buyers for the building would arrive via the picturesque avenues along Central Park and not have to traverse grotty 57th Street.

Field's bet on overseas buyers paid off big. A wealth adviser would call her from Russia, and within days she would be traipsing around New York with a group of Russian-speaking guys "with hands the size of tractors," wining and dining them at Il Mulino, the classic Italian restaurant on East 60th Street, then heading in a caravan of black cars across the park to see the building. "It was so productive because I was so good at it. I had some hubris in this," she laughed.

A petite, neatly coiffed blonde, Field was approaching retirement age, but her energy was that of a twenty-year-old surfer riding the wave of a hot market. A former stay-at-home mom and, before that, an air hostess with Pan Am, she'd cultivated her connections over a decade, starting by schmoozing with wealthy moms at her children's Upper East Side private school. Sensing an enormous opportunity in Asia, she brushed up on Chinese customs and signed up for Mandarin classes at the State University of New York's Confucius Institute for Business. (The going was tough. After months of Mandarin classes, she said she still mangled basic phrases. Eventually, she decided to pack it in and hire her instructor to be her team's personal translator.) She began making multiple trips to China each year to meet with wealth managers.

After appearing on what she described as a "cheesy state-owned television channel" in mainland China to talk about real estate opportunities in New York, she received a call from a nineteen-year-old Chinese student at Stanford University in California, who said his mother had seen her on TV and wanted her to show him apartments in New York for after graduation. She initially assumed he was in the market for what amounts to a "starter apartment" in ultra-wealthy circles and spent his spring break showing him properties priced at around $2 million. His mother, however, was not satisfied. She ended up buying her son a $21 million apartment at the Time Warner Center. Ms. Field assumed the whole family intended to use the property when they visited, but that was not their intention.

"The family was so excited that when it came time to close, they came to the United States and toured it. The mother turned to me and said, 'We're so very happy with this. Thank you for helping our son. Could you find us one for me and my husband now?'"

For Field, learning the Chinese way of doing business was challenging. The Chinese had wildly different negotiating styles from the American buyers she had worked with—they were always driving a bargain until the very last moment—and their desire for privacy trumped anything she had seen from the American billionaire set. "Even if their money was already offshore—and a lot of it came out of Hong Kong and London—they did not want their family, their friends, their business associates, or their government knowing what they were doing."

On the other hand, many of the buyers who came from China were keen to adapt to the American way of life. When one of the buyers she worked with at One57, a Chinese family whose son was planning to attend college in the States, asked her to show them weekend homes in nearby Greenwich, Connecticut, where the market had been slow, she landed them a $15 million country house, down from its original $26 million asking price. After the deal was already in contract, the family inquired about getting the seller's furniture thrown into the deal for free. While the request was unorthodox, the seller, desperate to be rid of the house, which had been sitting on the market for years, agreed. The family wanted everything, from the decorative pillows and picture frames to the crystal decanters in the bar and the liquor they contained.

At the closing table, the buyers attempted yet another retrade. The family, speaking in hushed tones, asked Field to step outside for a quick conversation. While they had been touring the property to inventory the furniture the seller should leave behind, their daughter had fallen in love with the seller's cat.

Field was horrified. The deal was done, she said. If the buyers really wanted a cat for their daughter, she would take them to a pet store or a shelter following the closing and their daughter could pick out as many cats as she would like. It would be her closing gift to them as their agent.

"No, she really loved *that* cat," they said.

Field went back into the room to break the bad news to the sellers.

"I say this with my extreme apologies. Please do not take this disrespectfully," she remembers saying. "But their daughter fell in love with your cat."

The seller threw her hands in the air. "Thank God," she said. "I hate that cat. She can have it."

For Field, the learnings from the deal were twofold. For one, she came to respect what she described as the centuries-old, fine-tuned, and well-choreographed negotiating skills of the Chinese, which she said left Americans in the dust. While Americans had the stomach for maybe three rounds of negotiations, the Chinese would go longer and harder every time. She also learned that many of the buyers she represented were hungry to fit into this new American culture. "I soon came to realize they were buying these people's lives. Not just a house," she said. "This was their opportunity to totally become American."

CHAPTER 7

Inventing an Icon

It was the summer of 2011. While Gary Barnett was gearing up for the launch of One57, Richard Ressler, the billionaire co-founder of CIM and the financial savior of Harry Macklowe's planned tower for the former Drake Hotel site, had been summoned to Macklowe's minimalist apartment at the Plaza hotel to meet with star architect Rafael Viñoly.

Ressler had already told Macklowe that he would sign off on Viñoly to design the building they would soon begin calling 432 Park Avenue, but Macklowe wanted to make sure that the principals at CIM were adequately wowed by the highly lauded Uruguayan architect's concept for the tower.

Macklowe and Viñoly were cut from the same cloth—each a showman capable of mounting a charm offensive of gargantuan proportions. Viñoly, who died in 2023, was then in the midst of designing a commercial skyscraper in London, which would later become known as the Walkie-Talkie for its distinctive top-heavy shape, and had designed the Tokyo International Forum, a civic complex in Japan. He and Macklowe had developed a friendship and would occasionally meet for dinner and swap ideas about architecture, art, and design. (Macklowe's longtime friend and sailing buddy Renzo Piano had also been considered for the project. Though the partnership didn't ultimately pan out, the Pritzker Prize winner had pitched Macklowe by sketching out a rough design for the building on a box containing a bottle of grappa and sending it to his office.)

Standing by the window of the Central Park–facing Plaza apartment, Viñoly, dressed all in black and with multiple pairs of designer reading glasses perched atop his mound of thick gray hair, pointed out at the city skyline and proceeded to outline in heavily accented English a vision for a slender geometric tower that would permanently transform it. Much taller than Barnett's One57, which was now well under way, the skyscraper would be seen from miles away, from as far afield as the George Washington Bridge, the Long Island Expressway, or even Citi Field.

Suddenly, as he continued to wax rhapsodic about his design ambitions, Viñoly, a classically trained concert pianist, plopped down at a grand piano in Macklowe's living room and began to play, providing his own musical backdrop to the presentation. To Ressler, the California moneyman, it was over-the-top theatrical, completely at odds with Ressler's own brass tacks personality. None of this was necessary. Viñoly already had the job.

The Uruguayan wouldn't be the only creative in the room, however. As time went on, it became clear that Macklowe considered himself as much the architect of 432 Park as Viñoly. Convinced of his own design sensibilities, Macklowe told Viñoly the two of them should collaborate like the producers of a movie.

Macklowe's vision for 432 Park married high architectural drama with references to the worlds of fine art and design. With a geometric design reminiscent of a waffle, its exposed concrete grid-like pattern would be precise and symmetrical, with six uniform windows punched into each side of the tower. Improbably, the design was inspired in part by a wastebasket, albeit an elegant wire grid-like metal one designed by the Austrian Josef Hoffmann. Macklowe and Viñoly agreed that the concrete design based on the same principles would offer the kinds of wide-open views offered by a glass curtain tower but without the cold look of curtain glass, which they associated more strongly with commercial office buildings. Viñoly believed that, living at these heights, residents would need to feel protected and enveloped by something stronger than sheer glass, and he knew that a building of this scale would require greater levels of structural support. The concrete grid design would serve both purposes.

Other inspirational sources were more grandiose than a trash can. The 10-by-10-foot recessed picture windows would be a nod to the famous coffers in the cupola of the Pantheon in Rome, the grid-like design on the building's exterior harking back to the twenty-eight radicals carved into the Roman temple's concrete dome. They would act as a kind of proscenium stage, with New York City as the show.

The purity of the design plans for 432 Park continued on the inside. The exposed structural frame of the building would be bonded to a slim concrete core, negating the need for any interior columns, leaving the apartments free of any structural interruption. The windows were to be lined with bench seats on which residents could recline and observe the views. Macklowe was inspired, he said, by the "widow's walk" platforms popular on the roofs of homes built in nineteenth-century New England coastal towns like Nantucket. The myth goes that the low-fenced platforms were used by women watching, perhaps fruitlessly, for their husbands' whaling ships to return from sea.

Macklowe was obsessive about preserving access to the windows. While he drew inspiration in terms of the layouts from classic Park Avenue architects such as Rosario Candela, he detested how frequently furniture was pressed against the perimeters of classic Park Avenue apartments. Why, he thought, would anyone want to have to peer over an armchair to observe the views? "I abhor couches against the wall," he said. By installing the window seats, Macklowe believed you could completely predetermine how the apartment's occupants would circulate. At cocktail parties, guests could mill around by the windows with a place to sit, rather than be confined to a seating area in the middle of the room.

While they agreed on much, Macklowe and Viñoly each possessed a sizable ego, and at times they came into conflict. Viñoly argued against the bench seating by the windows, contending that it detracted from the simplicity of the design. But Macklowe insisted.

The two men also argued over the pinnacle of the tower. Macklowe felt there should be some kind of architectural or design flourish at the top, such as a spire or light show. Viñoly again advocated for simplicity. He couldn't stand the idea of what he described as "putting a hat" on the building and believed there should be nothing that even remotely resembled a gimmick. It was Viñoly who won that round.

Tempers occasionally flared. It became Ressler and his CIM partners' job to keep the peace between the two and serve as the tie-breaking vote when the men could not agree. "Even prima donnas can't sing alone," said one person involved in the tower, describing the dynamic. "The truth is that CIM owned the thing and Harry didn't."

Later, Viñoly would be forced to issue a very public apology to Macklowe and CIM after he spoke too freely at an event hosted by the brokerage firm Douglas Elliman at the building in 2016. As part of a discussion designed to market the building, Viñoly had said he considered the design to have a couple of "screw-ups" and interior elements that he would "rip out." Macklowe was furious, and Viñoly was forced to issue an awkward public apology for his "inartfully" expressed comments toward his "dear friend."

Beyond aesthetic quibbles, the building's design also posed significant engineering challenges. At 1,396 feet, it would be the tallest residential building in the Western Hemisphere, much taller than One57's 1,004 feet, and building it would be a feat of modern engineering. Macklowe and Viñoly grappled with how to keep the slim tower, rising on a relatively small footprint, from swaying in the wind, tapping a team of leading engineers and technical consultants from around the world to weigh in. While its slenderness connoted exclusivity—there would only be one or two units per floor—the last thing Macklowe needed was billionaire buyers putting their checkbooks away because they felt queasy on a windy day.

For developers, building an ultra-skinny tower is far more expensive than building a more conventionally proportioned one. The more spindly a building is, the more vulnerable it is to the elements. If wind causes the building to sway too much, it could cause damage such as broken joints, leaks, and broken windows. It could also jam up the building's elevators.

Traditionally, engineers have found that buildings with a height-to-width aspect ratio of more than 5 to 1 are particularly sensitive to the effects of wind. Macklowe's building was so tall and situated on such a small site that it would have an aspect ratio of 15 to 1. By comparison, some of the world's tallest towers are built on much larger sites. One World Trade Center is tall, but it is not skinny. Thanks to its huge floorplates, it has a base-to-height ratio of just 7 to 1.

The only reason Macklowe could even consider building his high-rise on such a small parcel of land was thanks to recent advancements in skyscraper technology. For one, a change in the New York City building code in 2008 paved the way for the use of stronger steel and ultra-strength concrete made using microsilica and fly ash. Developers also benefited from advances in elevator speeds, made possible by algorithms that could help better consolidate passenger traffic, and from new computer systems that could simulate the weather conditions and the way the building would perform once constructed.

While most of the time the movement from the wind at 432 Park would be imperceptible, engineers projected that the building could drift from side to side as much as a foot or more during hurricane-force conditions, which might send its more sensitive occupants reaching for their sick bags. While such swaying would not represent a safety hazard, it could be a dealbreaker for buyers and a potential source of liability for the developers.

For Macklowe and Viñoly, the idea was not to prevent sway

entirely—that would be impossible—but to mitigate it. With that in mind, the pair set off on a trip with the building's chief structural engineer, Silvian Marcus, a quirky expert with a thick Romanian accent, to Canada's Western Ontario region to visit the Boundary Layer Wind Tunnel Laboratory, an experimental facility with two state-of-the-art wind tunnels, where they could simulate the effects of wind on a scale model of the building. In the tunnel, they could test wind-induced structural loads, cladding pressures, pedestrian-level winds, and ventilation requirements as well as rain and snow effects on the tower. It was the same facility where the Burj Khalifa was put through its paces.

Tests showed that more would need to be done to mitigate the effects of the wind at 432 Park. The trio brainstormed potential solutions. Marcus, the structural engineer, suggested rounding the edges of the tower, which would reduce the wind pressure and drag on the building, but Viñoly balked at the idea, saying that it would completely ruin the design.

Instead, they settled on a more unusual solution. They would leave some floors of the building completely open to the elements, allowing the wind to pass through. This series of gaps in the tower—five in all—would effectively confuse the wind and reduce the crosswind forces that could rock the building. Marcus compared the strategy to cutting holes in the sail of a boat. While the sail would ordinarily facilitate the movement of the boat, the wind would rip through the holes, ensuring that the boat did not move. It was a clever workaround.

The other major investment was a pair of more than 600-ton tuned mass dampers, enormous counterweights positioned at the top of the building. Supported on cables and hydraulic cylinders, the enormous concrete weights were designed to counter the building's movement and keep it within acceptable limits. On windy days, these hulking metallic creatures would shriek and grind as they swayed slowly back and forth in opposition to the force of the wind.

The champagne might slosh a little in the glass, but the glass itself would never topple.

MACKLOWE WAS JUST as exacting when it came to his vision for the tower's interior.

Beyond the luxury design, the building would feature a suite of amenities specifically catering to the 0.001 percent. For wealthy buyers, Macklowe believed, 432 should be a place where they could not only live but where they could entertain, conduct business, and, most important, be pampered. To that end, Macklowe planned an elaborate spa cum fitness and wellness center, dubbed the 432Club, which would have a sauna, a steam room, and a massage room as well as a 75-foot indoor swimming pool.

There would also be a high-end private restaurant with a landscaped outdoor garden terrace overlooking 56th Street. For decades, private dining rooms had been a sought-after amenity at some of the city's fanciest buildings, particularly in prewar co-ops. While frequently unprofitable as a result of their limited audience, these spaces were often a hit with buyers. The restaurant at 15 Central Park West, a known venue for spotting Fortune 400 CEOs and unrivaled in its exclusivity, had upped the ante spectacularly with its Veneziano stucco walls and farm-to-table menu when it debuted in 2003. Now Macklowe would top it. Shaun Hergatt, an Australian who headed the Michelin-starred restaurant Vestry in SoHo, was hired as chef. The design for the space would be open plan, giving residents direct access to the people preparing their food.

Private boardrooms, too, would be available on the tower's lower floors. For pied-à-terre owners on business in New York, they would provide a quiet place for private meetings and for local dealmakers looking for a haven away from prying eyes.

A residents' library would comprise a curated selection of books on the works of artists like Ai Wei Wei and Matisse as well as on designers like Valentino and Manolo Blahnik and architects like Richard Meier, Christian Liaigre, and of course Rafael Viñoly. The luxury publishing company Assouline, a producer of beautiful coffee-table books founded in Paris and known as a mouthpiece for the art world and high-end fashion industry, would help select the books.

There would be a screening room, and residents would have the option to purchase climate-controlled wine cellars and private staff apartments for assistants and secretaries. Each of the residences would feature a private elevator landing as well as a separate service entry for deliveries or for housekeepers to come and go discreetly. The elevator cabs were to be finished in tan leather by Hermès. Macklowe, an avid sailor, had the idea for those while cruising on a friend's nicely appointed powerboat in Croatia. The living spaces would have 12.5-foot finished ceilings, solid oak floors, white marble kitchens, and bathrooms fitted with book-matched slabs of Italian statuario marble and freestanding egg-shaped soaking tubs. The tubs, pictured in renderings against the background of the 10-foot-square window overlooking the Manhattan skyline, would become a hallmark of the tower. Brokers would eventually pose in the tubs for shots for their Instagram pages.

When Matthew Bannister and his business partner, Keith Bomely, got the call to pitch for the 432 Park project's marketing in the summer of 2011, the branding experts arrived early at Macklowe's office, spreading across the conference room copies of the brochures their company, DBOX, had created for other real estate developments for Macklowe to peruse. The most impressive brochures, those for the priciest and most luxurious buildings, were placed at the head of the table, where Macklowe was expected to sit, while the less impressive ones were scattered on the other end of the table where they wouldn't catch the developer's eye.

Macklowe glided into the conference room, leaned across the table, and immediately picked up the worst brochure he could have chosen. It was low-budget and flimsy, created years earlier for the developer of a rental building in Koreatown who had skimped on quality. Bannister immediately cursed himself for even having brought it to the meeting.

Macklowe examined the brochure, unimpressed.

"What makes you think you could do the marketing for this project?" he asked the pair, the implication being that they could not.

Bannister, convinced that Macklowe had ruled them out already, sought ways to salvage the meeting and convince Macklowe that he and Bromley spoke his language. A longtime student of art and architecture, he rolled the dice on a hunch, comparing the building to the Austrian modernist Josef Hoffmann's wastepaper basket. The building's design, he told Macklowe, minimal and repetitive as it was, gestured more to the worlds of Hoffmann and the American conceptual artist Sol LeWitt than it did to any reference point in the architectural world.

Macklowe's eyes lit up at the eerily precise reference to Hoffmann, whose wastepaper basket had indeed informed his vision for the building's design. His demeanor softened.

Bannister was relieved. "It's a beautifully designed object, but it is a trash bin," he said later. "If we had been wrong, that would have been quite a crash."

Bannister and Bromley had the job.

Macklowe quickly became one of the pair's most exacting and difficult clients. It was clear from the get-go that he wanted to mount a marketing campaign far more extreme than any real estate developer had done before. Everything must be completely original. The duo found early on that it was almost useless to talk through their ideas with him because he didn't want to hear idle chatter. The way to get Macklowe excited was to show him their ideas visually on storyboards and just stay silent, allowing Macklowe's imagination to run wild.

Their task was tricky: Through the marketing, DBOX needed to articulate the provenance of and inspiration for the building's design. The building was tall, slender, repetitive, and minimalist, with a concrete exterior, but it was so much more than the sum of its parts, Macklowe would say. It took its cues from the worlds of fine art and modernism. In some ways, it was useless to do market research, since Macklowe himself was perhaps the best representation of what would likely be the building's buyer base—wealthy, discerning, and with an appreciation for art and culture.

For 432 Park, there would be no typical marketing video boasting the property's high-end finishes and amenities, shuffling between shots of marble bathtubs, glistening pools, and besuited doormen. Instead, Macklowe would employ an Emmy Award–winning film crew to produce a roughly four-minute artistic film that showcased the building in a more abstract light, incorporating many of the elements that the team had storyboarded. The cost: more than $1 million.

The image of the 10-by-10-foot window became the focal point of their efforts. They imagined a dancer within the window frame, reminiscent of Leonardo da Vinci's Vitruvian Man, the famed drawing of a human figure inside a square and a circle. They looked to the work of the American artist James Turrell, known for his series of "skyspaces," signature light chambers with ceiling apertures that open to frame the heavens. Each image was laid out on Macklowe's conference room table, where the trio debated how they might be sequenced.

Macklowe felt that the film should venture into the surreal and that DBOX should be open to including nonliteral elements. They toyed with the idea of setting it to "Pure Imagination," the song sung by Gene Wilder's Willy Wonka in the 1971 film *Willy Wonka and the Chocolate Factory*.

In the end, the film was set to the Mama Cass song "Dream a Little Dream of Me" and featured Philippe Petit, the French high-wire artist best known for his gravity-defying walk between the Twin Towers of the World Trade Center in 1974, tiptoeing on a wire over Midtown Manhattan from the Empire State Building to 432 Park.

The production of the 432 Park marketing materials had the scale of a Super Bowl ad. The shoot spanned several days at Silvercup Studios and required a staff of more than seventy people. Petit walked a tightrope in front of a giant green screen. They used the same type of automatron filming rig that had been used in the filming of *Jurassic Park*.

Through a series of dreamy vignettes, the viewer follows a beautiful brunette from her sprawling country estate in Southern England all the way to her penthouse in New York, traveling in a Rolls-Royce, a Learjet, and a helicopter. Spliced throughout are images of luxury—chandeliers, crystal decanters, grand pianos. A camera pans over the woman sitting in a bathtub filled with diamonds. An enormous CGI King Kong peers through one of the tower's distinctive windows.

There are references to the building's design inspirations, too. Mies van der Rohe's Barcelona Pavilion transforms into the building's swimming pool. The ceiling of the Pantheon morphs into one of the building's geometric window frames. The film culminates in a cocktail party inside the 432 Park apartment, where guests including Spiderman and Al Capone mingle with Petit over cocktails. In the film's final moments, a guest dressed in a King Kong costume removes his mask to reveal that he is Harry Macklowe.

Viktoria Hofstaedter was just twenty-one years old in 2013 when she answered a Craigslist ad looking for a model and dancer. The unlikely gig would take her to a film studio in Brooklyn as an enormous marketing machine revved into gear, setting up a photo shoot that would generate the defining image of 432 Park Avenue.

The crew dressed her in a selection of dramatic outfits, from a ribboned black satin dress to a sheer lace leotard, and she struck a series of ballet poses on her toes inside the frame, holding them for as long as she could. A man attached strings to the ends of her gowns to hoist them into the air, making her feel like a real-life marionette. There were wind machines and lighting rigs, and a 10-by-10-foot window frame had been constructed for her to pose inside. She felt like a celebrity as teams of people ushered her around, offering her a robe and water. She wasn't used to this kind of treatment.

In one particularly dramatic image, Hofstaedter is poised on her toes, thrusting her tiny 5-foot-3-inch frame forward and her arms into the air like a bird taking flight, as her diaphanous pink gown billows out behind her. That was the image that would be used on the cover of the 432 Park marketing book.

Naturally, Macklowe also served as the editorial director for the inch-thick art book with essays about the city and design, including a piece on New York kitchens by the former *New York Times* restaurant critic Ruth Reichl and a "compendium of spectacular baths" by Wendy Goodman, the design editor of *New York* magazine. He also commissioned photographs of models posing in the building's residences sporting outfits by Balenciaga, Gucci, and Giorgio Armani. On the cover, there was Hofstaedter, rising on her toes on a windowsill overlooking the city at night.

The foreword pointed to the building as a new architectural icon for the world. "The famous towers that have ruled the New York skyline thus far will find a new companion, and rival, in 432 Park Avenue," it said.

It wasn't until the image appeared in splashy newspaper and magazine advertisements around the world—when the building's sales effort kicked off—that Hofstaedter realized that she had been a part of a project that would be so significant to the New York skyline. She was able to use the images to secure a much-sought-after green card so that she could continue to work in America.

Years later, when gazing at the Manhattan cityscape after the tower was completed, she felt a tug of ownership over the building of which she had unwittingly become the face. But she was never invited to step inside.

IN THE SPRING of 2013, One57 sales director Dan Tubb was out grabbing a sandwich at a local deli when he ran into his biggest competitor on a bustling Madison Avenue street corner. Richard Wallgren, Macklowe's 432 Park Avenue sales director, looked dapper as usual in a well-fitted suit and round glasses à la Le Corbusier. The two men caught each other's gaze.

He likely knew the answer would be no, but Wallgren hazarded the question nonetheless. "It'd be really good to get in and take a look at your sales office," he said, gesturing toward the Fuller Building just down the street, from which Tubb and his team were doing a roaring business at One57.

"Yeah, and for me to see yours as well," Tubb responded, aiming at nonchalance.

Both men knew it was never going to happen.

By early 2013, the competition between One57 and 432 Park was heating up. While 432 Park had not yet officially launched, word was leaking out about early deals being signed there. Barnett could feel Macklowe breathing down his neck. Tubb and the sales team at One57 scrounged for information about the finishes, floor plans, and sales office experience at Macklowe's rival tower, trying to figure out ways to undermine their pitch.

When Tubb finally got a resale broker friend to stealthily send him some images of floor plans at 432 to show Barnett, he "felt like 007," he said. "There was a real arms race mentality with regard to trying to get information and trying to make sure that what you had was ahead of the crowd."

For his part, Macklowe would say later that he never had any interest in seeing competing towers and never actively scoped out One57 or any of the other towers. When he attended a party at a private residence at One57 years later, he intimated that he was unimpressed.

"I don't like to go to other people's buildings because I don't want to be critical," he said. "I don't want to compare myself to somebody else, because I have the courage of my designs and my convictions. And I know they're right."

The sales office for 432 Park was located in Macklowe's offices at the GM Building, which overlooked the Plaza and the southeast corner of Central Park. Clients would be greeted in a bright white and gray marble lobby, then led into an art-gallery-like showroom filled with renderings of Macklowe's prior projects.

If Macklowe saw himself as an artist, the showroom was like his own museum retrospective. "When you go to an art gallery, and you see a retrospective, what you're looking at is not simply the development of the artist's work. You're looking at one painting talking to another painting, because you're seeing the progression of his ideas, the progression of his thoughts," he said. "So the building that I designed in 2016 is considerably better than the building I designed in 1961, by dint of more knowledge, by dint of a greater understanding."

There were models of the kitchen and bathroom at 432 Park as well as a scale model of Midtown, complete with the new building, so that buyers could see how far it would tower above its neighbors. One area of the showroom comprised a pristine white seating area with Eames-style chairs and a large screening facility for buyers to watch the sales video and view the floor plans.

CIM proposed hiring a brokerage like Douglas Elliman or Corcoran to handle sales, but Macklowe wanted to keep them in-house, where he could control the buyer experience.

Leading sales was Richard Wallgren, a storied figure in the new development world who had made his name heading up sales at 15 Central Park West, widely considered the most successful condominium project in New York's history at that time. A former investment banker, Wallgren had a famously fat rolodex. He had done stints at Salomon Brothers and Union Bank of Switzerland, where he specialized in handling commercial mortgages. Now, he was on staff at Macklowe Properties.

With Wallgren at the helm, Macklowe was free to insert himself into the sales process as he saw fit. Outside agents who brought buyers to the building would occasionally complain of Macklowe's proximity to the sales process. He would sometimes pop in to perform his own spiel to their clients. That typically involved impromptu recitals of Macklowe's self-penned ditties or his own unique brand of dirty jokes, which often involved rabbis, sex, and disgruntled husbands complaining about their wives and didn't always land well with the high-net-worth purchasers. One agent reported that his client quietly turned to him during one of

Macklowe's most elaborate routines. "Let's get out of here, this guy's crazy," he said.

Still, an early rush of buyers quickly proved out the concept. That was thanks in large part to CIM, whose executives leveraged their own rolodexes to bring in a swarm of friends-and-family buyers who would score early deals at sweetheart prices, allowing the developers to quickly declare the property's offering plan effective.

Early buyers included Fawaz Al-Hokair, a Saudi billionaire property mogul and the owner of a portfolio of malls in the Middle East and the local franchise rights in Saudi Arabia to brands such as Zara, Banana Republic, Nine West, and Topshop. Al-Hokair would go on to purchase the building's most prized apartment, a roughly 8,300-square-foot six-bedroom penthouse on the building's 96th floor, for $87.66 million. His U.S. representatives would give it an orange color scheme and fill it with designer furniture from the likes of Bentley, Fendi, Louis Vuitton, and Hermès.

There was Mitch Julis, a co-founding partner of the Los Angeles hedge fund Canyon Capital Advisors, who paid almost $60 million for a full-floor apartment on the building's 79th floor. He and his wife, Joleen, both major collectors of Asian art, tapped the Japanese architect Hiroshi Sugimoto and brought in a team of Japanese artisans to turn the space into a temple of Zen, with cedar shutters, sixty-year-old bonsai trees, and a traditional Japanese tea room with tatami mats for kneeling. The process reportedly took four years and included multiple trips to Asia as well as the shipping of rare materials from Japan, such as stone that was salvaged from an old Kyoto tram station. Julian Velasco, the former curator of the bonsai collection at the Brooklyn Botanic Garden, imported and shaped two very old ficus trees grown in Florida for inclusion in an indoor garden designed by Sugimoto.

Other early buyers included the private equity executive Jonathan Sokoloff, who formerly worked at Ressler-linked Drexel Burnham Lambert, as well as the New York real estate magnate Joe Sitt, whose company controlled large swaths of Fifth Avenue retail, and Jamie McCourt, the ex-wife of the former L.A. Dodgers owner Frank McCourt. There was also the British Iranian art collector Mohammed Afkhami, whose Magenta Capital Services had acted as the exclusive adviser to CIM and other private equity and real estate firms on more than $15 billion of capital placement in the Gulf region, Brunei, and Malaysia.

To Macklowe's consternation, the building would also eventually be home to Jacob Arabo, or Jacob the Jeweler, who purchased a pair of units with his wife, Angela Arabo, for close to $24 million in 2016.

There were $60 million in purchases by Hillel "Helly" Nahmad, the son of a billionaire art collector, who had been arrested in 2013 and served time in prison for his role in running an illegal sports gambling business.

Later, celebrity couple Jennifer Lopez and former Yankee slugger Alex Rodriguez moved in. The baseball great was left red-faced when a picture of him scrolling on his phone while sitting on the toilet at the tower was taken by an onlooker from a neighboring building and leaked to the press. He took it in good humor, telling *Good Day New York* that he did his "best thinking" in the loo and clearly needed to invest in "some good blinds."

Before long, among the city's high-end brokers, a distinct sense had set in that the Park Avenue tower had stolen the limelight from One57. It was just as Macklowe had planned. Now it seemed that every billionaire on the planet wanted to take a look. They included the likes of Amazon founder Jeff Bezos, who sources said considered 432 Park seriously, returning to the sales office several times before ultimately choosing to live farther downtown, near Madison Square Park.

Howard M. Lorber was another of the early buyers. The executive chairman of the New York City real estate brokerage Douglas Elliman and a friend of CIM's Richard Ressler, he accepted the offer of a friends-and-family deal early in the project's construction. At the time, he was living in an apartment at the Sherry Netherland, an opulent 1927 hotel and condo building on nearby Fifth Avenue, and wanted a little more space. Though afraid of heights, he inked a deal for the building's 67th floor because he saw it as a no-brainer investment. His deal penciled out at around $4,000 a foot, significantly less than what he believed the building would ultimately command.

In fact, Macklowe had originally predicted that the building would sell out at prices of $2,500 to $3,500 a foot. They were already surpassing those figures. So getting in early, at a sweetheart rate, was on Macklowe's mind too. In January of 2013, Harry announced to his unsuspecting wife, Linda, that he had signed contracts to buy two units at 432 Park Avenue, a larger one in his name and a smaller one in hers. He saw it as a good investment, since he had the promise of an insider price. He believed that they could buy them and flip them for a profit. It was also a chance to own a piece of a building that Harry might well have considered the pinnacle of his life's work.

All seemed sunny with clear skies at 432 Park—but it wouldn't stay that way forever.

CHAPTER 8

Make Way for the Billionaires

Joel Diamond was moving on up in the world.

It was the 1970s, and the young record producer had just scored a string of hits with the English pop star Engelbert Humperdinck. As Humperdinck began to soar in the charts, Diamond was determined to leave his noisy basement studio on First Avenue—and he had his sights set on a veritable palace in the sky, a penthouse unit in 220 Central Park South, a rent-controlled white brick building at the south end of the park.

At 220, Diamond reigned supreme, though he could barely afford his $1,200 a month in rent. The single twentysomething, a bachelor of his era, with shoulder-length wavy blond hair and tight-fitting jeans, lived above high-rolling television executive neighbors and took to hosting celebrity-studded parties with the likes of Regis Philbin, Salvador Dalí, Andy Warhol, Sammy Davis, Jr., and Joe Pesci. His New Year's Eve parties were famous; at midnight, he would gather all his friends to watch the fireworks over the park. Sometimes, after drinks, they would walk a few blocks south to Studio 54.

As Diamond's success grew—he would go on to work with artists like Gloria Gaynor and executives like Clive Davis—he plowed more than half a million dollars into turning the rental apartment into a slick bachelor pad, complete with a mirrored ceiling in the bedroom. He wasn't shy. When the actress Candice Bergen moved into the penthouse next door at 240 Central Park South, he strained to catch a glimpse of her. On a day when he was feeling particularly bold, he wrote her a letter asking her out on a date and left it, along with flowers, at the front desk of her building. (He received no response.)

Diamond had better fortune when his friend Barbara Creaturo, a senior editor at *Cosmopolitan* magazine, persuaded him to be featured in the magazine as Bachelor of the Month, and she included his address in the article. In the picture that accompanied the piece, Diamond reclined in his office, his shirt unbuttoned to almost his navel. (Another man who would later receive this dubious honor in the pages of *Cosmopolitan* in the 1980s was Jeffrey Epstein.)

"I got over five thousand letters," Diamond recalled. "I got letters from girls in mental institutions, jail, everything."

"I'd like to say how delicious you appear to be," one potential suitor wrote to him. "Relax—slam the door—draw the drapes—distill a quart of scotch—and turn out the lights!"

For rent-stabilized tenants like Diamond, the roughly 120-unit building, located near Columbus Circle and boasting large terraces and expansive views over the park, was a dream come true. The Central Park South address meant having a front row seat to some of New York City's most valuable vistas without the eye-popping rent check to match. It drew an eclectic mix of New Yorkers, from entertainers to advertising executives, lawyers, and publishers.

"Once you got those apartments, you didn't move," said longtime resident Cathy Marshall, a teacher and single mother. "When I used to tell people I met that I lived on Central Park South, they automatically assumed I was rich. They had no idea that it was a rent-stabilized apartment."

At the time, New York's unusual rent stabilization laws applied to some buildings constructed prior to 1974. Qualifying buildings had to contain more than six units and developers would opt into the program in return for tax exemptions—a decision many land-lords would regret in the decades that followed, as New York's ap-peal and population exploded anew in the 1990s and 2000s. Having a rent-stabilized unit meant that the maximum rent increase per year for one- and two-year leases was set by the city's Rent Guide-lines Board, which would work to ensure that the housing stock within the program remained affordable and rarely raised it more than a couple of percentage points at a time. It also provided certain protections against eviction. The rent stabilization program differed from the more stringent rent control program, which froze rents completely at a certain price. It was under that program, for in-stance, that longtime New Yorkers like Thomas Lombardi, whose family moved from Italy to Manhattan in the 1940s, were still pay-ing as little as $55 a month for an apartment in SoHo in 2012.

Once units became rent-controlled or rent-stabilized, landlords could return them to market rate only under certain conditions. In the case of rent stabilization, those conditions included if the units were vacated or if the building was subject to demolition.

Diamond's landlord at 220 Central Park South was Sarah Ko-rein, one of New York's most powerful female real estate execu-tives. A rare breed in the real estate boys' club, Korein, formerly Sarah Rabinowitz, moved to New York from Palestine with her husband, Isidor Korein, a Hungarian engineer, in the 1920s. Early in life, she was a Hebrew teacher at a local nursery school, but after the purchase of her family's own walk-up apartment building in Flatbush, Brooklyn, in the 1930s, she got a taste for real estate in-vesting.

She presented as "more Dresden doll than Machiavellian nego-tiator," according to an obituary in *The New York Times.* "But buy-ers or sellers who assumed they were sitting across the table from sweetness and light did so at their peril."

Korein died in 1998 at the age of ninety-three, and by the mid-2000s, 220 Central Park South, one of her former trophies, had fallen into disrepair. Diamond, the record producer, had moved out in the early 1990s. After he had glue traps set out to catch a cockroach in his apartment, he returned a week later from a trip to discover squawking mice in every trap. It turned out the rodents had been breeding inside his radiator. He took it as a sign that he should finally make the move to Los Angeles, the center of the music business.

Other residents were complaining too. In the spring of 2004, at approximately two in the morning, tenant Donald Glasgall was awoken by a loud noise in his apartment. As he opened his eyes, he realized that he was being hit by a torrent of hot water from above. A water pipe in the ceiling had burst. Clambering out of bed, the ailing seventy-five-year-old made a beeline out of the bedroom and rushed to grab containers from the kitchen to catch the falling water. It was too late. His bedroom was soaked. A bookcase collapsed under the weight of his collection of waterlogged books.

Glasgall dialed the night man downstairs in the building's lobby.

"We know," the doorman said, gloomily informing Glasgall that some of his neighbors' units were flooding too.

The building was ripe for demolition. In 2005, the Korein family sold it for roughly $132 million, a sum that, while staggeringly high by most measures, had everything to do with the value of the underlying land and its prime position on the park, as opposed to any value left in the white bricks themselves. The new owner was a partnership between the Clarett Group, led by Veronica Hackett, one of the city's only active female developers, and the major real estate company Vornado Realty Trust, led by the New York real estate magnate Steve Roth.

The following spring, residents of 220 Central Park South arrived home to letters slipped under their doors, informing them that the building had a new owner and that eviction proceedings were forthcoming. The new owner planned to tear down their building and replace it with a gleaming new residential skyscraper with for-sale condos.

The new owners were big fish—and talking a big game—but there was one problem. If assemblage was one giant hurdle in the effort to procure a viable development site, a related but distinct challenge was dealing with New York's byzantine rent stabilization system.

The building's tenants, many of whom didn't want to move, would not be easily cast aside. Many were of retirement age and had lived in the building for decades. For them, moving would mean a rupture in the fabric of their lives. They were like old trees, said one former resident. Their roots went so deep that if you dug them up, they would die.

The residents included colorful characters like Ronald Pecunies, an aging minority owner and COO of Mercedes-Benz of Greenwich, Connecticut, who lived there part-time with his glamorous mistress, Emel Dilek. Pecunies had met Dilek at a charity event in her native Germany in 2004. After months of courtship, he flew her to the United States, got her a work visa, gave her a job, and put her up in his Central Park–facing apartment. Dilek would insist it was love, even though Pecunies was nearly fifty years her senior. "People can say whatever they want," she would later tell the *New York Post* over tea at the luxurious Pierre Hotel. "I had something that was Romeo and Juliet. Some people don't find that in a lifetime."

Other prominent tenants had backgrounds in the law and in real estate. They included Jean E. Shimotake, a partner at the prestigious law firm White & Case, and Leighton Candler, a leading luxury real estate agent who had handled the $46 million sale of Brooke Astor's duplex apartment at 778 Park Avenue, one of the city's most expensive deals at the time, and who would eventually go on to represent Michael Dell at One57.

The seasoned New Yorkers of 220 Central Park South knew that being a rent-stabilized tenant meant they had serious leverage against developers and could potentially extract a payout in exchange for vacating. They quickly formed a tenants' association to strategize what their next steps should be. "Nobody is an idiot when it comes to real estate in New York," said Connie Collins, a longtime resident of the building who received the letter. "When you're living in a rent-stabilized apartment, they can't just say 'You have to leave now.' That's not how it works."

IN STEVE ROTH and Veronica Hackett, the eccentric residents of 220 Central Park South had encountered formidable adversaries.

Known for his bare-knuckle style of negotiation, Roth looked like Hollywood's idea of a New York City real estate magnate, with well-tailored suits and tufts of gray hair on the side of his otherwise balding head. If you entered the ring with him, there was a significant chance you wouldn't get out alive.

A native of Brooklyn, he was the son of Fred Roth, a small apparel manufacturer who made children's dresses, and graduated from Dartmouth before starting his career building industrial facilities in the New Jersey Meadowlands. In 1964, he founded Interstate Properties, an outfit geared toward purchasing, rehabilitating, and leasing strip malls.

Roth soon came to believe that the bigger value in retail brands was the underlying real estate, not the retail operations themselves. He took on the Vornado name in 1979, when he bought a stake in the company which operated the beleaguered New Jersey discount department store chain Two Guys, with an eye toward liquidating the department store business and monetizing its real estate holdings. He waged war against board members who opposed the plan and wanted to save the chain. Roth would ultimately triumph, shutting down all the chain's stores. It was carnage—and a financial home run for his company.

He employed the same strategy in the 1980s with the publicly traded New York department store chain Alexander's, which had its flagship on Lexington Avenue and 59th Street. This time, Roth spent years trying to convince the longtime family owners of the chain that the value of their real estate far exceeded the profit-making potential of their stores. Later, Roth would face off against Donald Trump in a six-year battle for control of the company.

Again, Roth came out the victor, successfully pushing the chain into bankruptcy, shutting down its eleven New York stores and letting go of its roughly five thousand employees. The move was seen by some Alexanders insiders as merciless, especially since some believed that the struggling retail chain could still have been salvaged and the jobs saved. But the move was a Steve Roth special, an illustration of his determination to extract every ounce of blood from a deal. A reporter for *Boston* magazine once described Roth's business model thus: "See a vulnerable animal, shoot it, and then sell the fur for more than the thing was ever worth alive."

Roth's dealmaking continued apace in the 2000s, as the mogul gobbled up Manhattan office towers and soon entered the fray in some of Manhattan's most hotly contested commercial deals, bidding for sites like the 110-story Twin Towers in Lower Manhattan. He was eventually bested by Larry Silverstein, whose winning bid for the site closed just months before the 9/11 attacks would destroy the towers. In 2007, Roth purchased a majority stake in two trophy office buildings, the Bank of America building at 555 California Street in San Francisco, which counted Goldman Sachs among its tenants, and the Axa Financial Center at 1290 Avenue of the Americas in New York, from a partnership led by his pal Donald Trump. Trump retained a 30 percent interest in the building, making them inadvertent partners.

He also had a history with Macklowe. As one of the subordinate debt holders on the Equity Office portfolio when Macklowe hit the skids in 2008, Vornado had opposed a workout plan which would have given Macklowe more time to repay his debt on some of the properties.

As Vornado assembled a portfolio worth tens of billions of dollars, Roth continued to live up to his cocky reputation, once famously referring to friend and rival Sam Zell as a "baldheaded chicken fucker." As the head of a public company, he might have been expected to toe the line with investors or conduct business in a more sanitized, corporate manner than his competitors like Macklowe and Barnett, but he often shrugged off the traditional expectations of public CEOs, even declining to communicate with analysts through quarterly earnings calls until 2012, a decision that contributed to the air of mystery around the company. For a company of Vornado's size to shirk off such protocols was extremely unusual.

For all his success in office and retail developments, Roth rarely messed around with condos. He liked to hold on to assets for the long term. He didn't like the idea of building units that others might quickly profit on themselves. Once, when he turned the Alexander's flagship into a mixed-use office and residential complex that would serve as the global headquarters of Bloomberg L.P., he had included a condo portion known as One Beacon Court on the top floors. When one of the buyers at the building, the hedge fund manager Steve Cohen, listed his unit there for $85 million (after buying it for just $24 million), Roth seethed at having lost out on the potential upside.

Roth's other least favorite thing was the press. Though he strove to keep his family's personal life private and almost never granted interviews, it was near impossible to remain completely under the radar given the line of work of his wife, Daryl Roth. By the 2000s, Daryl, the daughter of a car dealer from New Jersey, was on her way to becoming one of the most esteemed producers on Broadway, bankrolling Pulitzer Prize– and Tony Award–winning plays and musicals such as *Kinky Boots, War Horse,* and *August: Osage County.* She bought a building that had housed the Union Square Savings Bank and turned it into the Daryl Roth Theatre. The couple's son Jordan, a self-described "couture devotee" and "theaterista," acquired his own Broadway theater chain. He arrived at red carpet openings in dramatic ensembles with sequins, ruffles, capes, and bows, providing a striking counterpoint to his father's nononsense image.

Veronica Hackett, too, was a force to be reckoned with. A native of Vero Beach, Florida, and the eldest of seven siblings, her first job out of college was tracking troop movements and rice shipments for the CIA during the Vietnam War. Ambitious and nononsense with tightly cropped dark hair, she started out in New

York as an executive assistant to the head of a corporate finance department at a small investment bank while simultaneously studying for a master's degree in finance at New York University. In the 1970s, she had been appointed the first female lender in Citibank's real estate division, then went on to run the global corporate real estate services division at Chemical Bank.

By 2000, she had gone out on her own, starting Clarett Group with former colleague Neil Klarfeld. They formed a partnership with the financial giant Prudential, with a strategy to identify prime sites, lock them down, and then find a financial partner to help bankroll the developments. They would put up a little equity of their own, while the financial partner would shoulder the rest. In the 220 Central Park South site, Hackett had seen possibility in an old building with fabulous views. Having secured the site, she turned to an old friend—Mike Fascitelli, at the time Steve Roth's protégé and rumored successor—to put up the rest.

She knew Vornado had deep pockets.

TECHNICALLY, THE BUILDING'S new owners had the right to evict the tenants when their leases expired. Under state law, they could do so as long as they demonstrated that they had plans in place to finance and build a new building. By 2008, the state had already ruled that the developer could proceed with evictions despite the tenants' protests.

But they had a secret weapon in their face-off with Vornado and Clarett. They called him "the barracuda."

Retained by the association in order to mount an appeal to the ruling, attorney David Rozenholc was a legend in the world of landlord-tenant buyouts. A gruff, portly man with a short, graying beard, Rozenholc was born in 1945 in Kyrgyzstan to a Polish father who had been recently released from a gulag in Siberia. He spent much of his childhood in Israel before moving to the Bronx as a teenager. Starting in the 1970s, he had been a pioneer in the world of tenant representation as the director of litigation at South Bronx

Legal Services, where he represented residents of buildings in a neighborhood that had become a flashpoint of poverty and urban decay where landlords were steamrolling low-income tenants.

Rozenholc was no stranger to a tough fight or even intimidation tactics. Once, while in housing court representing South Bronx tenants who were on a rent strike because of conditions in their building, Rozenholc looked to his right and saw the opposing landlord pointedly counting out bullets in his hand.

Rozenholc's reputation as public enemy number one for developers was cemented in the mid-aughts when he secured a settlement for Herb Sukenik, a then seventy-something-year-old recluse who had lived for three decades at the Mayflower Hotel on Central Park West. The hotel was slated to be demolished to make way for 15 Central Park West, and the developers, Arthur and William Zeckendorf, were buying out or relocating the remaining rent-stabilized tenants who lived on the building's upper floors. Sukenik, a physicist who lived alone in a roughly 350-square-foot room with a small corner kitchenette overlooking the park, was the final holdout.

By the time Sukenik was introduced to Rozenholc, he already had a provisional agreement with the developers to give up his unit. In exchange, they would buy a two-bedroom apartment facing the park at another high-end tower, the Essex House condominium on Central Park South, where they would allow him to live for only $1 a month in rent for the rest of his life. Rozenholc encouraged him to try to renegotiate. "I said to him, 'I can get you a lot of money as well as the apartment,'" Rozenholc recalled. "But he said he didn't care about the money."

But Rozenholc persisted. "I said to him, you're a scientist, why would you want to give the money to a landlord? Why not start a foundation or something?"

Negotiations with the Zeckendorfs dragged on for months, but Rozenholc and his client held firm even as relations with the brothers grew tense. Meanwhile, the developers, seeing that Sukenik was playing hardball, started demolishing other parts of the building around him. They turned half the lobby into a noisy construction site. Still Sukenik stuck around.

Finally, having pushed the Zeckendorfs to the breaking point, Rozenholc brokered a record-breaking $17 million settlement. It was more money than Sukenik, who also got a lifetime lease at a nearby apartment building overlooking Central Park as part of the deal, had ever dreamed of. Two months earlier, a tenant in the same position at the building had listened to another lawyer and sold out for less than $1 million, according to Rozenholc. The settlement made the front page of the *New York Post*.

When Rozenholc's name came up, landlords shivered. His secret: understanding leverage. He told tenants to think like developers and to do their own math. They should consider the zoning, what the developer paid for the site, the cost of constructing the new building, and how much they could reasonably expect to make from the sale of new apartments. Based on that analysis, they could extrapolate how much a developer could afford to pay to buy them out of their lease and still have enough money left over to make the project worthwhile.

Rozenholc was known for dragging cases on for years, if the situation called for it. (As of the time of the publication of this book, he still had a case ongoing since 1984.) "If my clients do not end up in a better position, I won't settle," he once told a reporter. "And if you fuck with me, I'll fuck with you for sport."

For the 220 Central Park South tenants, Rozenholc took over from their previous lawyer to mount a Hail Mary appeal of the state's decision to allow the evictions. While the chances of the appeal's success were limited, and his leverage minimal, he knew that every second he could delay the developer from moving ahead with the project meant a potentially greater payout for his clients. Vornado and Clarett had already made some of them a $350,000 offer to leave, but he was confident he could extract more.

His advice to the tenants was simple: They should drag out negotiations for as long as possible, because as long as the building stayed up, Vornado and Clarett would bleed money on real estate taxes and other carrying costs and would get more and more desperate to hammer out a deal. "We wanted to be the biggest pain in the neck to the buyer," said Cathy Marshall. "Every time they presented an offer, Rozenholc would find things wrong with it."

When Veronica Hackett, Roth's partner at Clarett Group, asked to meet with the tenants' association, Rosenholc advised the residents to attend the meeting, which was held in one of the building's common spaces, but to remain stone-faced. Don't smile, he said, and most definitely don't laugh.

The meeting, Marshall said, was a memorable one. "They said, 'You're little people. We're a big corporation. We're going to win,'" she recalled. "We were frightened."

To Marshall, Veronica Hackett seemed cold and detached, a no-nonsense type who showed zero empathy for the tenants' situation. "She didn't give us the impression that she was breaking up our homes that we had lived in for so long. This was purely a financial deal. This was purely money," Marshall said, describing the residents' skepticism. "She tried to intimidate us."

Delays to the project weren't entirely of the residents' making. The global financial crisis also put a temporary kibosh on the plans. Still, the tenant-landlord fight dragged on for close to five years as some of the residents continued to hold their ground and negotiate as a group.

By the end of 2010, however, Roth and Hackett, seeing Barnett and Macklowe move ahead with their buildings and eager to finally move ahead on their own, came to Rozenholc with a new offer: roughly $1.56 million per remaining tenant. Given that there were about twenty-five of them, that represented a roughly $40 million payout by Vornado and Clarett.

The attorney called the remaining residents to Cathy Marshall's apartment, where he presented the developers' offer to them. He told them he felt that they couldn't push the numbers any higher.

Some of the tenants felt that they still had room to negotiate further, but the decision was put to a vote. Ultimately, the group decided to accept.

"I stayed there for five years fighting," Marshall said. "Some people died. Some people got cancer. It came to a point where Rozenholc said, 'This is it.' And we trusted him and we took it."

The white brick building—where Joel Diamond has hosted untold celebrity parties and stared up from his bed at his mirrored ceiling—was finally coming down. But there would be one more hitch in Roth and Hackett's plans.

BY 2012, VORNADO and Clarett had mostly completed the demolition of 220 Central Park South, with one important exception: a parking garage at the base of the building. It was the lone obstacle to the new tower's construction, and it was quickly becoming a thorn in Roth's side.

For years, even as Roth struck deals to remove the group of residential tenants from 220 Central Park South, the garage operators had resisted Vornado's moves to buy them out of the lease, which ran through 2018. It didn't make sense—until it did.

Roth soon learned that just months before Vornado and Clarett had purchased the building in 2005, the garage operators had been approached by none other than Gary Barnett, now Roth's chief rival along the Billionaires' Row corridor, with an offer to buy a stake in the lease.

It was early days, but Barnett, basking in the success of One57, had been quietly putting the finishing touches on another site assemblage, at 217 West 57th Street, which could support a second 57th Street tower. The assemblage, which sat right behind Roth's proposed tower at 220 Central Park South, near the corner of 57th and Broadway, encompassed two of the buildings that had once been at the heart of New York's Automobile Row, the B. F. Goodrich Company buildings at 1780 Broadway and 225 West 57th Street. The smaller of the two buildings, the one on 57th Street, had been home to a car showroom operated by Stoddard-Dayton.

Depending on what Roth chose to build on his site, the Vornado building could potentially block the Central Park views from the second new Extell tower. In an act of pure chutzpah, Barnett had acquired a 49 percent stake in the limited liability company that controlled the garage from Kenneth and Gary Rosenblatt, brothers who ran Champion Parking, a third-generation family company with interests in garages all over the city. As an owner of the garage business, he could refuse to move, stalling Roth's plans.

A rivalry between the two men had been brewing for months. In his annual letter to shareholders that year, Roth had made it clear that Vornado had its eye on Barnett and had been watching the deals roll in at One57. "We hear that the 1,000 foot tall, direct park-view apartment tower under construction on 57th Street is pricing at $6,500 per square foot," he wrote. "Our 220 Central Park South site, just down the block, is better."

When Roth found out about Barnett's trickery, he was furious. That July, he took aim at Barnett, through the proxy of Champion Parking. Vornado and Clarett served the parking garage operators with a notice of default on their lease, a precursor to an eviction, citing an alleged breach of the terms of the garage's certificate of occupancy. The breach was based on a small technicality: the certificate allowed for a total of forty-four parking spaces to be designated primarily, though not exclusively, for residents in the building above. Because that building no longer existed—Vornado had torn it down—there were no residents to serve, the developers said. As a result, the landlords said, they had been issued a violation by the city's Department of Buildings.

The garage operators quickly responded with their own lawsuit, alleging that the whole gambit of the lease default was a sham. For his legal representation, Barnett tapped a familiar face: Rozenholc, Roth's now long-term nemesis. "I thought it would enhance my negotiating position," Barnett laughed later.

Barnett and his fellow litigants, through Rozenholc, claimed that the parking garage violation was a pretext by the developers to clear the site so that they could proceed with their new tower—and that one of the landlord's own attorneys had actually been the one to request that their own client be issued a violation by the buildings department. When the department then neglected to issue a violation for over nine months, the landlords had followed up to inquire into the whereabouts of their own punishment.

By the fall, the developers of 220 Central Park South had issued Champion a second notice of default, this time using a different strategy. They claimed that by selling a 49 percent interest in the company that operated the garage to Barnett in 2005, Champion had violated the terms of its lease, which precluded the company from reassigning the lease without the prior written consent of the landlord. They also claimed that the Rosenblatts had given Barnett control over any negotiations on the lease regarding a buyout. Barnett, for his part, said he had purchased an interest in the garage only so as to provide parking for the residents of his nearby projects and would be willing to reverse the transaction if it was found to trigger a breach of the lease. He accused Vornado of having "animus" against him because he had bought up a number of air rights close to the building that Vornado could have used to expand its tower. In a sworn affidavit, he claimed to have rejected offers made by Vornado to buy some of those rights. The "defendant's present efforts to terminate the lease are motivated, at least in part, by a desire to extract a more favorable deal from me on those property interests," he said.

Insults were flying, in the form of legalese. In court documents, Rozenholc accused the developers of having "unclean hands" and of "creating 'straw man' arguments" regarding competition with its rival, Gary Barnett. The developers had tried "to paint a dark picture of Barnett," he wrote. "The effort here is to stand the facts on their head and contend that Barnett is only involved in the garage to gain leverage against Vornado regarding its competing residential project between 57th and 58th Streets. But Barnett had acquired his interest in the garage and other nearby properties before the landlord acquired the building."

Furthermore, Champion argued, the sale of the 49 percent interest in the garage business did not constitute a transfer of the lease, since the Rosenblatts maintained a 51 percent interest and continued to manage the garage. It was an internal transfer, not an external one.

In 2013, a judge issued an injunction on the garage operators' behalf, preventing Roth from terminating the lease. In her ruling on the injunction, then Manhattan Supreme Court Justice Donna Mills said the case was "rife with the palace intrigue that attends high-end real estate development in Manhattan."

Despite the tone of the court filing, Barnett was lobbying Roth behind the scenes that they both might be better off if they worked together. He proposed putting an office building on Extell's site and a residential tower on Vornado's, arguing that the two buildings would be the best in their respective categories: the best office building in New York City and the best residential building. At times, it looked as though Roth might be amenable to the idea, but the pair could never quite agree on how to split the baby, or the relative values of their respective pieces of the deal. As time dragged on, Roth grew more and more frustrated. "There were a couple of times that Steve got really annoyed with me," Barnett would later say in his typically understated way, declining to go into specifics.

While he wasn't opposed to a settlement in principle, Barnett took a hard line in the negotiations, telling Roth that the money meant a lot less to Vornado than it did to Extell. "Central Park Tower is my business," he recalled telling Roth. "You've got a $30 billion office company, it doesn't make a damn bit of difference to you. I've got to pay the bills."

Meanwhile, Roth's exasperation spilled over in earnings calls. "We've not taken the old rental apartment house down to the garage where we have an irritant, as I think everybody knows," he told analysts on a call in February 2013. "Well, he may be an irritant to us, but we're an irritant to him because we're in front of him, so I think everybody knows the dynamics of the situation."

"You can imagine the way those negotiations went. There may have been a few expletives involved," said Vornado analyst Alex Goldfarb.

The dispute was not settled until near the close of that year, when Roth's Vornado agreed to pay a hefty $194 million to buy a separate small parcel from Barnett's Extell on the block as well as other air rights for its own building, and Barnett agreed to relinquish his hold on the garage. Both developers actually agreed to shift their planned towers slightly in opposite directions so that both could enjoy better views, though some of the view planes at both men's towers would remain partially obstructed. In fact, the buildings were so proximate that Lendlease, the construction company involved in building both towers, devised a special electronic communications system to prevent the tower cranes constructing the two buildings from overlapping.

Barnett had played hardball, but he hadn't intended to make an enemy of Roth. He had long admired the Vornado chief's deal-making acumen. It was just business, after all, and Barnett wasn't looking for things to end on a sour note. For that reason, Barnett said, he made any settlement contingent on his and Roth's having dinner together, just the two of them.

As the year drew to a close, the two men dined at Tevere, a kosher Italian restaurant on the Upper East Side with exposed brick walls, white tablecloths, and Romanesque wall murals. Roth soon delivered the evening's catchphrase: "Take good care of my money, Gary." Even as the conversation drifted from the deal, Roth repeated the phrase like a mantra several times. "Take good care of my money, Gary." It seemed he couldn't let the deal go.

Following the dinner, Barnett watched as Roth headed toward his car, which was idling by the restaurant. As he moved to get in, Roth turned back one last time.

"Take good care of *your* money, Gary," he said.

To Barnett, it seemed like a moment of graciousness from one of the hardest-nosed dealmakers in the business.

CHAPTER 9

Throwing Shade

On the afternoon of October 29, 2012, Gary Barnett was holed up with his family at his modest home in Queens when a panicked call came in from one of Extell's executives. Barnett was among the more than fifty million people across the Northeast bracing for the arrival of Hurricane Sandy. The massive storm was barreling northward toward New York City on what was increasingly looking like a collision course. Officials had announced plans to cease subway and rail service across the region, and Mayor Michael Bloomberg had instructed New Yorkers to stock up on supplies and stay home.

Heeding the warnings, Barnett had suspended construction at his sites across the city and gone home to Queens to wait out the storm. Now the executive on the other end of the phone was imploring him to turn on the TV.

What Barnett saw made his blood run cold.

On practically every news channel, broadcasters were locked on the image of One57. Breathless newscasters described an alarming development: The boom of the project's construction crane had snapped and was now dangling precariously a thousand feet above the street. Crumpled and seemingly warped, it was twisting in the wind and looked as if it might break off entirely and plummet to the ground.

Barnett's mind started racing. If the giant crane fell, what else might it take down? Debris raining down on the street might cause mass casualties. And then there was what lay beneath 57th Street: a natural gas main. If the crane fell on the main, could it cause an explosion?

Suddenly, Barnett's cell phone was ringing again. On the other end was Mayor Michael Bloomberg.

"Gary, what's going on?" the mayor asked.

Barnett didn't have a great answer. He told Bloomberg that he had spoken to the top brass at Lendlease, the company handling One57's construction, prior to the storm and they had assured him that all equipment was secured. Knowing that the storm could cause havoc, operators had set the crane at a supposedly safe angle of roughly 60 degrees, intending for it to move with the wind rather than resist it. Should it have been set even lower?

Barnett knew now wasn't the time for conjecture. Authorities should close the street, evacuate neighboring buildings and shut off the utilities, he told Bloomberg. He needn't have bothered. They were already on it, Bloomberg replied.

Residents of nearby apartments were given just minutes to pack up as many belongings as they could carry and evacuate, though many had no obvious place to go amid the storm. With the street closed and the subway service suspended, they walked for blocks and blocks to find cabs to take them to the homes of friends and family or local hotels.

"That evening, on 20 minutes' notice, my wife and I found ourselves dragging a hastily packed suitcase and a sopping wet dog down Central Park South, walking toward the home of a friend who'd offered us shelter," the author Michael Gross, a resident of the nearby Alwyn Court co-op, wrote in *The New York Times* of the debacle. "Some of our neighbors, who range from demi-celebrities to a bedridden 95-year-old living in a rent-regulated apartment, weren't so lucky. At least one ended up in a public shelter."

As the hurricane raged around them, representatives from Lendlease and the city hiked up the stairs to the upper portions of the building, which were open to the elements, battling 90-mile-per-hour winds and piercing rain to assess the situation. Firefighters were already up there examining the flailing boom. Barnett immediately drove into the city, where he stood at the edge of the cordon surveying the damage to the building, which seemed significant. As the crane had whipped around, the building's glass curtain wall had been smashed in places and shards had fallen to the ground.

In the end, Hurricane Sandy would claim the lives of more than forty New Yorkers, with thousands of homes destroyed and millions left without power. At One57, it would take nearly a week before the boom was fully secured to the side of the building and the street reopened. To get the boom down, it would have to be broken up into pieces and lowered to the ground in the site's construction hoist, a kind of giant construction elevator for high-rise buildings that operates on a pulley system.

The incident cost Extell "many millions" of dollars, Barnett would later say, in large part because the company's insurance provider denied coverage. The policy, with Zurich Insurance Group, included an exclusion for any losses related to "contractor's tools, machinery, plant and equipment" that were not meant to become a permanent part of the project. In other words, the crane was their problem. Ever worse for Extell, in the ensuing months the company would be slapped with lawsuits from residents of neighboring buildings and offices, who cited losses related to their temporary displacement owing to the street closure.

Barnett came to see the crane incident as a turning point for the fortunes of One57, the moment where he began to see a dropoff in sales. "We lost our luster," Barnett said later. "People said, 'Oh, that's the crane building.' It's not the best marketing. By the time we got back into the market, it was harder to pick up."

FOR MORE THAN a year, One57 had been the only game in town. By 2013, with talk of the impending launch of sales at 432 Park Avenue, it was clear it was about to have company.

That spring, Extell announced that One57 was 70 percent sold. From the outside, the announcement may have looked like a victory lap, but, in truth, company executives were facing a new reality. Sales at the building were beginning to level off.

The crane incident was just part of it. The other problem, brokers said, was that the remaining inventory was the building's hardest to sell. Many of the initial buyers had gravitated toward the full-floor apartments on the upper levels of the building, which had uninterrupted views of the park. The leftover units were predominantly on the low and middle floors of the building, where park views were obstructed by the Essex House hotel tower on Central Park South. After all, One57 might tower *above* the park, but it wasn't quite *on* it. For these kinds of prices, buyers didn't want to be looking into the back of another building.

To the sales team, it was quickly becoming clear that the market might not be as endlessly deep as it initially seemed. Were there actually enough billionaires to go around at these prices? To the team's chagrin, Barnett hadn't seemed to have gotten the memo. He was intent on *increasing* prices for the remaining units.

Emily Sertic, the One57 sales representative, said she mentioned to Barnett that raising the prices on those units with lesser views would stunt the progress of sales.

Barnett said it didn't matter. Buyers could come in and negotiate. "I said, 'Gary, they won't negotiate or make an offer if we can't get them in the door because they think the price is too high,'" Sertic recalled. "I was very forthright about that and I was correct."

As the months rolled on, Sertic noticed the volume of appointments dwindling. The sales office phone was ringing less frequently, with long gaps between showings.

Barnett, who was a numbers whiz, insisted on daily sales calls, which became a painful exercise for the salespeople in light of the declining activity. On those calls, he would cross-examine the sales team on the deals they were trying to make, asking them, on the fly, to justify numbers, quote comparable sales, or calculate prices per square foot. He wanted essential, critical information distilled into pithy explanations and didn't appreciate verbose explanations or unnecessary narrative flourishes.

As competition began to emerge along the corridor in 2013, the Extell sales team was forced to assess the building's strengths and shortcomings in comparison with new towers and find ways to hone their sales pitch. "432 Park was very, very real competition," Sertic said. "A lot of times, it was us or them."

Compared to 432 Park's swanky Park Avenue address, the 57th Street corridor felt low-grade, so the One57 sales team would play up the building's closer proximity to 15 Central Park West and Time Warner Center, buildings that had helped establish luxury pricing in the area. They would also play up One57 residents' access to the hotel amenities of the Park Hyatt, since 432 Park did not have a hotel component. That might particularly appeal to pied-à-terre owners who didn't have full-time help when they visited New York, they thought.

Another complication: As construction on One57 neared completion, the sales team was no longer selling a fantasy on the strength of floor plans, renderings, and imagination. The building was a brick-and-mortar reality. While it helped to have a product that was ready for buyers to move into, showing them around unfinished units, some of whose views were blocked by construction rigging, wasn't ideal.

With a nearly finished building, the team could also no longer brush off criticisms relating to the design. They worried that the finished lobby, with its dark lacquered woods, looked cold, dark, and small compared to the lavish lobby at 15 Central Park West, which looked more like the sanctum of a cathedral than the entrance to a condominium, with English oak paneling, fluted columns, and a central oval ceiling cutout that appeared to open to the sky. Sometimes Sertic would skirt buyers through the hotel lobby and then into the residential side of the building via a back corridor in order to avoid the residential lobby altogether.

The façade, too, which had been divisive from the time the tower's renderings were initially released to the public, turned out to be even more of an issue now that the building was approaching completion. It was clear that de Portzamparc's distinctive blue waterfall design didn't appeal to everyone.

In 2014, the real estate blog *Curbed* would dub the tower "the worst building of the year." It quoted architecture reviews from far and wide, including one by *New York* magazine's Justin Davidson, who called the building "clumsily gaudy." The *New York Times* critic Michael Kimmelman described the tower as "chintzily embellished, clad in acres of eye-shadow-blue glass offset by a pox of tinted panes, like age spots."

"Good job, Gary Barnett," the *Curbed* writer signed off, "on your big ugly blue tower."

One of Barnett's most notorious critics appeared to agree. "One 57 [*sic*] is one of the worst looking buildings I've seen in a long time, in particular its very ugly 'skin,'" Donald Trump tweeted about the tower.

Perhaps the building's most notable critic was the architect himself. De Portzamparc was said to be unhappy with how the building had turned out, privately accusing Barnett and the Extell team of compromising on quality and cutting costs by opting for a cheaper glass for the undulating waterfall façade than he had recommended, according to people familiar with the situation. After the initial launch, he largely declined to participate in press for the building, refused interview requests, and kept a notably low profile.

While de Portzamparc publicly denied his disappointment, Barnett was clearly rankled by what he perceived as the architect distancing himself from the building.

"I said, 'You're running away from the building because you got a bad review from the *New York Times* architecture critic, who always had an agenda,'" Barnett recalled later. "He hated rich, rich buildings. But he said, 'No, it's not true.'"

Architecture critics weren't the only ones weighing in. As the construction of One57 neared completion, New Yorkers began to take notice of the giant new tower, with some dubbing it "the billionaire building." Cabdrivers and Midtown office workers gossiped about the prices of the apartments, and the narrative began to take on a life of its own. *It's all Russian money. The buyers are all Chinese. No one even lives there. A Saudi prince bought the penthouse. No, it was a Qatari royal.* No one seemed to know fact from fiction.

Barnett observed the chatter around the building with dismay. As talk swirled about foreign oligarchs stashing their cash in dark, empty apartments, he wished he could correct the record. After all, the buyer of the project's most expensive apartment, Michael Dell, was an American. "We would have loved to publicize that," he said later. But, wary of breaking his word to the buyer about keeping his deal confidential, he kept his mouth shut.

In a city with an enormous wealth gap, the skyboxes for billionaires were simultaneously an object of fascination and loathing. To some, these new towers were eyesores that the city should have prevented. And to many New Yorkers, the amount of wealth being poured into the building seemed obscene, especially amid an ongoing housing shortage and a mounting homelessness crisis. New York's shelter system was reaching breaking point by the end of 2013, with a record more than 52,000 people living in the system, including about 22,000 children.

THEN THERE WERE the shadows.

In October 2013, the journalist Warren St. John wrote an op-ed for *The New York Times* decrying the shadows the seventy-five stories of One57 were casting over Central Park, observing that visitors to a playground on the south end of the park now found themselves cut off from the midafternoon sun. With 432 Park now rising up near the park's southeast corner, access to sunlight and blue skies above Central Park was under assault. St. John warned that, with even more new buildings planned for the corridor, few

New Yorkers knew what was coming, in terms of their changing Midtown skyline. "There has been remarkably little public discussion, let alone dissent, about the plans," he wrote.

The public's ignorance of what was coming was linked to the fact that the city had had little control over what could be built. St. John suggested that most of the towers were abusing the rules surrounding "as-of-right" buildings, meaning that so long as a developer had assembled the necessary site and the air and development rights, they could build as tall as the zoning code in the area allowed. Theoretically, every building on the 57th Street corridor was subject to the input of the public, since the zoning regulations under which they were built were subject to public debate. But the public had no input whatsoever into how the buildings would actually look.

An environmental review and public consultation were not required, and the city had no say whatsoever in the design. Most of the new buildings were also located within what's known as the Manhattan Special Midtown District, which has special zoning regulations that allow for some of the largest buildings in New York.

With detractors like St. John ramping up their public criticism, Billionaires' Row, as it was starting to be widely known, had suddenly become a topic of heated public debate. And Barnett, as the developer of One57 and now a forthcoming second tower, was, for better or worse, the face of the phenomenon.

It wasn't Barnett's first brush with being publicly characterized as a greedy developer. The year prior, he drew a series of negative headlines after installing separate entrances for affordable rental tenants and luxury condo buyers at a property he was developing on Riverside Boulevard. The press dubbed the entrance for affordable tenants, "the poor door."

Barnett defended the move, saying that "poor door" was just the media's way of dramatizing what was inherently a run-of-the-mill financial decision.

"Ask any of the thousands of people who are applying for that [affordable housing], and they don't give a damn," he told WNYC.

TAKEN INDIVIDUALLY, the impact of One57 in terms of its shadow-casting potential may not have been enormous. But critics worried that the tower would set a precedent for future skyscrapers that could block the views of the sky from numerous locations within the park and shroud landmarks like the carousel, ball fields, and even the Central Park Zoo in shadows throughout the day.

According to a report released in 2013 by the Municipal Arts Society, Barnett's second planned tower for Billionaires' Row—the one he had gone through the parking garage debacle for—could be capable of casting shadows as long as 4,000 feet, or three quarters of a mile, in certain conditions. The society, a powerful lobbying organization known as MAS, had helped block the demolition of New York City landmarks such as Radio City Music Hall and Grand Central Terminal.

MAS also had decades of experience defending Central Park from shadows. In 1987, when plans were filed to replace the Coliseum with a pair of towers standing fifty-eight and sixty-eight stories tall, the society filed a lawsuit, arguing that the city had granted the project a zoning bonus so that it could build larger structures than would be typically allowed, without regard to the effects on the local neighborhood. It also organized an event called "Stand Against the Shadow," at which roughly a thousand protesters dispersed into the park with black umbrellas to draw attention to areas that would be cast into shadow by the proposed development. They formed a human chain from the Columbus Circle entrance to the park to 69th Street and Fifth Avenue, then lifted the umbrellas one by one for dramatic effect.

"One would hope that the city would act as a protector of sun and light and clean air and space and parkland," said one of the organization's board members, former first lady Jacqueline Kennedy Onassis. "Those elements are essential to combat the stress of urban life."

The issues raised by the city's long debate over shadows posed an interesting question: If the New York skyline was going to be altered so irreparably by ultra-high-rise towers, shouldn't New Yorkers have some say in what was being built? Weren't these buildings, by virtue of their visibility, the property of all New Yorkers to some extent? Wasn't their design everyone's business?

As it stood, the public would have no access to the new slate of Billionaires' Row megatowers. None of them included any plans for publicly accessible areas near their pinnacles, such as an observation deck or a Windows on the World–style restaurant in the sky. They were going to be prominent buildings—structures the average New Yorker would not be able to overlook—but off-limits.

Only a small number of the towers that would eventually permeate the Billionaires' Row corridor were subject to any additional design scrutiny from the city. One was a planned tower by the architect Jean Nouvel and the real estate developer Hines at 53 West 53rd Street adjacent to the Museum of Modern Art, the design of which had to go before the City Planning Commission only because the developers were requesting a variance to the zoning code that covered the area. The planning board chair, Amanda Burden, a graceful, wafer-thin woman with a precise blond bob and a long-time confidante of then mayor Michael Bloomberg, overruled the project's height, then planned at around 1,250 feet, the same height as the Empire State Building minus the antenna. She was unhappy with the design, which called for a matrix of steel beams tapering up the skyscraper like a spider's web. The development team had failed, she said, to design something that was as great as or greater than the Empire State Building, and the project was therefore unworthy of approval. As a result, 200 feet were lopped off the top of the design, effectively disqualifying the project from the Billionaires' Row race to the sky.

Then, inevitably, the planning board's verdict incurred its own backlash—again playing out in *The New York Times*. In response to the rejection of the proposal, Nicolai Ouroussoff, an architecture critic for the *Times,* accused Burden of the "disturbing" act of "treating the Midtown skyline as a museum piece."

"Both the Empire State and Chrysler buildings, built during the Great Depression, were celebrated in their time as emblems of the city's fortitude," Ouroussoff wrote. "And now a real alternative to it, one of the most enchanting skyscraper designs of recent memory, may well be lost because some people worry that nothing in our current age can measure up to the past. It is a mentality that, once it takes hold, risks transforming a living city into an urban mausoleum."

It seemed someone would be unhappy no matter what the outcome. In a subsequent report, the MAS warned that the supertalls along Billionaires' Row were being planned at such a rapid clip that they caught the public off guard and called for a reappraisal of the zoning around key open spaces such as Central Park that would allow for more consideration of the impacts of development. By creatively skirting zoning constraints through buying up air rights from neighboring properties, developers had been exploiting half-century-old zoning codes that were written before it was even possible to build such tall, narrow buildings on tiny lots, the report argued.

Its authors also maintained that developers were outsmarting controls designed to regulate the height of buildings by including empty floors, which do not count against the floor area limits of their sites, thereby allowing them to build higher and maximize their views of the park. At 432 Park Avenue, for instance, there would be nineteen full floors of mechanical and structural voids, ten of which would be used for vortex shedding or aerodynamic design purposes. Altogether, these lent an extra 313 feet to the tower's height, the report said—and that height was exempt from zoning calculations.

"If the problems these developments pose aren't addressed, what's at risk is a city that is darker, drearier, and more austere than its denizens deserve; a place where ordinary New Yorkers can't find an affordable apartment while faceless corporations stockpile vacant investment properties," Elizabeth Goldstein, president of MAS, wrote in the report.

But the debate was about more than shadows.

BARNETT HAD BENEFITED financially from being a pioneer on Billionaires' Row, but he was conscious that for many New Yorkers, including some in local government, his role in transforming the skyline made him an antagonist.

Aware of the delicate relationship between developers and local authorities and eager to maintain good relations, Barnett agreed to appear on a panel in February 2014 where the issues surrounding the supertall debate would be discussed. He would present his case for the buildings in the presence of his detractors, including the journalist St. John, Landmarks Conservancy president Peg Breen, and Margaret Newman, executive director of the Municipal Art Society. It was the preservationist vs. developer match-up for the ages.

Interest in the forum was so intense, ultimately drawing a crowd of roughly four hundred people, that it had to be relocated from the 143-seat Museum of Arts and Design Theater to the much larger Celeste Bartos Forum at the New York Public Library, with its grand 30-foot-high elliptical glass dome and dramatic crown-molding-embellished archways. The public seemed finally to be waking up to the fact that a new cohort of supertall towers was going to change their view of the city forever.

Barnett said he decided to attend the meeting against the advice of his public relations team because he's always believed in rational argument, even if it involves sitting in front of an unfriendly audience. "If you don't speak rationally to people with an opposing viewpoint, you can't change things," he said later. "People are ignorant. They just hear these slogans about blocking the sun and rich people taking over the world and they think it sounds right. If nobody corrects them, they don't get educated."

During the forum, the case against Barnett's buildings was neatly laid out by St. John and the other activists. In an impassioned speech, St. John invoked the same criticism from his *New York Times* op-ed, recalling taking his daughter to the Heckscher Playground in Central Park near 65th Street only to have the weather grow suddenly chilly. The shadow of One57 had drifted over the playground. Everyone left.

Having awaited his turn to speak, Barnett took to the podium that evening in his trademark black turtleneck and rimless glasses, pitching his own defense to the crowd.

"My name is Gary I'm-a-glutton-for-punishment Barnett," he announced, which produced a few chuckles amid the crowd's hisses.

He laid out his counterarguments. These buildings created jobs, he said, and surely a tall slim tower was better than a wall of small chunky ones. "Does the possibility of a small, minute shadow out- weigh the possibility of giving our fellow New Yorkers a chance at a better life?" he asked.

"The shadows cast by tall, slender buildings—which is what most of the buildings going up are—are very brief. Maybe they're ten minutes in any one place and cause no negative effect on the flora or fauna of the park," he argued. "The net additive effect of shadows on the park is at most a couple of percent, from a space- time viewpoint."

But the crowd, largely made up of preservationists, politicians, urbanists, and members of the local community board, didn't seem to be buying it. "These buildings will make a lot of money for de- velopers," said Assemblywoman Linda B. Rosenthal, who repre- sented the Upper West Side. "And that's their right. But we need something back."

THE SHADOW DEBATE compounded Barnett's public perception problems at a time when his name was already being dragged through the mud in the city tabloids. It had all started the previous spring, when he found his name splashed over the New York *Daily News.*

A TOWERING INSULT read the headline in the city's so-called "hometown paper" in June 2013, alongside a picture of a gleaming One57.

The piece, written by the paper's editorial team, took issue with Extell's use of the city's 421-A tax abatement program, a state program that allowed New York developers a tax break on their projects in return for funding the creation of affordable housing. "At a cost of $1.3 billion, Extell Development is erecting the 1,004-foot spire between Sixth and Seventh Aves. as what *The New York Times* called a 'global billionaires' club.' And you, and Mr. and Mrs. Taxpayer, are subsidizing the project with tens of millions of dollars," read the piece, positing that the project's inclusion in the deal had been the result of a mysterious backroom deal in Albany. "One57 is the poster child for misplaced public aid," it said.

A second editorial ran in the *Daily News* less than a month later, calling on a newly formed state anticorruption commission, known as the Moreland Commission, to probe the tax break in light of donations made to New York governor Andrew Cuomo, a popular figure among developers, by Barnett's Extell just days before the governor signed the bill allowing the developer and four others to make use of the 421-A program. The paper pointed to two $50,000 donations to the governor's campaign by corporations linked to Extell on the very same day in late January 2013 that Albany passed a housing bill containing the tax breaks, and another $100,000 donation made by Barnett to a state Democratic Party account that Cuomo had used to finance ads pushing his agenda, less than three weeks after the bill was signed into law.

"This giveaway to One57 has all the makings of a perfect case for Cuomo's Moreland Act commission: large campaign contributions changing hands, lawmakers operating behind closed doors, special interests gaining undeserved benefits and taxpayers getting the shaft," the article read.

It seemed the commission took note.

That summer, Extell was slapped with a subpoena from the commission, which had been established by Cuomo himself to investigate public corruption amid a string of high profile arrests of New York State legislators. It requested extensive materials, including emails and any other communications between Extell executives and lobbyists and elected officials that pertained to the tax break.

The controversial 421-A tax abatement program had been around since 1971, when it was created to incentivize the development of underutilized or unused land by dramatically reducing the taxes on newly developed land. At the time, city officials were contending with a mass migration of New Yorkers to the suburbs and feared a major slump in the production of new housing as a result of inflation and the imposition of rent stabilization laws.

Over the decades, the program was revised and renewed several times with a view to linking the tax exemption to the production of affordable housing. At one point, developers could qualify for the abatement in two ways, either by purchasing certificates from affordable housing developers who would then use the proceeds to offset their construction costs on other projects or by including affordable units in their own buildings. The latter became known as the 80/20 program, because developers would be required to set aside 20 percent of their units for low-income New Yorkers. It was the same program that led to the "poor door" phenomenon. The certificates side of the program was discontinued in 2008.

To critics of 421-A, One57 was a physical manifestation of the problems with the program. While the building was not necessarily representative of the types of projects that took advantage of the abatement, it drew outsized attention because of the prices it commanded. Why, critics asked, did a building on Billionaires' Row, where apartments had traded for as much as $100 million, need a subsidy that would cost the city $65.6 million of property tax revenue over a decade? They argued that there were more cost effective ways of creating affordable housing.

A review of the 421-A deal at One57 by the city's Independent Budget Office in 2015 showed that the abatement the project received generated 66 units of affordable housing in the Bronx at the cost of $905,000 per apartment. By the IBO's estimates, that was a bad deal. The agency contended that, had the city provided an affordable housing developer with a cash grant equal to One57's tax expenditure, nearly 370 affordable units at a cost of $179,000 per unit could have been created.

More specifically, though, the controversy around One57 centered on a 2013 move by state legislators, as detailed by the *Daily News* editorials, to allow five specific projects—One57 among them—to be grandfathered into the program under the pre-2008 rules. This meant that the developers could purchase certificates to fund offsite affordable housing rather than including affordable units in their own buildings. The five projects hadn't qualified under prior legislation because they were situated in high-density zones.

As a result of its inclusion in the program, One57 was able to offer its buyers a 95 percent reduction in property taxes in 2014 and 2015. Over ten years, they would save about 56.5 percent—which for some buyers would amount to hundreds of thousands of dollars.

Publicly, Barnett shrugged off the Moreland Commission investigation. Donating to state officials was perfectly legal and par for the course for anyone doing business in New York, he contended, and he and Extell had done nothing outside of the parameters of the law. The deal, he said, had sign-off from the city and the state. "Nothing was done in the dead of night here," he said.

Melissa DeRosa, then a spokeswoman for the governor, told the *Times Union* that, though the checks were not logged until January 28, they had actually been cut earlier in the month and that the governor's office would have supported the bill with or without the provision that benefited Extell.

The week the subpoenas were issued, Barnett's spokesperson issued a statement to *The Wall Street Journal* saying that the company was happy to "cooperate fully with any agency trying to improve government." Behind the scenes, though, Barnett fumed to colleagues about who he posited was really pushing the 421-A controversy narrative: the New York *Daily News* publisher and fellow real estate titan Mort Zuckerman. "That was a vindictive act by Mort Zuckerman," Barnett said later, claiming that Zuckerman had a vendetta against him.

Before the financial crisis, Zuckerman's Boston Properties and the Related Companies had locked up a site in New York's Theater District, on Eighth Avenue between 45th and 46th streets, at a cheap price with plans to build an office tower, but had let the contracts lapse amid the global financial meltdown. Before Boston and Related could restart the project, Extell had quietly bought an interest in the land. According to Barnett, Zuckerman, who still hoped to proceed with the project, was furious when he found out that Barnett, who had previously sold him air rights for the project, had scooped it out from under him.

But as far as Barnett was concerned, it was just business. "You can't put a Reserved sticker on New York real estate," he said. "It doesn't work like that. You walk away from it, somebody else can take it."

For a while, the pair talked about teaming up to develop the site together, just as Barnett had tried to do with Roth after the parking garage debacle, but they could never reach an agreement over the terms. Zuckerman, Barnett said, never got over the perceived slight. After all, five projects had been grandfathered in under the new 421-A legislation in 2013, but the *Daily News* seemed laser-focused on just One57. It could have been because of the headline-grabbing prices but, although he had no proof, Barnett couldn't help but think that it was Zuckerman, the paper's publisher, who was pushing the stories.

"He held a grudge," Barnett said. "This was his way of trying to get back at me."

Barnett thought of calling Zuckerman and confronting him head-on about the *Daily News* editorials, but then he thought better of it. "Someone said to me, 'Don't get in an argument with someone who buys ink by the barrel,'" he said.

Barnett needn't have worried. After less than a year and numerous allegations of interference by Cuomo in its activities, the Moreland Commission was abruptly and permanently disbanded. In a preliminary report issued in December 2013, prior to the disbandment, investigators said that, without further work, they could not draw any "premature" conclusions on whether or not the extension of the 421-A program had involved any improper action.

"It is clear," the report said, "that the combination of very large campaign contributions and very narrowly targeted benefits to those same donors creates an appearance of impropriety that undermines public trust in our elected representatives."

DESPITE HIS TROUBLES, Barnett was ready to double down on Billionaires' Row. By the end of 2012, he knew that, despite the headwinds he was already facing in the market—and the proverbial public square—he was ready to move ahead with building his second tower on the corridor.

That winter, as they chatted at the launch of another Extell building on Riverside Park, Corcoran Sunshine president Kelly Mack asked him why. "Gary, you literally just built the most successful project in New York. You changed everything and you proved all the naysayers wrong," she said, referencing the success of One57. "Why don't you just sell the other site to someone else? You can get a ton of money and be done with it."

Barnett smirked. "That's probably a good idea," he said.

But Mack knew that was never going to happen.

Within a few weeks, Barnett would sign a deal with department store chain Nordstrom to open their first full-scale New York City store, a roughly 400,000-square-foot, seven-story commercial establishment, at the base of his new building at 217 West 57th Street. It was the deal Harry Macklowe had wanted for 432 Park. Nordstrom had agreed to buy its portion of the building in a deal valued at more than $300 million, which would form the cornerstone of the financing for Barnett's newest creation.

Known as Central Park Tower, it would be the tallest primarily residential building in the world. Taller than his own One57. Taller than Harry Macklowe's 432 Park. Much taller than Steve Roth's 220 Central Park South.

On Billionaires' Row, they were now engaged in a full-on race to the sky. Acknowledging the phallic nature of the towers, Macklowe would later be quoted as saying that the race was driven by a certain level of "penis envy."

PART II

Turbulence

CHAPTER 10

"Too Much Money"

David Juracich knew he had "too much money." He had so much money that he didn't know how to spend it.

The Melbourne native had made a small fortune working for nearly two decades in the financial industry as a broker trading interest rate swaps, financial instruments designed to help major corporations protect against and profit from future swings in rates. It was one of the most profitable and controversial fields in finance.

Tall, affable, and boyishly handsome, with a full head of wavy sandy-colored hair, Juracich had once been a state champion Aussie rower. He spent most of the nineties on trading floors in Tokyo, acting as a conduit between Japanese traders and the foreign markets. It was an experience he compared to the roaring twenties in Shanghai, "crazy, amazing years of money, growth, opulence and a great time."

He was a regular on the Tokyo club scene back then, and fellow traders would share stories for years about his antics, each adding their own more outlandish flourish until the tales became legendary and detached from reality. On his first day in Japan, some waggish British swap brokers had christened him "Wavey Dave" for his hairstyle, and the nickname stuck. (The Japanese traders called him

Wavey-san.) Thanks to his far-flung travels, and the international dynamics of the money markets, people would remember Juracich wherever he went. He would be walking down the street in Stockholm when suddenly someone would yell "Wavey!" and remind him that they had met in some bar or nightclub in Dusseldorf or Singapore. He would rarely remember.

In 2003, when Tradition, the brokerage he worked for, asked him to relocate to New York, Juracich thought it would never match up to the riotous experience he had had in Tokyo, but he found himself pleasantly surprised. By the time the mid-aughts rolled around, he said he felt like America was "on steroids."

Juracich worked hard and played hard, and, in New York at least, the cost of partying was way, way up. He ponied up thousands of dollars for tables at charity balls and tapped his expense account to pay ungodly sums for table service at the best clubs. "In most other places in the world, a guy can be let in for sixty or eighty dollars entry and then buy some drinks," he said. "Here, you couldn't get in anywhere unless you committed to a bottle service table for four thousand. I couldn't get my head around it. There was so much money around."

Juracich lived on the corner of Spring and Lafayette streets in the trendy Manhattan neighborhood that had been rebranded in the midnineties as Nolita (North of Little Italy), and from there he could walk downtown to his Financial District office each day. He played hard, but he worked hard, too. He logged long hours, starting each morning around four thirty and getting home around six thirty in the evening. As the debt markets exploded over the Bush and Obama administrations, the times were busy and profitable— but exhausting.

As he wined, dined, and partied his way around New York, Juracich began to sniff out his next career steps. He was almost forty and thinking of settling down. By 2007, the real estate market in the city was as hot as it had ever been and, with Wall Street bonuses sky-high, it seemed everyone he knew was making money flipping apartments or investing in real estate deals. It sounded like a much easier life than the Wall Street hamster wheel, where you were only as good as last quarter's figures. "I kept hearing about people buying some warehouse apartment in Tribeca for $1.4 million, putting $500,000 into it and selling it eight months later for $5.5 million," he said later. "I'm like, 'What the hell is going on?' I want my piece of that."

Juracich began doing his homework. After long days at work, he went online to research real estate opportunities and meet with brokers and developers. In 2007, he was introduced by a broker to an aspiring real estate developer named Michael Stern.

Stern was by all estimations an unknown quantity among the ranks of New York developers at that time. Still in his twenties, he was much younger than some of the best-known Manhattan builders—he was less than half Harry Macklowe's age, for instance—and he and his company, JDS Development Group, had almost zero track record. However, he carried himself with so much confidence that anyone might have been forgiven for assuming he was a veteran.

From the steady stream of designer cars Stern rolled out each time they met, Juracich assumed he had been somewhat successful already. Short and heavyset with a mumbling, quiet demeanor, Stern struck the Aussie as hardworking and no-bullshit. Stern said he had built a million square feet of low- and mid-rise residential projects in Florida and more than one thousand units across the outer boroughs, in neighborhoods like the Rockaways, Flatbush, and Forest Hills, and was ready to do something bigger.

By "something bigger," Stern meant a luxury rental building in Brooklyn's up-and-coming Gowanus neighborhood, taking advantage of rezoning that had paved the way for residential development. Stern was looking for capital, and Juracich came with a string of banking contacts that could help the pair cobble together early financing for this project and future ones. As Brooklyn was booming with young professionals priced out of Manhattan and heading across the river, the strategy and reasoning behind the project made sense to Juracich. He trusted his gut and invested a modest $2.7 million of his personal funds. It would be a test to see whether the partnership worked—Juracich would put up some cash and the "reassuring, very confident" Stern would "steer the ship."

THE FOLLOWING YEAR, when the financial markets went into free fall following the collapse of Lehman Brothers, Juracich thought the sky was falling. "I was leaving work every night and I'd see people walking the streets and eating in restaurants and I'd want to shake them and yell at them that the end of the world is coming." He assumed the economic carnage—which, of course, traced its origins to the real estate industry, in the form of subprime mortgages—would spell the end of his brief foray into property investing. But Stern had different ideas. By the close of that year, he was already trying to persuade the Australian to double down on a second deal with him, despite the fact that the Gowanus project was stalled. With values slumping, he said, now was the time to pounce and reap the rewards later.

Stern was now setting his sights even higher—zeroing in on the old New York Telephone Company building in Manhattan's Chelsea neighborhood, which he had been touring the very day of the Lehman Brothers collapse. The 1920s-era brick Art Deco high-rise, designed by the architect Ralph Walker, was owned by communications giant Verizon, which was trying to unload it amid a selloff of some of its monolithic offices used to house copper wire for landline telephones. With the market plunging toward rock bottom, there were few buyers, and Stern had negotiated an unbelievable price of just $25.25 million, far less than what he believed the building was truly worth. He wanted to turn it into condominiums.

If Juracich had been on the fence about the deal, it was a steak that convinced him.

On a cold Tuesday evening that winter, as he considered Stern's proposal, he had invited a client out for a late-night dinner at Del Frisco's, a posh steakhouse near Rockefeller Center. They couldn't get in. "The world is falling apart and they're telling me it's an hour and a half wait for a table for us to spend $300 on a steak and $1,000 on a bottle of wine," he marveled.

Sure, the economy was limping along, but he was making more money than he ever had. Wall Street, and by extension money brokers, were making record profits. He decided then and there: "My company's making money, all the banks are making loads of money. We're going to be safe and Manhattan's going to be safe. So I'm going to buy this property," he said.

Over the next few months, the duo went out to raise the funds needed to close on the Chelsea building, with Wavey mortgaging a rental apartment he owned in Chelsea to contribute to the deposit. He called on his banking contacts for $250,000 or $500,000 at a time in a bid to raise initial capital. He took a casual approach befitting his reputation. "Feel free to tell me to take a hike," he would say, or "Just putting this out there."

By the following year, just days before Stern and Juracich were slated to close on the Chelsea building, the pair still didn't have all the money they needed, thanks in large part to a hedge fund's pulling out of the deal last minute. Despite having obtained several extensions from Verizon already, there was a $3 million gap in their capital stack, and their nonrefundable 10 percent deposit, roughly $2.5 million, was on the line.

They asked Verizon for another sixty-day extension but were denied. It turned out that Verizon had union contracts tied to the shedding of office space and had to close the deal.

With just days before the closing deadline, Stern and Juracich feared they might have to default on the deposit. But then they were introduced to a potential savior: Kevin Maloney, a founder of a national development firm named Property Markets Group, which had the capital to plug the hole quickly.

By the time Maloney was approached by a broker about the deal, everyone had already seen the Verizon building, Maloney said, including his own business partner, Elliott Joseph. Joseph thought the building had good bones, with great light and air and high ceilings, but with just 88,000 square feet of salable space, the project was simply too small for the mathematics of the deal to work, he said. Stern was now asking them to take a second look. He said that the project could be a lot bigger than the 88,000 salable square feet they had been quoted; if they moved around the elevators and stairwells, they could wind up with more than 120,000 square feet of salable space. That could spell significant profits.

Maloney was intrigued—if the space really could be reconfigured, the deal had a lot more potential upside than he originally thought—but he told the broker that Stern would need to show PMG's team how he planned to pull off the reconfiguration.

"The broker said, 'You know, if you do this, you've got to close in three days. This guy's on his third or sixth extension and the seller is pissed,'" Maloney recalled later. "I said, 'Tell him, if it's 120,000 feet like he says, we'll write the check and close with him.'"

And close they did. There was barely time for any due diligence and no time for paperwork; in fact, Maloney wired the nearly $3 million before a formal contract could be drawn up and signed. The relatively paltry sum would secure for Property Markets Group a 50 percent equity stake in a deal that, if Stern was right, could be enormously profitable.

Stern and Maloney had met only a couple of times, and for his part, Maloney said he knew at that time that he was putting his money on an untested partner. "I think he was kind of working out of his car at the time," Maloney said later. (Stern denied this.)

It was the ultimate shotgun real estate marriage, but the potential for winnings was so good that Maloney was willing to jump first and ask questions later.

THE NEWLY ANOINTED partnership was on a winning streak, thanks to the crash. Just a year after JDS and PMG closed on the building, Starwood Capital Group, the real estate private equity firm led by W Hotels founder Barry Sternlicht, bought a roughly 30 percent stake in it for $42 million. One of Sternlicht's associates reportedly went up to the roof of the Verizon building, strolled around for fifteen minutes, took in the views, and said, "Get this done."

The Starwood deal was evidence of how much the market was already starting to rebound since Stern had locked in the roughly $25 million price a couple of years earlier. It also spoke to how an active deal could suddenly bestow a sense of desirability on a property that hadn't existed before. Financiers often experienced FOMO—the fear of missing out.

Juracich couldn't imagine another scenario in which a company with the cachet and deep pockets of Starwood would invest in a group of guys with close to zero experience in the development business. But Starwood had money on its books to put to work, and there were few active projects in which to stash it.

Despite their nearly nonexistent track record, Stern was also able to lure the architecture firm Cetra Ruddy, known for its thoughtful restorations of historic New York City buildings, to work on the project. In a regular market, they would never have been able to afford the firm, but it was a dry season for architects, too. "You usually don't go from doing shitty apartments out in the back of Queens to something like this," Juracich said. "We just jumped over all that. And that was all because of the crash."

Among the city's top residential brokers, the repositioning of the building would eventually result in its being seen as one of the most tasteful in the city. Debuting as Walker Tower in the spring of 2012, it was a resounding commercial and critical success. Led by Stern, who spent the most time of all the partners on the physical job site, the developers rearranged the building's distinctive setbacks, punching new windows and replacing the brickwork on its north and south façades with ornamental stainless bronze that was seen as simultaneously timeless and trendy. By the time the units went on sale, the market was crying out for inventory, and Walker Tower was one of the most appealing projects in town. The developers sold out the apartments for roughly $4,000 a square foot, more than twice the roughly $1,800 they had initially projected, and the apartments drew big-name buyers like the actress Cameron

Diaz and the cosmetics maven Laura Mercier. The project propelled Stern's reputation; he had entered the ranks of the boldest names in real estate.

For Stern, Juracich, Joseph, and Maloney, it was a windfall, and each accepted some of the profits, which collectively totaled more than $400 million, in the form of their own sprawling apartments at the building. Wavey would secure one with a large terrace with views straight to the Empire State Building where he and his new wife, a glamorous platinum blond real estate broker named Catherine, were hoping to expand their family. Stern used some of his earnings to add to his growing collection of designer cars, which by then included '60s muscle cars, vintage German cars, and modern sports cars like an Audi R8 Spyder and a Mercedes AMG GT S.

The partnership was so successful that Wavey, Stern, and PMG agreed to partner on several more projects, including another high-end condo in Hell's Kitchen known as Stella Tower on which they also joined forces with Starwood, an Art Deco–inspired condo near Chelsea's High Line park, and an ultra-luxury rental building on the East Side near the United Nations. With the win seeming to prove his partner's competence for dealmaking, Juracich steered away from the details, letting Stern take the wheel. And his ambitions were growing even higher.

In 2013, the pair, again with Maloney and PMG on board, would embark on their most ambitious undertaking yet: a supertall spire next to the historic Steinway & Sons concert hall and piano showroom on West 57th Street. Within less than five years, Juracich had gone from complete real estate neophyte to an investor in a business proposition that could forever alter the skyline of the city.

It was a decision he would come to view with deep regret.

CHAPTER 11

New Kids on the Block

To the New York City real estate world, Michael Stern seemed to have come from nowhere. How was it possible that a kid no one had heard of a couple of years earlier was suddenly trying to build one of the tallest skyscrapers in the world? The truth was that no one, including his own partners, seemed to know very much about him.

Michael Zev Stern grew up in an Orthodox Jewish family in Far Rockaway, a neighborhood on the eastern part of the Rockaway peninsula in the New York borough of Queens, where his father owned an auto body shop and his mother was a nursing executive. His parents divorced when Stern was a teenager, an act that amounted to a scandal in their Orthodox community, which was not accepting of divorce.

Stern had graduated from high school, but just barely, and didn't have a college degree.

"I was a pain in the ass," he would say later in an interview with the real estate trade magazine *The Real Deal*. "According to my mother, I used to go around knocking over [store] displays and kicking old ladies in the shin." He later claimed he had been expelled from at least four schools as a teenager, citing his penchant for dressing in leather jackets and riding motorcycles. "They didn't like that very much," he said. "They kicked me out for being a quote unquote 'bad influence.'"

STERN SAID HE had cut his teeth as a construction manager on some multifamily buildings in Miami in his early twenties before setting up his own company back home in New York. As for the seed money for his early projects, he claimed to have saved up the earnings from the sale of an online business that sold weaves and hair care products to Black women, though, in numerous interviews over the years, he resisted going into any level of detail on the company or the sale. Stern was never keen to go into his past, preferring to gloss over it in broad strokes.

At the time of the Walker Tower purchase, Stern, then only about thirty years old, had been in the midst of a divorce battle. At around age twenty, he had married Yael Hirsh, an Orthodox Jewish divorcée eighteen years his senior who did work in the wig business, selling head coverings to Jewish women whose religious beliefs required that they hide their natural hair.

Their split in 2009 was messy—so messy that Hirsh eventually requested an order of protection against Stern, testifying in court that he had threatened her physical safety on several occasions, an allegation that Stern denied. In a motion made to the court during the divorce case, Stern asked that the marriage be declared null and void because he and Hirsh had never intended to be married but had participated in a religious ceremony solely to deceive members of their community who disapproved of their nonmarital relationship.

In later litigation between the couple and Stern's mother, Hirsh alleged that Stern may have forged her name on documents that added his brother as an owner of her house in Lawrence, New York, which she had gotten from her first marriage and on which she was then facing foreclosure.

"There was a mystery about Michael Stern. He was not part of

NEW KIDS ON THE BLOCK

the inherited class. He also didn't have the family pedigree or credentials of someone who went to an Ivy League or had a residency at the private equity firms," said Amir Korangy, publisher of the real estate magazine *The Real Deal*. "To tip the scales against him further, he was young and physically appeared brutish."

And, by the time the Steinway project got underway, he already seemed to have made some enemies.

I was wrapping up my workday on a Tuesday in March 2021, when I got an email from an unfamiliar sender. "Heard you're writing a book. . . ." the subject line read.

If that wasn't enough to capture my attention, the email address certainly was: michaelzsterncriminal@gmail.com.

In the coming days, the mysterious person behind the inflammatory email address unloaded heaps of documents to me, using Gmail's confidential mode, a method by which you can prevent the recipient from forwarding or downloading messages or attachments. They included copies of lawsuits filed against Stern, documentation of private loans the developer had received, and even what purported to be a private investigator's report on Stern that included allegations of a criminal past. No one would admit to having commissioned the report, and the investigations firm didn't respond to numerous requests for comment. Stern denied any suggestion of criminal misconduct.

But this person, whoever they were, clearly had serious beef with Stern. It would soon become clear that they weren't the only one.

PMG FOUNDER KEVIN Maloney had all the many years of experience Stern lacked. Though he was spending more time in Florida, he had been in the New York real estate ether for decades, starting out in finance at Chemical Bank before going on to run real estate for the now defunct Ensign, a $2 billion federal bank. When he went out on his own in the early 1990s, he worked on a few deals with Gary Barnett and partnered with another major New York

City power player, Ziel Feldman. He would later tell tales of how they cobbled together small deals in the early days, in a tiny office with no heating and Home Depot card tables for desks.

Tall, with a long, thin face and graying hair, Maloney had a knack for spinning a story and a taste for the good life. He was rich and had a private Piston prop plane, a house on the beach in Golden Beach, Florida, an apartment in London, and a ranch near Aspen. Not unlike the eccentric billionaire Stuart Mott, he kept chickens on the terrace of his sprawling luxury penthouse on West End Avenue. He said he met his wife, a statuesque young British brunette named Tania, on the side of the road in Miami. She was standing beside a silver Porsche being frisked by two policemen, who suspected her of drunk driving. Maloney knew one of the cops and pulled over. It turned out she was just a terrible driver, he would say.

Like Stern, he had been a rebellious kid. The son of a lawyer for the Marine Corps, at age fourteen he had taken an unregistered family farm truck without permission, loaded it with beer and shotguns, and gone out with his friends to shoot mailboxes. He was soon stopped by state troopers.

The partnership between Stern and Property Markets Group was far from a match made in heaven. As the success of Walker Tower made headlines, Maloney quickly came to resent how much attention and adulation Stern was receiving for it, both among the investment community and in the real estate press, which wrote lengthy profiles depicting Stern as a young upstart rising quickly into the big time and only mentioned PMG as an afterthought. The hard hats worn by the construction workers on their projects all said JDS Development, not Property Markets Group.

Maloney bristled, too, when Stern left him with what he deemed the worst of the remaining apartments at Walker Tower as a dividend. Stern and Wavey Dave had gotten the better ones for themselves, as had his own partner in the project, Elliott Joseph. While Maloney didn't plan to actually live there, he didn't like getting the short shrift.

"They were all smart enough, early on, to go pick their apartments. And I actually got two apartments at the end. Because they were kind of really, you know, not great apartments," he said.

In time, Maloney said he wasn't satisfied with the level of transparency Stern was providing about spending on the project and asked Joseph to keep close tabs on the finances. "If you're my partner and my accounting staff doesn't get the monthly budgets and costs and contracts and all that, I start to dig in. It's just human nature," Maloney said later. "I just want full disclosure. If you're my partner, it's your job to protect the project, yourself, and me. It's us against the world, right?"

Sometimes, when the PMG team was clashing with Stern, photoshopped memes of Stern would circulate in the company's office, making fun of the young developer, according to people familiar with the situation.

One such meme depicted Stern speaking at a conference. The speech bubble above him read "Thank you for coming today. Just to clear the air, it's true that I created, designed and constructed Walker Tower. I also invented Post-It notes and discovered Penicillin." It was a jab at Stern's perceived tendency to take credit for work he hadn't done.

In another, a speech bubble poked fun at what the PMG partners deemed Stern's propensity for stretching the truth. "Ladies and gentlemen," it said. "For my first trick, I will say something that is actually true!"

Maloney's and Stern's respective recollections of their time working together would eventually sound as though the two were singing from two different hymnals. As they presented contradictory narratives of the same events, it became difficult to parse fact from fiction. Maloney would accuse Stern of stretching the truth; Stern would accuse Maloney of embellishing for the sake of a better story. One of their former partners used a quote from Cormac McCarthy's *Blood Meridian* to illustrate the point: "Men's memories are uncertain," McCarthy wrote, "and the past that was differs little from the past that was not."

For his part, Maloney would later compare his early relationship with Stern to the honeymoon period of a romantic relationship.

"It's like dating someone," he told *The Real Deal*. "In the beginning, everything is great, and then you start to see the cracks."

THEIR FORAY INTO Billionaires' Row started small. Starwood, who had become a major investor in Walker Tower, owned a small, narrow lot on 57th Street with dead center views over Central Park, and CEO Barry Sternlicht wasn't sure what to do with it. He invited Stern to take a look.

Despite Starwood's acquisition of air rights, the sliver of a site, located next to the landmarked Steinway Building, was so small that it was doubtful it could support the construction of a tower of more than 700 feet, roughly half the height of 432 Park. On Billionaires' Row, that was tiny. Even so, Stern and Maloney agreed to take it on.

They tapped their contacts to buy a majority stake in the site, at 105 West 57th Street, for $40 million in 2012, then later bought out the entire thing.

Juracich maintained an interest in the project through a side deal with Stern but did not have a direct equity stake.

They again tapped Cetra Ruddy to design a tower on the vacant lot.

But Stern wasn't satisfied. Because the site was so small, the building would be just 43 feet wide with sharp raked setbacks. At the top, there would be space for just a 30-by-40-foot box—and that was before you factored in elevators and mechanicals. The floor plans would be small and cramped and would never command prices comparable to those garnered at One57 or 432 Park.

It would have worked, but it wasn't the kind of big ticket project that Stern aspired to build. It would have close to zero permanent significance to the New York skyline.

It seemed like a long shot, but up until the very last minute,

Stern held on to the notion that he could still enlarge the site, by purchasing either the Steinway building next door or the site on the other side, which was home to the Buckingham Hotel. The former would make for an especially complex equation, since the distinguished neoclassical Steinway building, the piano company's international flagship, was protected by the city's Landmarks Preservation Commission and could not be demolished or altered.

STEINWAY & SONS, a longtime family business, was founded in 1853 by the German cabinet and piano maker Heinrich Engelhard Steinweg, who had immigrated to the United States three years earlier amid political unrest at home. Steinweg, a veteran of the Battle of Waterloo and an expert in woodworking, had built his first piano in his kitchen in 1825 as a gift for his new wife; he quickly developed a booming business in the United States, setting up the first Steinway factory on Tribeca's Walker Street. The company, run by Steinweg (who by this time had anglicized his name) and his sons, was known for continually experimenting with the design and construction of the instruments and held more than one hundred technical patents. Its pianos were often seen in the homes of the city's wealthiest residents.

After Steinway died in 1871, his sons took over. For decades, they operated Steinway Hall, a prestigious concert hall and showroom near Union Square, which housed the New York Philharmonic.

But after the industrialist Andrew Carnegie built his iconic Carnegie Hall on 57th Street in 1891, the Philharmonic relocated there, shifting the center of gravity of New York's classical concert scene uptown. Manufacturers of musical instruments began opening up impressive showrooms along 57th Street. Steinway & Sons soon made plans to follow.

Around 1924, Steinway commissioned Warren & Wetmore, the architecture firm behind the landmark Grand Central Terminal, to design a new Steinway Hall on West 57th Street. Whitney Warren, one of the founders of the firm, was a cousin of William K. Vanderbilt, chairman of the board of the New York Central Railroad, and the pair had high society connections all over town.

The building's basement level was used as an area for artists to test concert grand pianos; the first and second stories housed a reception hall and sales rooms; and the fourth and fifth floors had rental music studios. The upper twelve stories of the building were rented to organizations with links to the arts, such as Columbia Artists Management and the Louis H. Chalif Norman School of Dancing.

The interior, too, was built to impress.

The first-floor reception area's 35-foot-tall octagonal domed rotunda, decorated with allegorical murals done in eighteenth-century style and complemented by a crystal chandelier, made for a dramatic entry, where Steinway representatives met with would-be customers before moving them into the sales rooms. Four arches on the perimeter of the rotunda were carved from white marble quarried in northern Italy, while the pilasters came from Tinos in the Cyclades archipelago of Greece. The floors were yellow Kasota stone, an American limestone, embellished with little rectangles of green marble from the Alps. The space was filled with luxury furnishings—wing chairs and desks modeled on pieces in the British Museum. Theatrical portraits of Mendelssohn and Schubert hung on the walls in gilded frames, and an octagonal Czechoslovakian rug was sprawled out on the floor. "The architects were instructed to use only the finest materials available," purred a writer for *Architectural Record* in 1925. "Steinway Hall has thus the dignity and distinction befitting the tradition of its owners."

Steinway Hall would become a magical, storied place where generations of pianists practiced and performed. It hosted recitals for beginners as well as legends like Rachmaninoff and Emanuel Ax. In short, it was a trophy space—but that wasn't why Stern couldn't get it out of his head.

Stern and Maloney were about sixty days out from breaking ground on the Cetra Ruddy building, but in the back of his mind,

Stern was still dreaming of Steinway. It was music to his ears when, at what seemed like the eleventh hour, the commercial real estate broker Darcy Stacom informed him that the piano company was finally interested in selling its building. Upkeep on the landmark building had become a financial burden, and the company, Steinway Musical Instruments, was losing about $5 million a year on the property.

With the Steinway building in hand, Stern and Maloney could merge the footprints of the two sites and apply for approvals to build a much taller tower. The market looked ripe. Down the street, it looked to the world like Barnett had proved out the concept, trading at number levels never seen before. Sales seemed to be moving swiftly at 432 Park. The numbers, Maloney said, were crazy. "Gary really was the pioneer. We followed suit," he said. "We were second or third to the game."

But they were gambling on the fact that the game still had a few innings to go.

WHEN STERN SHOWED the plans to his landmarks consultant Valerie Campbell, an attorney who had formerly served as general counsel to the Landmarks Preservation Commission, she burst out laughing.

The application to build the tower in a manner that would overlap with the landmarked Steinway Hall was largely without precedent. The city's Landmarks Preservation Commission was known to automatically reject out of hand almost any application that would require tampering with an existing landmark. The exterior of the Steinway building had long been designated as a protected landmark by the commission. The idea that they might be allowed to demolish a portion of the existing landmark and then thread a new tower through it seemed preposterous.

But Stern's architects thought they could appeal to the commission's desire to see more thoughtful, contextual development in the city. They argued that while it was possible to build a tower on the adjacent vacant lot as-of-right, or without the commission's permission, the footprint was such that the resulting tower would have to have a much more significant bulk of frontage on the streetfront, which would in turn have a greater visual impact on the landmarked Steinway Hall next door. If the commission allowed the team to build through the center of Steinway, they could set the bulk of the tower farther back from the street, thereby mitigating that impact. From the streetfront, passersby would see only a low-rise glass atrium fronting the tower.

In hearings with the commission in October 2013, the architecture team, led by Gregg Pasquarelli of SHoP Architects, set forth their vision for the new 1,428-foot tower. They said it would be inspired by the great landmarks of New York and built with materials in the vein of those used in Steinway Hall: bronze, glass, and terra-cotta. It would have a long series of miniature setbacks at its pinnacle, which the architects compared to a feather, and twenty-six twisting terra-cotta pilasters interlaced with brass filigree that would wind up its façade.

The proposal also came with an upside for the commission, since Stern was promising to carry out a "meticulous renovation" of the interior of Steinway Hall, which had fallen into some disrepair. He also threw his weight behind an idea to designate the entire Steinway Hall interior as a landmark, which would make any future changes subject to approval by the commission.

Response to the partnership's plans for the project among conservationists and neighborhood groups was mixed. The critics included Christabel Gough of the Society for the Architecture of the City, who slammed the plans as inappropriate and described the proposed tower as "a space needle on top of a piano showroom." However, in an early hearing, the majority of commissioners seemed to lean toward approval.

Stern and Maloney faced one notable adversary: Commissioner Margery Perlmutter. A no-nonsense lawyer and an architect by training, the curly-haired Perlmutter was never afraid to be a dissenting voice. When the commission created a historic district aimed at preserving tenements in the East Village the prior year, Perlmutter was the only member to vote against the designation, insisting that most of the buildings didn't warrant preservation.

In the early hearing, Perlmutter reportedly seemed perplexed by the broad support for the project. She declared that she found the proposal inconsistent with the commission's usual modus operandi and that there were plenty of more appropriate sites in the city on which to build a tower of this scale. The developers worried that she might swing the other commissioners to her way of thinking.

But Maloney had a trick up his sleeve when it came to the face-off with Perlmutter, a potential trump card that could take her out of the equation altogether. Perlmutter, in her capacity as an attorney, had been a consultant on a project he and another partner had worked on several years earlier, on Sullivan Street downtown, and he figured that if he pointed out the onetime client-attorney relationship, though it was now concluded, it could be seen as a potential conflict of interest. He hoped it might result in Perlmutter's having to recuse herself from matters involving his firm. As he expected, after a gentle nudge from their lawyers, Perlmutter conceded the conflict and recused herself from the vote.

As they carried out the vote, one commissioner remarked how small the building's floor plates would be given the small scale of the site itself, saying he couldn't imagine anyone who could afford to live there actually wanting to do so. However, that was not the commission's concern. The project was approved unanimously.

Thus, by the end of 2013, a new entrant had arrived to compete for attention on the burgeoning Billionaires' Row corridor, with plans to build a tower that would eclipse One57, 432 Park, and 220 Central Park South, and add to the mounting pile of expensive inventory along 57th Street.

The new tower, which would be known as 111 West 57th Street, would be 1,428 feet tall, trumping 432 Park by 31 feet. It would be the world's skinniest skyscraper and, for a brief time, the world's tallest residential building.

WITH THE APPROVALS in the books, Stern and Maloney now proceeded to the next challenge: finding the money to build the tower.
This project would make Walker Tower, which by most measures
had been a significant New York condo project, look like small
potatoes. The costs might amount to billions of dollars, not millions. To secure the construction loans they needed to build their
tower, the pair needed more equity than either of their firms could
reasonably provide. And so they began recruiting a motley crew of
characters to provide a cash injection.

The moves they made in this early phase would set the stage for
a series of complications that would derail the project later.

ACCORDING TO MALONEY'S account, Masood Bhatti, a friend of
Maloney's and formerly a senior executive in the real estate division
at Lehman Brothers before the crash, pointed them to an investor
out of Connecticut, a former banker who was looking to do real
estate deals.

A little-known entity, the banker, Richard Bianco, headed an
investment company known as AmBase Corporation, based in the
affluent Greenwich area. While he had little real estate experience,
he had been active on the fringes of the financial world for decades.
A small but stocky Italian with olive skin and white hair, he was
perhaps best known for having successfully faced off with the federal government over the demise in the 1990s of one of his company's subsidiaries, Carteret Savings Bank of New Jersey.

The roughly twenty-year legal battle, which dragged on through
appeal after appeal and turned Bianco into a proficient litigant, was
one for the record books. The complicated litigation hinged on a
policy called "supervisory goodwill" rolled out by government regulators during the savings and loan crisis of the 1980s to encourage
banks on strong financial footing to absorb weaker ones. As part of
that policy, the government had allowed the healthy banks to count

any "supervisory goodwill" they bought toward their regulatory capital. Carteret availed itself of the goodwill policy to acquire several troubled banks in the 1980s, so in 1989, when Congress abruptly eliminated the goodwill provision, it was left high and dry, Bianco had argued. It had to hurriedly off-load bad branches and increase its reserves against troubled loans. Despite returning to profitability by 1991, the bank was still low on capital, and it ultimately failed in 1992.

Bianco blamed regulators, whom he accused of breach of contract, saying that the elimination of the provision is what caused the bank to collapse. He spent roughly $10 million and two decades fighting the federal government in court.

At the time, Bianco's company's sole asset was its claim against the government, but Bianco was determined to stay in the fight to make his shareholders whole again. He felt that the law was in his favor, and that the government had breached its contract. "He had the tenacity to stick to it when other people threw in the towel," said one person close to Bianco.

A judge eventually sided with him in 2012, issuing a $205 million judgment in favor of AmBase and the FDIC. Faced with an appeal, they settled with the government for $180.65 million. Roughly $87.5 million of that money went to AmBase shareholders, including Bianco and his family, in the form of dividends. Bianco also got a $13.6 million bonus for his work on the settlement. The remainder of the money was now available for AmBase to invest in Steinway, which it did, buying a 59 percent stake in the project for $56 million in June 2013. It was an enormous bet on a single project for a company with little to no New York real estate chops. Bianco had battled for two decades for that cash, and now his company was betting it all on one horse.

Maloney also turned to his buddy, Arthur Becker, for cash. Becker was a former Bear Stearns banker turned real estate adviser and artist who was perhaps best known as the ex-husband of the fashion designer Vera Wang; the couple, who split in 2012, had been married for more than two decades and had two adopted daughters. Becker was not a trophy husband, however. He had made a lot of money himself in 2011 when he and some partners sold their company Navisite, a data center firm that provided hosting and cloud services, to Time Warner Cable for $230 million. He was fascinated with money. His art pieces, predominantly sculptural wall installations, were often fashioned out of cash. He made origami butterflies, roses, little Buddhas, and human skulls out of international currency. Over his fireplace he hung a giant collage made from large-scale printed money and money bands.

He was interested in the Steinway project and knew an overseas investor, another former partner in Navisite, who he thought might put some money in the project, too.

The investor, Andy Ruhan, a UK-based businessman who lived in upscale Buckinghamshire outside London, was flashier even than Maloney. He had been a champion racing driver and owned a stake in the Lotus Formula One team as well as a pair of luxury superyachts.

No stranger to risk, Ruhan had faced death in 2002. He was surveying a potential real estate site in Shropshire when his personal helicopter fell hundreds of feet from the sky after losing power. The legend spawned by the close call made Ruhan famous; emerging from the wreckage with more than a hundred fractures, he had crawled on his hands and knees across two fields and flagged down a motorist, who had called an ambulance. He'd reportedly been fitted with steel eye sockets, cheekbones, and jawbones as a result of the crash.

It didn't slow him down for long. Quickly back in his racing gear, the businessman, who was grizzled with white-blond hair, had won the famed GT Cup Championship motor sporting event at the UK's Brands Hatch racetrack in 2011 in a Porsche after almost spinning out of control during one particularly fraught lap of the race. "He's that kind of guy, right?" Maloney remembered. "He had a big yacht. He went to Marbella. It's like that TV show *Lives of the Rich and Famous*."

The source of Ruhan's fortune appeared to run the gamut. Described by the *Times* of London as "the most successful property tycoon you have never heard of," the newspaper said Ruhan had made a killing by buying up and then selling data centers and hotels, and he reportedly had a stake in a company that installed and maintained cables on the ocean floor as well as in a game reserve in South Africa. He had also been involved in financing the construction of a residential skyscraper in the United Arab Emirates known as Dubai Pearl.

Becker ultimately invested more than $20 million in the Steinway project in 2014 through a Delaware-registered entity called Atlantic 57 LLC, for which he was given a 26.3 percent stake in the tower. Becker would then agree to pass most of his profits on to an entity controlled by Ruhan.

In truth, Becker and Ruhan had little intention of holding on to their stakes in the project for the long term. Instead, through a series of loan agreements and promissory notes exposed through an investigation by *The Real Deal,* Ruhan ultimately promised 49.9 percent of his profits to a company tied to a pair of Russian investors, Serguei Adoniev and Albert Avdolyan, who were looking to put money in the tower. Though it was legal for Becker and Ruhan to include the Russian investors—their actions were inherently no different from those of a bank syndicating a commercial loan—their involvement was initially not made known to the wider investor pool at 111 West 57th Street. Industry insiders said Adoniev's unsavory track record would have been a red flag to potential lenders. "We were not aware of this until it was reported in the news media and still have no idea exactly how they structured it," Stern said later.

Adoniev, one of Russia's wealthiest men and reportedly close to Russian president Vladimir Putin, had a track record of murky business dealings. Imposing-looking, with a shoulder-length mane of dark hair, he reportedly started out as a banana importer, and an investigation by the *Los Angeles Times* showed that he had also come under scrutiny from the FBI over a possible connection to 1.1 tons of cocaine seized on the Russian-Finnish border in 1993.

In 1996, a federal grand jury handed down an indictment against him and some of his then partners related to allegations that they had bribed a top Kazakhstan official to help secure a contract for him to provide 25,000 tons of Cuban sugar to the former Soviet republic. However, after receiving most of the $6.7 million due on the contract, they allegedly never sent the sugar. Instead, he and his partners took the money and ran, using it to buy designer cars. After being deported back to Russia following a plea deal, Adoniev reemerged around 2007 as an early investor in mobile broadband in Russia, co-founding the start-up Yota with Avdolyan. In 2012, they struck a deal to sell it to Megafon, one of the country's largest mobile phone operators, and from there their fortunes only grew.

Avdolyan was well connected in Russian business circles and a major shareholder of the Russian chemical giant Usoliekhimprom and of construction equipment firm Gzkomplektservice, a subsidiary of energy giant Gazprom. In 2009, he reportedly bought a $13 million home in Beverly Hills, completely refitting it with soaring walls of glass, porcelain, and gold and incorporating a wet bar, a massage room, and a cavernous home theater. Yota became a sponsor of Ruhan's Lotus Formula 1 racing team, and the Yota-Phone emblem was emblazoned on the car's wing.

Structuring the loans as promissory notes meant that Adoniev and Avdolyan would get all the benefits of being equity investors in the Steinway deal without being listed as owners.

Adoniev and Avdolyan weren't the only international investors interested in the deal, though. Soon Maloney was approached by an even more questionable money man.

CHAPTER 12

The "Prince"

Later that year, Kevin Maloney was sitting in his company's New York office on West 17th Street when, as he tells it, he got a call from a broker pal. The broker said he was with a powerful client— "the prince of some massive oil country," as he put it—who wanted to buy a stake in the new supertall tower Maloney and Michael Stern were building on the Steinway site, which was now going by its official moniker, 111 West 57th Street. The prince, the broker declared, was coming over to chat.

New York has long been a draw for foreign leaders, even royalty, to plunk down cash for choice properties, whether for second homes or simply as investments. Prince Nawaf bin Sultan bin Abdulaziz al-Saud, a prominent member of Saudi Arabia's royal family, famously owned a home with three bulletproof panic rooms, saltwater aquariums, and a six-person Jacuzzi at the Heritage at Trump Place on the Upper West Side. Another Saudi prince, Mohammad bin Fahd, would be the eventual buyer of Joan Rivers's opulent Manhattan condo, inspired by the lavish style of Louis XIV, for $28 million. Entities connected to the late Queen Elizabeth II have also been tied to the purchase of more than two dozen units, many located around the United Nations complex on the East Side.

Still, Maloney was skeptical. After years of dealing with phony condo buyers and time wasters, he was not easily convinced of anything. He had met with dozens of guys who claimed to be princes or billionaires, but he found that they usually just turned out to be "grifters."

"They come in, they tell a story, you entertain them for a couple of days. And when they gotta write a check, they disappear," he said. "There are people in the world that go around pretending to be something, actually engaging people in contracts and trying to buy stuff. But they don't have enough money for dinner."

Within a few hours, however, the so-called "prince" had arrived at Maloney's office in a motorcade of three shiny black Escalades with diplomatic or foreign plates. He was flanked by what Maloney described as "two ex-military guys with tattoos up to their necks" and holstered weapons on their belts, and accompanied by an attorney. Inside Maloney's office, the visitor introduced himself to the developer, offering a Middle Eastern–sounding name that meant nothing to Maloney at the time.

This guy's really got this show down, he thought to himself.

The "prince" looked nothing like what one might have expected of a senior Saudi royal. There were no white robes or headdresses; he sat across the desk from Maloney in ordinary streetwear. With his flowing dark hair and ripped physique, he looked more like a trainer from a local gym than a man with billions of dollars at his fingertips. Only the armed guards standing by the door indicated that he was someone of importance. He wasted no time getting to his ask, offering Maloney a deal that seemed to make absolutely no sense, Maloney said. He offered to pay him and his partners $250 million for a 50 percent stake in the Steinway project. To Maloney, an offer like that fell firmly into the category of *way too good to be true*. After all, the partners had only about $150 million invested so far; the proposal being floated would allow them to make all their money back overnight, net a $100 million profit, and still retain a 50 percent stake in the project. To make it more absurd, the project hadn't even broken ground and didn't yet have a construction loan.

Maloney nodded along, even though he was fairly certain this was a hoax. On the slim chance that the prince was legitimate, he would agree to bring the deal to his partners. As he rose to leave, the visitor asked Maloney one last question. He was looking for a place to stay when he came to New York and wondered if the developer knew of any great apartments. At the time, Maloney had just two units remaining at Walker Tower, the Art Deco former New York Telephone Company building, whose successful conversion into condos had supercharged his partnership with Stern and David Juracich. Maloney warned his visitor that the properties were extremely expensive, but he agreed to walk him the few blocks to have a look at them. The whole posse, about six men in all, walked down the street to the building, the guys with guns leading the way.

When the prince strode into the five-bedroom penthouse at the top of Walker Tower—which boasted a private south-facing terrace and views of the Chrysler Building, the Statue of Liberty, and the Empire State Building—he only glanced at the kitchen and didn't so much as check out the bedrooms.

"How much?" he asked, standing in the middle of the living room.

"Fifty-five million," Maloney said.

"Will you take fifty-one million?"

Maloney accepted, the two men shaking hands on the spot, though Maloney was confident the money would never materialize.

As Maloney walked the prince to his car, he noticed that a yellow boot had been applied to one of the Escalades for failure to pay parking tickets. Maloney looked at his visitor and smiled. *This doesn't bode well,* he thought. *The grift is up.*

Seeing the boot, the would-be royal gestured to his security guys to remove the license plates from the car. Then, as Maloney looked on in astonishment, the man and his entourage all piled into the other two Escalades and drove off, leaving the third car behind.

When Maloney got back to his office and googled the "prince," he was shocked to be proved wrong. He was none other than Khadem al-Qubaisi, the same top aide to the Abu Dhabi royal family who had led the financing of Gary Barnett's One57. As head of Abu Dhabi's International Petroleum Investment Company, he had been involved in negotiating the bailout of Barclays Bank in 2008 and had negotiated a multi-billion-dollar investment in Daimler AG, the owner of Mercedes-Benz, for his boss, Sheikh Mansour bin Zayed al Nahyan, the United Arab Emirates' deputy prime minister and a member of the royal family.

Since then, al-Qubaisi had also become a nightclub impresario. Among his many business ventures was his role as chair of a company called Hakkasan, which ran clubs in Las Vegas, including the Omnia Nightclub at Caesars Palace, famous for its UFO-style chandelier suspended over the dance floor. The company was known for luring top DJs like Calvin Harris and Tiësto, who would sign exclusive contracts to play at the clubs.

Only then did it occur to Maloney that this guy might be legitimate.

Shortly after his brief visit to the penthouse, al-Qubaisi wired a $15 million deposit for the penthouse. The impulse deal would break the price record for a Manhattan condo south of 34th Street at the time. The story would become legend among the Walker Tower partners, with Stern's recollection varying significantly from Maloney's.

In Maloney's version, the abandoned Escalade was still sitting on the street near his office weeks later, covered in a mess of tickets. At some point the mirrors were picked off.

REACHING A DEAL on Steinway proved much more challenging.

Maloney said he took al-Qubaisi's $250 million offer to Stern and the other partners, who, unsurprisingly, were all eager to get it done, given the advantageous terms. Then Maloney went to Dick Bianco, the Connecticut investor who was bankrolling the project. "I said, 'Dick, I got the deal of the century. I know you're gonna kiss my ass for this one.' . . . And he's like, 'Yeah, I'm not doing that.'"

Maloney couldn't wrap his mind around Bianco's refusal to sign off on the deal. In his view, Bianco was looking a gift horse in the mouth. He later conjectured that Bianco, seeing an opportunity, had been trying to use the situation to extract a bigger piece of the pie for himself.

Both Becker, Vera Wang's ex-husband, who had invested in the project, and Stern would say they tried to talk Bianco into accepting the deal, as did Ruhan, the former champion racing driver who had put money in the project, who even flew in from London to try to persuade him in person. They couldn't understand why he wasn't biting. And so they were in a holding pattern: Bianco versus everyone else, with nobody willing to budge.

"It's unfathomable," Becker said. "I don't know if it was the vanity of being associated with one of these supertalls that made him feel that he was successful. I can't imagine that it was the economics."

Ultimately tiring of the endless back-and-forth negotiations, the "prince" lost interest. The too-good-to-be-true deal was dead.

Still, with the Landmarks Commission approval behind them and the initial capital lined up, it still looked like full steam ahead on the tower.

The partners just didn't see the freight train hurtling toward them from the other direction.

CHAPTER 13

Supply and Demand

In the year following the launch of sales at Gary Barnett's One57, the luxury real estate market experienced an unprecedented upswing across Manhattan. A string of big ticket closings reflected a tidal wave of demand for ultra-luxury homes on 57th Street and far beyond.

The following year, 2012, had been one for the record books. In May, the billionaire investor Howard Marks paid $52.5 million for a thirty-room spread at 740 Park Avenue. In June, the casino mogul Steve Wynn dropped $70 million for a duplex at the Ritz-Carlton on Central Park South. In November, the entertainment executive David Geffen paid $54 million for a duplex at 785 Fifth Avenue. The average price per square foot for a Manhattan luxury apartment ballooned by close to 40 percent, and there was a widening chasm between the prices for new development units and the prices of resales.

Developers and home sellers across the city began to vie for a piece of the action, listing units for record sums. In 2013, Florida Panthers owner Vin Viola put his Upper East Side townhouse on the market for $114 million, making it the most expensive ever to come on sale in the city. And Kyle Blackmon, the agent behind the record Dmitry Rybolovlev deal at 15 Central Park West, listed a co-op apartment at the iconic River House building on the East Side for $130 million, another listing price record.

By 2014, Gary Barnett had completed construction of the 1,004-foot One57 and early buyers were already moving into the blue-hued Christian de Portzamparc tower that now rose high above the south end of Central Park. Foundation work was under-way on Barnett's second project, the still taller Central Park Tower, which would eventually soar to 1,550 feet. Macklowe's 432 Park, too, was also nearing completion; the 1,396-foot modern concrete spire topped out in October 2014 and the glass was being installed. And, at 220 Central Park South, with the parking garage fracas finally resolved, Steve Roth's construction team had begun foundation work on his 953-foot limestone tower. Together, the developers were contributing to a global surge in supertalls, which would double in number to one hundred by the end of 2015, up from just fifty at the end of 2010.

Developers were known for their herd mentality, but this kind of hyperlocal stampede was out of the ordinary. The new towers represented a new species of New York skyscraper in terms of pric-ing, architecture, and height. "It is a new market category, it is being called Billionaires' Row," the appraiser Jonathan Miller told *The Wall Street Journal* that spring. The moniker, which had first been used in the newspapers around 2013, had well and truly en-tered the lexicon.

Thus, by the time Kevin Maloney, Michael Stern, and the part-ners behind 111 West 57th Street got moving with their site at the end of 2014, they were already very late to the party. The building would now join at least seven other ultra-high-end condominium projects under construction or planned near or along the 57th Street corridor.

The new projects included a mix of brand-new towers and condo conversions of aging but graceful office towers. Each had its own unique selling points and potential drawbacks, but what they all had in common was the market of intended buyers: the same jet-setting international billionaires and ultra-rich New Yorkers who had pushed the high-end market to record-setting heights in recent years. "Billionaires' Row was based on the assumption that these high-net-worth individuals created a market that was infinitely wide and deep and could support a tremendous amount of new product coming into the market," Miller, the appraiser, observed later.

Meanwhile, the Zeckendorf brothers, the brains behind 15 Central Park West, were hard at work on their own contribution to the corridor, a nearly 800-foot Robert A. M. Stern–designed limestone spire at East 60th Street between Park and Madison avenues that aimed to replicate the success of their original "limestone Jesus." With only about thirty units, the project was small, but the pricing was mighty. The penthouse was expected to go for roughly $100 million. Thanks to an air rights deal the brothers had struck with a church on the corner of Park Avenue and 60th Street, the new building would also be able to claim a coveted Park Avenue address, something they reckoned would be a major selling point for buyers.

Sales were also slated to launch at 53 West 53rd Street, the luxury skyscraper down the street from the Museum of Modern Art designed by the star architect Jean Nouvel. Plans for the tower had survived the real estate bust of 2008 and were now being revived by developer Hines in partnership with Goldman Sachs Group and Singapore-based Pontiac Land Group. Though shorter than some of the other towers at just 1,050 feet, thanks to planning chief Amanda Burden, the roughly 140-unit project, built on land once owned by MoMA, would make a distinctive mark on the skyline with its unusual façade, which comprised a web of diagonal concrete beams that gave the appearance of a spider's web.

Every developer active on the 57th Street corridor was eyeing new opportunities to build or to renovate and reposition existing buildings as homes for the 0.01 percent, aiming to springboard off the early success of One57 and 432 Park. Those plans extended to conversions of hotels and even office buildings.

After paying $1.1 billion for the granite office tower known as the Sony Building at 550 Madison Avenue in 2013, the New York developer Joseph Chetrit was working with the architect Robert A. M. Stern to convert it into luxury apartments, with a triplex penthouse valued at as much as $150 million. Similarly, the Russian-born developer Vladislav Doronin, perhaps best known for his one-time relationship with the supermodel Naomi Campbell, was eyeing a purchase of the top floors of the historic Crown Building at the southwest corner of 57th Street and Fifth Avenue as the prospective location for a condominium project tied to his luxury hotel brand, Aman. The building, designed by Warren & Wetmore, the defunct but famed architecture firm behind Grand Central Terminal and the original Steinway building, was famous for its Beaux-Arts style, with 1,363 ounces of 23-karat gold leaf and Vicenza statues adorning the exterior and a green copper pinnacle that was lighted at night. It had been previously owned by Philippine president Ferdinand Marcos and first lady Imelda Marcos.

Perhaps the most significant of this new batch of plans was by the New York developer Steve Witkoff. He wanted to raze the aging but iconic Park Lane Hotel on Park Avenue South, designed by the architecture firm Emery Roth & Sons for the late real estate titan and New York icon Harry Helmsley. Brokers said the site, which was near the Plaza hotel and had unobstructed views over Central Park, was one of the city's most valuable.

The Park Lane had been home to Helmsley's widow Leona Helmsley's sprawling private penthouse. The infamous so-called Queen of Mean, Helmsley lived in the private apartment with her dog, a Maltese named Trouble, to whom she left $12 million upon her death. The pricey spread had its own personal indoor pool, crystal chandeliers, and an enormous master suite with a king-size bed draped in satin. It had a salon where Helmsley would sit while the celebrity hairdresser Frédéric Fekkai styled her short tresses, surrounded by the mannequins that seamstresses used to make her custom outfits. Helmsley had died in 2007, however, and by 2014, the hotel had fallen into disrepair.

Witkoff had closed on the building in 2013 in a deal bankrolled by Jho Low, a baby-faced Malaysian financier with ties to Malaysia's prime minister, Najib Razak, who had recently arrived with a splash in New York City. Known for throwing lavish parties and cavorting with celebrities, Low was quickly becoming a fixture in the New York tabloids. He was photographed popping expensive champagne at a party with Paris Hilton, and in a foray into Hollywood he had helped finance Leonardo DiCaprio's 2013 film *The Wolf of Wall Street*. For his New York bachelor pad, Low, through a tangle of LLCs, had acquired an apartment at the Time Warner Center that had once been home to the celebrity power couple Jay Z and Beyoncé.

Low's pockets were deep. Indeed, it was the Malaysian's willingness to put up a hefty $100 million nonrefundable deposit that had convinced the Helmsley estate to take Witkoff's offer over several competing bids. Low had funded 85 percent of the deal, while Witkoff brought in New Valley, an investment company headed by his friend and Elliman chairman Howard Lorber, and Harry Macklowe to help shore up his own 15 percent position. For Macklowe, the minority stake was a chance for him, like his rival Barnett, to move forward quickly with a second tower on the Billionaires' Row corridor while the market was still humming.

Witkoff and his partners envisioned tearing down the Park Lane and erecting a new tower designed by the Swiss architects Herzog & de Meuron in its place. Every unit would be a vertical glass mansion with Central Park views, and the five penthouses, each expected to ask more than $100 million, would each have its own private outdoor swimming pool, at Low's suggestion.

By 2014, four years after Gary Barnett had laid the first stone, it was Billionaires' Row 2.0.

WITH HIS OWN Central Park Tower, Gary Barnett was also thinking bigger and bolder than he had at One57. He looked to the Middle East for inspiration, tapping Adrian Smith + Gordon Gill

The construction of One57, starting in 2010, marked the beginning of a condo development frenzy that would completely transform the blocks immediately to the south of New York's Central Park. *(SeanPavonePhoto/iStock)*

Now known as Billionaires' Row, the corridor, chock-full of supertall buildings, has come to symbolize an influx of wealth from around the globe into the city. *(Wade Zimmerman Photographer)*

Pictured on his penthouse terrace, Joel Diamond, then a young record producer, was among the rent-stabilized tenants at the original 220 Central Park South. The building was torn down to make way for a new tower by Steve Roth's Vornado Realty Trust.
(Silver Blue Productions, Ltd.)

Jacob Arabo, better known as Jacob the Jeweler, owned one of the townhouses next door to the original Drake Hotel. He refused to sell it to Harry Macklowe, even after lengthy negotiations.
(Johnny Nunez/WireImage)

The Drake Hotel opened in the 1920s and was popular with celebrities, including rock bands like The Who and Led Zeppelin.
(George Rinhart/Corbis via Getty Images)

The image of Gary Barnett's One57 was beamed across television screens in 2012 when the construction crane snapped during Hurricane Sandy. Barnett pinpointed the incident as a turning point for the building's fortunes.
(Peter Foley/Bloomberg via Getty Images)

Developers on Billionaires' Row grappled with how to keep their skyscrapers steady in the wind. At 432 Park, they left gaps in the façade to allow the wind to pass through.
(DBOX for CIM Group and Macklowe Properties)

Construction union boss Gary LaBarbera, pictured with then–New York governor Andrew Cuomo in 2018, had enormous political influence but faced a decline in union market share. At 111 West 57th Street, he clashed publicly with developer Michael Stern over Stern's decision to use nonunion subcontractors on the project.
(Lev Radin/Alamy Stock Photo)

Hedge fund billionaire Bill Ackman was among the highest-profile early buyers at Barnett's One57. He and some investor friends inked a contract to buy a $91.5 million unit, known as "the winter garden," in 2012.
(Chris Ratcliffe/Bloomberg via Getty Images)

Gary Barnett and Steve Roth clashed in 2013 over a parking garage at Roth's 220 Central Park South, which is one street over from Barnett's second Billionaires' Row building, Central Park Tower. Eventually, both men agreed to shift their buildings slightly to maximize the views from both towers.
(Krblokhin/iStock)

At Central Park Tower, a hundredth-floor private club offers views over Central Park.
(Evan Joseph)

Barnett gave an uncharacteristically dramatic presentation at the Central Park Tower topping-out ceremony in 2019. A few months later, he would have to shut down the sales office because of the pandemic.
(Anuja Shakya for The Real Deal*)*

A rift between Billy Macklowe (pictured with his mother, Linda) and his father, Harry, spilled over into negotiations with Los Angeles private equity firm CIM over the Drake Hotel.
(Patrick McMullan via Getty Images)

Ukrainian businessman Dmytro Firtash was among the potential equity partners who expressed interest in the Drake project.
(Simon Dawson/Bloomberg via Getty Images)

Harry Macklowe dressed as King Kong for a marketing video designed to promote the apartments at 432 Park Avenue. The video cost over $1 million.
(DBOX for CIM Group and Macklowe Properties)

Ballet dancer and contortionist Viktoria Hofstaedter appeared in a marketing campaign for the building. The picture was taken at a film studio in Brooklyn, where she struck a series of ballet poses *en pointe* inside a purpose-built frame designed to look like the windows of the tower.
(DBOX for CIM Group and Macklowe Properties)

Vornado's Steve Roth, pictured with his wife, Daryl, and former president Donald Trump, leveraged his impressive rolodex to find buyers for his tower at 220 Central Park South.
(Billy Farrell/Patrick McMullan via Getty Images)

Billionaire hedge funder Ken Griffin set the record price for a U.S. home when he paid nearly $240 million for an apartment at Roth's tower.
(Reuters/Alamy Stock Photo)

The deal was brokered by Oren (front) and Tal Alexander, a flashy brother duo making a mark in New York at the time. The deal supercharged their careers.
(Seth Browarnik/WorldRedEye.com)

Emirati businessman Khadem al-Qubaisi was fundamental in providing financing for Barnett's One57 and once offered to buy a stake in 111 West 57th Street. He is now serving time in prison for his role in a global Malaysian sovereign wealth fund scandal. *(WENN Rights Ltd./Alamy Stock Photo)*

Kevin Maloney (center) and Michael Stern (right) first collaborated on Walker Tower in Chelsea. By the time they started working on 111 West 57th Street, their relationship had turned sour. *(Marc Patrick/BFA.com)*

David Juracich, known to his pals as Wavey Dave, was among the investors burned by the delays and litigation at 111 West 57th Street. He is pictured with his wife, Catherine Juracich. *(Brendon Cook/BFA.com)*

The developers of 111 West 57th Street agreed to restore the interior of the original Steinway Hall as part of their project. The offer helped sweeten their case to the city's Landmarks Preservation Commission. *(Peter Murdock)*

In 2019, Harry Macklowe had pictures of himself and his fiancée, Patricia Landeau, displayed on the façade of the retail space at 432 Park. He said it was a gesture of love, but some speculated that it was motivated by spite. *(Timothy A. Clary/AFP via Getty Images)*

Visitors to New York City can now look up at 432 Park from observation decks at 30 Rockefeller Plaza (pictured) and the Empire State Building. These towers, constructed in the 1930s, kicked off the city's original race to the sky. *(Spencer Platt/Getty Images)*

Architecture to design it; Smith had been one of the architects behind the design of the Burj Khalifa in Dubai, the tallest building in the world. The firm's expertise was in designing very, very tall buildings.

If the Steinway Tower from Michael Stern and Kevin Maloney was going to beat out Harry Macklowe's 432 Park Avenue to become the tallest residential tower in the world, that record wouldn't stand for long. Central Park Tower would quickly usurp it.

But exactly how tall should Central Park Tower be? Initial plans for the tower incorporated a spire, a subject of heated debate in the world of supertalls. Historically, some critics have argued that a spire or antenna should not count toward the recorded height of a building because it can't be occupied, while others countered that such structures should be considered a continuation of the architectural form of the building. The architecture critic Michael Kimmelman once compared including an antenna in a building's height to "counting relish at a hot dog eating contest."

For Central Park Tower, the architects, Gordon Gill and Adrian Smith, initially proposed a simple, futuristic spire for the crown of the building that would have brought the structure's total height to 1,787 feet, surpassing 1 World Trade Center, then the tallest building in the city. The trade center's height, including its spire, came in at 1,776 feet. The height, a symbolic nod to the year the Declaration of Independence was signed, was intended as an homage to the indomitable, defiant spirit of a city rising from the ashes of 9/11. Smith and Gill suggested that Central Park Tower could continue this symbolic tradition with a further nod to American greatness, picking 1,787 feet as a salute to the year the U.S. Constitution was signed.

While the idea of having the tallest building in the city held undeniable appeal, Barnett rebuffed the recommendation, fearing it could be seen as disrespectful, given the painful history of the 9/11 attacks at the World Trade Center site. Instead, for Central Park Tower, he encouraged the architects to opt for something more subtle. They ultimately settled on a height of 1,550 feet, still

300 feet higher than the Empire State Building and enough to make sure that Extell could bill the tower as the tallest primarily residential building in the world. By comparison, 432 Park was only 1,396 feet and the Steinway Tower was slated to be only 1,428 feet.

But just because it would be the tallest residential building didn't mean there would be great views in every direction. With 220 Central Park South now under construction to the northwest of Barnett's Central Park Tower site, it was becoming clear how much Roth's building would still block the views in one direction from the lower floors of Barnett's new project. If the fundamental impetus for Central Park Tower was its views, Roth's project was literally standing in the way.

Barnett and his architects hatched a plan that would help mitigate the issue. If Extell could secure additional air rights, they devised a way for the new building to cantilever eastward over its neighbor, the headquarters of the Art Students League of New York. The cantilever would hang about 290 feet in the air, stretching out nearly 30 feet to provide more expansive Central Park views for the residents of Central Park Tower's lower floors. It was a shift in perspective that Barnett believed would give the building's values a significant boost.

The cantilever idea seemed crazy at first. It would require a total reworking of the design, an enormous amount of money, and for Extell to do potentially dangerous construction work directly above an existing and occupied building. Designed in the late 1800s by the architect Henry J. Hardenbergh, who had also designed the Dakota apartments and the Plaza hotel, the French Renaissance–style headquarters of the Art Students League was one of the most ornate buildings on the 57th Street corridor and was designated on the National Register of Historic Places in 1980. The city's Landmarks Preservation Commission, in its decision to protect the low-rise limestone building, noted its "great charm and restrained elegance," pointing to its heavily decorated cornice, roofline balustrade, and arched main entrance flanked by "tall, candelabra-like spindles executed in stone." Artists like Jackson Pollock, Robert Rauschenberg, Norman Rockwell, and Georgia O'Keeffe had all honed their craft at the center, which was filled with work and exhibition spaces as well as an arts and crafts store.

Before Extell could move ahead with constructing a cantilever over the landmark building, they'd need sign-off from the city's notoriously hard-to-please Landmarks Preservation Commission. Building a portion of the tower that appeared to have nothing supporting it from below would also involve installing behemoth supporting sheer walls to channel the load through the building's central core and incorporating a lattice of thick steel beams that would extend into the foundation of the tower.

However, the cantilever came with other upsides. Shifting the building's core toward the east side of the lot also meant that the space near street level earmarked for the flagship Nordstrom department store would be uninterrupted by the building's structure elements, such as elevators and electrical lines.

During one of their meetings, the architect Gordon Gill sketched out a rough design for the cantilever. He compared the look of it to the contrapposto pose of ancient Greek sculpture, a figure standing with most of its weight on one foot as its shoulders and arms twisted off-axis. Beside it, he scribbled "The Art of Levitation."

"I remember us walking away from that meeting going, 'Boy, that would be fantastic, but I don't know if it will pencil out,'" Gill said. "Then they called us and said it penciled out."

Barnett would ultimately estimate the cost of the cantilever at as much as an additional $300 million, but he was betting that the improved views would add at least that much to the total value of the units. "It may be worth it, it may not be worth it. We'll see," he said.

By 2014, Barnett had struck a deal with the Art Students League, whose members voted in favor of accepting $31 million for the air rights. He had even garnered the necessary approvals from the Landmarks Commission, which, despite strong community op-

position, ruled that the cantilever would not detract from the landmark beneath it.

It looked as if the residents of Central Park Tower were going to
have better views than expected.

WITH THE PIPELINE of projects on Billionaires' Row growing fuller
with pricey projects like Barnett's, real estate watchers began to
warn of an impending surplus of high-end Manhattan condominiums.

Were there really enough real-estate-hungry billionaires out
there to absorb hundreds of new condo units that would each run
in the tens to hundreds of millions of dollars? At Central Park
Tower alone, Barnett had twenty units that would be priced at least
$60 million apiece.

At the very least, brokers cautioned that the onslaught of new
product was likely to result in a shift in buyer behavior. When
spoiled for choice, buyers tended to feel less urgency to purchase
and to take more time over buying decisions. They were also more
likely to feel that they had room to negotiate prices, since there
were plenty of other options to choose from in the market. Already,
at One57, where sales had been under way for three years, sales
activity had plateaued.

In November 2014, thousands of industry insiders gathered at
the New York City Real Estate Expo at the Hilton Hotel in Midtown. They packed tightly into a hotel conference room until it
was standing room only.

As one of the event's most hotly anticipated panel discussions
got under way, the topic turned to Billionaires' Row, and one of
the panelists, a major New York City landlord named Ofer Yardeni, didn't mince words.

"If real estate was a publicly traded company and I could short
its stock, I would very happily short 57th Street," he said. "The
market there has stopped. It hasn't just declined 5 or 10 percent. It's
just stopped."

Remarks like these reinforced the unmistakable feeling that the mood around Billionaires' Row had shifted.

But Barnett, in the throes of planning his second Billionaires' Row tower, downplayed those concerns.

"I don't think people really understand the depth of demand at the super high end of the market," he told the audience at a real estate panel event the following spring. "People say there's a lot more buildings coming and that's true, but a number of those buildings are wannabes."

In other words, rather than easy money, Billionaires' Row was going to have its winners *and* its losers.

CHAPTER 14

The Best Building in New York

Vornado chief Steve Roth received an unlikely visitor in his office on Seventh Avenue: the fashion designer and *Project Runway* star Zac Posen.

Posen, the "P. T. Barnum of New York Fashion Week," as a *New York Times* writer once dubbed him, had rocketed to fame in the 2000s as a wunderkind in the city's fashion scene, quickly becoming a favorite of celebrities like Natalie Portman, Rihanna, and Jennifer Lopez. In addition to running his own label and his TV gig, Posen, then in his thirties, would eventually take a number of lucrative side hustles over the years, including redesigning uniforms for Delta Air Lines.

Posen had come armed with a variety of custom blazers for Roth to take a look at, but they weren't for the Vornado boss. They were for the doormen at 220 Central Park South.

Bringing in an internationally recognized designer for staff uniforms might have seemed like an unnecessary expense for most developers, but Roth was determined that his new project at 220 Central Park South would be the world's premier residential address, besting those of Barnett, Macklowe, and Stern. That meant paying attention to every detail, down to what the men and women opening doors and delivering packages would wear. (The fact that Posen had become friendly with Jordan Roth, the developer's flamboyant Broadway producer son—the pair would go on to collaborate his elaborate outfits for the opening nights of shows like *Moulin Rouge, Frozen,* and *Funny Girl*—surely didn't hurt the designer's prospects of landing the uniform designing gig.)

At 220 Central Park South, where sales quietly launched in the spring of 2015, prospective buyers and investors who visited the sales office were told that many of the design flourishes were specifically selected by Steve Roth, who, while a more conservative dresser than his son, had his own eye for design. In fact, Steve Roth was firmly the judge and the jury when it came to design, programming, and buyers. As an established member of the billionaire class in New York, he could speak peer to peer with prospective buyers, and much like Harry Macklowe, he made decisions based not on the advice of brokers or designers so much as on what he personally liked. And he was prepared to spend heavily in pursuit of making the building a brick-and-mortar masterpiece. His idea of a "masterpiece," however, diverged considerably from Macklowe's.

After a lengthy period of deliberation, Roth had eschewed a modern glassy tower in favor of a classic limestone design by Robert A. M. Stern in the vein of the architect's prior success, 15 Central Park West. Observers would come to describe the building as "15 Central Park West on steroids," for it was also reminiscent of the earlier project's form, with a lower-rise "villa" in front and a taller tower behind. The exterior would be clad in an Alabama "Silver Shadow" limestone similar to the stone used at the Zeckendorf project.

By emulating the classic design of 15 Central Park West and evoking the tradition of the storied limestone-clad co-op buildings of Park and Fifth avenues, Roth was betting that he could draw the same clientele that had made those buildings such roaring successes. It was the conservative choice, a proven formula, and stood in dramatic contrast to Barnett's, Macklowe's, and Stern's more daring, idiosyncratic designs, which were already dividing opinions across the city. If his competitors' sensibilities were firmly "new money," Roth was evoking the old.

For the building's common areas, Roth tapped Thierry Despont, the wildly successful French designer who had helped oversee the restoration of the Statue of Liberty and who had designed the interiors of globally renowned hotels like the Ritz Paris, Claridge's, and the Carlyle. While billionaires like Bill Gates, Calvin Klein, and Mickey Drexler called on Despont to design their private homes, the architect rarely took on a condominium development. (One of the few exceptions was the residences at the famed Woolworth Building in Lower Manhattan.)

The expansive lobby would be the most dramatic in New York, simultaneously an homage to some of New York's most storied apartment buildings and yet more luxurious and fantastical, a fortress of taste and sophistication. When entering, residents would pass through a reception area with a black lacquered desk with a built-in clock and a large round table dressed with flowers. They would then enter a more intimate living-room-style space with a large black lacquered wood fireplace and decorative stone floors in black and gold. Above the fireplace hung a photographic portrait of Anne of Cleves by the Japanese artist Hiroshi Sugimoto. The valuable photograph was part of a series by Sugimoto, who shot wax figures of Henry VIII and his wives based on portraits from the sixteenth century.

An adjoining library was decorated in deep reds and mustards, with wood-paneled walls and a seating nook framed in black lacquer. Above the sofa hung a vivid portrait of a woman, her face split into quadrants of yellow, red, green, and orange, by the Spanish artist Manolo Valdés. Vornado—at the direction of Roth—had acquired the artwork at auction specifically for the building. Pieces by the artist have commanded up to about three quarters of a million dollars.

In keeping with the amenity-loaded trend of new luxury towers, 220 Central Park South would feature a double-height common lounge area on the second floor. The space was designed to include a roaring fireplace with a carved stone mantel, classic moldings, plush beige sofas, and a backlit bar area. A wrought iron balcony on the gallery level would lead to a billiards and poker room and a plush red velvet screening room. Outside the screening room, a small pantry would have its drawers continuously restocked with snacks like Junior Mints and Milk Duds. The common area led to an urbane dining room with classic leather club seating and a landscaped terrace for outdoor dining. The restaurant, open only to residents and their guests, would be operated by Michelin star auteur chef Jean-Georges Vongerichten, well known for his prestigious restaurants around the globe. The building's common space would also include a gym, a juice bar, a basketball court, a golf simulator, and a children's play area. The men's locker room was clad in deep red leather, and the entrance to the onsite porte-cochère was framed by roughly 20-foot golden gates.

All these elaborate finishes would come at a hefty price. In 2015, Roth announced to investors that constructing and finishing the building was costing the developer about $5,000 per square foot, a mammoth figure for a New York City condominium project and roughly double what Macklowe and CIM were spending at 432 Park. Only $1,500 of that $5,000 could be attributed to the cost of the land. Roughly $3,500 was attributable to the hard and soft costs of actually building the tower. But to Roth, it was all worth it. In his mind, there should be no question about whose building was of the highest quality.

That spring, Roth appeared alongside Barnett and other real estate developers on an industry panel at Bloomberg LP's headquarters in Midtown to discuss Asian investment in U.S. real estate, sponsored by China's Chamber of Commerce. Introducing himself to the assembled crowd, a besuited Roth, legs crossed and leaning on the arm of his chair, announced that his firm was building the "best condo project in New York, arguably."

"Arguably," Barnett said, piping up to defend his own Billionaires' Row projects.

"Don't be jerky," Roth retorted, swatting away Barnett like a fly. "It's not even close."

IT WAS PERHAPS no surprise that the notoriously publicity-shy Roth had agreed to appear on the China Chamber of Commerce panel. For it was thanks in large part to a far-flung backer, the Bank of China, that he could afford to take his time over every detail at 220 Central Park South.

The bank, one of the four biggest state-owned commercial banks in China, had provided Vornado with a $950 million loan for the construction of the building with an interest rate of just 2 percent, lower than the rates Roth's fellow developers were being charged elsewhere on Billionaires' Row—and, indeed, far below what any American homeowner was likely to get on their mortgage, even in the halcyon days of historically low rates. In addition, Vornado had obtained a $750 million loan facility, a de facto line of credit with an interest rate of just 1.15 percent, from a consortium of lenders that included J.P. Morgan Securities, Merrill Lynch, and Wells Fargo. Vornado could draw down on the money as needed to build the tower and didn't need to rely on expensive mezzanine financing like so many of his competitors.

Those rates gave Roth, whose company had taken sole control of the project from Veronica Hackett's Clarett Group following the financial crisis, a sharp advantage over his competitors.

That Vornado's money was so cheap was down to the company's strong balance sheet, experts said. Lenders could rely on Vornado's ability to meet its debts, since by the end of the first half of 2015, the company had $3.1 billion in liquidity, including $2.4 billion undrawn on its additional $2.5 billion in revolving credit facilities. In other words, Vornado had great credit.

For its part, Bank of China had become a significant player in keeping the U.S. commercial real estate market afloat in the wake of the great recession. It was one of several foreign or nontraditional lenders who stepped in to fill a gap in the market after U.S. banks reduced their average loan amount following the great recession. Others included the Children's Investment Fund, which financed 432 Park, and Bank of the Ozarks, a small community lender from Arkansas that issued loans on a string of prominent Manhattan condo projects in the mid-2010s.

"[Bank of China] picks their spots and do a few big deals a year with their favorite customers," said Michael Gigliotti, the commercial real estate finance broker at JLL. "They can pick and choose." Such a big fish was likely more inclined to do a deal with the likes of Vornado, which, as a public company, was obligated to provide a level of transparency into its business that privately held competitors like Barnett, Stern, or Macklowe were not, Gigliotti said. Lenders "can just look at *Bloomberg* and find out how Vornado is doing every day," he said. "With Gary Barnett, they have no idea what's going on in his empire."

As 2014 drew to a close, Vornado's top brass assured analysts and investors that demand would be high for 220 Central Park South despite the flagging sales at One57. While he was wary of what he described as "premature gloating," Roth said he was sure that every major broker had a handful of clients anxious to get in and tour the building. "With respect to One57, which, I guess, was the building that started the market movement, they're down to cats and dogs there," he said. "They've sold all the good products, and they have some odds and ends left, and so it's not that surprising . . . that sales are slowing. That's predictable."

ROTH'S EYE FOR detail extended to far more than design. From day one, he ran 220 Central Park South as his own personal fiefdom, taking firsthand interest in the buyers who came through the door of the sales center.

A number of brokers who brought buyers to view the plans would later complain to reporters and fellow agents that they had been subjected to autocratic, co-op-level scrutiny. Some, with seemingly well-qualified prospective buyers, struggled to get an appointment at the sales center. Others were turned away based on responses to a preliminary questionnaire before they could even see the sales office. Some foreign buyers were told they would have to appear in person in the sales office, even if they lived overseas.

For brokers who did gain access, a small number reported that Roth, whose office was on the same floor as the center, would casually pop in to say hello and then ask what some deemed intrusive questions about a client's business and lifestyle. For some prospective buyers, it felt as though they were trying to gain entry to a country club rather than buy a place to live in the middle of Midtown Manhattan.

For wealthy buyers and their agents, purchasing in the building had transformed into an exercise in pleasing Roth, who was simultaneously feared and revered. Roth may not have had Harry Macklowe's singular panache, but his legend loomed large and his personality cast a shadow over the whole sales process.

One broker who brought an ultra-wealthy Middle Eastern buyer to the building, and who spoke on the condition of anonymity for fear of angering Roth, said the developer met with their buyer personally and asked questions about his background and where he currently lived. The would-be buyer, who had very deep pockets, found Roth charming and liked the building but did not commit immediately to purchasing a unit. A few months later, when the buyer decided he would like to take a second look at 220, the broker was informed that it wouldn't be possible. Some vague reasons were given about shuffling layouts and evolving schedules.

"It's total speculation, but it just didn't seem like Steve liked him," the broker said. "My impression was that he was not who Steve felt should be in the building and he was turned off that the buyer wasn't falling over himself to make an offer."

Over time, a theme started to emerge. Across the industry, brokers began to speculate that Roth didn't want foreigners in the building, especially Russians. One industry insider with knowledge of the situation said he believed Roth had turned away contracts valued in the hundreds of millions at the 125-unit building from buyers with ties to the former Soviet Union. Many were not even offered appointments. The insider speculated that, as the head of a publicly traded company, Roth didn't want to take the risk of foreign money coming into the building and the potential scrutiny it might bring over its origins.

If this factored into Roth's thinking, it would be no surprise. In early 2015, an investigative series by *The New York Times* documented how the Related Companies, the developers of the Time Warner Center, had sold units to a string of wealthy foreigners, including Russians, some of whom were found to be the subjects of government investigations around the world and some of whom had been arrested for or found guilty of illegal activities. For people in the real estate industry, the series, named "Towers of Secrecy," gave front page treatment to something they already knew: that lawyers, brokers, title insurance professionals, and developers were willfully turning a blind eye to potentially dirty money flowing into real estate in New York, Miami, Los Angeles, and beyond.

Roth didn't want those kinds of headlines about Vornado.

"Whether it's know your customer rules, money laundering, you name it, he just decided he didn't want foreigners in the building," said one person who had a client turned away. "But it's not like he said 'No, I'm not going to allow this foreigner into the building.' He just never sent out a contract. And he never indicated why he wasn't sending out a contract."

The insider said Roth's team circled back to some of those buyers when deal volume began to slow later in the sales process, but none of them were interested in giving the developer a second chance. "Practically every single one of them said things you couldn't print," the person said. "They basically showed him a bird—and not a pretty bird."

Some in the industry cautioned that the developer should tread carefully or risk running afoul of the city's fair housing laws, which prohibit discrimination by housing providers on the basis of a person's race, familial status, color, national origin, religion, disability, or sex. He couldn't simply turn buyers away because they were Russians, they warned. And several high-profile agents said they had actually boycotted the building because of Roth's approach.

They felt that they couldn't afford to bring high-net-worth buyers to the building only to have them rejected for reasons unrelated to their financial strength. "We would have lost our credibility and their trust," said one top agent. "It could have come off as a pretty big insult, and I didn't want to be a part of that. We had plenty of other properties to show them."

In some ways, Roth's was a strategy perfectly formulated to play on a person's desire for acceptance and approval—the desire to be the person inside the velvet rope, to have their tastes and inclinations validated by their peers. It was an exacting process, and one that Barnett and Macklowe didn't have the social capital to support at their own buildings. 220 Central Park South was quickly the hottest reservation on Billionaires' Row.

"If you're asking people to pay $50 million or $100 million for an apartment, they'll want to know that they're not moving into a place that's going to be filled with a bunch of flippers, or where everyone is going to rent out their apartments to someone else," said the Vornado analyst Alex Goldfarb. "It's like a club. You want to be a member of one that is really strict on who they allow in."

If 220 Central Park South was like a club, the club's first rule was that you didn't talk about the club or who else was a member. In contrast to their peers at the other Billionaires' Row towers, the marketing team for 220 Central Park South employed a seemingly counterintuitive strategy for selling units: They wouldn't really market the project at all.

Vornado didn't launch any kind of public-facing marketing campaign, run splashy advertisements, or even release interior renderings of the building to the media. Roth held no press previews of the building and answered no questions posed by the real estate media. Every detail of the building, from the identities of the buyers to the choice of cabinetry in the kitchens, was a tightly held secret. Reporters who asked permission to republish renderings of the exteriors of the tower were denied and brokers were asked not to post images on social media. Rumors circulated that Roth had fired a construction worker when he caught him snapping a picture from inside the tower.

The idea was to maximize the project's exclusivity and cement the sales team's reputation for discretion. The message was that 220 Central Park South was a place where billionaires could rest assured they would be completely shielded from the glare of the public gaze. "We have not run a single advertisement and I don't think we will," Roth told the Bloomberg audience at the event.

If Roth was manning the pearly gates to 220, his top lieutenants were the Corcoran Group chief executive, Pam Liebman, and one of her top real estate agents, Deborah Kern.

Kern's father-in-law had been Roth's roommate at Dartmouth College, and the two hit it off immediately. Like Roth, Kern was smart and tough and didn't beat around the bush. A tiny brunette with delicate features and a refined London accent, she wore leather jackets and animal-print boots and could quote prices per square foot for nearly any high-end building in the city off the top of her head. She had worked in the music business and was well versed in dealing with the high rollers of the finance world. Her husband, James Kern, was former senior managing director at Bear Stearns and a veteran of J.P. Morgan.

Liebman, who had helmed Corcoran since its founder, Barbara Corcoran, had sold the company in 2001, was a veteran of the industry. She was popular with developers for her straight-talking, suffer-no-fools business style and her encyclopedic knowledge of the New York apartment stock, as well as her proficiency on the golf course and her fondness for sucking down a late night bourbon.

Securing the project had been a massive win for Corcoran. Liebman had won over Roth by promising that she would make the building a personal priority rather than assigning it to the firm's dedicated new development division, Corcoran Sunshine. She would later say that press reports had vastly overstated Roth's scrutiny of the individual buyers and that she rarely saw him meet them in person.

Louise Sunshine, a onetime top consigliere to Donald Trump and a granddaughter of the founder of Barneys New York, was brought in to consult for a short time. Sunshine was already in her seventies and walked with a cane, her beloved little Cavachons never far behind, but she ruffled feathers with her confrontational style and her tendency to insult the junior staff. Her tenure didn't last long, however. Though she denied it, insiders said Roth was upset after she mentioned her work on the project in an interview with *The Real Deal* magazine. She had broken rule number one.

IF ROTH'S APPROACH successfully kept the "wrong" kind of people out, it brought in the "right" kind of people in droves.

On an earnings call with investors in early 2015, Roth announced to analysts and investors that he already had commitments for more than $1.1 billion worth of apartments, representing about a third of the building—within two months of launching sales. "What has been accomplished in five or six weeks has never been done before," he boasted, calling the response from buyers "extraordinary and unprecedented."

By the third quarter of 2015, Vornado had sold more than half of the building's units. The buyers were a smattering of the top names of American finance, art, and entertainment.

Dan Och, the billionaire investor and art collector who founded the hedge fund Och-Ziff Capital Management, snared one of the building's penthouses for nearly $100 million. The purchase represented a considerable upgrade from Och's prior apartment at 15 Central Park West, which he purchased for nearly $22 million. Och, who founded his company in 1994, had long been one of the most influential figures in the investment world and also a subject of controversy. In 2018, protesters gathered outside his former building to protest an investment made by Och-Ziff in a small African miner with links to Zimbabwe president Robert Mugabe's government.

Och wasn't the only big name migrating from 15 Central Park West in search of even more luxurious surroundings. The musician Sting and his wife, Trudie Styler, were among the building's earlier buyers, making a deal with Roth to completely customize four floors at the top of the property's front "villa" into what essentially amounted to a townhouse in the sky. It would have terraces on every level and a four-story spiral staircase that would have to be delivered in pieces. The couple would be one of only about ten or eleven owners in the villa component, adding yet another layer of privacy. They paid $65.57 million for the unit and tapped the architect Lee Mindel, who also designed a model unit for the building, to oversee the construction.

Soon after, the couple would sell their vibrantly colored futuristic apartment at 15 Central Park West, which also had sculptural spiral staircases and fluorescent lighting, for $50 million. A debate ensued over whether a portrait of a nude reclining Trudie above the bed should be removed for showings. The unit was purchased by Karen Lo, a Hong Kong heiress whose family started the Vitasoy beverage empire.

Perhaps the most unlikely buyer at 220 was Ofer Yardeni, the real estate bigwig who, more than a year earlier, had told participants in the New York Real Estate Expo that if he could, he would short Billionaires' Row. The Israel-born Yardeni, who founded the real estate giant Stonehenge Partners, had evidently since changed his tune, shelling out about $22.2 million for a three-bedroom apartment overlooking Central Park. "It just shows you the mystique that Steve created, that Ofer is buying there after everything," Barnett said later. "It's like, 'Well, all the other big shots are there, so I've got to be there too.'"

It was a run that put One57's initial sales blitz to shame. Roth was collecting $50 million sales like Imelda Marcos had collected shoes. Speaking on a panel at a real estate conference that October, Barnett told the crowd that the unit sales at One57 had averaged about $6,500 a foot. By contrast, Roth's units were averaging about

$8,500, he said. Barnett appeared magnanimous about his rival's success, but there was envy there too. "If I had a magic wand, I'd want to be Steve Roth," he proclaimed, breaking out in a grin.

BARNETT, OBSERVING THE activity at Roth's tower, viewed his rival's success through two different lenses. Thanks in part to the sales bonanza at 220 Central Park South, Vornado's stock price was surging in 2015 to levels not seen since before the financial crisis.

While the debut of 220 had made One57 look like an old spinster sister to the new princess of Billionaires' Row, the prices Roth was fetching indicated fresh interest in the corridor. Barnett knew that could only help him at his new project, Central Park Tower, conveniently located across the street from 220.

If One57 had been a gamble in the depths of the 2008 financial crisis, Barnett was dramatically upping the ante with Central Park Tower. Even with One57 still not sold out after four years on the market, Barnett was now plotting a building with nearly twice as many units and even higher prices amid talk of an industry-wide wave of new condo supply. To some, it seemed to defy logic.

Barnett wasn't just shooting for the stars with the proposed height of the Central Park Tower, which would be the second-tallest building in New York, after One World Trade Center—and taller than any residential building in the world. He was also setting prices at astronomical heights. In 2015, he projected that the building would produce total sales of $4.4 billion, including the $400 million from the sale of the base to Nordstrom and $4 billion from the sale of the apartments. Those numbers were without precedent. Even 15 Central Park West, then widely considered the most successful condominium in U.S. history, had a sellout of only about $2 billion, and One57 was panning out to achieve something similar. Roth was projecting just $3 billion for his new tower at 220 Central Park South.

The project mirrored One57 in more ways than one. As in 2009, Barnett was once again hard up for the cash to actually build it. The same lenders that were too anxious to put their toes in the

water again following the financial crash were now once again fearful. This time they worried that there was a surplus of inventory
and that they were growing overexposed to a potentially frothy
luxury Manhattan condo market in which buyers were waking up
to the fact that prices had become completely detached from the
intrinsic value of the real estate. By 2015, the average number of
days it took to sell an apartment in a new development had increased by nearly 50 percent from the previous year.

That spring, Barnett took to the stage in the ballroom of a hotel
in the Israeli city of Tel Aviv. Across from him was Sophie Shulman,
a reporter from the Israeli daily business newspaper *Calcalist*. Shulman didn't pull punches.

A year earlier, Barnett had raised $300 million by floating cor-
porate debt secured against a segment of Extell's portfolio on Israel's
bond market. The portfolio included the remaining unsold units at
One57 as well as those planned for its more ambitious sister building, Central Park Tower.

"We all were pretty skeptical last year when you came," she told
Barnett in front of the assembled audience. "We didn't understand
why a famous person in the New York real estate market, who is at
the center of the most sophisticated financial market, has to come
to Israel for money."

Still, Barnett waxed optimistic, citing Vornado's success at 220
Central Park South. "In the last six weeks, they've sold over a billion dollars' worth of apartments and they're continuing to see tremendous demand," he told Shulman of Roth's company. "People
thought we were hot, then they thought Macklowe was hot. They
said, 'How long can it continue?' Now Vornado has taken it to the
next level. It's not clear to me that we have to see a turndown in the
New York market."

In truth, Barnett was once again in a tricky position. Some of
the major banks were tightening the spigot on their luxury condo
construction lending or stepping back from the market altogether.

If Barnett's One57 had kicked off the Billionaires' Row race to
the sky, would Central Park Tower now represent its demise?

CHAPTER 15

Starting Wars

When a small mock-up for the façade of 111 West 57th Street was delivered and installed on the roof of the old Steinway building, Michael Stern and his architect, Gregg Pasquarelli, rushed up to see how the terra-cotta and bronze would look in the light.

They grew silent, both marveling at how the ornamentation glimmered in the morning sun. They believed it would put the competing towers down the block, which looked to them as though they were shrink-wrapped in blue plastic, to shame.

Stern turned to his architect, his eyes lit up with delight. "When this building is finished," he said, "no one will believe it's real."

Like Macklowe, Stern had grown up driving into the city with his father; the new tower planned for the Steinway site was his opportunity to add a new landmark to the New York skyline he had been enchanted by as a young boy. His tower would take its design cues from some of the city's best-known skyscrapers—the Chrysler, the Empire State Building, 30 Rockefeller Center—merging their Art Deco history with the high-rise architecture of the future. The east and west façades would be clad in terra-cotta and elegant bronze filigree, creating a dynamic play of light and shadow, while a bronze-framed glass curtain wall along the north and south façades would take full advantage of the sweeping, centered views over Central Park and the Manhattan skyline. The building would have a roughly 170-foot feathered steel crown at the top, a modern-day twist on the Chrysler Building spire. It would narrow until it appeared to dissolve into the sky. A writer for *The Atlantic* would later compare it to "the love child of a dustbuster and a Mach3 razor."

The building was one of the most ambitious architectural undertakings the city had ever seen, in terms of both engineering and architectural flourish. It was also one of the most expensive.

The terra-cotta for the undulating façade would be sourced from Germany, then formed in twenty-six digitally fabricated custom molds made in China. The whole thing would then be assembled in Mexico before being shipped to New York.

But the tower's most striking feature would be its slender footprint. With only a roughly sixty-foot-wide base, the Steinway Tower would have the distinction of being the world's skinniest skyscraper, built on a site much narrower than any of the others on Billionaires' Row. It was a skyscraper that would fit in many Americans' backyards.

Working with a width-to-height ratio of 1 to 24, the developers also faced a host of expensive problems relating to how to brace the skyscraper against the wind. It was the same issue Macklowe had faced, but on an even more extreme scale. Before the tower could even begin rising, 192 gigantic steel rods with expanding anchors would have to be drilled down into the bedrock beneath the city. They would help the building withstand an uplifting force of more than 57,000 tons. A 730-ton mass damper would need to be installed at the summit, and a small number of floors would be left vacant to allow the wind to pass through, the same techniques that had been used at 432 Park. It was technology that hadn't existed even a few decades prior.

Making the building more expensive still was Stern's insistence that the apartments' sight lines shouldn't be broken up with structural columns. Because the tower was so skinny, every inch of floor

space was valuable. The wealthy buyers would want open, uninterrupted floor plans, he said. That meant installing an elaborate shear
wall system that called for 1.3 million cubic feet of high-strength
concrete to be poured onsite. Carving out space around the structural core meant the building's full-floor apartments would ultimately be shaped like dumbbells, with a narrow middle throughway
and two long arms of square footage on either side.

The interiors were to be designed by William Sofield, a celebrity interiors guru known for designer boutiques and the homes of
stars like the fashion designers Tom Ford and Ralph Lauren. The
finishes would take their cues from the materials of the Gilded Age.
The kitchens would have custom-designed cabinetry finished in a
light hand-rubbed finish and château-gray oak and countertops and
backsplashes in stepped Cristallo quartzite, while the bathrooms
would be finished in gold quartzite with handmade freestanding
polished nickel bathtubs and hand-cast bronze fittings and sconces.

Throughout the building, there would be nods to the site's musical past. An elephant motif was inspired by the ivory used to make
the original Steinway piano keys. It would take a local artist more
than three months to paint a mural for the entry hall depicting a
pair of elephants escaping the Central Park Zoo to reclaim the metropolis of Manhattan.

The project would comprise just sixty units—fourteen in the
landmarked Steinway Hall building and forty-six full-floor and duplex residences within the 91-story tower behind. But despite the
small number of apartments, Stern wouldn't compromise on the
level of amenities. His plans called for an 82-foot indoor swimming
pool housed in a dramatic ballroom-style space with an arched
double-height ceiling and surrounded by Kentia palms. A common
residents' area would include a fitness center, sauna and treatment
rooms, a private dining room, meeting rooms, and a bar area inspired by the legendary King Cole Bar at the St. Regis hotel, with
its ornamental balcony and custom murals in gold, silver, and au-
bergine. The space would be decorated with original works by
Picasso, Miró, and Matisse.

Despite the now challenging market, Michael Stern and his partner, Kevin Maloney, had successfully secured a $725 million construction loan from AIG and Apollo Global Real Estate Finance, the private equity firm's real estate finance arm, paving the way for the rise of their supertall. With construction lending beginning to dry up, arranging the financing had taken about a year longer than they thought.

AIG had taken the senior loan position with $400 million, while Apollo provided a riskier higher-interest-rate mezzanine loan for $325 million. Apollo Global Real Estate Finance would later sell a large chunk of that mezz loan to another Apollo fund, which managed the money of the Qatar Investment Authority.

For Apollo, which had a relatively tiny piece of the real estate debt space in comparison with competitors like Blackstone, the deal was one of the largest loans it had made to a residential project. The company saw it as a way to show the market that it wasn't afraid to take on big ticket development projects. In an earnings call following the deal, Apollo's chief operating officer acknowledged that the company remained cautious about the overall health of the Manhattan real estate market, given the potential issues of oversupply, but was happy with its own basis. He projected that the apartments would be marketed at somewhere between $7,000 and $10,000 a foot, well above Apollo's break-even point, which he pegged at around just $2,500 a foot.

On the surface, the project seemed to be moving ahead smoothly but by 2015, the developers of 111 West 57th Street, who had lost close to a year lining up their financing, could sense that the market was beginning to shift under their feet. Sales had stalled at Barnett's One57 and slowed at Macklowe's 432 Park, and still more ultra-luxury product was coming down the pike across the city.

Behind the scenes, all hell was about to break loose.

MICHAEL STERN WAS being ushered quickly by a bodyguard out of the glitzy Art Deco lobby of Walker Tower on West 18th Street into a Range Rover that idled by the entrance. A small group of construction union workers routinely loitered outside the building, and Stern didn't like to linger.

He hadn't moved quickly enough this time.

"Hey Michael, let me ask you something," shouted one of the men as Stern exited the building, looking businesslike in a long coat and tie. "How do you feel about the people that are going to die on your job because of your greed?"

The man pointed a camera in his face and peered at him threateningly through the car's rear side window before the Range Rover raced off.

It was 2015, and, much to the chagrin of Kevin Maloney, Stern and the unions were at war.

Stern had made a bold and unusual decision: He was attempting to build the Steinway Tower using a mix of union and nonunion contractors, or in what's known in the business as an "open shop" environment, which he believed would reduce the costs of construction and maximize profits.

For generations, the construction of Manhattan's big buildings had been marked by the presence of union workers, from carpenters and joiners to engineers and crane operators. Designed in the late nineteenth century to improve working conditions and laborer safety in cities like New York, Philadelphia, and Baltimore, the construction unions dominated the industry by the 1950s, by which time more than half of construction workers in those cities were card-carrying union members. By the 1980s, the unions had accumulated significant political influence, and the vast majority of residential high-rises in the city were built using exclusively union labor.

While the industry had been pivoting toward open shop construction for more than a decade—rising costs of construction materials and land were leading developers to cut costs—the "open shop" approach envisioned by Stern for Steinway had rarely been attempted on such a scale, and certainly not in such a high-profile location. The decision quickly put a target on Stern's back with the unions.

Gary LaBarbera, president of the Building and Construction Trades Council of Greater New York, was the face of the union opposition. Built like a tank, with a booming voice and a thick neck that hung over his collar and a cigarette in hand, the six-foot-three Long Islander started out as a member of Local 282 of the International Brotherhood of Teamsters in the 1980s, working as a forklift operator, and was one of the first members of 282 to graduate from the Labor Studies program at Cornell University. In a union best known as the onetime stomping ground of the Gambino crime family, LaBarbera developed a reputation as a new kind of labor leader who could clean up corruption. His father was a Teamster before him, and he carried his late father's union initiation card, from 1949, in his wallet. He would say that he hadn't chosen the labor movement, it had chosen him.

As the head of the building trades, LaBarbera spoke the language of the blue collar worker, rattling off the foundational union talking points. Being a union man, he would say, was about having a strong moral compass and believing that there needs to be equity in the workplace. A hard day's work should be awarded a fair day's pay and workers should be able to retire with the dignity that comes with appropriate pension benefits. He prided himself on being able to operate in two universes, in sophisticated financial negotiations with wealthy real estate power players in the boardroom and bellowing from a podium on a packed New York City street to the cheers of his working class union audience.

For LaBarbera, the stakes were high. While 90 percent of the construction workforce was made up of card-carrying union workers in the 1970s, those numbers had dwindled to around 40 percent by the mid-2010s, thanks in part to growing construction costs and a new generation of developers who didn't have the same longstanding loyalties as their predecessors. The unions' monopoly was endangered. If Stern could pull off such an ambitious tower using open shop construction, what would stop other developers from finally jumping ship and doing the same?

LaBarbera took a hard line straight out of the gate, openly accusing Stern in the press of being greedy and grandstanding on an issue he was too inexperienced to understand. He suggested that in using what he called "unscrupulous" subcontractors, the developer was being careless with safety on his construction sites, which could lead to accidents.

Stern did not shy away from the fight. He openly derided the building trades, which he contended were charging too much and didn't actually have the superior safety record to the nonunion shops that they claimed. He contended that the unions were merely surviving through intimidation. "If you look at the contractors in both union and non-union . . . most of the big-union concrete contractors are run by a bunch of guys who sat in jail for years," he told the *Commercial Observer* earlier that year. "They're mafia-affiliated. Long, lengthy criminal records, safety issues, etc."

An illustration of Stern on the cover of the real estate industry publication depicted him flashing his middle finger, which was shaped like the new Steinway Tower, while a union rat clung to it for dear life. The publication characterized the dispute as "Waterloo" for the union's grip on New York, a kind of litmus test for what it was possible to build without them.

The dispute bubbled over at public events. When Stern attended a gala or conference, a huge inflatable union rat known as Scabby was often positioned outside the venue. When he spoke on an industry panel, he was sometimes interrupted by union protesters. In October 2014, more than five thousand union protesters shut down 57th Street in a rally to protest his company. On several occasions, crowds demonstrated outside his personal residence.

Meanwhile, LaBarbera did nothing to discourage his guys, saying that he would never try to dissuade anyone from exercising their First Amendment right in any way that was lawful. After a while, Stern said he began to feel threatened—and he told friends he had hired off-duty policemen as bodyguards. For close to a year, three or four of them would escort him around town as he went to meetings as well as accompany his children when they were out in public.

The two men met privately numerous times, although their negotiations weren't as hostile as appearances would suggest. In negotiation mode, the tensions that had fueled their public spat were diffused. Stern said he knew that much of LaBarbera's rhetoric was theatrical posturing. "He would go on the dais and, you know, curse me out and this and that. He would text me before that and say, just so you know, ignore everything I'm about to say."

Still, he grew weary of the continuing heckling, complaints to the Department of Buildings, and calls to his lenders and partners, and frustrated at what he saw as the difference between LaBarbera's public and private personas.

LaBarbera later accused Stern of "immaturity and hubris" and said he came to believe that Stern had been negotiating in bad faith and never planned to make a deal.

For his part, Maloney wasn't impressed. He said later that he didn't think the cost savings Stern predicted from the use of nonunion labor was worth the fight, and he wasn't convinced that there would be large enough specialized nonunion subcontractors to get the massive job done on schedule. "People talk about there being a 30 percent or 40 percent savings, but there's also a time cost in not having enough staff," he said. "You might need fifty plumbers and [the subcontractor's] only got twenty. So now it causes delays in the schedule that trip up everybody else—the mechanic, the sprinkler guy, the finish people."

He said he didn't appreciate how Stern had made the project a flashpoint of union debate. Having faced off against the unions himself decades earlier, he said he knew firsthand how volatile a situation like that could become. "This is what starts wars," he said he thought when he saw the *Commercial Observer* magazine cover.

He speculated that the dispute had become more about individual egos than the actual economics of the site.

"You're just never going to win that way. So I kept my head down," he said of Stern's approach. "I said to him, 'You're just inflaming these guys,' I told him. 'They're gonna bonk you in the head with a pipe.'"

THE PRESSURE OF getting the Steinway project off the ground
took a toll on Stern and Maloney's already fragile relationship. It
wasn't just the unions. Other cracks that had developed privately
between the two men during the tail end of their Walker Tower
project began spilling into the public sphere.

For one thing, Maloney believed Stern was too interested in the
spotlight. "I don't know that it's productive for any developer to
stand up and get too much on his soap box, saying, 'look at all the
great things I did,'" Maloney told *The Real Deal* of Stern's approach
in the spring of 2014. "I don't think it's appropriate to take credit
for work that you don't do. You're more magnanimous if you give
credit to your architects and to your partners."

Maloney also griped to partners about what he perceived as
Stern's lack of focus. The delay in getting a construction loan for
Steinway meant that the partnership had had to cover the costs of
extending its land acquisition loan for longer than the partners had
anticipated, paying interest and taxes. That meant Stern and Maloney started issuing what's known as capital calls, an industry term
for when a sponsor calls on their investors for extra money to meet
an unforeseen circumstance or budget increase.

As costs started to escalate, the pair traded insults in a string of
emails later cited in court documents.

Maloney told Stern that he didn't want the project to wind up
over schedule and over budget: "Fifty percent over budget and [a]
year late."

"You not paying attention," he wrote. "6 months waster [*sic*] w
no staff on the job."

"You are clueless and uninformed as usual," Stern replied, calling Maloney's company a "two-bit organization" filled with "criminals and morons and secretaries," according to court records. "Why
don't you parade investors through something you have built instead of taking credit for MY work? You are an ingrate as I have

made you lots and lots of money. Easy to throw potshots from Florida. Fuck you."

With every day that went by, the market looked like a less fertile ground for the type of high-end product they were building. "There were issues pretty much from the start," said an attorney for one of the project's early investors, who spoke on the condition of anonymity. "But things really started to spiral down once the market turned."

Dick Bianco, the Connecticut investor whose company, AmBase, held the majority stake in the project's equity, quickly started to bristle at the rising costs too.

The prior year, 2014, the partnership had repeatedly called on AmBase via capital calls to inject more money in the project. Under the terms of the agreement, AmBase would have to meet those capital calls or risk having its percentage stake in the overall project diluted. AmBase had answered the calls, contributing an additional $1.085 million to the joint venture in March, $5.595 million in June, and $5.842 million in July.

When the partnership issued yet another capital call that December, AmBase was on the hook to contribute an additional $10.3 million, but Bianco pulled the brakes. The demands were getting too rich for his taste and his company's coffers were almost empty. He contributed just $1.5 million to the pot, far short of the partnership's requirements. He also demurred when the partnership issued two more calls in February and April 2015, forking out just $1.1 million of the $14.1 million that was asked.

At the end of 2014, after investing more than $70 million, Bianco finally put his foot down. AmBase would not be investing any more money in the project. "Given the continuing development risks of the joint venture, and the company's financial position, the company should not at that time increase its already significant concentration and risk exposure to the 111 West 57th Street property," the company said in its annual SEC report.

In March 2016, Kevin Maloney blindsided some of his partners by announcing that sales at 111 West 57th Street were on hold.

In an interview with *Bloomberg News,* he said that the team was hitting the pause button on marketing the project until later in the construction process. He attributed the change in strategy to a faltering luxury market in Manhattan, which had made wealthy buyers more hesitant to sign deals without physically seeing a completed project. Across the city, brokers reported finding that buyers no longer wanted to buy from floor plans or too far out from delivery. If they were going to put down a meaningful deposit, they wanted to know for certain that the building would be finished, wanted to see and touch the finishes themselves. "If the market were red-hot, people would be buying off plans, throwing checks down, and it'd be great," he said in the interview. "But if you have a market where you think marketing would be ineffective for now, why would you launch and spend the money? Wait."

Perhaps more surprised than anyone else by Maloney's announcement was Pam Liebman, the chief executive of the Corcoran Group, whose brokerage had been retained to market the units for sale and was contractually obligated to hit certain sales benchmarks by deadlines set forth in the contract with the partners. The Fifth Avenue sales office now complete, she had onsite staff actively working to woo buyers. What the hell was going on? How was her team supposed to sell units when the developer was telling the world that the units weren't for sale?

While Stern said he bristled that Maloney hadn't discussed it with him before going public in the press, he agreed that pausing the public marketing campaign made sense. At the time, sentiment around inventory on the 57th Street corridor was growing even more toxic, with columnists sounding off in the papers about how there was too much supply and too few billionaires to go around. In such an environment, he believed it wouldn't serve the partners to declare to the market exactly when sales had launched. If they said they were launching now and sales were slow, it could hurt their future prospects, since buyers might start to believe there was something wrong with the tower. If they paused their public efforts, they could continue to sell quietly, then launch with a splash later when the market began to recover and the building was closer to completion. The market would be none the wiser.

Meanwhile, Stern felt like he was chasing foreign buyers who always seemed just out of reach. Chinese buyers couldn't get their money out of China thanks to their own government's capital controls, and Middle Easterners seemed to have dried up since the Trump administration took over. The impending vote on Brexit had also made European buyers anxious. The entire landscape seemed to be shifting under his feet.

But soon, Stern had bigger problems than Pam Liebman.

A month later, in April 2016, he and Maloney were slapped with a lawsuit from AmBase.

Dick Bianco, tired of the cost overruns at the project, had sued in the New York State Supreme Court, alleging that Stern and Maloney had devised a scheme to increase their own ownership interests in the joint venture at AmBase's expense, all while minimizing their own financial exposure.

AmBase's refusal to pony up yet more cash meant that the partners had moved to reduce its stake in the project, from about 60 percent to 45 percent. Bianco argued that such a sizable reduction in his stake was unfair.

It was all a scheme, AmBase alleged, to drive up development expenses and then issue unnecessary capital calls to cover the purported costs. He also alleged that the developers had funded their own portion of the capital calls by illicitly obtaining financing from undisclosed third parties, thus limiting their own risk while putting the financial burden on AmBase.

The lawsuit brought into stark focus how sour the relationship between Bianco and the developers had become.

AmBase alleged that it had made repeated inquiries to Stern and Maloney seeking further explanation for the capital calls but never got a clear answer. Bianco felt he was being kept in the dark, too, about major decisions being made about the project.

One such decision concerned setting pricing for a number of the units. The developers had filed paperwork with the New York

State attorney general's office showing that initial pricing would begin at $15.5 million for units on lower floors and go up to about $57 million for the highest available unit, a four-bedroom duplex penthouse on the 74th floor. (They hadn't announced pricing for the top two residences, on the 80th and 82nd floors, which were likely to be the most expensive.)

He also learned that Stern and Maloney had spent $9 million constructing a lavish multilevel sales office for the project on Fifth Avenue, complete with a scale model of a luxury apartment, and tapped the marketing firm Corcoran Sunshine—the same firm that Roth and Barnett had used for their projects—as the exclusive sales representative for the property, all without his involvement.

Bianco grew suspicious, wondering if they were self-dealing—steering business to affiliates—without his knowledge, according to the suit. When he checked in with Stern and Maloney, they would often be in Miami, where both had significant business interests. Bianco wanted to know how they could really be paying close attention to the critical details of the development if they were not continuously onsite.

"At a certain point, the investors got concerned about Michael overspending. That no cost was too high," said an attorney for one of the project's investors. "They were concerned that he was overspending to the point where the project would no longer be financially viable."

Complicating the issue was that Stern, as the project's contractor, was also taking fees on the construction side, meaning that, as Bianco saw it, the more elaborate the project became, the more money his contracting company would make. Stern's construction company was entitled to a quarterly fee of roughly $641,000, with total payments capped at about $6.4 million, according to the lawsuit. It was also entitled to seek reimbursement for payroll and other expenses. In other words, the increasing spend was benefiting Stern, while AmBase felt it was being left in the cold.

Stern was furious. With a project of this scale, he argued, it would have been impossible to predict the costs exactly, and some level of overruns and capital calls was to be expected. Any reasonable or remotely sophisticated investor would see that. Besides, Bianco had gotten into the deal so early that it would have been impossible to adequately lay out the costs for him.

"When he brought him into that deal, we hadn't even hired an architect yet. We didn't have a design, we hadn't gone through landmarks, we didn't even have construction drawings," he said. "We had a conceptual budget but it wasn't based on a real design."

He accused Bianco of viewing partnership decisions as a means to exploit the other partners. They were "train stops for extortion," he said.

But the war between the partners was just getting started.

CHAPTER 16

Disdain in Paradise

Harry Macklowe should have been in his element. It was May 2016 and he was in Florence, Italy, standing in the main sanctuary of the Palazzo Vecchio, one of the city's most important civic buildings. The more than 170-foot-long Salone dei Cinquecento, or Hall of the Five Hundred, dated to the fifteenth century and rose to a height of nearly 60 feet, with extravagant gold-paneled ceilings, towering sculptures, and intricate wall frescoes. Artwork on display inside included the masterpieces *The Genius of Victory* by Michelangelo and *The Deeds of Hercules* by De Rossi. It was like a scene from *The Da Vinci Code*.

The hall was heaving with people, and they were all cheering for Macklowe—or at least for his boat. The occasion was the World Superyacht Awards, the boating industry's answer to the Oscars, and the developer's new yacht, *Unfurled,* had just triumphed in the Sailing Yacht of the Year category. It was the kind of occasion Macklowe typically reveled in.

Macklowe, who had long had a love of sailing, and his wife, Linda, had commissioned the construction of the yacht from scratch. A 151-foot aluminum boat with a teak deck, it had been designed by the acclaimed naval architect German Frers and built in the Netherlands at Vitters Shipyard. For the developer, the boat, valued at around $23.5 million, had been a longtime passion project, and winning the award was like having his efforts rubber-stamped by the yacht world's top brass. As he and Linda took to the stage to receive the trophy, he in a tuxedo and she in a jeweled black ensemble, they beamed and interlocked arms, a picture of marital bliss.

Behind the scenes, things were not quite so blissful. The Mack-lowes had had a busy spring filled with travel. First, they had gone for two weeks to Japan, a longtime dream of Linda's, where they had toured galleries and temples and eaten at the best restaurants in Tokyo and Kyoto. Unfortunately, Harry had come down with pneumonia during the trip. When the pair returned home, he felt Linda was less than sympathetic to his illness. He felt he was being ignored, and the feeling wasn't at all unfamiliar.

Harry believed that Linda resented his success. When people would approach them on the street to congratulate him on his accomplishments—which, he insisted, happened frequently—he said he would turn to introduce them to his wife, only to find that she had walked on. When he had asked her to attend the topping out ceremony of 432 Park, a celebration of the structure's having reached its full height, she had refused, he said.

For nearly two years, the marriage had been running on fumes. That was thanks at least in part to another woman. Harry had met Patricia Landeau, a French former fashion executive and the president of French Friends of the Israel Museum, at a private showing of his art collection in 2011 and then at a friend's dinner party two years later. He was instantly besotted with Landeau, whom he found elegant and sophisticated. He would boast that her ancestry dated back to the sixteenth century, whatever that meant. It was language that might have been more aptly used to describe the provenance of a piece of antique furniture.

While Linda ignored him, Landeau wanted to stay up all night talking with him, he said. With the hope of new love, Harry's dissatisfaction with his marriage and his life became all the more acute.

With Patricia, he told friends, he was as happy as a pig in shit. With Linda, he was miserable.

"I tried to make it work, but my life I knew was with Patricia," he said later. "I was very dissatisfied with the life that I had here with a small social world and people that I found not to be very stimulating, not at the level where I wanted to be."

Severing the ties between the longtime married couple would not prove easy. Harry and Linda's portfolio of assets had grown vast over their more than half a century together, including a highly notable collection of art from twentieth-century masters. Their holdings consisted of at least 165 pieces, including works by Willem de Kooning, Jeff Koons, Mark Rothko, Cy Twombly, Jackson Pollock, and Andy Warhol. In addition to their apartment at the Plaza, which spanned 14,000 square feet on the seventh floor of the iconic hotel building, providing an expansive "above the treeline" view of the entirety of Central Park, there was the house in East Hampton, a modernist property built in glass, steel, and limestone on more than two acres with frontage on the exclusive Georgica Pond. There were also the two units they were still under contract to buy at 432 Park. Then there was the jewelry, the silver, the book collection, the cars, and of course the yacht.

There was also Harry's stake in a number of high-profile real estate projects across the city, including 432 Park. In addition to his hope certificate on the residential portion of the building, Harry had acquired the retail space at the base of the building from CIM in 2016, along with Sheikh Hamad bin Jassim bin Jaber al-Thani, the former prime minister of Qatar, for $411 million.

They were in deep. But Harry Macklowe was undeterred.

That summer, after returning from dinner with his brother and sister-in-law, Harry said he sat Linda down to talk in their apartment at the Plaza. Their nearly six-decade marriage, he told her, was over.

"Tomorrow I am going to Paris," he later recalled telling her. "I haven't seen Patricia in six months, but I love her and I'm going to be with her. I want you to know that everything I have will be split right down the middle. There are no secret bank accounts. There's nothing. My office is an open book."

Linda, who had known about Patricia for some time already, had questions, he said.

Would Harry be moving to Paris permanently? He responded that he would not. Patricia would move to New York to be with him. (Page Six would later report that he had been secretly putting Patricia up in a Park Avenue apartment for two years.)

Was he represented by an attorney?

No, he said, he was not.

Macklowe said he was hoping to keep the exchange and the subsequent split as "straightforward" as possible. "I wanted it to be definite," he said. There was no "I'm sorry."

For Linda's part, she rejected the narrative Harry was constantly painting, that she had never cared for him and had all but pushed him into the arms of Patricia. She contended that it was far from the truth. She said that in reality, Patricia was really just the latest in a long line of women.

Harry's idea of splitting the assets, she said, was that he would keep his business and the boat, and everything else would be sold. Selling their assets would mean Linda would lose her home at the Plaza, her country house, and her art, which she had spent decades collecting and wanted to leave to the children. Harry would also net more on the sales, since he could apply net operating losses from his business to the proceeds to reduce taxes, she said.

Complications like those would make the following months anything but straightforward.

SHORTLY THEREAFTER, Macklowe found himself riding the high-speed train the *Eurostar* from Paris to London to attend a business meeting. Patricia had accompanied him on the trip. As the couple disembarked at London's St Pancras Station, Macklowe said he scoured the terminal until he found his driver, a tall man standing by the exit waiting for him.

Suddenly a woman popped out from behind the driver.

"Are you Mr. Macklowe?" she asked in a posh British accent.

He replied in the affirmative.

An envelope was thrust into his hands. He had been served with divorce papers.

Macklowe was in a state of shock. He said he had no idea how Linda could have known he was on the *Eurostar* or why she would go to the expense of serving him in Europe when she could easily have waited until he returned to New York. He said he suspected that she had hired a private investigator to follow his and Patricia's movements.

It was the beginning of what would be one of the ugliest and most expensive divorces New York had ever seen—one that would shed a bright light on the reality of Harry's stake in 432 Park.

And it was just one piece of a brewing family drama that would engulf the Macklowes.

THAT NOVEMBER, Billy Macklowe's general counsel, Jason Grebin, got a call from Harry Macklowe's attorney, Keith Corbett.

The elder Macklowe was gearing up to sue his own son.

It was just a few months since Harry had announced he was leaving Billy's mother. Caught up in what was quickly becoming a bitter and messy divorce battle, Billy was siding with his mother. Harry believed Billy was too immature to accept that the marriage was over. "At fifty-two years old, he couldn't reconcile that. He was like a sixteen-year-old idiot," the elder Macklowe said later.

Now the bitterness had spilled over into their respective businesses.

When Harry and Billy had gone their separate ways in business in 2010, after the debacle with the CIM deal—Billy setting up his own firm, William Macklowe Company, and Harry resuming the top spot at Macklowe Properties—Harry had transferred his ownership in Macklowe Management, a separate company that provided administrative, payroll, and human resources to both men's firms, to Billy. While he no longer owned it, the two had made a gentleman's agreement that Macklowe Management would continue to provide such support to Harry's company. But there was one small snag: Macklowe Management owned several domain names that Harry thought were rightfully his, Macklowe.com and HMacklowe.com.

Suspecting that Billy could be reading his emails (which were routed through Macklowe.com) in the midst of the divorce, and eager to take ownership of anything that bore his name, Harry was now demanding that the domains be transferred to him, and Billy so far had not complied. Harry was threatening to sue for breach of contract, unfair competition, misuse of company funds, and usurping control of the domain names. The Macklowe name, he said, was so deeply associated in the public's mind with Harry's company that it could not be used by Billy's now competing firm.

It all seemed petty, but the way Harry saw it, it was a battle for control of the family name. That was his legacy and a brand that he had built over decades. Billy, on the other hand, thought Harry should see his only son as his true legacy.

The threat of legal action that November 14 set off hours of desperate negotiations between lieutenants on two sides, with Billy determined to avoid an embarrassing public lawsuit. By close to midnight, it looked as if the crisis had been averted and agreement reached.

"Are we good?" Grebin, Billy's attorney, asked Corbett, Harry's legal counsel, in an email at 11:51 P.M.

Then, less than thirty minutes later, a follow-up: "How about a confirm so I can go to bed?"

He got no confirmation.

The following day, Grebin finally heard back from Corbett in the form of an email attachment: a lawsuit. Harry was suing his own son for $300 million.

CHAPTER 17

Selling Billionaires' Row

They were brothers who described themselves as best friends—and they were taking the real estate world by storm.

Tal and Oren Alexander were part of a new wave of agents who started redefining the high-end real estate business in the 2010s. Before shows like *Selling Sunset,* they were already fluent in the language of social media and personal branding, posting about their major deals and their travels around the world. They would fly with their clients in private jets, watch tennis at Wimbledon, spearfish in Panama, snowboard in Aspen, and ride dune buggies in the Saudi Arabian desert. They dubbed themselves "the A Team," and Oren even drove around Miami in a black Mercedes AMG S63 with a Florida plate reading A TEAM—O.

They fit right into an industry filled with former soap stars and models. Oren was the more classically good-looking, with dark hair and olive skin. Tal was handsome too, and more dogged in his fight for a deal. He had honed his competitive spirit in the sporting world, playing Division I tennis at Hofstra University, at one point contemplating a professional career on the court.

They understood the business, too. Born in the mid-1980s in Miami Beach, Florida, they had been raised in a real estate family.

Their father, Shlomy Alexander, started a business that provided security and concierge services to commercial and residential buildings, then went into real estate development himself, building mansions in Miami. On weekends, he would take the boys to construction sites.

The duo's antics quickly became a source of gossip in the industry, which was split on whether to aspire to the same lifestyle or ridicule it. For Tal's thirtieth birthday, the brothers hired a professional production company to film a compilation of their adventures in the Hamptons for the occasion, set to the soundtrack of Travis Scott's hit "A-Team." In the video, they were seen traveling by seaplane, partying on a speedboat, and dining in all-white ensembles at a Hamptons megamansion.

But the brothers' success could not be disputed. At just twenty-one, Oren had already sold an $8.2 million penthouse at the Park Imperial on West 56th Street, and the pair had gone on to sell ultra-luxe units across the city, from SoHo lofts in buildings like 102 Prince Street to soaring aeries at the Time Warner Center in Midtown. In Miami, they sold a $47 million home built by their father on Indian Creek Island to a mysterious Russian billionaire.

Competing agents accused the brothers of being nepotism babies and indiscreet publicity junkies, but the brothers saw it as part of their job to be ubiquitous at events for the rich and famous. The Alexanders believed in spending money to make money. They showed up at the World Economic Forum at Davos in Switzerland, at the Super Bowl, at the Allen & Company Sun Valley Conference, at Art Basel in Miami and the Frieze Art Fair in London. Often, clients came too. Once, the developer Michael Stern joined the pair in Las Vegas to watch a fight between Conor McGregor and Floyd Mayweather, Jr.

"The hashtag that we live by is #nevernotworking," Tal said. "I meet some high-net-worth individuals on the ski lift in Aspen around Christmas time. The following year, I'm doing a deal with them in New York or Miami. That stuff happens all the time. We're just playing one big game of connect the dots."

The Alexanders went into the real estate brokerage business straight out of college. Initially, Oren did sales while Tal started his own boutique brokerage focused on rentals, a much less lucrative side of the business. Tal eventually wanted a piece of the sales action, which threatened to drive a wedge between the two. Howard Lorber, the chairman of the real estate brokerage Douglas Elliman, who was friendly with the Alexander family, helped defuse the situation. Ultimately, the brothers agreed that they would form a team and split all their commissions fifty-fifty, regardless of who closed the deal.

However, it wasn't always smooth sailing. In August 2014, as Billionaires' Row began to take shape, Tal said he was left "depressed" and contemplated quitting the business after the government of Qatar pulled the plug on a $90 million deal he and his brother had brokered for them for an Upper East Side townhouse owned by the Wildenstein art family. The brothers had already gone public with the potentially record-setting deal when it went into contract, but the Qataris had walked away prior to the closing, leaving them red-faced.

The brothers' detractors speculated that they had blown up the deal by blabbing about it all over town. After all, the oil-rich nation, which had eyed the house as a potential consulate, might have wanted to keep a low profile amid political scandals surrounding the World Cup at home.

In a post on his blog, the prominent New York real estate agent Leonard Steinberg called the Alexanders "young, less experienced brokers who have learned a very painful lesson," saying that they had caused damage to their credibility and a huge loss to their own income.

However, the Alexanders maintained that the Qataris had wanted to release the news of the contract and had even planned to throw a party at the townhouse prior to the closing. The deal was not a closely held secret. "I get why people made it out to be the press," Tal said later. "People want to see you fail. That's just the way the world works."

But less than a year later, the brothers would land a deal that would lead to their biggest press hit yet, with a deal at 220 Central Park South that would completely change the luxury real estate landscape in New York.

THE ALEXANDERS WERE primarily resale brokers—which meant that they brokered transactions between parties in established buildings. Deals with buyers that they brought to new developments like those on Billionaires' Row were only a few among many deals they would typically close in a given year. Once they were finished with a deal in one building, they'd move on to the next.

Dealmaking in new developments like those on Billionaires' Row carries headaches that resale transactions in established buildings do not. Brokering a sale in a new development sometimes means waiting years to see a cent of commission, since closings in buildings like those on Billionaires' Row don't start until sales have reached a certain threshold and the construction is near completion.

For instance, when the luxury real estate agent Michael Graves did a $52.95 million deal with Brazil's richest healthcare billionaire, Edson de Godoy Bueno, for a full-floor unit at One57 in 2013, he had to wait for more than a year and a half for the transaction to finally close and collect his multi-million-dollar commission. The wait can be stressful. Graves recalled constantly worrying that something could happen to derail the closing and cause his buyer to walk away from an admittedly hefty deposit.

He worked to keep Bueno happy and protect his relationship with the billionaire. If Bueno or one of his friends came into town, Graves made sure their trip ran like a "Swiss watch."

"I felt like at any given moment, something could break in the news that turned him off of New York and caused him to walk away from the deal," Graves said later. "I recognized how delicate this dance was and I was just mindful of the fact that until it was fully executed and signed, any number of things could go wrong."

For the onsite brokers who worked on the buildings full-time, selling on behalf of developers like Barnett, Macklowe, and Roth, the job of selling real estate looked completely different. In contrast to brokers like the Alexanders and Graves, those agents would live and breathe a building exclusively for several years on behalf of the developer, typically until more than 70 percent of the apartments had been sold. They worked directly for the developers or for new development marketing firms like Corcoran Sunshine, which then assigned them to suitable projects.

Being an onsite broker is a longtime niche of the real estate brokerage world. With a few exceptions, such onsite positions rarely draw the most successful brokers, who are often unwilling to give up their lucrative resale businesses in order to dedicate 100 percent of their time to selling out one building, which can take years. Going onsite typically means accepting a base salary of a few hundred thousand dollars a year, plus a small commission on each deal, which comes only after the deal closes, often years later.

During the first year of their exclusive agreement to market the units at 111 West 57th Street, for instance, Corcoran Sunshine was slated to earn a consulting fee of $10,000 a month until the building's offering plan was accepted and the sales office opened. After that, its compensation would be derived from the sale of the apartments. Corcoran negotiated a commission equal to 2.125 percent of each unit's net purchase price, which was to be paid at the time of the closing. Based on the expected $1.45 billion sellout price of the building, the firm expected to earn roughly $30 million from the sale of the units. Those proceeds would be divided up among the company and the onsite agents, who would remain with the building until it was almost sold out.

While that would be a lot of money to any regular person, it would represent a significant pay cut for the industry's top agents, who could net several million dollars on just one major resale deal. As a result, developers typically choose an up-and-coming agent who has yet to build a large book of business and who can use the assignment to bolster their own personal brand and build a client base for the future. (Once the sales process is completed, onsite agents often find themselves becoming the de facto agent for resales in the building, since they already have a relationship with all the owners, which can significantly propel their careers.)

On the flip side, some agents have come to regret taking an onsite assignment, particularly in cases where the market has taken a nosedive. They've given up their freedom to sit all day every day in a sales office, where there can be a lot of downtime between showings and sales calls, and where they must answer to the whims of their developer bosses, who can dictate their hours and vacation schedules as well as how much they can negotiate on prices and concessions.

An onsite sales agent must be comfortable selling to anyone. Jeannie Woodbrey, the onsite sales agent at One57, once said she could go from selling to a pig farmer from Middle America to selling to a hedge fund billionaire an hour later. "You have to be a chameleon," she told *The New York Times.*

Insiders say the perfect onsite agent is physically attractive, sophisticated, styled to perfection, and savvy enough to close deals without an ounce of vulgarity. A European accent can be an added bonus.

At 520 Park Avenue, for instance, the Zeckendorfs selected Louis Buckworth, a formerly UK-based nightclub impresario turned New York real estate agent with high society connections, who perfectly fit the mold of an in-house sales agent.

Buckworth checked all the boxes: handsome, dapper, intelligent, and, perhaps most important, British. Prior to moving to the United States, he ran the trendy Firehouse bar and restaurant in London's South Kensington neighborhood, which had its own nightclub named after his then wife, Chloe Delevingne. Delevingne, a prominent socialite, is the sister of famed British model and actress Cara Delevingne, known for her distinctive thick eyebrows. They and sister Poppy hail from one of London's best-connected high society families. Their grandfather, Sir Jocelyn Stevens, was a drinking pal of Princess Margaret.

When Buckworth married the socialite in 2009, the glamorous affair drew guests including the Duchess of York, Princesses Beatrice and Eugenie, the actress Joan Collins, and Spice Girl Geri Halliwell. Though the union didn't last—Chloe went on to remarry Buckworth's former friend, the property developer Edward Grant, who reportedly lodged at the couple's home in South London after they were married and had been an usher at their wedding—it yielded a slew of high society connections for Buckworth.

In 2012, he had brokered a deal to sell the penthouse at the storied Plaza hotel on the corner of Central Park for $25.4 million to the British property developer Christian Candy, whom he knew from his days on the London club scene. Then, in 2015, he sold another of Candy's New York homes, an Italian Renaissance–style limestone mansion on East 70th Street, to the financier Leon D. Black and his wife, Debra, a Broadway producer, for $50.25 million.

If some brokers parlayed their high society connections into dealmaking wins, others had to get more creative.

TAL AND OREN Alexander had preternatural skill for sniffing out the real estate market's newest whales.

One strategy of theirs was to pay close attention to what was happening in the art world, the theory being that billionaires who were actively shelling out hundreds of millions for the Old Masters might also be willing to spend big on real estate.

In 2015, the art markets were starting to buzz about one man in particular: the hedge fund billionaire Ken Griffin, who had paid a record $46 million for Gerhard Richter's painting *Abstract Picture, 599*.

That put him square in the Alexander brothers' sights. Clearly, he was in the mood to spend money, and they had a particular home in mind for him: a penthouse at Steve Roth's 220 Central Park South. The pair had prior notice of the project's launch thanks to a relationship with Louise Sunshine, the new development executive advising Steve Roth on sales strategy.

Somehow, though he wouldn't reveal how, Tal tracked down Griffin's cell phone number. (One source claimed he bought it and other phone numbers from a former FBI agent, but a spokesman for Griffin disputed that account, saying that Alexander had simply mailed the marketing materials to his office.) Once Tal got the billionaire on the phone, he was delighted to find that Griffin was interested. A couple of months later, when the hedge fund magnate made it to New York on business, his visit coincided with the first day Roth was taking appointments with prospective buyers for the tower.

For the billionaire investment magnate, a deal at 220 Central Park South was the peak of a spending binge that started around 2015 and continued through 2022. His buying spree would roil both the real estate and art worlds, setting a new bar for prices around the world. The luxury real estate, luxury goods, and art markets were reaching historic highs, thanks, at least in some small part, to one man. His purchases would eventually read like a laundry list of the most prestigious residential properties in the world.

In 2015, he bought a pair of Miami apartments atop Faena House, a high-end building that had drawn a who's who of the New York finance world, including Apollo Global Management's Leon Black and the former Goldman Sachs chief executive Lloyd Blankfein. In South Florida, they called the building, designed by the Pritzker Architecture Prize–winning firm Foster + Partners, the Billionaires' Bunker. If combined into one, Griffin's roughly 12,500-square-foot apartment would have had terraces spanning nearly 10,000 square feet and a 70-foot-long rooftop pool. It was the most expensive residence ever sold in South Florida.

In his native Chicago, Griffin made a deal in 2017 with the developer Jim Lechtinger to customize a massive four-story, $58.75 million penthouse for him at No. 9 Walton, an under-construction building in the city's downtown area. Dubbed Chicago's "Tower of Power," the building was widely considered to be the city's most luxurious, with spa services and an in-house driver and car, and the scale of the Griffin apartment was beyond anything the industry had seen before.

In 2019, Griffin bought a $122 million London townhouse that dated back to the 1820s and was formerly used by MI6, the British intelligence agency, for interviewing potential agents.

In February 2020, he bought a seven-acre estate on storied Meadow Lane in the Hamptons—an enclave well known for its rich and famous residents, from the fashion designer Calvin Klein to the billionaire hedge funder Dan Och—for $84.45 million.

In 2021, he bought a mansion on Miami's Star Island for $75 million. The following year, he added another mansion in Miami's Coconut Grove area for $107 million, setting a new Miami record. In nearby Palm Beach, he also assembled one of the largest waterfront sites in the country, just south of President Trump's Mar-a-Lago resort, with plans to build a house for himself and one for his mother. He would ultimately spend upward of $350 million putting the site together over several years.

Then there was the art collection, which was on its way to rivaling Macklowe's. In February 2016, Griffin paid the entertainment mogul David Geffen's foundation $500 million for a pair of paintings by Jackson Pollock and Willem de Kooning in one of the art world's largest ever private deals. And in 2021, he paid $43.2 million for a first-edition copy of the U.S. Constitution.

In Griffin's world, it was raining money.

Griffin, a legend in the financial world, was the founder and chief executive of Citadel, a hedge fund which was based in Chicago and that, by 2015, had close to $24 billion in assets under management. Born in Daytona Beach, Florida, the son of an engineer at General Electric, he had started his first business in high school, running a mail order education software firm out of his parents' house. By college, he was buying stock options and convertible bonds and lobbying Harvard to allow him to install a satellite dish on the roof of his dorm so that he could receive stock quotes faster. He launched his first fund in 1987, just days after his nineteenth birthday, and by age thirty-four, he was the youngest self-made person ever listed on the Forbes 400, with a net worth of $650 million.

The timing of Griffin's spending spree lent to the public intrigue. The deal for the New York apartment was signed less than a year after Griffin filed for divorce from his wife of more than a decade, Anne Dias Griffin. A few months later, the couple, who share three children, were publicly quarreling over a prenuptial agreement, which she said she was coerced into signing the night before their wedding. Her lawyers argued that the agreement should be voided and that, given Griffin's vast fortune, she should be awarded $1 million in monthly expenses, including $300,000 for the use of a private jet, $160,000 for hotels, and $2,000 in stationery costs. Dias Griffin was also a Harvard graduate and had worked at Soros Fund Management, the hedge fund turned family office founded by George Soros, before starting her own firm in 2001, then returning investor capital about a decade later to concentrate on the couple's charitable foundation.

Griffin's attorneys argued that Dias Griffin had plenty of time to review the proposed prenup weeks before the wedding and that she had consulted her own legal team prior to signing. Eventually, the two settled out of court in October 2015, narrowly avoiding a very public trial.

For all his easy spending, Griffin wasn't an easy buyer. For one thing, he didn't want one of the 220 Central Park South's existing floor plans. Rather, he wanted to create his own custom quadruplex in the middle of the building. He didn't want to be at the top; the perfect spot, he said, was in the center of the tower, where the views would skim the treetops of Central Park. He also required a special, ultra-high speed internet connection.

Griffin's custom pad would arguably be to 220 Central Park South what Ackman's Winter Garden was to One57—the best but not the highest unit in the building.

Douglas Elliman's chief executive, Howard Lorber, the head of the firm the Alexander brothers worked for at the time, was brought in to face off in negotiations against Pam Liebman, the sales chief for the building and the chief executive of the Corcoran Group. Negotiations took place over several hours at Roth's office in Midtown as the parties drilled down on the details.

"He was a ball buster," said one person of Griffin's approach.

That June, the Alexanders finally reeled in the ultimate billion-dollar whale when Griffin agreed to pay $239.96 million for his custom apartment at the building, more than doubling the previous record price for a New York City apartment, set by Michael Dell at One57. Griffin had also paid more than twice what Ackman, his competitor in the cutthroat world of corporate finance, had paid at Barnett's building.

The deal made 220 Central Park South the darling of Billionaires' Row and Roth the king of the corridor. To design his unit, Griffin would later work with a revolving door of architects, including stars like Peter Marino, Thierry Despont, and the firm of Olson Kundig. He seemed unable to settle on just one.

FOR ANY REAL estate agent, landing Ken Griffin as a client would be like finding the Holy Grail. A commission on a single deal of that scale could tally up to more than $7 million.

The day the contract was signed, the Alexanders were in Basel, Switzerland, for the annual art fair, drinking champagne at a party thrown by art dealer Larry Gagosian's gallery.

When the lawyers confirmed the deal had been inked, Tal looked at his brother.

"How does it feel to have sold the most expensive home in the world ever?" he said.

Technically, it wasn't (there was once a larger deal in Monaco). But that didn't matter.

Tal would go on to find his own perch on Billionaires' Row, renting an apartment at 432 Park from one of his clients. He said he took his lead from real estate agents like Kyle Blackmon, who had purchased the small apartment at 15 Central Park West before selling Sandy Weill's penthouse for $88 million in 2011. He realized the access that living in a top-tier building could bring. "If people want to buy in this building, they would be making a mistake not calling me," he said. "I have more context than anybody else in the marketplace. I have off-market opportunities that no one else has access to."

It was an extension of the Alexanders' strategy of aiming to live like their clients, riding with them in the elevator and dining alongside them at the in-house restaurant. "I'm not just some broker who's, you know, flapping my wings outside of these buildings, looking to just broker transactions," he said later. "I actually live, eat, sleep and breathe it."

Tal's sun-bathed corner apartment had a flavor of *Architectural Digest* meets *Penthouse,* a touch of the pornographic along with heart-stopping views over Central Park and the city skyline. On one wall, he had hung a piece from the controversial artist Richard Prince's collection of Instagram paintings. It depicted a young peroxide blonde wearing only a thong, leather hot pants, and Playboy rabbit nipple coverings, handcuffed to the Australian viral artist Jesse Willesee. On an adjacent wall was a photograph of another topless peroxide blonde, nipples exposed. She was snorting diamonds through a $500 bill.

The Griffin deal had helped him get there.

"I would like to know if there was ever a better cold call made in the history of cold calls," Tal said.

PART III

Falling Back to Earth

CHAPTER 18

Shadowy Figures

Kolawole "Kola" Aluko was beaming in his gray suit with a purple checkered shirt and tie as the opening bell rang out at the Nasdaq exchange's studio in Times Square in September 2013. Appearing alongside a group that included the actor Jamie Foxx, the Nigerian oil magnate was celebrating the Made in Africa Foundation, which he had co-founded several years earlier. Now he was launching a $500 million fund to spur new infrastructure projects on the continent and said he was chipping in $50 million of his own money to get the ball rolling.

"I thank everyone here for believing in our vision," the normally soft-spoken Aluko told the gathered onlookers, heralding the dawn of a new era in African development. "Africa is open for business."

By all accounts, he could afford it. Rolling in money from a series of oil extraction contracts his company had inked with the Nigerian government, Aluko landed on the global stage with a bang in the early 2010s. He was spotted partying with the actor Leonardo DiCaprio and lounging in the sun on the top deck of his 210-foot megayacht, which he named the *Galactica Star*. The tabloids speculated that he was dating the supermodel Naomi Campbell after the two were photographed arm in arm leaving a posh restaurant in Paris, he in a red fedora and she in skyscraper heels, then later taking in a winter-wonderland-themed Christmas attraction in London's Hyde Park. Seemingly eager to amass the traditional trappings of wealth, he had acquired fancy watches, exotic cars, and high-end real estate, with homes in New York, Santa Barbara, Los Angeles, London, Switzerland, Canada, and Dubai.

In 2014, Aluko had closed on the purchase of what was arguably his most lavish home, a full-floor, 6,240-square-foot spread on the 79th floor of Gary Barnett's One57. Aluko had purchased the unit, which offered soaring views over Central Park, through a shell company listed in New York City public records as One57 79 Inc. The price: $50.916 million.

Aluko was one among dozens of buyers who had helped One57 achieve record prices as the market reached new peaks. But by early 2017, a few years after his moment in the spotlight at the Nasdaq opening bell, Aluko's wild ride had come to a screeching halt. Nigerian authorities had declared him a fugitive, and the apartment at One57 had become a point of focus in an investigation by U.S. and Nigerian officials into his business dealings.

As the U.S. Justice Department laid out in a civil complaint filed in July 2017, Aluko and an associate allegedly conspired to pay bribes to Nigeria's former minister for petroleum resources, who oversaw Nigeria's state-owned oil company, between 2011 and 2015. In return for these improper benefits, the minister used her influence to steer lucrative oil contracts to companies owned by Aluko and his associates.

That summer, the Justice Department announced that it would seek the forfeiture and recovery of both the apartment and the *Galactica,* alleging that the assets represented the proceeds of foreign corruption offenses that had been laundered in and through the United States. "The United States is not a safe haven for the proceeds of corruption," Acting Assistant Attorney General Kenneth Blanco declared in a statement.

By this point, the Nigerian's lavish lifestyle was looking depleted. Aluko had failed to pay common charges and mortgage payments on the unit in One57 and owed the city roughly $60,000 in back taxes. Lenders quickly filed to foreclose on the apartment. A corporate entity controlled by Aluko had obtained a $35.3 million mortgage on the property from Banque Havilland SA, a private bank headquartered in Luxembourg and owned by Spotty Rowland, a British property developer and financier perhaps best known as an investment adviser to Prince Andrew, the Duke of York. The full repayment of the loan was due within a year, but the borrower hadn't repaid, Rowland's bank alleged in court documents.

It was the largest New York residential foreclosure anyone could remember, and it generated a series of negative headlines for One57, to the chagrin of Barnett, who still had plenty of units left to sell at the tower.

IN THE YEARS since One57 debuted, international figures with sometimes murky backgrounds had become a small but consistent staple of the Billionaires' Row buyer pool. The brokers representing them often professed ignorance at the source of their clients' wealth. Sometimes, brokers would deal exclusively with a buyer's representatives and be kept in the dark about the buyer's true identity. Purchasers were registered under trusts, limited liability companies, and other legal vehicles that could shield their identities.

Since they were declared legal in New York State in 1994, LLCs—legal business entities that provide a shield against potential liability as well as certain tax advantages—had become increasingly popular. By the 2010s, they had become de rigueur in the New York condo world, with close to 70 percent of buyers choosing to use one. For celebrities and public figures, LLCs served as a way to keep their names out of the press, since property deeds are publicly available through the city's Department of Finance website. Reporters trying to trace down the true owner of an expensive home would often find it was owned by a shell company with an address that led to a real estate law firm or wealth management firm. Some purchasers took a playful approach to the formation of their LLCs, selecting names like "Why The Face," "We Nailed-it," and "Who Needs Enemies."

But for some, LLCs offered more than the promise of anonymity. They also provided a potential vehicle for corruption, tax evasion, money laundering, and the concealment of assets or illicit gains, a way for bad actors to move money around the globe unchecked. In some cases, one LLC would lead to a string of further LLCs with addresses in international tax havens like the Cayman Islands or Guernsey, holding companies based in the British Virgin Isles, and Swiss bank accounts.

Some of those buyers had never set foot in the apartments they were buying. The real estate agent Vickey Barron said she had seen ultra-luxury apartments lying empty for years after purchase, completely unfurnished. In some cases, wealthy buyers on Billionaires' Row paid millions to well-known designers to furnish their homes and then never stayed there. "They spend all this time curating a space with beautiful pieces and then they never even sit on the sofa," she said.

For many of the buyers, their apartments were third, fourth, or even fifth residences. They were places they visited infrequently, or simply places to park cash. The buyer of the penthouse at 432 Park Avenue, the Saudi retail mogul Fawaz Al-Hokair, never set foot in the unit before or after the purchase, and even years after some of the buildings were completed, neighbors observed that the towers remained largely dark at night. No one appeared to be home. An analysis by *The New York Times* using Census Bureau data found that in a three-block stretch from East 56th Street to East 59th Street, between Fifth Avenue and Park Avenue, close to 60 percent of the apartments were vacant for at least ten months a year—and that included co-ops in the area better known for primary residences.

Those purchases had been a boon to developers like Barnett, who often didn't see it as their job to vet a prospective buyer's origins or the source of their wealth. He contended that it was a bank's job to meet so-called "know your customer" requirements and that developers were ill equipped to do that level of due diligence. If the money turned out to be dirty, Barnett reasoned, the apartment would always be there for authorities to grab.

"The good thing about having these people investing in real estate is that the Department of Justice now has something they can sell and probably get hundreds of millions of dollars out of," he told *The Real Deal* in 2016. "If that was art or jewelry, it would be long gone. It would be out of the country. This way, they can get the goods."

Still, the Aluko ordeal showed how quickly one shadowy figure could start to tarnish a building's reputation. While the foreclosure of his unit in 2017 had nothing fundamentally to do with the quality of the real estate, most luxury agents agreed that it cast a shadow over the tower. For all the downsides of life in buildings run as cooperatives—a system in which buyers acquire shares of the resident-controlled entity that owns the building's equivalent to their unit rather than, strictly speaking, the unit itself—the rigorous financial checks instituted by co-op boards often weeded out the financially unfit, thereby ensuring that mortgage defaults were an exceedingly rare occurrence. For the most part, this system, in place at many grand older buildings in the city, ensured that the owners didn't have to worry about living among supposed criminals and fugitives. The wealthy wanted to feel safe in their beds at night.

In contrast, the Billionaires' Row developers risked running afoul of fair housing laws if they turned away buyers for reasons of personal preference, though Steve Roth seemed to have toed that line as closely as was possible. In condos, once a building is sold out, the buyer of each individual unit can also decide when and to whom they wish to resell their apartment. New residents don't require any permission or sign-off from the condo board.

Although Aluko was one of the more high-profile cases, he wasn't the only buyer hiding in the shadows. Macklowe was dealing with shadowy buyers at his tower too.

That same year, a company linked to Ye Jianming, a Chinese oil entrepreneur with ties to China's military, spent roughly $83 million on a New York City property buying spree. His purchases included a $50.55 million penthouse at 15 Central Park West that had belonged to former Barclays chief executive Bob Diamond and an 86th-floor apartment at 432 Park that was purchased for almost $33 million. Ye was chairman of a Shanghai-based conglomerate called CEFC China Energy, which had recently struck a multibillion-dollar deal for shares of Russian energy giant Rosneft. He was connected with Washington power players and had donated to top universities in the United States. That December, before he could finalize a deal to buy yet another property, an $80 million Upper East Side townhouse owned by Vincent Viola, the billionaire owner of the National Hockey League's Florida Panthers, Ye disappeared. Some news outlets reported he had been detained by Chinese authorities.

In more recent years, Ye, who is reportedly still in Chinese custody, has drawn scrutiny for links to the family of President Joe Biden. According to *The Wall Street Journal,* Ye was in business around 2017 with then Vice President Biden's son Hunter Biden and brother James Biden, and the pair helped Ye get his daughter into an exclusive Manhattan private school.

The federal government was starting to take notice of these types of sales, thanks perhaps in large part to the 2015 *New York Times* "Towers of Secrecy" investigation, the same one that may have spooked Steve Roth into excluding Russian buyers from his tower.

In 2016, the U.S. Treasury Department announced a new initiative that would require title companies to identify the true buyers of luxury properties in New York and Miami that were purchased through shell companies. The new rules applied to cash purchases of $3 million and up in New York and were designed to try to prevent money laundering.

While the initial version of the initiative lacked teeth—it had enormous loopholes, including that it didn't apply to wire transfers or to anonymous trusts—developers worried that it could deter buyers, such as celebrities or overseas billionaires, who felt strongly about keeping their transactions out of the public record. While their names would not be available to the general public, they would be reported to the Treasury Department, which could then theoretically share that information with foreign governments or other U.S. agencies. For foreign buyers looking to avoid scrutiny from their own country's tax or criminal authorities, that was a real drawback.

Agents with listings at One57 also worried that the Aluko foreclosure sale would close at a massive discount to what the Nigerian had paid, dragging down values in the tower. Those fears proved well founded.

That November, with Aluko still reportedly on the run—he and the *Galactica* were reportedly last seen at that point in the Bahamas, during the rapper Ja Rule's botched Fyre Festival that spring—the 79th-floor unit was purchased by David Lowy, whose father Frank Lowy had founded retail giant Westfield Corporation, and who already owned a unit on a lower floor of the building. He spent just $36.66 million, representing a 28 percent decrease compared to what Aluko had paid three years earlier.

Worse still for Barnett, it wasn't the only foreclosure at the building. Roughly twenty floors below, another One57 owner was also under pressure from lenders.

The *New York Post* reported that the 56th-floor unit, purchased in 2015 for $21.39 million, was owned by Sheri Izadpanah, an international businesswoman who headed a lifestyle concierge business in Dubai that provided personalized travel experiences, special event access, personal shopping, and styling services to high-net-worth individuals. (She denied owning any property in New York.) In a bid to sell the unit prior to foreclosure, the owner had listed it on the market for well over a year, dropping the price from $26 million to just $19.99 million. The unit was eventually seized at auction by the lender, a Canadian entity linked to Maurice Benisti's Point Zero Capital.

"It's like getting an awful stain on a gorgeous wedding dress," the real estate agent Tyler Whitman told *The Real Deal* in 2017. "Foreclosures happen—people fall on hard times and things go south. But for it to happen in a building like this is surprising. It's become abundantly clear that One57 did not turn out to be the investment everyone wanted it to be."

THE DEVELOPER STEVE Witkoff was similarly experiencing the

downside of doing deals with foreign investors who didn't turn out to be all that they claimed.

In January 2016, Witkoff had temporarily halted plans to tear down the Helmsley Park Lane Hotel on Central Park South, where he and Harry Macklowe had planned a new Billionaires' Row megatower. They had dubbed the project, which was supposed to top out at more than 1,200 feet, 1 Park Lane. At the time, Witkoff cited a lack of short-term confidence in the market. Instead, he said, he would hold on to the property as a hotel and reassess the project once the outlook improved. "The fact of the matter is, the velocity is not what it was," he told *Bloomberg*.

He wasn't the only one pulling the plug on plans to bring new condos to the area around Billionaires' Row. That same year, Joseph Chetrit abandoned his plans to convert the former Sony building into apartments, selling it instead for $1.4 billion to Olayan America, a division of Saudi conglomerate Olayan Group.

A year later, however, the outlook was even bleaker for Steve Witkoff. In fact, it looked as though the Park Lane project might be sold out from under him. His equity partner, the Malaysian financier Jho Low, whose party-boy habits had become tabloid fodder, appeared to be a fraud.

Just months after the developer announced that he would delay the project, the U.S. Department of Justice moved to seize Low's assets, including his Time Warner Center penthouse and his Los Angeles megamansion, as part of a massive civil forfeiture action. He was accused, along with others in the circle of people close to

Malaysia's prime minister, Najib Razak, of participating in a scheme to siphon off more than $3 billion from Malaysia's sovereign wealth fund—an economic development fund known as 1MDB that was supposed to invest for the benefit of the Malaysian people—for personal gain. According to authorities, the money Low had stashed in art and global real estate—and blown on champagne and parties—was dirty.

The money trail for 1MDB stretched from Malaysia to Abu Dhabi to the British Virgin Islands. One of its primary destinations: real estate on New York's Billionaires' Row.

Also cited in the Department of Justice's complaint was none other than Khadem al-Qubaisi, the Middle Eastern financier who had bankrolled One57, bought the record-breaking penthouse at Stern's Walker Tower, and offered to buy a stake in the Steinway project years earlier. Allegedly a key figure in helping to perpetrate the fraud, he was arrested by Abu Dhabi authorities. (Both Low and al-Qubaisi have long denied the allegations against them, although other figures implicated in the 1MDB scandal, including Goldman Sachs and the former prime minister of Malaysia, have paid large fines and served prison time.)

For Witkoff, a Bronx-born former real estate attorney who had climbed the ranks to compete with some of his best developer clients, the aborted Park Lane deal put him and his partners in an uncomfortable spotlight. Had they known that they were dealing with an alleged kleptocrat? And if not, why not?

With allegations of money laundering and kleptocracy hanging over Low, the Park Lane project had been essentially frozen. Now, three years after acquiring it, Witkoff and his partners were being forced by the DOJ to put the building on the market. "We woke up and were faced with these circumstances that we couldn't imagine would ever happen," Witkoff told *The Real Deal* in 2017.

The developer claimed total ignorance of the true source of Low's vast wealth. On paper, Low had looked like the perfect blue-chip partner, he said. He had attended Harrow, the elite British boarding school whose alumni included prime ministers and Nobel

Prize winners, and the prestigious Wharton School of Business in Pennsylvania. He had done business with major corporations like Blackstone and had a close relationship with Goldman Sachs, which had handled a bond offering on behalf of 1MDB. He came with references from prominent global leaders. Witkoff had also completed his own usual due diligence, checking on those references and running a background check. As far as he knew, the lenders on the project had run all the usual "know your customer" checks.

In 2013, as they finalized a deal for an acquisition loan, one of Witkoff's top executives had emailed Low about his source of capital. "We are getting down to the end with the lender, they are asking for specifics on where the money on your side of the deal is coming from given it is international money," the email said.

Low quickly responded: "Low Family Capital built from our Grandparents, down to the third generation now."

The Witkoff principal replied: "Ok, thanks Jho, just didn't know if there were any other minority investors on your side, I will let the bank know."

That was it.

The investigations didn't touch Gary Barnett. While al-Qubaisi had made the deal for the International Petroleum Investment Company (IPIC) and his Dubai-based real estate company Tasameem to invest in One57, that arrangement predated the alleged 1MDB scheme.

For Barnett, the Park Lane condo project would have been heady competition. Now, observing the calamity unfolding at Witkoff's project, he felt relief that he wasn't in the crosshairs. Before Low had signed on to bankroll Witkoff's project, he had talked to Barnett about co-developing the Helmsley Park Lane, too. At the time, Barnett had suspected that Witkoff had given the Malaysian playboy a better deal. Now he thanked God that he wasn't involved in that mess.

The ordeal showed that allegations of money laundering weren't confined to the purchases of individual apartments and exposed how easily illicit funds could find their way into the back end of

U.S. real estate projects. While Low had been hiding in relatively plain sight, it was obviously possible for bad actors from across the globe to cloak their investments in trusts and limited liability companies for the purpose of hiding ill-gotten gains among the already complex financial stacks behind major New York City developments.

In many ways, the commercial side of the real estate business was the perfect place to hide cash undetected, because of a general lack of oversight. Real estate developers, under no legal obligation to deeply vet their partners, largely left it up to the banks, which in turn typically didn't apply heavy scrutiny to transactions. Unlike deals for individual condominiums, there were also no publicly available records of these back-end deals, and with developers turning to foreign funding sources in higher numbers than ever amid a drought in construction lending, the problems seemed poised to grow. That Low and al-Qubaisi both had dealings with several of the developers on Billionaires' Row shows just how attractive a proposition the towers may have been for them.

When they did manage to consummate transactions, they left a mess behind.

The penthouse at Stern's Walker Tower, purchased by al-Qubaisi for a record-breaking $50.9 million in 2015, was ultimately sold in 2020 by the Justice Department for a comparatively paltry $18.25 million to Ron Vinder, a private wealth manager at Morgan Stanley.

The deal sparked a war between the government and the building's condo board, which was outraged by the agency's decision to let the unit go for what they considered a song. Naturally, other owners at the building worried that it could drag down their values and damage the building's reputation.

"The contract price can only be described as steeply distressed and unrealistic and one which could adversely affect the market value of other homes at Walker Tower," the board's attorney, David Berkey, told *The Wall Street Journal*.

In 2019, al-Qubaisi was convicted in Abu Dhabi criminal court on financial crimes charges and sentenced to fifteen years in prison.

Low's stake in the Park Lane project was eventually sold to Mubadala, the Abu Dhabi sovereign wealth fund, after Low, now a fugitive rumored to be living in China, agreed to drop his claims to the property in the U.S. forfeiture lawsuit. Witkoff and Macklowe got to keep their stake, but by 2022 they still hadn't made moves to redevelop it.

Macklowe said he resented the whole situation.

"I wanted to build another significant building, and because of the scandal, I couldn't."

CHAPTER 19

The Music Stops

R yan Serhant was naked.

Standing at a bank of floor-to-ceiling windows and facing outward toward the city, the shameless real estate broker pressed his palms against the glass and popped his butt toward the camera. He was baring his sculpted body for the edgy fashion and culture magazine *Flaunt,* which was doing a piece on the brokers from Serhant's television show *Million Dollar Listing New York.*

The furnished apartment featured in the shoot was located on the corner of the 39th floor at One57 and came complete with a shiny grand piano, leather wall panels, and a recessed bar. The original purchaser was trying to resell the unit for $10.5 million, and Serhant was the broker. He had said yes to stripping on a whim, hoping that the stunt might draw more eyeballs to the property, which had been on and off the glutted market for close to three years without an acceptable offer. "You couldn't resell anything unless you were drastically cutting prices," Serhant recalled of 2016. Desperate times called for brazen marketing techniques.

The foreclosures were just the latest blow for One57, which had been quickly overshadowed by the new towers on Billionaires' Row. Too much glitz had come onto the market at the same time, and the boom was dragging down values across Manhattan, but nowhere so much as at Barnett's tower. Buyers who had bought in early were seeing their values quickly plummet. The mighty had fallen.

Greg Young, a Connecticut philanthropist who had made his fortune as a commodities trader at Glencore, and who had bought a $31.67 million apartment at One57 in 2014 through the oddly, and somewhat ironically, named limited liability company Escape from New York, resold for just $23.5 million after numerous price cuts, a nearly 26 percent loss in just a couple of years.

When Frank Lowy sold his lower-floor unit following his purchase of the disgraced Nigerian tycoon Kola Aluko's higher-floor apartment, he took a 32 percent loss on the roughly $28 million he had paid.

Making matters worse, Barnett decided to finally sell a batch of thirty-eight units he had held on to initially as luxury rentals. Releasing them to the market at a time when velocity was slowing made his situation look all the more challenging.

Nikki Field, the agent who had thrived at One57 years earlier, told her clients not to sell their units at the building, hoping that the market for the tower would eventually return. "You're not selling until I tell you to," she recalled telling her clients. "We didn't get you in here to lose money."

If One57 had helped establish Billionaires' Row as a new asset class or investment vehicle for the super-rich, that asset class had turned out to be less liquid than some buyers might have hoped. It wasn't just One57. Luxury sales had slowed across Manhattan. Brokers across the city complained of a massive disconnect between what sellers thought they could get for their properties and what the market could actually command. Sellers, still mentally stuck in the market of two years prior, didn't want to accept that they had overpaid for properties and now could be forced to sell for a loss. But like it or not, they were chasing the market down.

At Harry Macklowe's 432 Park Avenue, the pace of sales had also slowed significantly. After selling more than fifty of the tower's roughly 120 units in the first two years, sales had slowed to a trickle: just six in 2014, fifteen in 2015, and eighteen in 2016, records show. In early 2014, the team had abandoned the idea of selling the units in-house and brought in the Douglas Elliman brokerage firm to help bolster sales, an indication that velocity was slowing.

Even Steve Roth's investors would have been forgiven for getting nervous. While Vornado had already contracted to sell the majority of units at the limestone-clad 220 Central Park South, still considered the premier property of the bunch, there was always the possibility that if the market fell far enough, buyers might walk away from their hefty 15–20 percent deposits. While a deposit on an apartment at such a high-end project could run to the millions of dollars, New York buyers had shown during the financial crisis that they were willing to turn their backs on that money should the market dip below those levels.

As deals at One57 started coming in at more significant discounts, John Kim, an analyst for the Bank of Montreal, which had provided some of the debt for 220 Central Park South, broached the subject with Vornado's investor relations team, who sought to reassure him that sales at their building were still going strong. None of the buyers seemed to be getting cold feet about the contracts they had signed.

In these dicey times, Steve Roth's one-man condo board approach—sizing up buyers to make sure they were a fit for the building—would serve them well. The multimillionaires and billionaires he had allowed into the building were specially vetted and had pockets so deep they were unlikely to walk away from their contracts even in the worst economic times, the investor relations team told him. Many of them had built up so much wealth that even a significant plunge in the stock market was unlikely to be a major concern for them.

But it was hard to shake the sense that the market had entered a significant slowdown, and one that extended beyond the condo market and affected everything from townhouses to storied, classic co-ops. Stories of money-losing deals began to crop up with frequency in the real estate press. U.S. Commerce Secretary Wilbur Ross sold his four-bedroom Midtown Manhattan penthouse for $15.95 million, down from the $18 million he paid for it in 2007. Rolling Stones legend Keith Richards sold his Greenwich Village penthouse for $9 million, a discount from the $10.5 million he paid four years earlier. Mary Solomon, the wife of then new Goldman Sachs chief executive David Solomon, scooped up an apartment at the storied El Dorado prewar co-op on Central Park West for $9.9 million; the sellers had paid $12.75 million in 2015 to buy it from Bruce Willis.

A slew of factors contributed to the market correction, though one felt more physically palpable than the others: To any New Yorker trying to get around by car and getting stuck in heavy traffic thanks to closed lanes and giant supply trucks taking up the road, it was clear that the city was in the midst of a construction frenzy. "You looked out over the skyline and you could see construction cranes everywhere. It was visceral," the appraiser Jonathan Miller said. "The physical appearance of cranes across the skyline did as much to slow down the market as anything else."

Developers emboldened by the early success of projects like One57 and 432 Park sought to replicate them in other areas of Manhattan, building ultra-luxury supertalls that would rival Billionaires' Row in terms of prices. High-rise condos were going up in the Financial District, at the southern tip of Manhattan, on the Upper West Side, and in NoMad, the moniker given by real estate insiders to the area just north of Madison Square Park. Clusters of new buildings had also appeared around the High Line, the new elevated park in Chelsea built on the site of a defunct rail line, and Hudson Yards, the Related Companies' massive new city-within-a-city development on Manhattan's Far West Side. Much of the inventory in these new towers was priced well beyond what had historically been achieved in these neighborhoods.

A study by Jonathan Miller showed that roughly 14,500 units had hit the market or were being prepared for market between

2015 and 2017, far outpacing the natural rate of absorption and close to twice the number that had come online in the years following the financial crisis. He estimated that it would take more than half a decade to sell the wave of inventory that had debuted.

Still, so confident were some developers that they could sell for big ticket prices that they had paid enormously high sums for land, betting that the prices would make up for it on the other end. As a result, the average price of land south of 96th Street nearly doubled between 2011 and 2015, to almost $600 a foot. In some cases, developers paid as much as $800 a foot for the best-located sites.

AS BILLIONAIRES' ROW sales garnered headlines around the world, the aspirational pricing phenomenon seemed to take on a life of its own, spreading to other luxury markets like Los Angeles and South Florida. Owners of high-end homes across the country looked to cash in on the trends they were reading about in the press, and each seller seemingly wanted an even higher sum than the last. By 2016, the national pricing arms race had truly begun.

In Florida, too, sellers were reaching for equally earth-shattering sums. A mansion in Hillsboro Beach, modeled after the Palace of Versailles, was listed for an eye-watering $159 million, and Netscape co-founder Jim Clark was listing his sprawling Palm Beach estate, known as Il Palmetto, for $137 million.

But Florida had nothing on California. In Los Angeles, a flurry of major properties came on the market for head-scratching sums. The Playboy Mansion, the sprawling Los Angeles estate where Hugh Hefner reigned supreme for decades, went on the market for $200 million. It was followed quickly thereafter by a Beverly Hills estate once owned by William Randolph Hearst and featured in the movie *The Godfather,* which was listed by its owner, the financially embattled attorney Leonard Ross, for $195 million. The British Formula 1 heiress Petra Ecclestone listed Spelling Manor, a roughly 56,500-square-foot Holmby Hills estate built by the late television producer Aaron Spelling, for $200 million.

The QVC handbag entrepreneur Bruce Makowsky put a $250 million price tag on an investment property he was building in Bel Air, which he named simply Billionaire. His fellow spec home developer Nile Niami told the world that he would ask $500 million, the biggest price tag for a single-family home in American history, for an under-construction home he was building on a hilltop nearby. It would have jellyfish tanks, a moat, and a Monaco-style casino, he said.

Some of the listings seemed destined, or at least designed, to command nine-figure prices. Spelling Manor, for instance, was one of the largest homes in the world, larger than the White House, and was built in French château style with a bowling alley, a wine cellar, a beauty salon, and tanning rooms. After paying $85 million for the property in 2011, Ecclestone had hired a team of roughly five hundred workers to complete a massive renovation in just a few months.

But the upswing in big-ticket prices emboldened sellers of lesser properties, too, and some began attaching equally stratospheric numbers to their homes. Everyone thought their property was just as special as the one they read about in the paper, and in order to secure listings, brokers would sometimes agree to list properties far in excess of their true value. If nothing else, brokers found that listing a property at an eye-popping sum was a way to garner exposure for the listing or even to boost their own profile as a luxury agent. They could always slash the price later, or so they thought.

New strategies arose to justify sky-high prices. Gimmicky add-ons were included in a property's asking price to help sweeten the deal. Homes came with a "free" Lamborghini or Rolls-Royce, a yacht with docking fees, season tickets to sports events, private chefs and butlers for the first year, and allowances for renovations. One New York broker offered the buyer two seats on a future flight to space—once such a thing became available. Makowsky's "Billionaire" house even came with a complimentary helicopter—an odd choice given that it was illegal to fly one in the area. Makowsky said he reckoned that if you could afford the house, you could afford the fine.

The penchant for overpricing quickly trickled down to other parts of the market. Suddenly a seller with a $5 million house wanted $8 million for it, and one with a $10 million house wanted $17 million. Real estate pricing, typically based on the study of comparable sales and market velocity, was never an exact science to begin with. Now, across the country, the playbook had been ripped up and was being replaced with a model that more closely resembled the art market, where pricing was more arbitrary and untethered to the intrinsic value of an asset.

To read the papers, one would have been forgiven for thinking the market was on fire. But the frenzy belied the true state of the market, which, at least in New York, was beginning to wane. A pileup of luxury homes was forming.

On Billionaires' Row, brokers justified the ultra-high prices by arguing that, compared to prices for high-end real estate in other leading cities like Hong Kong, Paris, and London, New York was still a relative steal. The most expensive home ever sold in the world at that time was a penthouse at La Belle Époque, a luxury building on the French Riviera in Monte Carlo with views over the Port Hercules and the ancient palace. It had been sold by the Candy brothers, the developers behind London's One Hyde Park, in 2010 for about $308 million. (The penthouse had formerly been the home of the billionaire banker Edmond Safra, who had died there in an arson attack perpetrated by one of his nurses.) The real estate blogosphere speculated that the buyer was either an Arab sheikh or a Greek billionaire, but no one could be sure.

Even once Billionaires' Row began selling in earnest, its top sales were still being surpassed by other top properties around the world. And it wasn't the only place wealthy foreigners were stashing their cash. In 2015, the Château Louis XIV, a new-construction 57-acre estate near Paris inspired by classic palaces in the region and replete with traditional frescoes, gold-leafed fountains, and marble statues, sold for about $305 million, reportedly to an entity linked to Crown Prince Mohammed bin Salman, heir to the Saudi throne.

Later, an estate on the Peak, an upscale hilltop district in Hong

Kong, reportedly sold for $361 million to Yeung Kin-man, whose private company Biel Crystal Manufactory made the screens for two of every three iPhones sold in the world and who reportedly had plans to tear it down and build his own family home from scratch.

But if scarcity was the cornerstone of a hot luxury market, the new dynamics on Billionaires' Row didn't bode well. On the eastern edges of the corridor, for example, there was the Zeckendorf Brothers' project, known as 520 Park Avenue, which launched sales in 2015 to early success, as the Zeckendorfs won out over competitors to sign contracts with several household name buyers.

One buyer was Ken Moelis, the head of the boutique investment bank Moelis & Company, a Wall Street rainmaker who had advised on Hilton's $26 billion sale to Blackstone in 2007. Moelis paid $62 million for a penthouse at the Zeckendorfs' tower. Other buyers included Frank Fertitta, one of the brothers behind the creation of the martial arts company UFC, and the British vacuum cleaner mogul James Dyson. Fertitta spent $67.9 million for his apartment at the building, while Dyson forked out $73.8 million. These were the kind of buyers Macklowe, Barnett, Roth, and Stern were courting. Every buyer who signed on to the Zeckendorf building was a loss for them.

Less successful, but still contributing to the inventory glut, was 53 West 53rd Street, the sculptural high-rise condo designed by the star architect Jean Nouvel for a site next to the Museum of Modern Art. The building, developed by a partnership between development giant Hines, investment bank Goldman Sachs, and Pontiac Land Group, a deep-pocketed family-run real estate and hotel company out of Singapore, struggled with lackluster sales that stemmed at least in part from the design, which included a significant exoskeleton on the façade that cut through windows and interfered with the sweeping views from the apartments. The idiosyncratic design didn't seem to resonate with prospective buyers who were spoiled for choice amid the inventory surge.

Foreign buyers seemed to be hitting the pause button, too.

Tighter capital controls overseas had made it challenging for some to buy in the United States. As part of a broader push to curb capital outflow within the ranks of its political and business elite, the Chinese government under Xi Jinping was cracking down on its citizens making overseas investments—tightening restrictions that could curb capital outflows and making it much more difficult for them to move any significant sum of money to the United States for real estate purchases.

Edward Mermelstein, the Ukrainian-born attorney, said he had already begun to see his business from Russia drying up starting as early as 2014. The Obama administration had ratcheted up sanctions on Russia and Crimea over what it called "continuing provocations" in Ukraine, freezing the assets on Russian individuals and corporations identified as closely linked to Vladimir Putin's inner circle. It also announced new restrictions on Russia's import of U.S. goods linked to its military capabilities. Mermelstein said it felt like a throwback to the Reagan era, when Russia and the United States were battling for domination. "We started seeing people saying, 'What do we need America for?'" he said.

Now, under newly elected President Donald Trump, there was fresh uncertainty from foreign buyers. A drop-off in oil prices and a surge in U.S. anti-Muslim sentiment was now keeping buyers from the Middle East on the sidelines, too.

Still, even as the market took a dive, most developers clung to their trophy price tags—and many even raised them.

"It's like the 'greater fools' theory," said Jonathan Miller, the appraiser. "Prices were continuing to rise but sales activity was collapsing. In other words, they were running out of fools to send the market further up."

BY THE END of 2017, though, it was impossible to ignore the signs. The market was going from bad to worse for New York real estate developers.

That November, newly elected house Republicans unveiled details of a complete overhaul of the U.S. tax code, the biggest in more than three decades.

"We're going to get this done because we told the American people, 'This is what we're going to do if we get this majority,'" House Speaker Paul Ryan told assembled press on November 2. "And guess what, we're doing it."

On the face of it, the Republicans' bill seemed to be a gift for the 1 percent: it called for chopping the corporate tax rate from 35 to 20 percent, compressing individual income tax brackets and ultimately repealing the estate tax. But the bill also contained some provisions that could be a drag on demand for high-end New York homes. It provided that New Yorkers would no longer have the ability to deduct income taxes or interest on high-end mortgages, and it almost completely eliminated what was known as the SALT (state and local tax) deduction.

Previously, New Yorkers could write off their property taxes by deducting the lion's share of their state and local taxes from their federal tax bill. It was a way for them to avoid double taxation and, without it, they would be taxed on money they had already paid to the state.

Since New Yorkers already paid higher taxes than most other states, they would be among the most affected by the elimination of the deduction. Higher income New Yorkers in particular would see their taxes ratchet up significantly. Many in the real estate industry feared that might send them fleeing to lower tax states like Florida and Texas.

In a head-scratching moment that seemed to invert the normal political dynamic around taxation, New York's Democratic governor Andrew Cuomo responded aggressively to the proposal, underlining the repercussions it could have for his state. "New York will be destroyed if the deductibility of state and local taxes is included in any final plan that passes the House," he tweeted.

For Manhattan real estate developers, the SALT proposal added to a growing tide of political sentiment that they feared was chasing away buyers.

Earlier that year, Mayor Bill de Blasio, who had won a surprise victory in 2014 on the promise of a more progressive-minded administration, had proposed a new so-called Mansion Tax of 2.5 percent on homes that sold for $2.5 million or more, intended to help generate cash to build more affordable housing in the city. For the city's highest-priced homes, the proposed tax could amount to millions of dollars. New York's real estate industry trade organization, the Real Estate Board of New York, had lobbied hard against its introduction.

Developers feared the proposal could sink the market further and deter pied-à-terre buyers who had the option to buy anywhere in the world. They cautioned that the growing backlash against the wealthy would cause the 0.1 percent to leave the city, and consequently result in fewer tax dollars flowing into the city's coffers. They pointed to Canada's west coast city of Vancouver, where foreign purchases of homes had taken a nosedive after a property tax was instituted for foreign buyers in a bid to increase affordability for local Canadians.

The open-for-business image that the previous mayor—Michael Bloomberg, a billionaire many times over himself—had helped New York project to the world, and that had formed the basis for the construction of Billionaires' Row, was gone. In its place had been erected a big sign that seemed to read BILLIONAIRES NOT WELCOME.

ONE MAN EYEING the declining market warily was Gary Barnett.

For the past two years, he had worked diligently to assemble enough capital to pay for the construction of Central Park Tower, the most ambitious project of his career. With mounting headwinds in the market and lenders having all but completely withdrawn from financing condominiums, that meant getting creative.

The capital stack for the building was looking like a hodgepodge of money he had cobbled together from a variety of nontraditional sources.

First, there was the EB-5 money. Like a growing number of New York developers, Barnett had leveraged a cash-for-visas program set up by the government to allow foreign investors to plow money into U.S. investments in exchange for a green card. Barnett used the program to raise $190 million in debt for the building, asking investors, mostly in China, to put up to $500,000 apiece to build the tower in exchange for a green card. The project would be one of the most expensive ever financed by the federal immigration program, which was created by Congress in the 1990s but had more recently, in the wake of the financial crisis, become a massively popular source of cheap financing for U.S. real estate developers, who sometimes took advantage of loose regulations to make projects look as if they were in low-income neighborhoods. The program was originally conceived to help create jobs in underprivileged communities, but much of the money ended up flowing into apartment and hotel towers in Midtown Manhattan. The late commercial real estate broker Howard Michaels once referred to the fundraising vehicle as being a form of "legalized crack cocaine" for real estate developers.

Then there was the approximately $300 million in equity Barnett had secured from SMI USA, the U.S. subsidiary of a Chinese sovereign wealth fund of the Shanghai municipal government. Formerly known as Shanghai Chengtou, the enterprise was best known for managing major infrastructure projects like tunnel and bridge work and urban water plants in Asia but also controlled the major Chinese real estate firm Greenland Group and had served as one of the developers of Shanghai Tower, one of the tallest buildings in the world. Central Park Tower was one of a handful of projects SMI had agreed to bankroll in New York.

Combined with the $400 million Barnett had generated through the deal with Nordstrom for their planned New York flagship at the base of the tower, and the cash Extell would put in from its own coffers, Barnett had raised close to $1 billion for the project.

Now he was in the market for the final piece of the puzzle— a massive $1.1 billion in construction financing. He was one of a wave of developers competing for attention from the banks at a time when they were writing very few checks. Willing the market to catch up with his aspirations, he had already started construction without it. The building was going vertical without the money to finish it.

The pressure was on, especially since the SMI deal came with strings. If Barnett couldn't secure a construction loan by July 2017, SMI had negotiated what amounted to a get-out-of-jail-free card that could force Barnett to purchase back its equity stake for the full $300 million plus interest. Those were harsh conditions even in a troubled market.

For Barnett, the shift in the financial markets was frustrating because, as he saw it, the fundamentals underlying his project were still strong. It wasn't that there was no demand for high-end condominiums, it was that the rush in supply had led to a general incertitude in the market over pricing, which was making buyers hesitant to commit. He believed that that situation would quickly correct itself.

The loan he needed for Central Park Tower was also exceptionally low-leverage, located at a position in the capital stack that he said largely guaranteed its repayment in full. He was asking the banks to finance his project to the tune of around $2,000 a square foot while across the street Steve Roth was still selling units at roughly $8,000 to $9,000. In other words, he could sell units at a quarter of what Roth's were trading for and the banks would still be repaid.

As Barnett saw it, the sharp conservative turn the banks had taken was not warranted. Rather, it was a product of the fear of regulation. The banks didn't want trouble, whether it be illiquid equity partners or construction issues, or regulators calling on them to put up greater reserves if the market dipped further. The projects they were financing in this environment needed to be buttoned up nice and neatly and relatively risk-free.

The uncertainty over the Central Park Tower loan was getting to investors in Extell's Israeli bonds, which were secured against collateral that included a swath of Extell's overall portfolio, including Central Park Tower. Barnett was one of a growing number of U.S. real estate developers who had tapped the Israeli bond market for generalized financing in the wake of the recession, raising corporate-grade debt at a low rate they could never score back home. It was typically debt that was issued against a selection of a company's portfolio of buildings—in other words, Extell was borrowing against a large pool of assets—as opposed to one singular project. For a developer, it required navigating complex regulatory procedures and becoming a publicly traded entity on the Tel Aviv Stock Exchange, but the reward was significant. The Extell portfolio comprised a number of stable rental buildings with steady income; Central Park Tower was by far the riskiest proposition, and the investors were watching it closely.

As concerns grew in Israel about the state of the New York condo market, the yields on Extell's bonds catapulted to 16 percent, as Israeli investors demanded higher returns in exchange for putting their capital at risk with the company, effectively making them junk bonds. The Israelis were worried that the building wouldn't get built.

Barnett had flown to Tel Aviv to meet with bondholders, but his visit did little to assuage their concerns. "He just put more fuel to the fire," Shahar Keinan of Brosh Capital, an Israeli hedge fund that owned Extell bonds, told *The Real Deal*. "He didn't say, 'Everything is going to be okay, don't worry.' He said, 'There are risks, I can't guarantee anything.'"

Asked later whether he ever thought about mothballing the Central Park Tower project, Barnett demurred. "In this business, once you're vertical there are no second thoughts," he said.

But unless he could find the funding he needed to build, he wouldn't get far.

CHAPTER 20

"Gone to Zero"

By early 2017, the developers of 111 West 57th Street were also running short on cash.

With the costs of the project still escalating and investors refusing further capital calls, Michael Stern and Kevin Maloney had reached the point where the balance of the loans the partners had secured from Apollo and AIG for the Steinway site would no longer cover the remaining costs of the project's construction. Known in commercial real estate as falling "out of balance," the situation meant that the financial firms could refuse to advance further loan proceeds for the project until the developers put up more money to bridge the gap.

A suitor had stepped in to top up their coffers. Baupost Group, a Boston-based hedge fund headed by the billionaire distressed-debt investor Seth Klarman, was willing to put up $100 million in mezzanine debt to cover the cost overruns and get the loan back in balance.

Klarman was a legend in the debt world, with clients like Harvard University's endowment. He had profited handsomely from the acquisition of liabilities stemming from the collapse of companies like Lehman Brothers and Enron and was a major holder of

Puerto Rico's debt load. His offer to Stern and Maloney wasn't pretty—the loan would have a steep floating interest rate, one that moves up and down with the market, of around 17 percent in the first year—but with the real estate market faltering and the sentiment on Billionaires' Row beginning to shift, there weren't a lot of better options on the table.

There was just one problem, and it was a familiar one: Dick Bianco, the Connecticut investor who had initially bankrolled the project and who had grown tired of the partnership's repeated calls for more cash, had to okay the Baupost loan. He was refusing.

Bianco, still warring with the developers in court over his diminished stake in the project, believed he was being conned. How, he asked, could the partners possibly need even more money to finish the tower? He pointed in court records to the costs of the gleaming sales center and to a $25 million distribution the developers had made to equity partners from the proceeds of the AIG and Apollo loan in 2015. If they had not spent so much on the sales gallery or paid themselves that distribution so early in the process, they would still have the funds to finish the building, he argued. Bianco wasn't about to have his place in the capital stack subordinated yet again because of what he perceived as their rampant spending.

Bianco believed that the costs had ballooned to such an extent that he could exercise a so-called "put" option in his contract with the developers. This would allow him to force Stern and Maloney to buy out his stake in the project for 20 percent more than he had paid in the event that the project's overruns were at least 10 percent above the previously approved budget.

As Bianco saw it, if they wanted the loan approved so badly, Stern and Maloney could buy him out at a good price or find someone who could. At the time, Bianco believed the dynamics of the negotiations were in his favor. After all, if the ship went down, in the event of a foreclosure, they were all going down with it. Stern, Maloney, and the other partners would also be wiped out along with him. If it came to it, they would declare bankruptcy, force a public auction, and recoup their equity value that way. Bianco was also skeptical that Apollo would really move to foreclose. He suspected that it was all theatrics.

For Stern's part, the developer said he was cursing himself for having accepted Bianco's money so easily. Back in 2013, he'd barely thought twice. He knew exactly the source of the Greenwich investor's wealth, so provenance wasn't an issue, and Bianco had been referred through a solid, existing relationship. "We didn't understand that he was a litigious, scorched earth, bad faith partner," Stern said later.

Maloney, who had a better relationship with Bianco, spent nights on the phone with him, pacing the floor of his Upper West Side apartment until he felt the edges of his expensive oriental rugs were wearing thin. He called in back-up from the project's other investors, including the developer Arthur Becker and the race car driver Andy Ruhan, who met with Bianco on several occasions in a bid to change his mind and accept Klarman's offer.

As the weeks wore on, the deal team at Apollo attached to the Steinway project was getting impatient. Word reached the partners that the lender was quietly shopping a piece of its mezzanine loan to another lender, an early sign that it was really moving to foreclose. If the bank did foreclose, it would wipe out all their collective equity in the deal, leaving them all with nothing.

"Are you out of your mind?" Maloney said he asked Bianco one night in the spring of 2017. "Don't let this happen. You're making a huge error." Maloney tried to convince Bianco that this wasn't theater. Apollo had given the partners months to figure out a way to put the loan back in balance on their own, but the lender could hold out for only so long. They had Apollo's investment committee and their own investors to answer to. At some point, they wouldn't hesitate to wipe out everyone above them in the stack.

Why, Maloney asked Bianco, would anyone give up a stake in an asset that could still be completed and sold for a profit, albeit a lesser one than originally set out, in favor of a long, painful litigation that had limited hope of success?

Still, he struck out. Some of the partners later said that they thought Bianco was just hoping for a big payout in exchange for his cooperation, and they weren't willing to comply.

Becker again tried to act as a mediator between Bianco and the partners. But as the clock ticked down, he felt increasingly agog that the unthinkable was about to happen. He, Ruhan, and the Russian partners to whom they had promised the proceeds of their investments would lose all the money they had put up for the tower.

"We were losing sleep for six months," Becker would say later. Negotiating with Bianco was like banging your head against a wall, he said. "At first, you think logic will work. When it doesn't, you get this weird feeling that you're dealing with either irresponsibility, intentional dereliction of duty, or some other thing that's hard to conceptualize. Maybe it's just stupidity. You can't fix stupid."

Becker theorized that it was the same defiant qualities that had made Bianco successful in his case against the federal government that were blinding him now. Any other reasonable person litigating against the government would have backed down years earlier, but in that case, Bianco had prevailed against an opponent with endless resources to defend itself. Maybe, Becker wondered, Bianco figured that if he just bore down hard and refused to budge, he would prevail once again, forcing Stern and Maloney to let him exercise his put option in order to right the ship.

Finally, in the late spring, Becker sat down with Dick Bianco at the offices of Bianco's legal team in Midtown. "Dick, if you bankrupt us, I'm going to be forced to sue you," Becker said he told him. Bianco rose from the table. "Are you threatening my family?" he asked Becker in a tone that reminded Becker of an Italian mafioso.

"I'm not threatening your family," Becker replied. "I'm just saying that, as a responsible party, I'm going to have to litigate if you make this decision."

Bianco stormed out of the conference room. Then, seemingly remembering that it was his own lawyer's conference room, he sheepishly returned and asked Becker to leave, Becker recalled.

Soon, it was too late for any more negotiation.

That June, Apollo assigned a $25 million piece of junior mezzanine debt to Spruce Capital Partners, a privately held New York–based real estate investment firm. Spruce in turn quickly filed to foreclose on the equity partners, demanding immediate repayment of the loan.

In an unusual move, Spruce had filed for what's known as a "strict foreclosure," which would allow them to take control of the project provided that the borrower didn't submit an objection within twenty days of being given notice of the foreclosure. If Stern and Maloney didn't object, Spruce could take over the project overnight, with no public auction, wiping out the interests of the entire partnership, including Stern, Maloney, Bianco, Becker, Ruhan, and the Russians. It would either finish the development itself, or find a new developer to take over—and, seemingly, the original partners and their investors would be left with nothing.

But to Bianco's horror and bemusement, Stern and Maloney didn't object. He couldn't figure out why. It seemed like a decision completely at odds with their own self-interest.

However, in the weeks following their discussions, as Spruce finally filed to foreclose on the project, it suddenly all became crystal-clear to Bianco. A recent amendment to the intercreditor agreement between Spruce and the other lenders, made without Bianco's knowledge, allowed Spruce to completely dissolve the current ownership of the project and create a new special-purpose vehicle to finish it. The new structure would essentially cut AmBase out of the deal completely, dissolve its full $70 million equity stake, and form a new venture with Stern and Maloney to complete the building.

Stern and Maloney had been cornered but found a way to wriggle free. Industry insiders said that Stern's reputation as an accomplished builder likely played to his favor in staying aboard, since the project was especially complex from an engineering standpoint. While lenders were often willing to step in and complete simpler developments like condo conversions or renovations, finishing a project of this magnitude and complexity would require a builder with serious chops—chops that Spruce didn't have. Stern and Maloney also held all the contracts with insurers and subcontractors, all of which would be expensive to reassign. "No lender wanted to step into those shoes," said one of the investors. The new structure of the deal allowed Stern and Maloney to finish the project.

The strict foreclosure was something Bianco could never have seen coming. Extremely rare, strict foreclosures are typically reserved for situations where there is little or no equity value left in a deal. Many New York real estate attorneys have never seen one in their career.

If Bianco was playing chicken, Stern and Maloney had just called his bluff.

But the saga was just beginning.

DAYS LATER, BIANCO'S attorney, Stephen Meister, rushed downtown to Foley Square and scaled the stone steps of the New York County Courthouse, a hulking granite building near Brooklyn Bridge with a massive Corinthian colonnade that made it look like a temple. He was in urgent need of a restraining order.

One of the scrappiest, most successful attorneys on the New York real estate scene, Meister was known for stepping into hairy situations that required last ditch Hail Mary legal campaigns. He liked to think of himself as representing the Davids against the Goliaths of the real estate world and would sometimes argue conspiracy or sabotage in a bid to buy his clients more time in eleventh hour situations. A boxing robe signed by Muhammad Ali hung in his office, a gift from a grateful client after a particularly bruising court battle over the deregulation of a rental apartment complex in Tribeca.

One of his most novel arguments was crafted on behalf of Donald Trump in 2008, when he argued that the financial crisis was an act of God (a term usually reserved for a flood or a hurricane) and therefore should result in the voiding of loans he had received from Deutsche Bank.

Now, with the vehemence of a rabid dog, Meister was arguing that the contract his client AmBase had with the Steinway partners meant that the developers could not proceed with the strict foreclosure without Bianco's approval, and that by allowing AmBase's position to be annihilated, Stern and Maloney had breached their fiduciary obligations to their partner. Appearing before a judge that afternoon, he urged the court to block the strict foreclosure until the case could be properly adjudicated.

At first, in a whiplash-inducing series of rulings, a preliminary restraining order was granted. Then, just over a month later, it was lifted by a judge who sided with Spruce that it had the right to move ahead with its action and AmBase did not have the standing, since it was not the legal borrower, to object to the foreclosure. Bianco had indeed lost everything.

"I feel that maybe you will lose your money," the judge said of AmBase, according to the court transcript. "But guess what? That's part of the gamble that you made."

He didn't take it lying down. The attempted restraining order marked the beginning of an extensive litigation between AmBase, Stern, and Maloney that would stretch at least six years into the future, with multiple lawsuits, numerous amended complaints, racketeering allegations, appeals, and discovery requests and would expand to include both Spruce and Apollo as defendants. Eventually the claims were so many that a judge would compare an amended complaint relating to the dispute to a copy of *War and Peace*.

Bianco's firm, AmBase, argued that it was the victim of an elaborate and long-running fraudulent scheme aimed at depriving it of its $70 million investment in the project. It accused Stern and Maloney of providing fraudulent budgets to debt and equity investors, lying about cost overruns, and denying it access to the books.

By 2018, AmBase said, the costs had shot up past the original $640 million budget to well over $900 million and counting. AmBase accused Stern and Maloney of improperly siphoning off partnership money into their own pockets. Though they were entitled to payroll reimbursements as the project's sponsors, as construction managers, they paid themselves over $3 million in payroll before the construction management agreement even went into effect, AmBase alleged in court documents. Between June 2013 and July 2017, JDS and PMG collected over $10.8 million in payroll and reimbursements. By the time of the foreclosure, they had received all of the $6.4 million they were entitled to as a construction management fee and at least $8.85 million of the $9.85 million development fee, AmBase said.

Moreover, AmBase claimed that Apollo and Spruce were in cahoots with Stern and Maloney and that Spruce had bribed them not to object to their foreclosure with an offer to allow them back into the deal.

Stern and Maloney both denied the allegations, both in court documents and numerous interviews, and the courts dismissed many of the claims, ruling either that AmBase did not have the standing to bring them or that it had not conclusively proved its claims. Apollo prevailed in an early suit brought by AmBase, with a judge ruling that it had a contractual right to split off a piece of the loan and assign it elsewhere without providing notice to AmBase.

But Bianco kept coming back for more.

The deal struck between Apollo, Stern, and Maloney had also left Ruhan, Becker, and their partners out in the cold. Becker said he and Ruhan had begged Stern and Maloney to get back in the deal, but were not offered acceptable terms. He was tempted to join Bianco's lawsuit but didn't know how to deal with the guy. He would wait and see how Bianco fared before he launched his own expensive litigation.

Still, despite his annoyance at the turn of events, Becker understood why Stern and Maloney were being allowed back in. Swapping out vendors and contractors would mean a pricey and prolonged reengineering of the project. "The devil you know is better than the devil you don't," he said.

By 2017, Ruhan was also facing issues at home. In 2013, the

same year he had invested in Steinway, he had separated from his longtime wife, Tania Richardson-Ruhan. Now they were embroiled in a messy divorce battle and at odds over what Ruhan was actually worth. He claimed he was insolvent, had fallen victim to an unrelated fraud scheme, and was having to sleep on one of his yachts. Richardson-Ruhan's lawyer insisted that Ruhan was still "phenomenally" wealthy and concealing assets from his wife. During the trial, it emerged that Richardson-Ruhan had been questioned about a plot to murder Ruhan, which had been investigated by police. (She denied involvement in the alleged plot.)

As for David "Wavey Dave" Juracich, the investor who had originally propelled Stern's career when he began investing in the young developer's projects years earlier, he had managed to maintain an indirect stake in the Steinway project, despite the foreclosure. But with no sign of any proceeds in sight, he too was running low on funds. With the exception of his original investment in Walker Tower, almost none of the handful of projects he had gone in on with Stern had been financially successful and their relationship had soured.

An exhibit related to a subsequent lawsuit revealed a 2016 text exchange between Juracich and a disgruntled pal who had invested in the project at his suggestion. In the exchange, Juracich admitted that he was facing financial ruin. The suggestion was that Stern had let down the very investors who had initially helped supercharge his career.

"I am on my knees financially," he wrote to his pal Warren Gilder, who had also invested in several Stern projects, by text that February. "Michael had stiffed me and not paid me money . . . I have nothing . . . everything on 57th st . . . and many other projects . . . has gone to zero."

CHAPTER 21

Knives Out

In March 2019, as New Yorkers made their way down Park Avenue, they would—if they looked up from their phones at the northwest corner of Park and East 56th Street—encounter a rather astonishing sight. Plastered on the façade of 432 Park Avenue and rising 42 feet into the air were a pair of giant portrait photos of Harry Macklowe and his new French wife, Patricia Landeau. In the black-and-white portraits, which looked liked stills from a Lynn Hirschberg screen test, a bespectacled Macklowe appeared to gaze at Patricia, who was beaming angelically at the camera, her flowing blond hair curling over her shoulders.

The portraits, taken by Studio Harcourt in Paris, framed the corners of the glass retail storefront owned by Macklowe and towered over pedestrians as they passed by the building. They were intended, Macklowe said, as a tribute to his new wife. He had asked her permission to go ahead with the bold declaration of love, and while, he said, she was wary of the public attention and annoyed by being dubbed a mistress in the tabloids, she allowed him to go ahead.

Not everyone saw it as a declaration of love so much as one of spite. REAL ESTATE MOGUL TAUNTS EX-WIFE WITH 42-FOOT-TALL

PHOTO OF NEW ONE read one *New York Times* headline about the stunt, insinuating that Macklowe was shoving his newfound happiness down his ex-wife Linda's throat. The *New York Post* dubbed it "The Height of Spite."

The characterization rankled Macklowe, who saw it as distinctly unsophisticated and, well, American. In France, where he and Patricia spent a significant amount of time, people had a more open and evolved way of looking at life and money, he insisted. His new wife had been married twice before and was best of friends with both of her exes. Why couldn't New Yorkers be a little more French?

Still, he loved the attention. "I was so proud of it," he said later of the portrait stunt, recounting how he and Patricia had stood on the corner that day, looking up at their own likenesses. "I said, I want to have my wife's and my picture up there every year."

When he and Patricia hosted their wedding reception at the former Williamsburgh Savings Bank later that month, guests who rode on the bus provided to transport them between the venue and the reception found a copy of the *New York Post* containing the picture of the building with its portraits of them on their seats.

Naturally, the *Post*'s Page Six gossip column reported on the wedding, too. According to their article, Patricia wore a pink and orange tweed Chanel dress that retailed for $8,150 with a calf-length fur coat, and carried a custom Edie Parker clutch that bore the initials of the newlyweds, HMP. Harry wore a Brioni suit with pink socks and a pink tie to match Patricia's ensemble.

The couple entertained two hundred people that night, including boldfaced names in the New York business world like Leon Black, Steve Cohen, Larry Silverstein, and even rival developer Steve Roth, the developer of 220 Central Park South. In a feat of self-promotion, the reception took place at Macklowe's own apartment at 432 Park, which had been transformed into a bright white candlelit ballroom for the occasion. Guests nibbled on baked potato topped with caviar from Paris's Caviar Kaspia.

The wedding marked the culmination of three years of bitter

fighting as Macklowe's divorce to Linda played out in the public eye—a battle that would reveal much about the financial roller coaster of developer Macklowe's prized tower that had played a role in inaugurating the race to develop Billionaires' Row.

THE JOKE WENT like this: A husband and wife still had a great sex life, he still sending her to the moon and back with his bedroom tricks after decades of marriage. But the thing was, they only ever got frisky in the dark. Then, one night, the wife, intrigued by her husband's latest move between the sheets, suddenly flipped on the bedside lamp, only to find that her husband was actually using a vibrator to pleasure her.

Furious at his deception, she told her husband to explain himself.

"Explain the kids!" he retorted.

This was one of Harry Macklowe's most memorable cracks during an impromptu comedy set he performed for journalists outside a Manhattan civil courtroom in the spring of 2017 as he and Linda duked it out in court over their marital assets.

In another of his rambling jokes, documented by the *New York Post,* a woman approaches a good-looking man lounging by the pool at the Fontainebleau Hotel in Miami. She tells him she hasn't seen him around there before. He's just gotten out of prison, he says. She asks what crime he committed.

"Well," he says, "I drowned my dog, I killed my wife, and then I set fire to our home where our children were sleeping."

"So," she responds, "you're not married?"

Ever the showman, Macklowe was putting on a performance—only now the venue wasn't a real estate pitch but rather his own divorce proceedings, whose eye-popping twists had caught the attention of the city's tabloid press. He told reporters outside the courtroom that his estranged wife never enjoyed his brand of humor—and that he had offered her a cool $1 billion to just walk away and allow him to be with his lover Patricia, whom he planned to marry. (Linda said she had received no such offer.)

Macklowe enjoyed being the center of attention. The impromptu courthouse steps routine would land Harry on the front page of the next morning's *New York Post* with the headline TAKE MY WIFE, PLEASE!

That summer, Macklowe had celebrated his birthday on a yacht off the coast of Sicily with Patricia, who presented him with a custom cake modeled after 432 Park that rose several feet into the air and was topped by a trio of heavy-duty sparklers.

The developer of 432 Park had quietly settled his other legal dispute a few months after it was filed—the one with his son, which involved control over their respective companies' online domain names. The terms were undisclosed. But his public head-to-head with Linda would only escalate that fall as the pair headed to court. And it was getting uglier and uglier.

"I found out that my wife was telling people, 'I want him dead, I want him dead,'" he said later. "She must have had a doll and was putting pins in it."

The couple's divorce proceedings would ultimately play out in a public trial that required seventeen days of testimony, spanning from September to December 2017, as Judge Laura Drager, the same judge who oversaw the divorce of former New York governor Eliot Spitzer and Silda Wall, determined how to fairly divide up their billions. She warned the couple that the proceedings were likely to be long and unpleasant, which turned out to be an understatement, but, dug in as they were, the case proceeded to trial.

The Macklowes' business and assets were complex, so coming to any agreement over how to split them was anything but straightforward. As such, a long line of real estate and art "experts" were paraded into the courtroom to weigh in on the value of many of the individual assets, many of whom presented conflicting valuations. In order to maximize their cut, each party argued that every asset awarded to the other was worth as much as possible, while each asset awarded to themselves was worth little.

One of the biggest, most contentious disputes between the parties involved *Le Nez* (*The Nose*), a sculpture by the artist Alberto Giacometti. In coming up with a valuation for the work, one art expert used as comparable auction sales two versions of a different sculpture by Giacometti sold in 1990 and 2010 and a sale of another version of *Le Nez* from 1992 with sale prices ranging from $25 million to less than $1 million. He pegged the piece's value at around $35 million.

Another estimated a much higher value, citing two auction sales in 2010 and 2013 of different sculptures by the artist that sold in the $50 million range and noting that there had been a recent surge of interest in Giacometti's work. She judged the sculpture's fair market value to be, conservatively, $65 million.

Ultimately, Judge Drager ordered that the piece, along with many of the other more hard-to-value items, be sold and the proceeds distributed equally between Harry and Linda.

Experts also differed on the value of the couple's impressive Plaza apartment, which was to be awarded to Linda. Linda's expert, the appraiser Jonathan Miller, argued that the unit's massive scale actually worked against it, since the apartment, for which they had paid about $60 million, was on a low floor of the building. He said that large luxury apartment buyers typically want to be on high floors. He noted that any prospective buyer of the apartment would likely incur significant renovation costs, since the apartment was designed specifically for the Macklowes' purposes, with enormous art walls and few bedrooms. He pegged the value of the apartment at about $55 million.

Harry's expert, Steven Schleider of Metropolitan Valuation Services, valued the apartment at almost double that figure, more than $107 million, which was more than the highest recorded sale in the city at that time. The judge ultimately valued it at $72 million.

Then there were their holdings at 432 Park. Linda filed a separate suit over the apartments they owned at the building, which were to be split into his and hers. She argued that a representative of Macklowe's company, acting on behalf of the sponsor, had improperly filed plans to reduce the scale of her unit by reconfiguring the floor to enlarge his own. She asked a judge to issue a restraining order stopping the developers from demolishing part of her apartment and to delay the closing until the matrimonial case was concluded and she could figure out how much money she really had. Ultimately, she chose to walk away from the unit at the close of the year.

Since neither Harry nor Linda wished to keep their house in East Hampton, the judge, valuing it at around $19 million, ordered that it be sold and the proceeds distributed between them fifty-fifty. Linda would keep the couple's books, valued at more than $850,000; the silver, valued at more than $400,000; and the jewelry, valued at $3.84 million. Harry got the cars, valued at $385,000, and, much to his delight, the award-winning yacht.

As the trial dragged on for months, with the legal bills piling up and the couple relegated to opposite ends of a long wooden table in a Tribeca courtroom, relations between the pair seemed even more hostile than ever. One reporter overheard Linda calling Harry an "asshole" as she walked by him on her way out of court. "Did the press hear that?" Harry responded, aghast.

For the purposes of the divorce, it was in Harry's best interests to plead poverty, thereby limiting Linda's potential haul. Somewhat ludicrously, Macklowe's lawyers pegged his personal net worth at *negative* $400 million as the result of deferred capital gains taxes from the sale of the General Motors Building in 2008. Linda's lawyers strove to counter that narrative, talking up the value of his real estate assets.

Throughout the proceedings, Harry also seemed determined to downplay any role his wife had had in his business life.

"Your wife testified that she helped you find architects. Is that true?" Peter Bronstein, his attorney, reportedly asked him in an exchange documented by *The Real Deal* magazine.

"I couldn't connect that at all," Harry said.

She perhaps had a role in entertaining clients, Bronstein posited.

"I searched my mind for that one, and I didn't have any recollection," Harry said.

Perhaps some role in coming up with design ideas?

"Husbands and wives talk, but as far as ideas, I don't know what that means."

Meanwhile, Linda told her lawyers she feared her husband would manage to cheat her out of her fair share of their assets.

"She has fears every day, every day she has fears," one of her attorneys, Adam Leitman Bailey, told a judge in the dispute over the 432 Park Avenue apartment. "She is in fear because he is so slick."

WHEN ASKED LATER, Harry Macklowe said he found the ugly divorce proceedings embarrassing, though it was hard to reconcile that with his earlier antics in the courtroom. He said he resented the Macklowe name being dragged through the muck.

But the proceedings had also cast an unwelcome spotlight on the true nature of his stake in 432 Park. While he was very much the face of the building, the divorce exposed that, thanks to his early financial issues, Harry had no equity in the residential portion of the tower. (He owned only a stake in the retail component, which he had purchased alongside Sheikh Hamad bin Jassim bin Jaber al-Thani, Qatar's former prime minister. The stake was attributed a value of $15.7 million.)

When Macklowe originally conceived of the project, he had projected making profits of about $400 million from the sale of the condominiums. While the divorce proceedings would include hours of fiery debate over what he actually made, everyone agreed on one thing: He made a heck of a lot less than that.

Harry did have a share of what's known in the real estate industry as the residential "promote," or a share of profits above a predetermined return threshold. When he had sold the site to the California private equity firm CIM in 2010, he had entered into a deal whereby he would receive payments from a CIM fund upon the future sales of the condos.

Harry's attorneys claimed that that agreement was amended in

2011 to allow CIM to bring outside equity into the deal, paving the way for a capital infusion by Citibank investors into the project the following year. They said that that $400 million deal had reduced CIM's equity to 39.41 percent. The amended agreement thereby limited Harry's potential earnings, since his promote would be calculated only from the payments that CIM received, not on 100 percent of the project. Those earnings had been further impacted by the flagging market, which had slowed the pace of sales significantly, his attorneys said.

Linda's attorneys, eager to drive up the value of Harry's promote, argued that it had never been diluted. They put into evidence filings that her husband had submitted to banks as recently as June 2016 in which he claimed that he anticipated distributions of roughly $428 million from the project. Harry claimed that those bank filings used old information from before the promote was diluted.

Ultimately, Judge Drager pegged the value of Harry's stake in the residential portion of 432 Park at the lowest possible estimate. After nearly a decade of work bringing the building to life, Harry's promote was valued by the judge at just $2.5 million. It may have been a humiliating sum, but it meant Harry Macklowe would be on the hook for less in his divorce.

Linda would later appeal that decision and lose.

MEANWHILE, AS 432 PARK finally approached completion in 2017—eleven years after he had bought the Drake Hotel, the site where the tower now stood—Harry had new headaches. As it came time to close on their deals and move into the building, some of the buyers were less than ecstatic about the condition of their apartments.

That January, a company controlled by Juan Beckmann Vida, a Mexican billionaire and majority owner of José Cuervo tequila, filed suit against the developers in a bid to get out of his 2013 contract to buy a $46.25 million unit on the building's 84th floor. Vida's company alleged that in November 2016, between the time of the contract signing and the scheduled closing, a "catastrophic" flooding event had occurred at the building, encompassing the tower's 83rd through 86th floors.

The suit alleged that the flood, which apparently resulted from a burst water pipe, heavily affected the unit, severely damaging multiple rooms, saturating multiple layers of insulation and sheet-rock, penetrating the walls and internal support beams and electrical wires, and infiltrating the marble and wood flooring throughout. Vida alleged that Macklowe and CIM had performed insufficient work to resolve the issues.

It wasn't the first issue with leaks in the Billionaires' Row super-talls. As developers pushed their buildings taller and taller and relied on new breakthroughs in engineering, they were encountering complicated technical challenges that they had never faced before.

In June 2015, a leak at One57 which originated from a "slosh tank," a mass damper that helped the building remain steady, resulted in thousands of gallons of water being released down the northwest side of the building and millions of dollars in damages to apartments on some of the highest floors of the tower.

Among those affected were Gary Fegel, a prominent art collector and the former head of the aluminum giant Glencore, the billionaire Cypriot shipping scion Polys Haji-Ioannou, and the hedge funder Mark Brodsky, according to a legal filing related to the incident.

But while Vida's company eventually closed on its 432 Park unit, albeit for the slightly lower sum of $44.6 million, it would soon become evident that the Mexican financier wasn't the only unhappy buyer.

Macklowe later acknowledged that there were major problems with leaks as closings commenced but claimed that the issues were typical of any new build. "There were tons of leaks. We probably had ten leaks from people building out their apartments, the workman leaving faucets on or toilets overflowing," he said. "It's the same in any new build. But you deal with it and we always repaired it right away."

Little did he know that those early complaints were only the beginning. The Park Avenue supertall had been promoted as the pinnacle of luxury, but it would eventually be dubbed in *New York* magazine a "Horrifying Hellhole."

CHAPTER 22

Casualties of War

Pam Liebman never wanted to go to war with her developer clients. It wasn't worth it. New York real estate was a small world. A client who crossed her today could be back tomorrow.

But in this case, she was willing to make an exception.

Her firm, the Corcoran Group, was the leading power player in Manhattan's new development space, having sold close to $40 billion in real estate through its Corcoran Sunshine new development arm, and she had helped craft the marketing strategies for Barnett's One57 and Roth's 220 Central Park South. More recently, Corcoran Sunshine had been leading sales at 111 West 57th Street, helping Michael Stern and Kevin Maloney come up with a rollout that could rival the splashy campaigns at neighboring Billionaires' Row towers. Now, however, in May 2018, with absolutely no warning, the Corcoran team had been unceremoniously kicked off the project by Michael Stern—and via a letter.

A notorious spitfire, the barely more than five-foot-tall blonde didn't suffer fools and was known to speak her mind freely. Suing a client was a bridge normally too far even for her, but the letter had her riled up.

"How could this happen? Why would he do that? He won't

pick up the phone," Liebman told Stern's partner Kevin Maloney by phone that day.

In the letter, Stern's JDS declared it was terminating the companies' exclusive marketing agreement because Corcoran hadn't hit a sales benchmark. Eighteen months had passed since sales launched and the building still wasn't even 25 percent sold. In fact, just four of a total of sixty units were in contract. A provision had been included in the contract that if a quarter of the units hadn't been sold within eighteen months of the launch, the developers could terminate the agreement early.

While Liebman couldn't argue with the numbers or the contract, she took issue with the blame. To the veteran broker, it seemed the developers couldn't have done more to sabotage their chances at sales if they tried. The infighting and protracted litigation between the partners and their lenders, not to mention the construction stops and starts, had generated horrible publicity for the building and led to uncertainty in the buyer community over whether the tower would ever actually be finished. Liebman had told Stern and Maloney in no uncertain terms that the claims and resulting press were hurting their chances with buyers.

Then, of course, there was Maloney's infamous interview with *Bloomberg* in March 2016, in which he had declared that the developers were delaying sales at the building for about a year in light of the declining market. As Liebman had indicated to the developers at the time, those remarks had left Corcoran in an untenable position, sending an unequivocal message to the market that the building was not open for business, even as its sales agents were still expected to meet the same sales targets.

To Liebman, it was beyond the pale. She decided to take action, throwing out her usual playbook and filing suit against the developers, adding to the mounting pile of litigation plaguing Stern and Maloney.

By now the Steinway project was in dire straits. All of the towers on Billionaires' Row had experienced degrees of financial tumult, most often their early stages as the developers courted financiers—

and a degree of financial uncertainty is par for the course in the real estate development world—but in comparison with the competing towers by Barnett, Macklowe, and Roth, Stern and Maloney's project was beginning to look like a train wreck. Over the course of the last three years, since they obtained financing for the project, they had burned through close to a billion dollars and the construction was still nowhere close to completion. If Stern and Maloney were ever going to finish their tower, they needed yet more money.

The following spring, the developers received a $90 million equity injection from Madison Realty Capital, a Manhattan-based investment firm known for stepping in to finance struggling projects teetering on the brink of bankruptcy. A well-known name among the city's hard-money lenders, the company, led by a pair of former Wall Streeters, Josh Zegen and Brian Shatz, was notorious for its hardball tactics and had been ensnared in several previous high-profile foreclosure battles. In other words, they were equally prepared to throw you a life jacket or let you walk the plank, depending on the circumstances.

In the case of Steinway, Madison was giving the developers its cash in exchange for a preferred equity stake that guaranteed the company a minimum return on its money. As part of the deal, Stern and Maloney were handed back a little taste of the project's potential profits, but the terms were not favorable. According to legal filings that documented the deal, Madison would receive 100 percent of the funds available for distribution at the close of the project until it received its capital back, as well as a preferred return of 25 percent a year, or 30 percent in the event of a default. Only then, if there were funds left, would Stern and Maloney see a cent. It was a similar structure to the hope certificate that Macklowe had negotiated with CIM at 432 Park.

But it was more than getting paid back first. The deal would also give Madison major decision-making power. In other words, Stern would need Madison's sign-off to make any significant moves, including refinancing, taking on new debt, or materially changing the budget and business plan.

To everyone who asked, Stern would insist he was still in charge but everyone knew that Madison and lender Apollo were calling a lot of the shots.

As Stern lost his grip, a new meme to fit the occasion began circulating among his partners: Michael Stern had been photoshopped into a picture with Kate Winslet on the sinking *Titanic*.

The onetime boy wonder of the New York development scene, who had shocked observers with his first-class renovation of the Walker Tower, making it one of the city's premier buildings, was now hanging by a thread from the supertall tower that he had envisioned taking his career to even greater heights.

MEANWHILE, DOWN THE street, it seemed that Gary Barnett had pulled a rabbit from his hat yet again.

In January 2018, Barnett's firm, Extell, announced that it had finally secured the construction financing it needed to proceed with his new Central Park Tower. The record-breaking financing deal gave Barnett the $1.1 billion he needed to finish the building. The announcement marked the end of Barnett's closely watched financing odyssey and meant that, for better or worse, the tower would be built.

As the market for construction loans tightened, most borrowers had no choice but to look beyond traditional banks to private equity firms and hedge funds, which would provide financing at a stiffer price. Barnett was no exception.

The developer had found an unusual way to guarantee all the financing he needed. He had bifurcated the building into two pieces, keeping a few of the highest floors separate from the rest. A $900 million senior construction loan by a syndicate of banks led by J.P. Morgan would be secured against the lower portion of the building. It was a massive loan, but even so it would cover only about $1,800 a foot in construction costs.

The remainder, secured against the top floors, came in the form of a $235-million preferred equity loan from the London-based hedge fund BlueCrest Capital Management. As part of the deal, BlueCrest would have the right to turn its investment into a pair of penthouse apartments in the building if Barnett did not meet repayment deadlines.

It was a creative solution—it's unusual for a developer to segment off a portion of their building and finance it independently—but an expensive one. BlueCrest was charging 11 percent on its money over a four-year term, while the interest rate on the bank loan was just 4.5 percent.

BlueCrest, led by British billionaire Michael Platt, was a relative newcomer in New York real estate, but it had already acquired some baggage. The hedge fund had earlier backed Gamma Real Estate, a lender on a stalled high-rise condo tower at 3 Sutton Place that had filed to foreclose on a Norman Foster–designed supertall tower project near the United Nations a year prior. The principals of that developer, Bauhaus Group, found themselves on the hook for tens of millions of dollars because of personal guarantees they had signed on loans tied to the condo projects. BlueCrest's role in the deal was exposed after the developer sued the company and Gamma, accusing them of engaging in an aggressive "loan-to-own" scheme.

Platt's name was splashed across the Page Six gossip column the following year when he was caught on video bragging shamelessly to his taxicab driver about being "the highest-earning person in the world in finance." In the video, seemingly leaked by the cabdriver or another occupant of the car, the Geneva-based financier had encouraged the cabdriver to google his name, mentioning that he had been featured alongside hedge fund magnate Marc Lasry in the television show *Billions*. Platt would later play off the embarrassing exchange as a joke.

For Barnett, the record-breaking construction financing deal was a hard-won victory. The delays had exacted a cost in terms of both money and effort, including time spent persuading his Chinese partner, SMI, to waive financing deadlines. The project's sales director, Jason Karadus, had left the project after just six months, frustrated by the building's failure to launch. While the sales team had been quietly marketing units since late 2017, the building still had not formally launched its sales campaign and the units weren't being advertised or listed publicly online.

The delays had also cost him at least one investor. Edward Mermelstein, the Ukrainian-born attorney, said he had a client who agreed early on to invest $18 million in the project in return for a half-floor apartment in the building, but the deal was contingent on Barnett's securing construction financing within a certain time frame. When he failed to do so, Mermelstein's client backed out of his purchase and Extell wired his funds back. "We dragged out for as long as we could but ultimately the client didn't feel comfortable staying on the deal," Mermelstein said. "It was taking too long."

BY THE FALL of 2018, however, Barnett was ready to start selling in earnest. As he geared up to swing open the doors of the Central Park Tower sales office, he strolled through the space for a final look with his design team, inspecting the recently completed kitchens and bathrooms. It was a wash of pink onyx and glimmering marble, but there was something missing.

The sales office needed to be unique, he told the team. It needed something extra. With so much competition out there, Extell needed to show buyers something that they couldn't see at every other new tower in Manhattan.

Barnett started spitballing. The company was already offering a dark and light kitchen palette, much as it had at One57, but now he was pondering a bolder kitchen option. Something metallic, perhaps. Something with texture. Something with a wow factor. It needed to really blow their socks off.

A few weeks later, Barnett found his wow factor in the form of a new hammered silver cabinetry for the kitchens. It was a bold choice, but "divisive" might have been a more accurate term. The finish might best be described as resembling a dark chrome-colored aluminum foil that had been crumpled and hadn't been completely smoothed out. The sales team couldn't possibly put this in front of wealthy buyers with a straight face. Barnett had to be stopped.

At least one member of his sales team said they tried to talk him out of it, but to no avail. Barnett, who was known among the brokerage community for his divisive tastes—one person's glitzy is another's person's chintzy—would stick to his convictions. The battered-looking silvery metal kitchens would be the centerpiece of the sales office's model unit. A few people would love it. Most would loathe it.

Barnett believed his building would be the best in the history of New York City, and he assigned it the price tags to match those aspirations. Only a handful of New York apartments had ever sold for more than $60 million. Now Barnett was bringing at least twenty to market at that price point. The triplex penthouse would ultimately ask $250 million, a number that was positioned to break Ken Griffin's penthouse record. The average price per square foot would top $7,000. That number was roughly in line with the original prices at 220 Central Park South and 432 Park, but Barnett had a lot more units to sell than both of those buildings, and he was facing much stiffer competition.

Everything about Central Park Tower was over the top.

Prospective buyers visiting the sales office on West 57th Street were led into a dimly lit room with 14-foot ceilings where New York City landmarks were projected on the walls—Yankee Stadium, the Statue of Liberty, the Empire State Building. The implication was that Central Park Tower would join their ranks.

"Is there any place that has symbolized individual success and collective ambition as boldly as New York City?" boomed a voiceover, set against a soundtrack of Gershwin's *Rhapsody in Blue.* "Here, the motto is ever upward, excelsior! A proclamation to aim for the stars, to succeed in the land of opportunity. And these buildings are the springboards, the platforms, the symbols of that success."

Central Park Tower was the "definitive New York skyscraper," the voiceover declared. "Fifteen hundred and fifty feet of steel, ambition, and aspiration, anchored to forty thousand square feet of Manhattan schist, the incomparable bedrock of New York City. A shimmering beacon of class, optimism, and chutzpah."

To woo buyers, Barnett had packed the 1,550-foot tower with high-end amenities, including a three-level Central Park Club complete with a residents' lounge with billiards, screening and function rooms, a 15,000-square-foot outdoor terrace with a 60-foot outdoor swimming pool and cabanas, an outdoor children's playground, a wellness center with a 63-foot indoor swimming pool, a fitness center, a basketball court, a squash court, and a sauna and steam rooms. On the hundredth floor, there would be a massive ballroom overlooking the whole city. The amenities were stealing a page from the best hotels in the world, but they were exclusively for residents—including the ballroom, which could be reserved for parties thrown by the owners.

The indoor pool, modeled after the Roman pool at Hearst Castle in San Simeon, California, would be decked out in midnight blue and gold, with mosaic tiles and a mass of twinkling lights on the ceiling designed to make swimmers doing the backstroke feel as if they were looking up at the stars, while the residents' lounge was inspired by a prestigious members-only club at Skibo Castle in Scotland, a place where the wealthy could gather without fear of prying eyes.

In the lobby, there would be an enormous custom crystal chandelier by the French glassmaker Lalique, high-gloss woods, brass accents, and a waterfall wall designed to give residents a moment of decompression as they stepped into the building from the hectic city outside.

The celebrity wedding and event planner Colin Cowie, a polished and suave South African known for designing events for celebrities like Tom Cruise and Oprah Winfrey, was tapped to oversee the building's lifestyle components, including its 100th-floor private club, which would have a private restaurant and a cigar room, in addition to the ballroom. For the restaurant, he was working to design a seasonal Mediterranean-style menu with the celebrity chefs Alfred Portale, Laurent Tourondel, and Gabriel Kreuther.

Cowie, who liked to say that his job was to "activate" the residents' five senses, had seemingly thought of everything, even down to how the building would smell and sound.

One afternoon, he and a team from Extell met with a "nose," or perfume artist, who had them sample a variety of scents that could represent Central Park Tower. They were choosing a signature fragrance that would be emitted throughout the building's common spaces, as well as a soundtrack for the lobby and shared spaces. Each scent was hosted in a separate conference room; as they moved from room to room, the team would clear their noses by sniffing coffee grounds. Eventually the team decided on a scent that incorporated rich jasmine, cedar wood, resinous amber, and rare iris flower.

For the building's lobby and elevators, Cowie hired a "musical curator" to custom-design a soundtrack for the building. In the mornings, the music would be lively, then gradually transition to something moodier, even a little "sexy," in the evenings.

They hoped that the song and dance would be enough to draw buyers.

BY LATE 2018, Barnett had been marketing the project quietly in the brokerage community for close to a year—and he was looking to cast as wide a net as possible to catch buyers.

The previous fall, he had hosted a party at the sales center for the city's top agents. Those in attendance described the event as lavish, a throwback to the peak of the market, with hand-rolled cigarettes and classic cocktails.

His sales team had also developed an "ambassador" program whereby top agents from Asia, Europe, and the Middle East were approached to help market the units to their global clientele.

Central Park Tower was ready for its close-up—all that was missing, it seemed, were the buyers. They weren't showing up in their droves the way they had done at One57. The days of juggling appointments with billionaires seemed in the distant past. Despite their best efforts, the Central Park Tower sales office was relatively quiet.

The delays in financing and construction had cost Barnett dearly in terms of market momentum. By late 2018, co-op and condominium sales had fallen to their lowest level since the economy last bottomed out in 2009. A *Wall Street Journal* analysis showed that sales were down 12 percent from 2017 levels and 22.5 percent from peak sales levels in 2013, with the steepest dip in the market for luxury condominiums. The culprits: a massive oversupply of new condo inventory, continuing political upheaval, and a volatile stock market. Rising interest rates and an ongoing trade war between the United States and China had sparked concerns about global growth, prompting dramatic upward swings followed by sharp reversals in stock prices. In October, the month of the Central Park Tower launch, the S&P 500 fell 6.95 percent, coming close to its worst month since the financial crisis.

During the fourth quarter of that year, ten of fourteen sales above $25 million were closings at Steve Roth's 220 Central Park South and the Zeckendorf brothers' 520 Park Avenue, all of which were holdovers from contracts signed years prior. They were throwbacks to the glory days of the top of the market.

Barnett, though admittedly frustrated, said he felt no malice toward Roth, who seemed to be printing money across the street. "I wish them all the best. I'm happy that he did it. It's great for the market. It's good for him," he said, though his tone began to sound a little defeatist. "I'm just saying that we weren't selling and we felt that we had the best building in town."

CHAPTER 23

Not a Good Look

In January 2019, Steve Roth cemented his reputation as the victor on Billionaires' Row.

Nearly four years after signing a contract, hedge fund titan Ken Griffin had finally closed on his apartment at Roth's 220 Central Park South, setting a new record for the most expensive home ever sold in the United States at roughly $240 million.

While news of the deal had already leaked to the press in fits and starts over a few years—Griffin had signed on so early that it took years before the building was far enough along for his unit to close—the January 2019 closing made it official: There was a new benchmark for luxury home prices in New York, and it was more in line with numbers in Hong Kong and Monaco than anything that the New York market had commanded previously. Roth had somehow leapfrogged what would normally be decades of natural price progression and more than doubled the New York record with his tower.

The New York purchase was a particularly audacious play even for Griffin. Even in Manhattan, where obsessive real estate market tracking trumps most other popular pastimes, the transaction drew an inordinate amount of press interest. It called attention to the vastness of one man's wealth at a time when the very existence of billionaires was being called into question by political heavyweights like Elizabeth Warren and Bernie Sanders. Sanders, who threw his hat in the ring for the presidential nomination for the 2020 election just a few weeks later, was drawing attention for his Democratic Socialist viewpoints, lashing out at "greedy" billionaires and at the growing wealth inequality in the United States, which he argued was eroding the American middle class.

Asked in an interview with the investor David Rubenstein about the purchase a few months later, Griffin shrugged it off, chalking it up to his desire to perhaps make New York his primary home one day. "The apartment represents the possibility that this might be home for me," he said.

More than just on Griffin, though, the closing also cast a bright surgical-grade light on 220 Central Park South and on the luxury real estate market, landing the building on the front page of *The New York Times* that January. The news was picked up across the globe, and the deal quickly became a key talking point in a political debate over the city's tax rolls. Some legislators expressed disgust that in a city with such a high degree of income inequality, a financier could pay so much for a single apartment and then not even live there full-time.

The city's complex and dated tax system, which dictated that tax assessors value co-ops and condominiums using the same system they used for rental buildings, often meant that the city undervalued high-end apartments in prime Manhattan areas. At just $9.4 million, the assessed value of Griffin's apartment placed upon it by New York City tax collectors was much, much lower than its actual market value. With an effective tax rate of roughly 0.22 percent, the valuation resulted in an annual tax bill for Griffin of just $516,500. Also, since Griffin lived most of the time outside New York, he was not subject to city or state income taxes. "It's ridiculous that this kind of astronomical wealth can exist in our city and never reach the people that actually live here," tweeted New York state senator Brad Hoylman in response to the news.

In a city where the political forces were drifting to the left, the Griffin deal fueled anti-real-estate, anti-billionaire sentiment. "It was one of the triggers that led to the downfall of real estate, in very harsh terms, in the political zeitgeist in Albany," said the appraiser Jonathan Miller.

The dichotomy between the wealthiest on Billionaires' Row and the mere mortals living in their updraft had rarely seemed more acute. Less than a block from the rear entrance of 220 Central Park South, Billionaires' Row residents were locked in a legal battle with the city to prevent a homeless shelter from opening on the pricey strip. In 2018, the city's Department of Homeless Services had announced that it would be gut-renovating the former Park Savoy Hotel on West 58th Street and turning it into a long-term residential facility for roughly 150 homeless men.

Residents of the corridor quickly formed a 680-member coalition, which included people who owned property or lived close to the location of the proposed facility, and filed suit against the city to stop the shelter from opening. They argued that the city flouted laws and regulations in a rush to open the facility in a building that was not fit for the purpose and that it didn't make sense to locate a shelter in such an expensive location. They claimed the cost of the shelter came in at more than $48,000 per year per resident, approximately 33 percent higher than the citywide average. Lawyers for the coalition framed the decision to put the shelter there as political maneuvering by New York City mayor Bill de Blasio, who had made a point of saying that he intended to house shelters in the privileged parts of town as well as in other communities.

"The city's decision to open this shelter at this location at this excessive cost, in a dangerous building and on a truncated timeline, was predetermined to meet the Mayor's political objective of locating such facilities in particular neighborhoods, no matter how expensive or nonsensical," the lawsuit read.

Their pleas fell on deaf ears.

Indeed, the political framework under which New York real estate players were used to operating was undergoing a dramatic transformation, thanks in large part to a blue wave the previous year that gave Democrats control of the New York State Senate in early 2019. While New York had already been a blue-leaning state, with Democrats in the driver's seat in the New York State Assembly, the Republican Party had held onto a razor thin majority in the Senate, stymying more progressive legislation for more than a decade. The fall of that majority fundamentally altered the political fabric of the state, emboldening legislators and allowing them to push through more progressive policies. For only the second time since World War II, Democrats controlled all three branches of state government. The status quo had been upended.

The reset in Albany put the real estate industry, which historically enjoyed a powerful lobbying position in Albany thanks to its ability to deliver big-dollar political donations, on the back foot, as progressive lawmakers weighed policies that would favor tenants over landlords, placed new emphasis on taxing the super-rich, and sought to further leverage the real estate tax rolls to fund new infrastructure development across the state.

In Albany's corridors of power, legislators had historically danced a delicate tango with the real estate lobby, eager to accept their money in donations without seeming to be in their pockets. After all, tax revenue from New York City real estate made up a significant portion of the funds to support critical city services.

Now it seemed that real estate was a dirty word and real estate dollars were toxic in politics. A growing number of elected officials were swearing off contributions from real estate interests. One report compared real estate money to the tobacco money of the twenty-first century.

Old guard officials' proximity to those interests was coming under the microscope, thanks to a new generation of politicians. Perhaps the most high-profile example was the then up-and-coming democratic socialist Alexandria Ocasio-Cortez, then twenty-eight, who successfully primaried longtime representative Joseph Crowley, long seen as a potential successor to Nancy Pelosi as Democratic leader of the House, for a congressional seat in 2018.

Ocasio-Cortez lambasted and vilified the real estate industry during her campaign, while simultaneously pillorying Crowley for filling his coffers with its donations. "Luxury real estate developers have decimated NYC affordability and way of life," she tweeted. "The ONLY way we change course is by electing candidates who aren't funded by them. I'm proud to not accept a dime from developers."

The reckoning over real estate was amplified by a number of high-profile criminal convictions in Albany. State Assembly Speaker Sheldon Silver had been convicted on charges of extortion and money laundering related to schemes in which he obtained millions of dollars in exchange for using his position to benefit two real estate developers, and former Senate majority leader Dean Skelos had been found guilty on corruption charges after using his position to pressure a real estate developer to provide his son with lucrative contracts. New York City Mayor Bill de Blasio was also under scrutiny for accepting donations from real estate interests to his political nonprofit group, the Campaign for One New York, which became the subject of an inquiry by the Joint Commission on Public Ethics.

The fracture in the relationship between real estate and politics came into stark focus that January 2019 at the Real Estate Board of New York's 123rd annual gala, hosted at the New York Hilton in Midtown. The raucous event, affectionately dubbed "the Liar's Ball" for its attendees' tendency to exaggerate and puff up their portfolios and sales figures, typically brings together more than two thousand real estate industry professionals to compare notes on the market over cheap steaks and bad wine, pick up deals, and gossip about one another. The din of the crowd typically reaches such a decibel level that featured speakers are forced to shout in order to be heard, though they are often ignored entirely. Real estate developers, typically an aloof bunch, debase themselves to hover in line to speak with powerful politicians, including the likes of Governor Cuomo, Senator Chuck Schumer, and Mayor de Blasio.

That year however, they didn't have the opportunity. Both Cuomo and de Blasio were no-shows.

UPON ASSUMING POWER in early 2019, the Democrat-led Senate quickly got to work, closing a loophole that allowed real estate interests unlimited donations to candidates and zeroing in on rent regulation reform.

They also focused their attention squarely on Billionaires' Row—more specifically, on a proposed pied-à-terre tax, which would place an annual recurring tax on homeowners who kept a residence in New York but for whom the city did not serve as a primary residence. In other words, Ken Griffin and the many others who had bought up the pricey units from afar.

As legislators prepared to roll out a $175 billion budget that March, the tax was a point of fervent behind-the-scenes debate. "You can call this a pied-à-terre tax. . . . I like to call it an oligarch tax," said Hoylman that February, standing on the steps of New York's City Hall alongside the bill's co-sponsor, Assemblymember Deborah Glick, and several members of the New York City Council, making a last-minute push for the bill.

Long championed by Senator Hoylman, the pied-à-terre bill had been on the table since 2014, when it was put forward by the Fiscal Policy Institute, a nonprofit, as a way to combat unsustainably rising housing prices and economic inequity and raise tax revenue to support public services, like the city's crumbling subway system. It would affect fifteen hundred nonprimary residences in New York City valued at more than $5 million, starting with a 0.5 percent surcharge on any amount over $5 million and rising gradually to 4 percent for homes valued above $25 million. The Fiscal Policy Institute estimated that it would yield approximately $560 million in new revenue for the city. While popular among legislators—after all, overseas residents don't vote—it had previously lost momentum and floundered thanks in part to ruling Senate Republicans.

Now the Griffin deal had lent it some much needed momentum and, in light of the new Democratic majority, it had political viability. It was risen from the dead.

Taken aback by the propulsion of the bill, the New York real estate industry was unprepared for this resurrection. They had to organize fast. With units still to sell at 520 Park Avenue, and a handful of other luxury condo projects across the city, William Zeckendorf tackled the issue head-on. "While the resurgent progressive movement is railing against President Donald Trump's ill-advised border wall, in New York City it is also seeking to build a poorly conceived tax wall around a city whose credo is to welcome everyone," Zeckendorf wrote in an op-ed for *Crain's New York Business.*

Zeckendorf didn't stop there. His firm hired Patrick B. Jenkins, a top New York State strategist with close ties to Assembly Speaker Carl Heastie, to help lobby the leaders in Albany against the tax. Together, Zeckendorf and Jenkins, accompanied by an economist from the Real Estate Board of New York, reportedly roamed the halls of the capitol, bending the ears of lawmakers on the proposal. They presented their evidence that the tax would produce less revenue than predicted and be an unreliable source of revenue given the volatility of the market.

To the real estate community, the push to tax buyers more heavily seemed ill-timed. They said it spoke to the market of four years prior, when Griffin had actually signed the contract at 220 Central Park South and when high-end real estate was still flying off the shelf. The market had nosedived since then, hobbled by oversupply and currency shifts. Increased taxation on buyers would be just the latest blow to an already struggling market.

They posited that even if some of these buyers were in the city only a few weeks a year, they likely contributed more to the local economy in that short time than the average New Yorker does in an entire year. In addition to paying taxes on the purchase of their homes, they drove city tax revenue by eating at the fanciest restaurants and shopping at the most expensive stores. At the same time, they barely drew on city services. Their kids didn't attend local schools and they didn't ride local trains and buses.

By the time the budget was announced, legislators had backed off the proposal, saying it would be too difficult to determine whether or not a given property qualified as a pied-à-terre. They did, however, implement in July 2019 a one-time transfer tax at the time of sale for anyone buying a New York City residential property for more than $2 million. The tax rate would rise steeply for the most expensive apartments and cap out at 3.9 percent for properties sold for $25 million or more.

Under the terms of the new transfer tax, known as the Mansion Tax, Griffin would have paid over $9 million in mansion taxes on his purchase, compared with the just over $2 million he was obligated to pay under the previous rules. Under the terms of the original proposed pied-à-terre tax of 2014, he would have paid an additional $370,000 plus 4 percent of any excess above $25 million, penciling out to around $8.6 million.

Hoylman touted the Mansion Tax deal as a victory and blamed the failure of the pied-à-terre tax on the real estate lobby. "They basically went to the playbook of how to kill a bill and flipped through every page," Hoylman told *The New York Times.*

Clearly, the real estate industry still had some shred of influence left. The existence of Billionaires' Row was proof of that.

Billionaires' Row was "a place where the biggest developers went to really show the size of their dicks," said Amir Korangy, the publisher of *The Real Deal.* "It was about height and over the topness. It was about doing the impossible, whether it was the size of the building or how unbuildable the project was. It was the last fuck you to Occupy Wall St., Elizabeth Warren, the progressive movement in New York City . . . and everyone else who thought that life is fair."

ONE BLOCK OVER, Gary Barnett, who had breathed a sigh of relief as the pied-à-terre tax was nixed, was hosting an event in September 2019 to mark the topping out of Central Park Tower. After five years of construction, the building had reached its full height of 1,550 feet, officially making it the tallest primarily residential tower in the world—besting Macklowe, Roth, and Stern's buildings. Guests, including partners, brokers, and a selection of the New York City press, were instructed to appear at nine A.M. in proper attire for an active construction site—preferably in pants, with no high-heeled, backless, or open-toed shoes. On the top floor of the building, guests in Central Park Tower–branded hard hats gathered in a space swathed in white tarps.

"These views are forever. . . . We brought you up here today to experience them firsthand," said Barnett as he addressed the audience from a purpose-built stage.

Then, in an uncharacteristic show of theatrics, Barnett pressed a button on the lectern beside him to drop the tarps surrounding the glass-walled unit and finally reveal the panoramic views, to an explosion of cheering from guests. "Here we go," he said.

Despite the slow progress in their sales efforts, the topping out marked a moment of undeniable progress for the Extell team. They were newly hopeful, knowing that units were typically easier to sell once a building was closer to completion.

Little did they know that in less than six months' time, they would have to shutter their sales center altogether.

CHAPTER 24

New York on Pause

On March 20, 2020, Kelly Kennedy Mack, the president of new development marketing at Corcoran Sunshine, sat on the edge of the sofa at her family's home on Long Island, glued to the television.

On the screen addressing a bank of cameras was New York governor Andrew Cuomo. He was announcing that he was taking the drastic step to put New York "on pause," owing to the rapid rise in the city's coronavirus case count.

The new virus had burst into the public's consciousness just weeks before, but to most it had seemed far off. Now the number of recorded cases was rising quickly across the state—at more than seven thousand, the total was seven times the number recorded in any other U.S. state. Now all nonessential workers were instructed to stay home effective immediately and not leave unless to seek food or medical care.

Cuomo told New Yorkers that the hospital capacity of their state would likely not be sufficient to meet demand. There was a shortage of ventilators and of protective equipment like masks, gowns, and surgical gloves. Ordinary New Yorkers were asked to send any masks they owned to local hospitals to protect nurses and

doctors on the front lines of the fight. The city and state were looking at the enormous Jacob K. Javits Convention Center and even
Central Park as potential locations for overflow COVID-19 pa-
tients. A massive U.S. Navy ship that served as a floating hospital
arrived in New York Harbor with an additional thousand beds.

An eerie silence quickly descended on the city that was supposed never to sleep. The streets, usually filled with bumper-to-
bumper traffic and blaring car horns, were empty and quiet.
Broadway went dark. Offices emptied. Museums closed. Children
didn't go to school. By April, the bodies of New York City COVID
victims were piling up in refrigerated trailers that had been con-
verted into makeshift morgues.

For many in the real estate business, all thoughts of dealmaking
vanished for the first few weeks of the COVID crisis. People hun-
kered down. Many of the wealthiest New Yorkers, and most of the
real estate industry, headed for the Hamptons, where they holed up
in their palatial homes, clashing with locals by overwhelming local
grocery stores and putting a strain on medical resources in small
luxury enclaves like Southampton. For those well-heeled New
Yorkers who didn't already own homes out east, a race to find one
ensued, driving up the prices of off-season rental homes.

For at least some of the Billionaires' Row developers, the disease
was hitting far too close to home. Barnett spent the early months of
the pandemic at his family's home in Monsey, New York, an enclave about an hour north of the city known for its large Orthodox
Jewish population. His brother contracted the disease early on and
was placed on a ventilator for two weeks. He survived—but barely.

When Barnett's own wife and children contracted the virus in
April, he decamped to the basement of his brother-in-law's house
around the corner, where he spent weeks in nearly complete isola-
tion from his family. For the feast of Passover that April, he stood
outside in the garden waving to his kids as they ate. "It was freezing
cold," he said.

Macklowe, having been friendly with then President Trump for
decades, had visited him in the White House just days before the

shutdown and had been horrified by the lack of masks on display. Now he holed up at his home in East Hampton with Patricia, watching Trump on television as he tried to handle the crisis. He and Patricia had an oddly good time, he would claim later, as the newlyweds spent their time cooking and cleaning together. "It was undisturbed. It was catharsis," he said. "I walked with my wife on the beach."

For Michael Stern, too, a strange sense of calm had taken over. Having fled to his waterfront home in Miami, he took the opportunity to get a handle on his health by getting up at four thirty for sessions with his personal trainer and starting a new regime of intermittent fasting. He lost more than forty pounds. He was also working on building a new mansion for himself on Miami's tony North Bay Road, which has drawn celebrities like Matt Damon and Jennifer Lopez. He tapped Bill Sofield, the interiors guru behind 111 West 57th Street, to design it.

With the world shut down, he knew there was nothing he could do to get sales moving at the project, no matter how hard he tried. Better still, every other developer was in the same position. The music had stopped.

"There was nothing anybody could do about it whatsoever. There was nothing a bank could do, there was nothing we could do," he said. "It was actually kind of incredibly liberating."

THE IMPACT OF the COVID shutdown on the Manhattan real estate market was swift and immense.

Developers all over the city were initially forced to send workers home in compliance with a state mandate. Even later, when construction was declared an essential business, it was difficult to get back up and running at the same pace.

New development sales offices were shuttered, leaving agents to rely on digital materials, such as virtual tours and renderings, to entice buyers. That was not particularly effective, nor were there many truly interested buyers in the first place.

Kelly Kennedy Mack, the head of Corcoran Sunshine, who had been watching Cuomo's speech that morning in March, was used to waking up to an email from her team, recapping all the contract activity across the company's vast portfolio of new developments. She would read through the list of contracts out, contracts signed, and deals closed on her phone before she even got out of bed. As COVID-19 ravaged New York, the emails kept coming, but the deals didn't. In fact, they were almost nonexistent. Between March 23 and August 16, sales of Manhattan homes were down 56 percent year over year. For properties priced at $4 million or above, sales were down about 67 percent. For those luxury homes that did sell in the second quarter, prices were down by about 11 percent.

Not since the days of the Lehman Brothers crash in September 2008 and the subsequent fallout had the market felt so unpredictable. COVID capped off what had already been a dark couple of years for the luxury market. It was kicking the market when it was already down. The developer Ian Bruce Eichner, interviewed in *The Wall Street Journal* that spring, would say that developers who had already been "catching a falling knife" were now "catching a falling sword."

That summer, the stakes only got higher, as thousands of people took to the streets across the country to protest the murder by police of George Floyd, a Black man in Minneapolis. In New York, mass protests in Brooklyn and Lower Manhattan led to clashes with police. Fringe groups turned to vandalism, setting fires and shattering the windows of stores in SoHo and the Flatiron District and looting and ransacking inside. On May 31, the worst night of rioting, more than four hundred people were arrested overnight in New York. Store owners boarded shopfronts, making once fashionable areas filled with boutiques into urban wastelands of plywood and graffiti.

Making matters worse for the real estate world, it was a presidential election year, which traditionally caused a slowdown in the Manhattan market as buyers sought to avoid purchasing during times of uncertainty. This time, the ugly matchup between President Donald Trump and former Vice President Joseph R. Biden, Jr., was inflaming a populace already reeling from the fallout of COVID-19. If the United States had once been a beacon of political and social stability to the world, and New York City its shining epicenter, that image had been well and truly shattered.

The exodus from Manhattan sparked a real estate feeding frenzy in Palm Beach, Florida, where ultra-wealthy New Yorkers picked up single-family homes for often record sums, resulting in what effectively amounted to a mansion shortage in the area. For many, Florida offered more space, better weather, and a tax shelter. Some well-heeled New Yorkers who had weighed the idea of escaping what they deemed burdensome tax policies at home in favor of Florida's more favorable environment now finally made the jump. When the Internal Revenue Service released data on the migration of taxpayers between states in 2020, it showed a surge in the number of American taxpayers moving to low-tax states amid the pandemic. Florida gained $23.7 billion in taxpayer dollars, while New York lost $19.5 billion.

The big ticket Florida deals came in quick succession. In Palm Beach, fashion designer Tommy Hilfiger and his wife, Dee Ocleppo Hilfiger, snapped up a mansion once owned by the former media baron Conrad Black for $46.25 million; the investment services entrepreneur Charles R. Schwab paid $71.85 million for a 1930s-era neoclassical lakefront property; and Scott Shleifer, a New York private equity executive and a partner at Tiger Global Management, paid $122.7 million for a contemporary oceanfront mansion built on a site once owned by President Donald Trump located near the Palm Beach Country Club. Ken Griffin, the billionaire hedge funder setting records on Billionaires' Row and who had talked about potentially one day making New York his home, would later announce that he was relocating his entire company to Miami.

His fellow financier Bill Ackman's plan to flip the One57 Winter Garden apartment to a foreign buyer also now seemed far-fetched. The foreign buyer pool had been dry for several years and now, even the oligarchs couldn't travel to the United States—and would they even want to be in New York City?

Divorced and remarried, Ackman tried to persuade his second wife, Neri Oxman, an American Israeli designer and a professor at the MIT Media Lab, to move in. The pair lived there briefly prior to COVID, but the apartment was simply too masculine for her tastes.

Ultimately, Ackman said to hell with it. He decided to rip out the Ingrao-designed finishes and replace them with a more neutral, modern design. The new design, which was being finished in 2021, would make the apartment look like a gallery at the Museum of Modern Art.

That summer, in a self-published essay that went viral, the comedy club owner and former hedge fund manager James Altucher declared that New York was dead forever. The city had been through hard times before, he wrote, but this time it would not bounce back. "Everyone has spent the past five months adapting to a new lifestyle. Nobody wants to fly across the country for a two-hour meeting when you can do it just as well on Zoom," he wrote on LinkedIn. "You can live in your hometown in the middle of wherever. And you can be just as productive, make the same salary, have higher quality of life with a cheaper cost."

Die-hard New Yorkers quickly rebuffed the "New York is dead" narrative, citing the city's incredible comebacks after 9/11 and after the financial crisis of 2008. The comedian Jerry Seinfeld, a New York icon, wrote a rebuttal in *The New York Times,* calling Altucher "some putz on LinkedIn wailing and whimpering" and declaring that he himself would never abandon New York. "He says he knows people who have left New York for Maine, Vermont, Tennessee, Indiana. I have been to all of these places many, many, many times over many decades. And with all due respect and affection, Are .. You .. Kidding .. Me?!," Seinfeld wrote in his ode to the city.

The Manhattan real estate developer Miki Naftali blew up the

Seinfeld editorial on a billboard that he erected on the side of one of his under-construction condominiums at 1045 Madison Avenue.

But some quietly wondered whether Altucher might be right.

WITH CONSTRUCTION NEARLY complete at Central Park Tower, Barnett was now truly up against the wall in terms of selling units.

As the end of 2020 approached, he knew he wouldn't hit the sales deadlines for the building set forth in his contracts with his construction lender, J.P. Morgan Chase. With activity at these levels, he had little chance of signing contracts on $500 million worth of apartments by the end of the year.

Normally, he would just have slashed prices in order to generate the sales he needed, but COVID had rendered that pointless. It wasn't that the prices were too high, it was that there were zero buyers active in the market at all. Travel to the United States from around the world had all but stopped. No one was around.

Barnett went to the banks for a reprieve but found that they weren't as flexible as he had hoped. They would waive the sales benchmark this time, but only if Barnett put up more cash reserves and paid down the loan. "The banks weren't particularly forgiving or understanding," Barnett said later. The COVID crisis had hit Extell's books hard, and executives scrambled to sell off other assets in order to free up money to pay down the loan.

The situation also forced Barnett to do something he had been desperately trying to avoid. That winter, he took out $380 million in mezzanine financing from Baupost Group, the same hedge fund that had offered money to Stern and Maloney when their loan fell out of balance, and Sail Harbor Capital. The loan carried a very high interest rate of 14 percent and put Barnett under a new mountain of financial pressure.

"I did not want to do that deal," Barnett said later. "That was a terrible deal."

Meanwhile, despite the pandemic being a major blow to Vornado's retail and office holdings, the closings kept rolling in at Roth's 220 Central Park South. Though buyers were not rushing to ink new deals, the company's investor relations team had been correct about the contracts they had already signed; buyers, many of whom had committed to the contracts during the heady days of the real estate boom, weren't walking away from their deposits, as some might have expected in these unprecedented times; they were closing. The building was like Teflon. Nothing ever stuck.

Roth would go on to close roughly $1 billion in deals at the building in 2020, as wealthy buyers kept their commitment to close on purchases despite the troubling conditions. By the end of the year, the building was almost sold out. It was a much-needed boon to Vornado's bottom line at a time when the value of the company's office portfolio was plummeting.

In an earnings call, Roth called the building "the financial engine feeding our liquidity and financial strength." Its financial success was perhaps a surprising indicator that the bad times wouldn't last forever.

CHAPTER 25

Tower of Hell

Sarina Abramovich and her husband, Mikhail Abramovich, retirees who made their money in the oil and gas business, bought a $17 million apartment at 432 Park Avenue in 2016 in order to be closer to their adult daughter. They expected that they would make the move later that year into the tower, which Abramovich reportedly said was being billed as "God's gift to the world."

However, when they arrived, they discovered that the building was far from finished.

Rather than entering into the lap of luxury, Abramovich found that in order to get to her apartment, she had to squeeze alongside a hard-hat operator into a freight elevator filled with steel plates and plywood. It was far from the "hoity-toity" experience she had paid for.

The problems with the building only worsened from there: a series of leaks, creaks, and breakages that Abramovich hadn't bargained for. In 2018, a leak caused by broken plumbing equipment on the 60th floor caused water to leak into her apartment several floors below, resulting in an estimated $500,000 worth of damage.

By early 2021, Abramovich had had enough.

After years of complaining to the developers about construction issues, and having spent months of the pandemic listening to the tower creaking in high winds, the "disgruntled" buyer—as Harry Macklowe referred to her in a subsequent interview—did what some of her neighbors deemed unfathomable. She went to the press.

In February 2021, she outlined the problems in Macklowe and CIM's building to *The New York Times,* which ran a front page story on the tower's alleged construction defects, citing millions of dollars of water damage from plumbing and mechanical issues, elevator malfunctions, and walls that "creaked like the galley of a ship."

She told the paper that she had been convinced that the building would be the best in New York but found that in reality it was all smoke and mirrors.

"Everybody hates each other here," she said.

For several years, rumors had swirled about elevator problems and leaks at 432 Park and homeowners had quietly faced off against the developer over the cost of repairs. Now she had exposed the issues to the world. The *Times* article, which was picked up by media outlets around the globe and inspired a raft of snarky responses on social media, was the ultimate in New York real estate schadenfreude. After all, the building had become so ubiquitous for its vast height that an Instagram account called "432parkseesyou" had begun documenting how the building could be seen from so far afield that it appeared to stalk New Yorkers around the city. For many, images—however accurate—of ultra-wealthy jet-setters getting stuck in elevators, crying over their damp Manolos in flooded custom-built closets, or drying out their soggy Cuban cigars at the tower were a source of great mirth. "I'm here for the residents of 432 Park with the tiniest and tallest violin," tweeted one gleeful reader. "Thoughts and prayers during your time of suffering."

Behind the scenes, a moment of reckoning was under way at the tower, thanks to an upcoming shift in the building's center of power from the sponsor to the residents.

The tension was tied to the way condo boards operate in New York. For a period of time after the construction of a new condo building in New York, the developer typically continues to control the condo board. During that period, the sponsor controls the building's funds and deals with remaining construction issues. Until residents take control of the board, they don't have access to the property's books and can't make any major decisions on behalf of the apartment owners without consent from the sponsor. In most cases, the New York State Attorney General requires sponsors to pledge in the offering plan for a new building that they will give up their right to control the board after certain sales thresholds are surpassed or a certain period of time has lapsed since the building's first closing.

Until the close of 2020, the residential board at 432 Park had been comprised of five representatives from CIM, the California firm that had come to Macklowe's financial rescue back in 2011, and one building resident, Howard Lorber, a pal of CIM chief Richard Ressler, whose company, Douglas Elliman, was heading up sales at the building. But the offering plan for 432 Park dictated that the sponsor's control of the board would end on the later of two dates: the fifth anniversary of the building's first residential closing, which would be December 2021, or the sale of 90 percent of the residential units.

With the building mostly sold out as the fifth anniversary of the first closing approached at the end of 2021, control of the board was finally set to be turned over to residents—allowing, finally, the opportunity for residents to force the sponsor's hand on the issue of the defects. One option, of course, was to sue.

The newly elected board comprised a who's who of real estate titans, many of whom, as frequent users of their apartments and longtime New Yorkers, took a keener interest in the day-to-day operations of the building than some of their more absentee foreign neighbors.

Leading the charge as chairman of the board was Meir Cohen, an Iranian-born real estate investor who made his fortune in the parking garage business and who had purchased a $14.9 million apartment with his wife, Glori, at the building in 2017. There was also Joe Sitt, a prominent New York real estate investor who at one point owned a chunk of Fifth Avenue's most valuable retail properties, and Jacqueline Finkelstein-LeBow, a principal of a real estate company named JSF Capital (her husband was the financier Bennett LeBow, whose company Vector Group was a majority owner of Douglas Elliman, the city's largest real estate brokerage). The LeBows had paid nearly $45 million for their spacious unit on the 64th floor of the building in 2016. The fourth seat was held by Eduard Slinin, the Ukrainian-born founder of AllState Limo.

Ryan Harter, a representative for CIM, was allowed to remain on the board as the fifth member so long as CIM continued to own at least one residential unit in the building.

With the new board installed, the question of whether it should sue the sponsor rippled through the building. While some cautioned that suing might result in a plunge in their own property values, others argued that, in light of the *New York Times* article, that horse had already left the barn. The hit to values was already inevitable.

If they sued now, they could at least force the sponsor into action—and, perhaps, light a fire under its insurance companies, guaranteeing a major payout.

IN SEPTEMBER 2021, the condo board at 432 Park Avenue filed a $125 million lawsuit against CIM and Macklowe.

The suit, explosive in its tone and allegations, posited that the building was one of the worst examples of sponsor malfeasance in the development of a luxury condominium in the history of New York City. The vote to bring the suit, conducted that September 23, was unanimous, with four of the five voting members voting to proceed. Harter, the CIM representative, recused himself.

The suit cited more than fifteen hundred alleged construction and design defects related to the building's common areas and accused the sponsor of denying responsibility, failing to properly address the problems, and ignoring its obligations to residents. Buyers paying tens of millions of dollars for apartments were promised ultra-luxury spaces, the filing alleged, but instead were sold a building plagued by breakdowns, failures, and safety issues.

Such a lawsuit was not without precedent. Legal disputes between residents and sponsors at New York City developments are par for the course in New York real estate. But the prominence of 432 Park and the grandeur of the apartments, coupled with the secrecy and mystique surrounding the billionaire class of owners, made the suit catnip for the media, which salivated over each allegation.

First there was the noise. The board complained of "horrible and obtrusive noise and vibrations" from the building, such as creaking, banging, and clicking noises. It compared the sound of dropping garbage into the trash chute to the detonation of a bomb. The noise was so awful that some residents were displaced from their units for as long as nineteen months while the sponsor tried to remedy the problems, the suit claimed.

Even Richard Ressler, the chairman of CIM, had allegedly admitted in an unguarded moment that the noise was intolerable and made it difficult to sleep during periods of even moderately inclement weather, the suit said. It alleged that Ressler had wanted the noise issues remediated before he personally moved into the building, but they remained nonetheless. (Attorneys for CIM denied the allegation.)

The suit also documented alleged incidents of severe flooding and water damage, which the board said had been treated with a "band-aid" by the developers. After the initial leaks in 2016, two further leaks in 2018 caused water to enter the building's elevator shafts, taking two of the four residential elevators out of service for weeks and damaging as many as thirty apartments, the suit said.

In one particularly dramatic incident, the suit claimed, a worker trying to fix the water infiltration issues drilled through concrete into the building's electrical wiring, causing an explosion and inadvertently shutting off the air conditioning to many of the apartments. The worker was thrown backward several feet through the air. It was the second arc-flash explosion at the building in three years under the sponsor's watch, according to the board.

Then there were the elevators. The suit alleged that the height and sway of the building was causing the elevators to malfunction, leaving residents and their family members trapped for hours. The elevators were programmed to slow down when high winds caused the building to sway, but sometimes they shut down entirely. One particular incident, referenced briefly in the suit but without any identifying information, involved the college-age son of board member Meir Cohen, who got stuck in the elevator for some time before the fire department was able to rescue him, according to people familiar with the situation.

Building staff had begun storing water and even an oxygen mask under benches in the Hermès leather-lined elevators.

The board accused the sponsors of being evasive and attempting to delay a potential reckoning over the issues. The filing alleged that the sponsors had refused repeated demands to produce engineering reports on the state of the building and that as a result, the residents had been forced to commission its own. The results, it said, were "shocking and disturbing."

Adding insult to injury for the residents, the cost of actually living in the building was exploding. Insurance premiums for the condominium were up by 300 percent and common charges were up 39 percent because of the sponsor's mismanagement, the board said.

The increases in the cost of common charges were related at least in part to the building's onsite restaurant, the costs for which were skyrocketing. Buyers purchasing in the building had initially gotten free breakfasts and had been required to spend only $1,200 annually at the restaurant. Now, not only had their free breakfasts been scrapped, but they were required to spend $15,000 a year, a more than 1,200 percent increase, to subsidize the restaurant's operations. That was because the sponsor had carried the cost of the restaurant for significantly longer than it had promised in the offering plan. While the residents had benefited from that extension, they suspected that CIM had continued to temporarily bankroll the restaurant only because it was still trying to sell units in the building and wanted to tout the $1,200 annual minimum spend to prospective buyers instead of the now far heftier sum.

In its legal response to the allegations, CIM said the building was "without a doubt, safe" and that it was not out of the ordinary for a new building to have some teething problems. "Like any other skyscraper, 432 Park's sophisticated symphony of systems needed to be fine-tuned when residents began to move into the building," the company told *The Wall Street Journal* in a statement.

In court papers, lawyers for CIM said the suit was "ill-advised" and "an effort to wrest unwarranted payments" from the sponsor, calling the building "a treasure." It claimed that the board had repeatedly prevented it from accessing the building to address any legitimate issues, which it said it was committed to rectifying, all the while manufacturing an ever-increasing list of demands, the vast majority of which were not required under the building's design, building code, or the offering plan. Rather, many of them were not defects at all but design preferences. The "public relations campaign" mounted by the board had been "value destructive" for the whole building, CIM's attorneys argued.

For his part, Macklowe branded Abramovich a "disgruntled woman" who was only tearing down the value of her own apartment by speaking out publicly about the issues the building faced, though he admitted that the build-out of her apartment had fallen significantly behind schedule. "She was told her apartment would be ready five times. Five times it was delayed," he said. "I don't blame her for being pissed off."

However, when Macklowe saw the lawsuit, he was shocked and bewildered that the board would vote to do something that would undermine the value of its members' own units, he said. Macklowe, who was planning to finally close on his own unit at 432 Park soon thereafter, hadn't expected that the dispute would reach that point.

"It's like a scorpion biting its back," he said that fall. "Why would they do something like that?"

THE NADIR OF the 432 Park dispute coincided with what was starting to look like a significant exodus from the building. It seemed
that more and more owners were putting their homes on the market. By the time the lawsuit was filed in September 2021, three of
the building's most valuable apartments were listed for sale. But
despite the increasing public acrimony over conditions in the building, the pricing seemed unrealistic and oblivious to the moment.

In the summer of 2020, Blessings Investments, a company with
links to the pharmaceutical mogul Meeta Patel, put an 8,000-
square-foot unit on the building's 82nd floor on the market for
$90 million, far more than the $61.9 million it paid in 2016, records show. Patel and her brother Amit Patel were the founders of
Auden Mckenzie, a British drug company that manufactured
generic versions of critical drugs. They sold the company for
£306 million in 2015. (Meeta's brother later got caught up in a
drug price fixing scandal related to his time at the company in 2020
and was banned by British authorities from holding a director role
at any UK company for the next five years. It wasn't clear if the sale
was related to those issues.)

The following summer, just two months before the lawsuit hit
and four months since the *New York Times* story damaged the building's reputation, the building's 96th-floor penthouse, owned by the
Saudi retail magnate Fawaz Al-Hokair, also hit the market, with a
price tag that raised eyebrows across the real estate industry:
$169 million, one of the highest asking prices in the history of New
York real estate and nearly twice what he had paid. In a video
posted to his YouTube channel, listing agent Ryan Serhant, dressed
in a luxurious green Tom Ford jacket, gushed over the unit, calling
it "the eighth wonder of the world."

Then, in September, after months of trying to shop it off market, Mitch Julis, co-founding partner of the Los Angeles hedge
fund Canyon Capital Advisors and one of the building's most

prominent buyers, listed his Japan-inspired apartment for $135 million, more than double the $59.14 million he paid for it.

Buyers, unsurprisingly, were scarce. The only major deal in the year following the lawsuit was the $70 million sale of the apartment owned by Patel, the British pharmaceutical magnate. It was purchased by Yossi Benchetrit and his wife, Gaëlle Pereira Benchetrit, who already owned an apartment on a lower floor of the building.

Meanwhile, brokers trying to do business in the building downplayed the issues, saying that glitches were to be expected in any new building and that they didn't go beyond the ordinary. They even played down the escalating costs of the restaurant.

"I don't think that this is the building that people should live in, if they can't afford to spend $15,000 a year in the restaurant," said Tal Alexander, one half of the flashy brother duo The Alexander Team, who was renting in the building. "It doesn't sound like a lot of money. Not to people like this."

One of his clients who was living overseas and didn't manage to hit the yearly spend found a creative way to circumvent the rules, he said. Since he hadn't eaten there frequently enough to hit the minimum, he made up for it by submitting to the restaurant a single bulk order for multiple cases of Pappy van Winkle bourbon.

CHAPTER 26

See You in Court

It was the eve of Halloween weekend 2020, and history seemed to be repeating itself on 57th Street.

The tower crane at Stern's 111 West 57th Street, the Steinway Tower, was spinning, what's known as "weather vaning," an intentional safety maneuver during high winds. But now something unintended had happened: the so-called "headache ball" at the end of the crane's hoist cable had come loose. It was smashing into the upper floors of the building's façade, raining a shower of debris down onto the city street below.

New Yorkers who had been dining in nearby restaurants, alerted by the sound of the ball crashing into the tower, sheltered inside for fear of being struck by a sheet of glass or aluminum debris, and the street was sealed to traffic by emergency workers. It seemed like déjà vu; the previous crane incident had taken place at One57 exactly eight years earlier to the day. But at over 220 feet tall, the crane at Steinway was the tallest freestanding crane in the history of New York City.

At 6:30 P.M. on a Friday evening, the approximate time the incident occurred, the street below was normally chockablock with city workers making their way home from their offices or scurrying to happy hours to meet friends. With the pandemic still raging, though, the streets were relatively empty. Michael Stern and his fellow developers had caught a lucky pandemic break.

Stern, en route to Miami on a private jet with his family, was quickly alerted to the news. After he dropped his family off in Florida, he hightailed it back around to New York to deal with the fallout.

The crane fiasco was just the latest in a series of construction incidents at the building that were casting an unwanted spotlight on Stern and his operation once again. Investigators determined that one of the cables attached to the crane, which was operated by US Crane & Rigging, one of numerous nonunion subcontractors Stern had selected for the project, hadn't been properly tied up. The following August, JDS would sue US Crane & Rigging and a subsidiary, NYC Crane Hoist & Rigging, for as much as $90 million, alleging that the ball had been left in an incorrect position, allowing it to spool up and strike the building. But Stern largely shrugged off the incident, saying that building skyscrapers thousands of feet in the air was inherently incredibly dangerous and that mishaps were to be expected.

He wasn't wrong about mishaps occurring. The prior year, 2019, JDS had been pouring concrete at the building when a hose had either loosened or broken, allowing the concrete to rain down over the adjacent Hampshire House condominium next door, a lawsuit by the condominium alleged. The concrete was corrosive and hardened, causing significant damage to the neighboring tower. (JDS denied the claims.)

And, as the union boss Gary LaBarbera had predicted, some of the nonunion partners Stern had tapped to work on the project had also proved less than upstanding. A concrete contractor named Parkside Construction was indicted in 2018 by the Manhattan District Attorney Cyrus R. Vance, Jr., on charges that it stole more than $1.7 million in wages from its workers, many of whom were undocumented laborers from Mexico and Ecuador. Authorities claimed that Parkside hid close to $42 million in wages from state insurance officials in a bid to avoid paying workers' compensation premiums.

Parkside co-owners Salvatore and Francesco Pugliese would later cut a plea bargain over the charges. Stern's development firm JDS was not charged in the indictments, since prosecutors had no evidence that the company was aware of the alleged scheme and Stern vehemently denied any knowledge of wrongdoing.

Stern had reeled in a couple of big deals at the building despite the COVID crisis, but sales velocity still wasn't what it should have been. Meanwhile, the building's investors and lenders had grown increasingly frustrated that, nearly seven years after the developers broke ground, the tower still wasn't finished. Maloney later attributed the delays in part to Stern's decision to use nonunion construction. "One of the big Achilles' heels at Steinway was that we were constantly screaming about labor and staffing the job," he said.

The construction union boss Gary LaBarbera pointed to the building as a poster child for the perils of using nonunion labor. "It validates everything I have said since I started in union leadership, that there is a value add to building with union construction trades," he said. "This is a graphic illustration."

Now, to add insult to injury, the building's preferred equity partner, Madison Realty Capital, together with Apollo, the private equity lender that had provided the project with its construction loan, were pushing for Stern to be sidelined.

Following the crane collapse, which delayed the construction by close to a year, Apollo brought on Steve Witkoff, the veteran New York City developer whose own project on the corridor at the Park Lane Hotel was still in limbo, as a construction consultant. Representatives from Witkoff would help oversee the completion of the tower and provide a review of the work that had been done so far, an unusual arrangement that provided an additional layer of oversight to keep Apollo's shareholders happy. To his consternation, Stern would from then on have someone from Witkoff's team looking over his shoulder as he signed off on construction decisions.

Corcoran Sunshine, the new development marketing firm that

had settled its lawsuit with Stern and Maloney after being unceremoniously fired from the project years earlier, was brought back in to help bolster sales.

DAVID "WAVEY DAVE" Juracich, whose first investment with Stern had proven to be a financial windfall, was also feeling the pain of the Steinway Tower's problems acutely.

From his apartment at Walker Tower in February 2021, Juracich was participating in what was quickly becoming an unfortunate fixture of his pandemic life: a virtual deposition. Stern was now engulfed in a mountain of litigation and, in light of the COVID crisis, most of the legal hearings had moved online.

Juracich felt exhausted and anxious for the day he could be clear of the whole saga. He was eager to detach himself from the real estate industry once and for all and was eyeing a move into other businesses, including Bitcoin mining.

The deposition in question was in relation to a lawsuit brought against an entity controlled by Stern and Juracich by two consulting companies that claimed they had been bilked out of money they were owed for helping to line up financing for 111 West 57th Street. A judgment had already been issued in the consulting companies' favor, but Stern and Juracich still hadn't coughed up the cash. The problem, Juracich told the attorney handling the pretrial deposition, was that there was no money left to give them. "The money that we earned has gone down a massive deep hole," he said in his deposition. "I can tell you where it is. It is in wiped-out projects . . . What a disaster. What a disaster."

Even in the context of a legal proceeding, Juracich seemed reflective. "The biggest fallacy and the thing that makes me laugh is that everybody believes property developers are so rich and they make so much money on every single development they ever do," he said. "You should be suing me right now and taking me to court for being so stupid that I lost so much money."

By the end of 2021, a consensus seemed to be emerging among

Stern's business affiliates. Many said they felt cheated and lied to. After years of communicating solely with Stern, some of them reached out to one another directly for the first time to compare notes, meeting in coffee shops and over Zoom from New York, Miami, and across the world. They found they had many of the same problems. They said Stern made promises to them that he didn't keep, oversaw projects that seemed to balloon in cost, and went dark when they demanded information about progress and financials. Some of them had independently turned to legal action.

"We don't expect publicity but we do expect information," said Maxim Serezhin, an investor in the Steinway project. "Michael is in a lot of ways a visionary, but in a lot of ways, visionaries sometimes lose track of reality."

Stern's vision—and, accordingly, his legal troubles—extended well beyond the fracas at 111 West 57th. At a condo he had built in 2017 in Brooklyn's tony Park Slope area, Stern had been fighting lawsuits on two fronts.

One of his equity partners, Largo Investments, had accused him of falsely inflating project costs and charging for expenses that did not exist in order to finance his own "lavish lifestyle of private jets, fancy car collections, and elaborate residences" and make up shortfalls on other projects. The company alleged that Stern had diverted funds from the project for his own use rather than making mandatory distributions to his partners.

Largo claimed that through the use of JDS's construction arm, the developer had ramped up the project management costs to $5 million, or 290 percent above the initial budget, thereby artificially depleting his partner's stake in the project, and tried to cover up the scheme by denying Largo's legal right to access financial and business records related to the project. The Largo suit, containing allegations that mirrored those by Dick Bianco and AmBase from the Steinway project, accused the developer of an "apparent pattern of defrauding his investors and real estate business partners," given the flurry of similar and recent litigation.

Another partner on the same Brooklyn condo project claimed

that Stern had improperly sidelined him from the development and substituted his own company's construction arm as the construction manager for the development by forging his signature on documents in connection with a construction loan. The partner, a company led by the Staten Island developer Domenick Tonacchio, had hired a handwriting expert, who allegedly confirmed that the signatures on the documentation were not genuine. The case had echoes of the allegations by Stern's ex-wife years prior.

In Florida, limited companies linked to the real estate companies Ackerman Development and Mink Development, which had invested in a waterfront condominium project by JDS in Miami Beach, had come forward with their own similar allegations. In a complaint, they alleged that Stern had exhibited a "pattern and practice of duping investors" to fund his projects "only for Stern to explode the project costs without authority, and siphon off the money, value, and publicity of the project for his own benefit through a variety of tactics in blatant violation of negotiated contractual and other legal rights."

Stern, who denied the allegations, was also in litigation for alleged missed rent payments at both his company's own office and the sales office for 111 West 57th Street.

The avalanche of litigation against Stern put his now longtime development partner Kevin Maloney in a difficult position, as a co-defendant with someone who had, over the years, been his adversary.

From his Upper West Side penthouse, Maloney had a direct view of the Steinway Tower as Witkoff oversaw the application of the finishing touches.

"If I could go back in time, I wouldn't have built that project for sure," he said.

CHAPTER 27

Seeds of Recovery

At Central Park Tower, a party was in full swing. A tuxedo-clad waiter poured bubbly onto an enormous tower of champagne coupes and classics from the Great American Songbook filled the air, courtesy of the renowned entertainer Michael Feinstein.

It was September 2021 and a crowd was assembled on the upper floors of the building to celebrate the hundredth birthday of the Manhattan fashion icon Iris Apfel, who wore an extravagant ruffled yellow ensemble for the occasion that made her look like a cross between Big Bird and Anna Wintour. Guests like Tommy Hilfiger and his wife, Dee Ocleppo Hilfiger, decked out in a pin-striped suit and a shimmering silvery disco ball dress respectively, posed with the centenarian cover girl for pictures, and guests snapped images of the nighttime skyline stretched out like a welcome mat beneath the tower.

Lending the space to the event hosts H&M and *Harper's Bazaar* for the evening was the latest move by Extell to generate fresh excitement about the building. Now that construction was basically complete and COVID cases were down dramatically in the city, the sales team was eager to get people in the space with parties, events, and open houses. The celebrity wedding and event planner Colin

Cowie had been spearheading the effort to design buzzy events for the building. The idea was to get as many people in the door as possible, the polar opposite of the strategy Roth had used to market 220 Central Park South.

The push came as Gary Barnett approached another deadline at the tower, the maturity date of his construction loan at the end of 2021. If he could generate enough sales by the end of the year, he could pay off the balance of the loan and not have to renegotiate it yet again.

Barnett needed a break. In all, Extell had seen losses of $190 million in 2020 and it had revised profit expectations at the tower significantly, according to filings it made related to the company's Israeli bonds. The company now expected that the project would yield just $845 million in gross profits, compared to the nearly $2 billion it had projected back in 2018, a more than 60 percent downgrade. The revision was based on a slight uptick in the costs of construction, from $2.8 billion to $3.1 billion, but mostly on a reduction in prices. Extell now estimated it could sell all the units in the building by the end of 2023 at a blended average of $5,750 a square foot, compared to the more than $7,000 a foot the company had originally forecast.

For now, the market seemed to be cooperating again. While many across the world had suffered horribly at the hands of the ongoing pandemic, the prior year had also been a massive wealth creation event for a small segment of the global population. As central banks injected trillions into economies across the world in a bid to keep businesses afloat, much of the stimulus flowed into financial markets, driving up the net worths of the super-rich and sending the stock market soaring higher. Billionaires like Amazon founder Jeff Bezos saw the value of their companies surge as consumers switched their behaviors amid the pandemic, boosting online services.

Another pandemic-era development was the sudden popularity of cryptocurrency. As the once fringe world of digital currencies seemed to enter the mainstream overnight, becoming a more accepted vehicle for investment, cryptocurrency prices soared, creating a lot of new wealth. Some of that wealth flowed into a new investment class of NFT art pieces. The explosion of the market for NFTs, which were essentially unique ownership codes tied to digital assets like images and video clips, accelerated as celebrities like Paris Hilton, Melania Trump, and Justin Bieber got into the NFT game. And the boom in alternative money minted a new class of billionaires. They included known entities like the Winklevoss twins, best known as Mark Zuckerberg's college nemeses, as well as newcomers like Brian Armstrong and Fred Ehrsam, who had founded the cryptocurrency exchange Coinbase, and Sam Bankman-Fried, the now disgraced creator of the competing exchange FTX.

At 111 West 57th Street, there was a contest between two wealthy buyers for one of the building's most expensive units, a 7,130-square-foot aerie on the 72nd floor asking $66 million. The developers had already accepted an offer on the unit when they got a second offer from Gavin Wood, one of the founders of Ethereum, the blockchain-based computer network. (The unit went to the first, unidentified buyer.) Tim Gong, an executive whose firm owned a major stake in the parent company of social media giant TikTok, bought two units at the building for $34 million.

At Central Park Tower, new buyers included Nicole Mendelsohn, the vice president of the global business group at Meta, Facebook's parent company, which was then in the midst of doubling down on the digital realm known as the metaverse.

The rise of the crypto billionaire upset the normal process for how brokers did their due diligence on buyers, forcing them to rely on screenshots of Coinbase accounts and gossip on the social networking site Reddit rather than on traditional bank statements or W2s.

The world's existing billionaires, too, had gotten even richer off the back of the global health crisis. As of April 2021, the Forbes list comprised a record twenty-seven hundred billionaires, an increase of nearly seven hundred from the year prior, with many of the newly minted coming from China. The Global Inequality Lab, a group founded by the French economist Thomas Piketty, found that just 2,750 billionaires controlled 3.5 percent of the world's wealth, up from 1 percent in 1995, with the most rapid gains happening amid the pandemic.

The great wealth transfer was of course bad news for most Americans, some of whom lost their livelihoods amid pandemic-related layoffs and business closures. But for luxury real estate developers, it spelled one important word: deals.

The turnaround in the luxury Manhattan real estate market seemed to happen virtually overnight. Just as quickly as it had disappeared, the activity came roaring back. It was as though a switch had been flipped.

Industry insiders pointed to the month of November 2020 as the tipping point, when the presidential election came to a long-anticipated end with President Joseph R. Biden's victory over Trump and Pfizer announced the results of its closely watched COVID vaccine trials, informing the world that its vaccine had a tremendously high efficacy of roughly 90 percent against COVID.

Combined, the end of a period of dramatic political uncertainty and a glimmer of hope in the fight against COVID provided prospective New York homebuyers with the assurance they needed to purchase.

Suddenly the phones in sales offices across Manhattan began to ring again with pent-up demand.

When Corcoran Sunshine president Kelly Kennedy Mack opened her morning contracts emails that winter, it seemed that every day had more deals than the last. She had gotten used to reviewing all the prior day's contracts with a single glance at her iPhone screen. Now she had to keep scrolling as the list of contract activity grew longer.

"This is amazing," she wrote back to her team. "I just had to scroll!"

Commentators that had rung a death knell for New York were forced to eat their words.

The year 2021 would ultimately pencil out to be the best on record for Manhattan's luxury market. By the end of the year, 1,877 contracts had been signed at $4 million and up, totaling almost $16 billion, according to real estate and data firm Olshan Realty. It was almost three times the number done in 2020 and twice as many as in 2019. Nationwide, at least forty properties sold for $50 million, a 35 percent increase from 2020, and at least eight sold for $100 million or more, a 300 percent increase.

The numbers shocked even the most optimistic New York brokers, who noted that foreign buyers hadn't even returned in force to the market yet. Activity in the New York market was at a record high based almost exclusively on domestic activity. Imagine where the market could go when the foreign buyers returned, they said.

But while demand was starting to come back, buyers were not willing to pay prepandemic prices—and the recovery was patchy. The underlying problem of oversupply were still there, particularly for developers of luxury high-rises. If anything, with more than a year of additional product on the market, the supply and demand dynamics were worse, keeping buyers firmly in the driver's seat. There was blood in the streets. And the savvy buyers could smell the bargains.

In order to capitalize on the renewed demand, some developers finally agreed to significantly adjust pricing to edge out the competition. On Billionaires' Row, the seeds of recovery seemed to have been sown unevenly at best.

Some of the city's best deals were to be found at Central Park Tower and at Barnett's original Billionaires' Row megatower, One57. At Central Park Tower, Extell was closing units at a roughly 25 percent discount from what the developer had initially projected in his 2017 offering plan. In some cases, they sold at even more dramatic discounts. One large four-bedroom unit, priced at $95 million in the original offering plan, sold for just $49.7 million. The idea, Barnett said, was to sell as many units as quickly as possible in order to pay down his loans, then raise prices later.

Also fueling the discounts was a flurry of major resale losses at neighboring One57. A resale at the building closed for $16.75 million that January, less than 50 percent of its original purchase price, a record resale loss for the tower. "Unfortunately, this was an estate sale and they decided to just dump it," Barnett told *Bloomberg News* of the situation.

But it wasn't the only one. Robert Herjavec, the technology entrepreneur who appears on the investment reality show "Shark Tank," grabbed a resale unit at the building for just $31.9 million from one of the companies linked to Chinese conglomerate HNA, one of the earliest major buyers in the building. The company had purchased the unit for $47.37 million six years earlier. In a statement to *The Wall Street Journal,* Herjavec cited his belief in New York's recovery to account for his purchase. "While I accept that COVID has created a nomadic, remote workforce, I also believe the energy of cities will bring people back," he said.

The deal was the second major loss for HNA at the building. The prior year, it sold a different unit for $17.2 million, far less than the $29.5 million it paid in 2014. In the intervening years, the Chinese conglomerate's fortunes had unraveled amid mounting debts stemming from its global shopping spree and scrutiny from Chinese authorities. It was on the verge of one of the biggest corporate collapses in Chinese history. One of the company's founders, co-chairman Wang Jian, had reportedly fallen to his death from a wall near the city of Avignon in France while trying to take a photograph during a business trip.

While HNA's troubles may have played a role in the rushed sales at One57, the discounts also spoke to how far the values in the building had fallen compared to the overall market. That was especially true in light of a series of resale transactions at 220 Central Park South in 2021, which showed that the building had maintained its value despite the crisis. Brokers continued to report that the Vornado building sat above the fray, its prestige trumping any obstacle the market had thrown at it so far and, now, benefiting the most from the rebound.

Among the deals at 220 Central Park South was a megawatt deal by the hedge fund manager Dan Och, who flipped his unit at the building for about $190 million to Joseph Tsai, the Taiwanese Canadian co-founder of Chinese tech giant Alibaba and owner of the Brooklyn Nets basketball team. It was roughly double what he had paid two years prior. The deal, the third-largest residential transaction in U.S. history, made headlines across the world.

Later, Tsai added yet more apartments in the building to his portfolio, bringing his total tally to around $350 million.

IN ALL, BY 2022, Barnett had sold close to $1 billion in units at Central Park Tower. It was a welcome improvement in overall activity, but the numbers were still not where he needed them to be. While he was still confident his investors and lenders would make it out safely, he knew that he might not extract all of the equity he himself had put in.

"I don't think we're going to see any real profits," he said.

It was a frustrating proposition.

"We're not in this business, and we don't take these kinds of risks and incredible effort and sleepless nights just to get our money back. You're in it to hopefully make significant profits," he said. "People see the finished product and the big headline numbers and it seems like you ought to be making a ton of money. They don't realize how expensive all of this can get."

In many ways, Barnett had become the poster child for New York's ultra-luxury condo boom, thanks in large part to the hype he created with One57. It now looked possible that his second building was falling victim to that hype.

CHAPTER 28

Resentment

On a crisp morning in November 2021 at the Upper East Side headquarters of the auction house Sotheby's, photographers in face masks angled to take the perfect picture of what experts said was one of the most iconic sculptures of all time.

It was Alberto Giacometti's *Le Nez* (*The Nose*), an arresting metallic image of a figure with a long thin Pinocchio-style nose suspended within a steel cage, the nose so long as to breach the cage's perimeter. In profile, the shape of the figure was reminiscent of a revolver, and the lights above cast a shadow that looked, from certain angles, like a New York skyscraper on the bright white auction house walls.

The nose was on the auction block. The estimate: between $70 and $90 million. "It presents so much psychological drama," Brooke Lampley, Sotheby's worldwide head of sales for global fine art, told the assembled press, noting that it was extraordinarily rare for a work of this magnitude to appear on the market. The majority of Giacometti's casts were owned by major museums around the world.

But those present knew that the real psychological drama lay in the reason the sculpture was for sale in the first place: The spoils of the war of the Macklowes were up for grabs.

Harry Macklowe had first seen the Giacometti sculpture in the mid-1960s, in his twenties, while touring the Maeght Foundation, a museum of modern art not far from the French city of Nice, he said. It was his first trip to Europe, and the sculpture made a lasting impression. Decades later, the developer said he could remember the piece in the same vivid technicolor that he recalled his trip to the Empire State Building as a boy. As he stared at *Le Nez,* he could see the artist's emotion, he could see grief. He could see a tortured Giacometti sitting in a chair with a cigarette hanging from one side of his lips as he took his forefinger and gouged the mouth of the figure from the clay. Macklowe said he found the experience overwhelming.

Decades later, when his now ex-wife, Linda, got a call from a dealer who had a twenty-four-hour exclusive to sell the piece, he told her to move on it immediately. "I don't care what price it is," he said he told her. "We'll buy it."

(Unsurprisingly, Linda's recollection of the Giacometti purchase differed from Harry's significantly. She said she saw Giacometti at MoMA while in high school, and when she was finally offered the sculpture, Harry almost killed the deal by trying to cut the New York dealer out of the transaction. Harry didn't really know that much about art. What he did know, he learned from her, she said.)

When the Giacometti finally hit the auction block in November 2021, it was a star lot in the first of two sales of the Macklowe collection, the high point of that year's art auction calendar. It was the biggest in-person sale held at Sotheby's since the start of the pandemic, and live bidding was blended with remote bids relayed in real time from London and Hong Kong via screens around the auction house headquarters. Representatives for the auction house stood in busy phone banks at the sides of the room, talking feverishly on the phone with prospective bidders as they cupped the mouthpieces with their hands to ensure their conversations could not be overheard.

The auctioneer started the bidding at $55 million. The assembled spectators looked on enraptured as two major whales emerged, issuing competing bids on the phone via Sotheby's representatives.

The sculpture would ultimately go for $78.4 million to Justin Sun, creator of the cryptocurrency Tron. That Sun was the buyer spoke to the moment perfectly. Cryptocurrency was reaching new heights, Bitcoin billionaires were flashing big checks, and an NFT craze was sweeping the globe. If foreign buyers hadn't yet returned to the real estate market in force, they were certainly making their mark on the art market.

All the while, Macklowe sat among the bidders and onlookers looking dour in a paisley pashmina and velvet loafers. Asked if he was sad to see the pieces sold, he said he considered himself only a temporary steward of the art and had never planned to take it to the grave. "I'm not an Egyptian," he said.

In all, across two separate auctions, the Macklowe collection would sell for $922 million, surpassing the $835 million record set by the sale of a collection owned by banking scion David Rockefeller and his wife, Peggy Rockefeller, in 2018. At the time, it was the priciest collection ever sold in auction history.

However, insiders said that Macklowe's share of that cash wasn't going into his own pockets. Rather, he had pledged at least some of the proceeds from the sale of his portion of the art to Fortress Investment Group, which had financed an assemblage he had been chasing in Midtown East, according to people familiar with the situation. Macklowe had spent an enormous amount of money conceiving a Gensler-designed office tower for the site, but was ultimately unable to assemble the properties necessary for the project to move ahead. Now he owed Fortress some money.

For all the equanimity he tried to exude, the developer had a bitter taste in his mouth.

"I was a very good husband and a tremendous provider," he said. "My ex-wife is walking away with $1 billion. My son had houses, cars, boats, and planes. . . . I'm very resentful, of course."

Epilogue

A Lasting Legacy

Invitations to real estate parties are a dime a dozen in this business, but this one caught my eye. In October 2021, I was among a few select members of the press to be invited to a cocktail party atop Brooklyn's first supertall, a more-than-one-thousand-foot, ninety-three-story tower built to incorporate the historic landmarked Dime Savings Bank of Brooklyn.

Upon arrival, I was ushered into the former bank building, an architectural gem built around 1906 in Greco-Roman style with a rotunda featuring a soaring dome surrounded by stately Ionic columns and an elaborate decorative ceiling, for cocktails and music. Then, I was whisked skyward in the construction elevator, where I could admire a view of New York City that had never been seen before. The building, the tallest in Brooklyn, had risen from the downtown Brooklyn skyline like a middle finger to Manhattan.

"Eat your heart out, Manhattan," read the invitation, calling the building a "cloud-scraping wonder."

In some ways, the project reminded me of 111 West 57th Street. Perhaps it was the way the developers had worked to incorporate the landmark building into the more modern supertall, which was clad in black steel, bronze, and copper. Or maybe it was the unapologetic ambition of the design, which would permanently alter the Brooklyn skyline.

It was one of a new generation of skyscrapers across the world that had taken inspiration from Billionaires' Row. In Miami, Chicago, and even Austin, developers and architects were planning the types of skinny supertalls that had made Billionaires' Row a global phenomenon. Even Jacob Arabo, or Jacob the Jeweler, was getting in on the action, partnering with an Emirati property company to construct a supertall residential skyscraper in Dubai with penthouses named for his signature Jacob & Co. timepieces, Fleurs de Jardin, Astronomia, and Billionaire. The Jeddah Tower, a one-kilometer building planned for Saudi Arabia, was also edging forward. The glass building was slated to be so tall that its architects planned to add a canopy to the base to prevent pedestrians from getting zapped by solar radiation. (The one exception to the supertall boom, perhaps, was China, where officials were now cracking down on the construction of buildings of more than five hundred feet, due in part to health and safety issues.)

Perhaps it was no surprise that the Brooklyn tower seemed familiar. With Steinway in the rearview mirror, it was the brainchild of none other than Michael Stern.

The party drew a mix of New Yorkers, from a few real estate agents I recognized to design honchos, publicists, models, and socialites. Some had heeded the advice on the invitation to dress warm and wear sensible, closed-toed shoes, while others had cast them aside, donning crop tops, colorful capes, and skyscraper heels.

Stern, aware by this point that my book would not necessarily be a favorable portrait of him, greeted me on arrival, and we posed somewhat awkwardly for a picture when a photographer passed by. Newly slender, he was dressed for the evening in Prada sneakers, jeans and a sweater, topped with a navy blue dress coat. As I began asking questions about the status of some of the legal wrangling at 111, he cautioned that I shouldn't believe everything I heard about him. "Little birdies," he said, often told lies.

It was chilly at the top of the building, with nothing to protect us from the elements. The top of the building was not enclosed, meaning the glass curtain wall hadn't yet been installed, so the only obstacle between us and a thousand-foot drop was some bright orange construction netting, which, frankly, didn't look sturdy enough to support many of us.

I didn't stay long. As a journalist, it's my usual tendency to try to remain as close to the action as possible, but as the socialites and models in skyscraper heels teetered close to the edge in pursuit of the perfect selfies, spiked seltzers in hand, I decided I'd rather spend the evening at home. I didn't want to be stuck answering questions for the cops if one of said socialites plunged to her death.

The risks were just too great when it came to these supertalls.

STERN AND HIS fellow Billionaires' Row developers had completely transformed one of the world's most iconic skylines, but only a select few would be able to enter these new kingdoms in the sky. While thousands poured in each day to their offices at landmarks like the Empire State Building and One World Trade Center, delivery drivers jamming up the elevators as they delivered hot lunches to the occupants, the towers of Billionaires' Row would add little to the culture or life of the city they had altered. They stood there a largely empty backdrop, a symbol of the decade in which they had been created.

Some would call them a waste of space, a holding vessel for money from around the world. If they didn't exist, the wealthy would probably trade gold bars, instead. For those who did live there, their occupancy could be compared to an art investor who chose to hang his Picasso on the wall rather than simply stashing it away in storage.

For the developers who made them possible, the towers would have a lasting impact on their legacies—though some had vastly more financial success than others. Undeterred, they all barreled ahead into future projects, even as, in 2023, gross inflation, a cryptocurrency collapse, and the threat of another financial crisis loomed large. Such is the developer mentality. "Developers develop until they can't develop anymore," said the appraiser Jonathan Miller. "If it ends badly, then a few years go by and they start over like nothing ever happened."

Vornado's Steve Roth was the most obvious victor of the race to the sky on Billionaires' Row, as his building at 220 Central Park South continued to post record deals even as sentiment around the corridor began to falter. Not one to shy away from self-praise, Roth has boasted about the building's performance multiple times over the past few years, telling analysts on earnings calls that the building was "unquestionably the most successful residential development ever." "We have achieved something that nobody ever thought could possibly be achieved," he said during a 2021 earnings call, even once comparing his company's performance at the building to "winning the Kentucky Derby by ten lengths."

The sweet taste of victory would not linger long. By 2023, 220 Central Park South was in the past for Roth. Instead, he was focused on his company's roughly 23-million-square-foot office portfolio, the value of which was under threat amid concern on Wall Street that workers weren't returning to their New York offices in anything close to their prepandemic numbers. Meanwhile, in a move that seemed to be in denial of the moment, his firm was vying for a deal with the city that would allow him to build yet more office towers around Penn Station.

Barnett had scored a win too: He had been the first developer to complete a Billionaires' Row megatower, and his early success had catapulted the market to new heights. Since then, however, the prospect of making any significant profit on his second building, Central Park Tower, had slipped away. As recession worries loomed, he struggled to keep sales momentum going. "We're not going to have $4 billion in sales. We were hoping to hit that kind of number, but there's no chance," he said in June 2022, adding that he was eager to pay down his debts and move on. "Our profitability here has definitely been hit in a big way."

Still, Barnett continued to swing for the fences, finally listing the building's triplex penthouse, which was positioned at a height of more than 1,400 feet, for $250 million. Its listing broker, Ryan Serhant, the "Million Dollar Listing New York" star who had dared to bare all at One57 years earlier, would say that from that unit one could see the curvature of the earth, though there didn't seem to be any scientific evidence to support that.

It was an unsatisfying conclusion, and Barnett, too, had moved on to other projects. He faced off against holdout tenants in an assemblage he was piecing together on the Upper West Side. After they refused to give in, he decided just to build around them.

Harry Macklowe, while still tangling with owners on the issue of his own liability over the alleged construction defects at 432 Park, could point to a minimalist pencil tower on the skyline and say it was his. And it was true. He had been its originator and champion. Though it didn't appear to have been a runaway commercial success for him personally so much as it had for CIM, which made profits of over $1 billion on the project, it was his baby, and in some ways, that was enough.

"A lot of my professional friends also feel it's the best building in New York, as far as architecture and design, because it has no artifice," he boasted in June 2022. "It hasn't tried to do something funny to make itself look distinguished or different. It's pure."

Meanwhile, even as Macklowe moved into the twilight of his life, he was struggling to sell units at yet another project, the condo conversion of a hulking former bank building at One Wall Street in Lower Manhattan.

Michael Stern continued to face off against his partners in a string of lawsuits. By 2023, his new Brooklyn Tower was also engulfed in litigation, as his onetime partner Joseph Chetrit alleged he was owed more than $17 million on the project. And after several failed attempts at settlement talks, he and Kevin Maloney, and their lender Apollo, would still be fighting their case against Dick Bianco over 111 West 57th Street seven years after the first suit was filed.

Maloney, whose company was already building a more-than-one-thousand-foot-tall Waldorf Astoria–branded tower in Miami, classified the Steinway project as a commercial failure, though with numerous projects going on at any given time, he said an occasional flop was to be expected. "People ask me if I make money in real estate. I tell them ten percent, probably fifteen percent of my buildings over the last thirty-five years have gone to zero," he said. "But I've had some home runs. And some doubles and triples."

In October 2022, Apollo partner Stuart Rothstein told analysts on a quarterly earnings call that the building still hadn't sold as many as half of its units.

While Stern said it didn't keep him up at night, Maloney felt that by 2022, the ongoing litigation with Dick Bianco had become an emotional burden on him, one that he didn't need at this stage of life. He said he was surprised Bianco didn't feel similarly, and that he hadn't run out of money to pay his lawyers. It crossed Maloney's mind that Bianco, now in his seventies, might litigate to the death, but he said he didn't want to win that way.

At a court hearing in July 2022, the white-haired Bianco sat at the back of a sweltering courtroom in a checked shirt, COVID mask, and brown shoes, gripping the arm of the courthouse bench with his thick, tanned hands as his lawyers continued to argue on his behalf. Occasionally he bowed his head and closed his eyes.

Somehow, though, Stern found a way to view 111 as a win. While the profits had been reduced tremendously, he argued that financial success was only one way to "keep score." More important, the building is "an architectural masterpiece, it's an engineering marvel. And I'm the individual most responsible for bringing it to fruition," he said of the tower. "That's very satisfying to me."

He paused for a moment, then added: "The trials and tribulations of how all these buildings get built—you barely remember them a few years later."

Acknowledgments

I am deeply grateful to a closely knit group of family and friends for making this project possible. Without them, I wouldn't be here.

I am fortunate to have found a wonderful professional home at *The Wall Street Journal,* where my kind and talented editors, Heather Halberstadt, Kris Frieswick, and Candace Taylor, gave me the space and support I needed to make this book a reality. Throughout this journey, they were always generous with their time, advice, and wit. I would also like to thank the paper's management, particularly Matt Murray, Kate Ortega, and Mike Miller, for allowing me to step away from my daily role in the Mansion section for a few months to focus my attention more firmly on *Billionaires' Row.*

My experience covering this topic for the *Journal* as well as for *The Real Deal* and the New York *Daily News* laid the foundations for this project, and I am thankful for the contributions of current and former colleagues and friends like E. B. Solomont and Konrad Putzier, who uncovered new revelations and helped further the reporting over the years, as well as to my former boss, *The Real Deal* publisher Amir Korangy, who has been my champion since he first hired me to work for him in 2011. Thanks also to all my colleagues and competitors whose work informed this book, including Stefanos Chen, Charlie Bagli, Terry Pristin, Jennifer Keil, Oshrat Carmiel, Vicky Ward, Peter Grant, Alexei Barrionuevo, Joshua Chaffin, Julie Satow, Adam Pincus, and the late Josh Barbanel.

Thanks to some of my protagonists for their time. Harry Macklowe, Gary Barnett, and Michael Stern made themselves available to me even when it was inconvenient and even when they didn't particularly like the nature of my questions.

Daniel Greenberg has been a helpful ally and guide to the book-writing business, which was entirely new to me. My editors at Crown, Paul Whitlatch and Katie Berry, have been trusted sounding boards and advisers and have slogged through numerous drafts over many months.

Special thanks go to a small group of close friends, notably Guelda Voien and Katie Mudrick, who have listened to me drone on endlessly about real estate development over drinks and dinners these past two years. A group text chat with some girlfriends in real estate also provided much laughter when I needed it—I can't repeat the name of the chat here.

To my parents I am most especially grateful. Without their constant love and support, I would be lost. The lengthy stays during the writing process at what my mum refers to as her "five-star hotel" in Northern Ireland were invaluable.

Finally, to my husband, John: I would never have pitched this book without you, nor would I ever have finished it. I love you, always.

Notes

This book is informed by interviews with more than one hundred people who were involved, either directly or indirectly, with the events described. It draws from personal recollections, notes, lawsuits, and personal communications including emails and text messages. The dialogue is rendered to the best recollection of those who were in attendance or were briefed on conversations. In some cases, recollections of the events depicted vary significantly; in those instances, I have provided the narrative around which there is the most consensus and noted the dissenting voices.

CHAPTER 1: SAVING HARRY MACKLOWE

3   **The firm he founded:** Charles V. Bagli, "G.M. Building Sells for $1.4 Billion, a Record," *New York Times,* August 30, 2003.

4   **He had then taken great pleasure:** Vicky Ward, *The Liar's Ball* (New York: Wiley, 2014).

5   **In 2007, the developer had completed:** Charles V. Bagli and Terry Pristin, "Harry Macklowe's $6.4 Billion Bill," *New York Times,* January 6, 2008.

5   **as the subprime mortgage crisis spilled over:** Terry Pristin, "Developer's Big Manhattan Move Faces a Time and Credit Squeeze," *New York Times,* August 22, 2007.

11   **As the night crept into the early morning:** Charles V. Bagli, "Macklowes Sell G.M. Building for $2.9 Billion," *New York Times,* May 25, 2008.

13   **The hotel itself had been a draw:** Ralph Blumenthal, "Police Check Led Zeppelin Party for Clue in Theft," *New York Times,* July 31, 1973.

CHAPTER 2: THE ORIGINAL PALACE CORNERS

15   **A grande dame of high society:** Christopher Gray, "Streetscapes: Edith Wharton; In 'The Age of Innocence,' Fiction Was Not Truth," *New York Times,* August 27, 1995.

16   **However, the intersection's status:** Julie Satow, *The Plaza: The Secret Life of America's Most Famous Hotel* (New York: Twelve / Grand Central / Hachette, 2019).

21   **The project, which debuted in 1975:** Douglas Martin, "Stewart R. Mott, Longtime Patron of Liberal and Offbeat Causes, Dies at 70," *New York Times,* June 14, 2008.

21   **One of Mott's interests was farming:** Leslie Maitland, "Quadruplex 57th St. Penthouse or Pie in the Sky?" *New York Times,* December 22, 1975.

23   **Opening in 1983 on Fifth Avenue:** Paul Goldberger, "Architecture: Atrium of Trump Tower," *New York Times,* April 4, 1983.

24   **By the late-1980s, thanks to the success:** Paul Goldberger, "Skyscrapers Battle It Out Near Carnegie Hall," *New York Times,* October 21, 1990.

26   **Some bemoaned the so-called "theme-parking of 57th Street":** Herbert Muschamp, "On West 57th, a Confederacy of Kitsch," *New York Times,* June 5, 1994.

CHAPTER 3: THE RABBI, THE JEWELER, AND THE DEVELOPER

33   **He was Rabbi Yoshiyahu Pinto:** Josh Nathan-Kazis, "Rabbi Pinto's Charity Spent Heavily on Luxury Travel, Jewels," *The Forward,* December 20, 2011.

34   **Jacob Arabo:** Lola Ogunnaike and Anemona Hartocollis, "Godfather of Bling Denies He Aided Drug Ring," *New York Times,* June 17, 2006.

37   **By 2008, Deutsche Bank was mired:** Jennifer S. Forsyth, "Property Mogul Poised to Take a Second Fall," *Wall Street Journal,* May 9, 2008.

38   **Cohen had his own designs on the property:** Laura Kusisto, "Unmasking Three Mismatched Heavies Who Won and Lost the Drake," *New York Observer,* June 7, 2011.

CHAPTER 4: THE CHESS MASTER

50   **With his slicked-back black hair and honed physique:** Tom Wright and Bradley Hope, *Billion Dollar Whale: The Man Who Fooled Wall Street, Hollywood, and the World* (New York: Hachette, 2018).

54   **Barnett left the meeting:** Craig Karmin, "Developer Courts the Global Elite," *Wall Street Journal,* December 7, 2011.

55   **Born Gershon Swiatycki in 1955:** Gabriel Sherman, "The Anti-Trump," *New York* magazine, September 22, 2010.

55   **He had gotten into the real estate business incidentally:** Devin Leonard, "Gary Barnett, Controversial Master of New York City Luxury Real Estate," *Bloomberg,* October 2, 2014.

62   **Starting in the late 1990s, Barnett spent:** Matthew McNelly Jones, "Finance of the Fallow Firmament: Valuing Air Rights in Contemporary Manhattan," DSpace@MIT, master's thesis, Massachusetts Institute of Technology, September 2015.

CHAPTER 5: CALIFORNIA DREAMING

68   **CIM had been founded in 1994:** Konrad Putzier, "Manhattan's New Skyline (*© CIM Group)," *Real Deal,* December 13, 2016.
69   **the company would post an annual return of 7.4 percent:** Craig Karmin, "New York Placing Tallest Order," *Wall Street Journal,* October 19, 2011.

CHAPTER 6: HITTING THE JACKPOT

82   **With the financing in place:** Katherine Clarke, "Thomas Juul-Hansen Is a Man of the Masses and a Star Architect in New York for the 1%," New York *Daily News,* June 6, 2014.
87   **The sellers of the penthouse:** Josh Barbanel, "Weill Takes Step Toward 'Downsizing,'" *Wall Street Journal,* November 10, 2011.
90   **While developers cooed over the Rybolovlev deal:** Elise Knutsen, "Who's Your Daddy: Did Dmitry Rybolovlev Buy the 15 CPW Penthouse for His Daughter?" *New York Observer,* December 19, 2011.
92   **Real estate reporters from the country's largest newspapers:** Josh Barbanel, "Storage Enters Stratosphere," *Wall Street Journal,* December 10, 2011.
97   **Negotiations with Nick Candy:** Alexei Barrionuevo, "Rising Tower Emerges as a Billionaires' Haven," *New York Times,* September 18, 2012.

CHAPTER 7: INVENTING AN ICON

113   **The production of the 432 Park marketing materials:** Julie Satow, "Selling Park Avenue Condos at $25,000 a Minute," *New York Times,* June 21, 2013.
118   **The process reportedly took four years:** Thessaly La Force, "In This Manhattan Apartment, Every Room Is a Testament to Japanese Tradition," *New York Times Style Magazine,* February 6, 2019.

CHAPTER 8: MAKE WAY FOR THE BILLIONAIRES

123   **Diamond's landlord at 220 Central Park South:** David W. Dunlap, "Sarah Korein, 93, Whose Dainty Bearing Masked a Tough Property Investor, Is Dead," *New York Times,* November 4, 1998.
124   **Other residents were complaining too:** Donald Glasgall v. Madave Properties SPE, LLC, New York State Supreme Court, 102777/2006.
125   **The residents included colorful characters:** Kate Briquelet, "Young Mistress Denies Claims She Was Out for Late Mercedes-Benz Exec's Money," *New York Post,* December 16, 2012.
126   **Roth soon came to believe:** Will Parker and Hiten Samtani, "Vornado Post Roth?" *Real Deal,* November 1, 2016.
128   **Hackett, too, was a force:** Hiten Samtani and E. B. Solomont, "The

Inside Story of 220 Central Park South, the World's Most Profitable Condo," *Real Deal,* November 18, 2020.

130 **Rozenholc was no stranger to a tough fight:** Will Parker, "The Closing: David Rozenholc," *Real Deal,* February 1, 2018.

130 **Rozenholc's reputation as public enemy number one:** Michael Gross, *House of Outrageous Fortune: Fifteen Central Park West, the World's Most Powerful Address* (New York: Atria / Simon & Schuster, 2014).

CHAPTER 9: THROWING SHADE

140 **As the hurricane raged around them:** Charles V. Bagli, "As Crane Hung in the Sky, a Drama Unfolded to Prevent a Catastrophe Below," *New York Times,* November 6, 2012.

140 **In the end:** "Impact of Hurricane Sandy," New York City Mayor's Office of Management and Budget, undated.

144 **Then there were the shadows:** Warren St. John, "Shadows over Central Park," *New York Times,* October 28, 2013.

CHAPTER 10: "TOO MUCH MONEY"

164 **And close they did:** Joshua Chaffin, "Michael Stern: The Highs and Lows of a New York Skyscraper King," *Financial Times,* April 17, 2020.

CHAPTER 11: NEW KIDS ON THE BLOCK

168 **In later litigation between the couple and Stern's mother:** Yael Hirsh v. Michael Stern, 2009-08896, Appellate Division of the Supreme Court of New York.

173 **Steinway & Sons, a longtime family business:** "Landmarks Preservation Commission Report on the Designation of Steinway & Sons Reception Room and Hallway," September 10, 2013.

176 **Response to the partnership's plans:** "Proposed Residential Tower Would Encroach on Site of Steinway Hall," *Cityland,* October 18, 2013.

178 **A little-known entity, the banker:** Konrad Putzier, "The Obscure Investor Who Could Sabotage NYC's Most Ambitious Planned Condo Tower," *Real Deal,* November 1, 2017.

178 **The roughly twenty-year legal battle:** Gretchen Morgenson, "The Bank Case That Refuses to Die," *New York Times,* October 1, 2011.

181 **In truth, Becker and Ruhan had little intention:** Konrad Putzier and David Jeans, "A Russian Oligarch's Guide: How to Hide $20M in a NYC Skyscraper," *Real Deal,* December 20, 2018.

CHAPTER 13: SUPPLY AND DEMAND

189 **Developers were known for their herd mentality:** Josh Barbanel, "New Tower to Join 'Billionaires Row,'" *Wall Street Journal,* March 24, 2014.

189 **by the time Kevin Maloney:** Paul Goldberger, "Too Rich, Too Thin, Too Tall?" *Vanity Fair,* April 9, 2014.

190 **Sales were also slated to launch:** Zoe Rosenberg, "At Last, Jean Nouvel's Supertall MoMA Tower Hits the Market," *Curbed,* September 18, 2015.

192 **Witkoff had closed on the building in 2013:** Tom Wright and Bradley
     Hope, *Billion Dollar Whale: The Man Who Fooled Wall Street, Hollywood, and
     the World* (New York: Hachette, 2018).
196 **With the pipeline of projects on Billionaires' Row growing fuller:**
     E. B. Solomont, "Revealed: Inside Gary Barnett's $4B Tower," *Real Deal*,
     July 7, 2017.

CHAPTER 14: THE BEST BUILDING IN NEW YORK

203 **Roth's eye for detail extended to far more than design:** Konrad
     Putzier, "At 220 CPS, Steve Roth Is the Bouncer," *Real Deal*, June 23,
     2016.
205 **If this factored into Roth's thinking:** Louise Story and Stephanie Saul,
     "Stream of Foreign Wealth Flows into Elite New York Real Estate," *New
     York Times*, February 7, 2015.

CHAPTER 15: STARTING WARS

217 **For LaBarbera, the stakes were high:** Kathryn Brenzel, "Are Unions
     Losing Their Grip in NYC?," *Real Deal*, March 1, 2016.
218 **An illustration of Stern on the cover:** James King, "Stern to Unions:
     You're Done in This Town," *Commercial Observer*, May 12, 2015.
222 **In an interview with *Bloomberg News*:** Oshrat Carmiel, "How to Sell a
     $60 Million Penthouse: Don't Try," *Bloomberg*, March 31, 2016.

CHAPTER 16: DISDAIN IN PARADISE

230 **That November, Billy Macklowe's general counsel:** E. B. Solomont,
     "Macklowes Locked in High-Stakes Tug of War," *Real Deal*, January 1,
     2017.

CHAPTER 17: SELLING BILLIONAIRES' ROW

233 **The duo's antics quickly became a source of gossip:** E. B. Solomont
     and Katherine Kallergis, "Cracking the Bro Code: Tal and Oren Alexan-
     der," *Real Deal*, March 18, 2019.
234 **The brothers' detractors speculated:** Hiten Samtani, "Qatar Scraps
     Plan to Buy $90 Million Townhouse in Manhattan," *Real Deal*, August 6,
     2014.

CHAPTER 18: SHADOWY FIGURES

247 **Kolawole "Kola" Aluko was beaming:** "Kola Aluko Launches AF-
     RICA50 Fund at NASDAQ, New York," YouTube, November 13, 2013.
248 **As the U.S. Justice Department laid out in a civil complaint:** Press
     release from the Department of Justice Office of Public Affairs, July 14,
     2017.
249 **In the years since One57 debuted:** Andrew Rice, "Stash Pad," *New
     York* magazine, June 27, 2014.
251 **Still, the Aluko ordeal showed how quickly:** E. B. Solomont and
     Katherine Clarke, "One57 Made Billionaires' Row. Will It Now Destroy
     It?" *Real Deal*, June 28, 2017.

252 **While the initial version of the initiative lacked teeth:** Will Parker, "The Biggest Weakness in the Treasury's New LLC Order? Wire Transfers," *Real Deal,* January 29, 2016.

253 **That November, with Aluko still reportedly on the run:** Philip Obaji, Jr., "The Crooked Playboy Who Courted Naomi Campbell, Threw a Birthday Bash for DiCaprio, and Rented a Yacht to Beyoncé," *Daily Beast,* July 23, 2017.

254 **In January 2016, Witkoff had temporarily halted plans:** Sarah Mulholland, "Manhattan Developer Ices Plans for Central Park Luxury Condos," *Bloomberg,* January 28, 2016.

254 **A year later, however, the outlook was even bleaker:** Peter Grant and Bradley Hope, "Prosecutors, Investors Propose Plan to Oust Malaysian Investor from Hotel Consortium," *Wall Street Journal,* February 1, 2017.

CHAPTER 19: THE MUSIC STOPS

259 **Ryan Serhant was naked:** Gus Donohoo, "My Other Home Is Spiritual Fulfilment," *Flaunt* magazine, February 16, 2017.

262 **A study by the appraiser Jonathan Miller:** E. B. Solomont, "By the End of 2017, Manhattan Will Have 5 Years of Excess Inventory: Analysis," *Real Deal,* March 18, 2016.

265 **Even once Billionaires' Row began selling in earnest:** Nicholas Kulish and Michael Forsythe, "World's Most Expensive Home? Another Bauble for a Saudi Prince," *New York Times,* December 16, 2017.

CHAPTER 20: "GONE TO ZERO"

278 **One of the scrappiest, most successful attorneys:** Jill Noonan, "At the Desk of: Stephen Meister," *Real Deal,* November 30, 2011.

278 **One of his most novel arguments:** Will Parker, "Stephen Meister: The Underdog's Lawyer," *Real Deal,* November 1, 2017.

280 **By 2017, Ruhan was also facing issues at home:** Maeve Sheehan, "The 'Ruined' Irish Millionaire, His Wife, a Bizarre Murder Plot, and the Battle for His Secret Fortune," *Irish Independent,* November 12, 2017.

CHAPTER 21: KNIVES OUT

284 **The joke went like this:** Julia Marsh, "Harry Macklowe Laughs After Offering Wife $1B to Go Away," *New York Post,* Page Six, April 5, 2017.

285 **The couple's divorce proceedings would ultimately play out:** E. B. Solomont, "Macklowe vs. Macklowe," *Real Deal,* November 1, 2017.

CHAPTER 25: TOWER OF HELL

320 **In February 2021, she outlined the problems:** Stefanos Chen, "The Downside to Life in a Supertall Tower: Leaks, Creaks, Breaks," *New York Times,* February 3, 2021.

322 **In September 2021, the condo board at 432 Park:** Stefanos Chen, "Residents of Troubled Supertall Tower Seek $125 Million in Damages," *New York Times,* September 23, 2021.

CHAPTER 26: SEE YOU IN COURT

329 **as the union boss Gary LaBarbera had predicted:** Press release from Cyrus R. Vance, District Attorney, New York County, May 16, 2018.

331 **The deposition in question:** Etage Real Estate LLC and Davla Consulting, Inc. v. Michael Stern and David Juracich, New York State Supreme Court, index no. 656322/2019.

332 **One of his equity partners, Largo Investments:** Largo 613 Baltic Street Partners LLC v. Michael Stern, New York State Supreme Court, index no. 652986/2020.

333 **In Florida, limited companies linked to the real estate companies:** Katherine Kallergis, "Michael Stern Accused of 'Duping Investors' in Monad Terrace Project," *Real Deal,* November 19, 2021.

333 **Stern, who denied the allegations:** 693 Fifth Owner LLC v. 111 West 57th Partners LLC and Michael Stern etc, New York State Supreme Court, index no. 155493/2020.

CHAPTER 27: SEEDS OF RECOVERY

335 **Barnett needed a break:** Chava Gourarie, "Extell Development Lost $206M in 2020," *Commercial Observer,* March 22, 2021.

CHAPTER 28: RESENTMENT

343 **In all, across two separate auctions:** Kelly Crow, "Macklowe Auctions Total $922 Million, Collection Surpasses Rockefeller Estate as Priciest Ever Sold," *Wall Street Journal,* May 16, 2022.

Index

Page numbers in **bold** indicate maps

Aabar Investments, 50, 51, 54
Abramovich, Mikhail, 319
Abramovich, Sarina, 319–20, 325
Abu Dubai, 255, 257
Ackerman Development, 333
Ackman, Bill, xx, 97–98, 315–16
Adoniev, Serguei, 181–82
Adrian Smith + Gordon Gill
    Architecture, 192–93. *See also*
    Central Park Tower
Afkhami, Mohammed, 119
The Age of Innocence (Wharton), 15
AIG and 111 West 57th Street, 215,
    273, 274
"air rights," 59–60, 62–65, 148,
    194–95
Alatau, 40–41
Alexander, Oren, 232–35, 238–39,
    242
Alexander, Shlomy, 233
Alexander, Tal, 232–35, 238–39,
    242–43, 327
Alexander's (department store chain),
    126–27
al-Hokair, Fawaz, 118, 326

Alibaba, 340
AllState Limo, 322
al-Qubaisi, Khadem
    arrest and conviction of, in Abu
        Dubai, 255, 257
    basic facts about, 50–51, 186
    One57 financing and, 51–52, 54,
        256
    Walker Tower unit purchased by,
        184–86, 257
al-Thani, Hamad bin Jassim bin Jaber,
    85, 228, 288
Altucher, James, 316
Aluko, Kolawole "Kola," 247–49, 253
Alwyn Court, 62
AmBase Corporation
    Apollo and, 280
    Baupost loan and, 274–78
    Carteret Savings Bank and,
        178–79
    lawsuit against Stern and Maloney,
        223–25, 249, 275, 278–80, 332,
        349, 350
    Saudi billionaires and, 187
    Walker Tower project and, 221

AOL Time Warner Center
  basic facts about, 31
  Chinese billionaires and, 102
  Low unit seized by government,
    254
  marketing of units at, 94
  Russian billionaires and, 90, 205
Apfel, Iris, 334
Apollo
  AmBase and, 280
  basic facts about, 68
  Bianco lawsuit against, 279, 280
  111 West 57th Street and, 215, 273,
    274, 275, 277, 295, 330
  Spruce and, 277
Apple cube, 4
Arabo, Angela, 119
Arabo, Jacob (né Yakov), 34–36, 119,
    346
Architectural Record, 174
Armstrong, Brian, 336
art
  Griffin and, 240
  Macklowes' investments in, 7, 8–9,
    228, 286, 341–43
  market for, and condominium
    market, 238
  NFT pieces, 335–36, 343
  sale of David and Peggy
    Rockefeller's, 343
  for 220 Central Park South, 200
The Art of the Deal (Trump), 24
Art Students League, 31, 194–96
Asia, supertalls in, 48–49
"as-of-right buildings," 145
Assouline (publishing company),
    110–11
The Atlantic, 213
Atlantic 57 LLC, 181
Auden Mckenzie, 326
Automobile Row, 27–28, 133
Avdolyan, Albert, 181, 182

Bailey, Adam Leitman, 288
Banco Santander, 54
Bankman-Fried, Sam, 336
Bank of America, 54

Bank of China, 202, 203
Bank of Manhattan Trust Building on
    Wall Street, xxix, xxx
Bank of the Ozarks, 203
Bannister, Matthew, 111–15
Banque Havilland Saudi Arabia, 249
Barnett, Gary. *See also* Central Park
    Tower; One57
  Aabar and, 51
  Ackman and, 98
  assemblage process and, 61–65
  background of buildings' residents
    and, 250–51
  basic facts about, xviii, 49–50,
    55–57, 61
  cantilever design of Central Park
    Tower and, 195
  characteristics of, 298
  COVID-19 and, 312
  on demand at super high end of
    market, 197
  financing of One57, 51–53, 54
  on lack of sales at Central Park
    Tower, 301
  Low and, 256
  on lower purchase prices (2021),
    339
  Maloney and, 169
  One57 rental units sales by, 260
  plans for One57 of, 82–83
  potential purchasers and, 97
  profits from Central Park Tower,
    340, 348
  Riverside Boulevard building,
    145
  Roth and, 133–37, 201, 209, 210
  sales and, 141–42
  supertalls forum panel, 149–50
  as symbol of Billionaires' Row, 145,
    150–51, 175
  217 West 57th Street assemblage,
    133
  220 Central Park South and,
    133–37
  Zuckerman and, 153–54
Barron, Vickey, 250
Bauhaus Group, 296

Baupost Group, 273–76, 317
Becker, Arthur
  basic facts about, 179–80
  Bianco and, 275, 276
  Saudi billionaires and, 187
  Spruce deal and, 280
  Steinway Hall and, 181
Belnord, 56–57
Benchetrit, Gaëlle Pereira, 327
Benchetrit, Yossi, 327
Bentham, Jeremy, xiii
Berkey, David, 257
Bernstein, Leonard, 31
Bezos, Jeff, 119
Bhatti, Masood, 178
Bianco, Richard
  basic facts about, 178–79
  Baupost loan and, 274–78
  lawsuit against Stern and Maloney,
    223–25, 275, 278–80, 332, 349,
    350
  Saudi billionaires and, 187
  Walker Tower project and, 221
Bibliowicz, Jessica, 88
Bibliowicz, Natan, 88
Biden, Joseph R., 315, 337
Biel Crystal Manufactory, 266
"the billionaire building." See One57
"Billionaire" house, 264
billionaires, increase in during
    COVID-19, 335, 336–37
Billionaires' Bunker, 239
Billionaires' Row. See also specific
  buildings
  areas exceeding prices on, 266–67
  Barnett as symbol of, 145, 150–51,
    175
  core of, 26
  defining, xvi
  description of (2008), 29–32
  developments halted, 254–55
  FAR in, 60
  fear of building glut, 196–97
  history and reputation of, 26–29
  justification for ultra-high prices,
    264–65
  as "last fuck you," 309

LLCs as purchasers of units,
    249–50
  as new market category, 189–90
  proposed homeless shelter and, 304
  residents' failure to occupy units
    on, 250
  supertalls inspired by, 346
Billions, 296
Black, Leon D., 68, 238, 239
"Black Mafia Family," 36
Blackmon, Kyle, 87–89, 91, 188–89,
    242
Blackstone, 5, 11–12
Blanco, Kenneth, 248
Blankfein, Lloyd, 239
Blavatnik, Len, 20
Blessings Investments, 326
Bloomberg, Michael, 53–54, 138,
    139, 269
Bloomberg News, 222, 293, 339
BlueCrest Capital Management,
    295–96
Boston, 127
Boundary Layer Wind Tunnel
    Laboratory (Canada), 109
Braun, Ayala, 56
Breen, Peg, 149
Brodsky, Mark, 290
Bromley, Keith, 111–15
Bronstein, Peter, 287–88
Brooklyn, first supertall in (Brooklyn
    Tower), 345–47, 349
Brown Harris Stevens, 87, 88–89
Buckworth, Louis, 237–38
Bueno, Edson de Godoy, 235
building trades unions, 216–19
Bulgari, 39–40
Burden, Amanda, 147, 190
Burj Khalifa (Dubai), 49, 109, 193

California
  income sources of wealthy residents
    in, 205, 253
  mansion listings, 263–64
California Public Employees'
    Retirement System (CalPERS),
    69–70

California State Teachers' Retirement System, 69–70
Calvary Baptist Church, 63–65
Campaign for One New York, 306
Campbell, Valerie, 175
Candela, Rosario, 106
Candler, Leighton, 99, 125
Candy, Christian, 238
Candy, Nick, 97
Canyon Capital Advisors, 326
"capital stack," 70–71
Carnegie Hall, 30
Carnegie Hall Tower, 24, 25
Carteret Savings Bank of New Jersey, 178–79
CEFC China Energy, 252
Central Park, shadows in
    from 432 Park Avenue, 144–45
    and MAS, 146
Central Park Tower
    "air rights" and cantilever design, 194–96
    amenities and furnishing, 299–300
    basic facts about, xxi, 155–56
    construction of, 270–71, 310, 317
    cost per square foot of, 271
    financing of, 210–11, 269–72, 295–96, 317
    height of, xxi, 189, 192–93
    hundredth birthday party of Iris Apfel at, 334–35
    location, **xxiii**
    marketing of, 296–99, 300
    profitability of, 340, 348
    projected sales at, 210
    purchase prices, 196, 298, 338
    residents, 336
    restaurant at, 299–300
    sales of units at, 297, 300–301
    triplex penthouse listed price (2022), 348
    220 Central Park South and, 194, 210, 211
    value of units sold (2022), 340
Champion Parking, 133–37
Château Louis XIV (France), 265
Chen, Guoqing, 93

Chen Feng, 93
Cher, 20
Chetrit, Joseph, 191, 254, 349
Chicago, 49, 239, 346
Children's Investment Fund, 80–81, 202–3
Chinese billionaires. *See also* specific individuals
    ability of, to make overseas investments, 267
    Citi Private Bank and, 79
    EB-5 visa program and, 270
    finances of, 223
    increase in, 337
    London real estate market and, 85
    as One57 purchasers, 93, 100–101
    real estate industry in New York and, 93, 100–101, 102
    Time Warner Center and, 102
Chou, Silas, 93
Chrysler Building, xxix, xxx, 41
CIM
    basic facts about, 68–69, 78, 79
    Children's Investment Fund and, 80–81
    Citi Private Bank and, 79
    Drake Hotel project and, 73–78
    on 432 Park Avenue's residential board, 321, 322
    432 Park Avenue's residents' lawsuit against, 322–26
    Harry Macklowe's lack of equity in residential portion432 Park Avenue and, 288–89
    profits from 432 Park Avenue, 349
Citadel, 240
Citi Private Bank (Citigroup Inc.), 79, 88
CitySpire, 24, 99
Clarett Group, 124, 129, 131–32, 133, 134, 202
Clark, Jim, 263
CMZ Ventures, 39–41, 43–46
Cohen, Arthur
    CMZ Ventures and, 39–41, 46
    Drake Hotel project and, 38
Cohen, Glori, 321

Cohen, Meir, 321
Cohen, Steve, 128
Coinbase, 336
Cole, Richard, 13–14
Coliseum, 28–29, 31
Collins, Connie, 125–26
Commercial Observer, 218, 219
"common equity," 71
condominiums
    art market and, 238
    Billionaires' Bunker, 239
    building of ultra-luxury outside of
        Billionaires' Row, 262–63
    construction issues and residential
        boards, 320–21
    cooperatives compared to, 19–20,
        251
    COVID-19 and, 313–17, 335,
        337–38
    decline in luxury market, 260–62,
        266–67
    early New York City, 18–19
    fair housing laws and, 205, 251
    57th Street and Seventh Avenue
        cluster, 24
    New York City taxation, 303
    profits and final sales of units,
        71, 73
    record prices for, 188–89
    record prices for New York
        (2011), 86
    regulation of, 91
    residents, appealed to, 20–21
    Russian billionaires as purchasers
        of, 89–91
    sales decline of (2016), 222
    sales of (2009), 52
    sales of (2018), 301
    sales of (2021), 338
    sales of (March—August 2020), 314
    "Tower of Power," 239
construction unions, 216–19
cooperatives
    air rights of, for One57, 62–63
    decline in prices (2015), 262
    Mott and, 21–22
    sales of (2009), 52

sales of (2018), 301
vetting of buyers, 19–20, 251
Cooper-Hohn, Jamie, 80
Corbett, Keith, 230
Corcoran Sunshine
    One57 and, 92, 94, 99
    111 West 57th Street and, 224, 236,
        292–93, 330–31
    220 Central Park South and, 207–8
Cosmopolitan, 122
COVID-19, 311–17, 335–37
Cowie, Colin, 299–300, 334–35
Creaturo, Barbara, 122
Cross & Cross, 30
Crowley, Joseph, 305
Crown Building, 191
cryptocurrency, 335–36, 343, 347
Cuomo, Andrew, 150–55, 268, 306,
        307, 311–12
Cuomo, Mario, 39
Curbed, 32, 143

Daily News, 150–51, 153, 154
Davidson, Justin, 143
DBOX, 111–15
de Blasio, Bill, 269, 304, 306, 307
Delevingne, Chloe, 237–38
Dell, Michael, xx, 99, 144, 242
Deripaska, Oleg, 46
DeRosa, Melissa, 153
design
    Art Students League headquarters,
        194
    Brooklyn's first supertall, 345–46,
        347
    buildings along Billionaires' Row
        (2008), 30–31
    Burj Khalifa, 193
    Carnegie Hall, 24, 30
    Central Park Tower, 194–95
    CitySpire, 24
    condominium cluster at 57th Street
        and Seventh Avenue, 24
    Crown Building, 191
    11 Madison Avenue, 78
    15 Central Park West, 142
    53 West 53rd Street, 190, 266

design (*cont'd*):
    432 Park Ave, xx, 104, 105–13
    Fuller Building, 92
    General Motors building, 3
    Harry Macklowe's interest in, 7
    Metropolitan Tower, 24, 25
    New York Coliseum, 28
    New York Telephone Company
        building, 162
    One57, 83, 142–43
    111 West 57th Street, xxi, 212–14,
        313
    Park Lane Hotel, 191
    Spelling Manor, 264
    Steinway Hall, 30, 173–74
    of supertalls and privacy, xiii–xiv
    as system of control, xiii
    3 Sutton Place, 296
    Tower Building, 47
    220 Central Park South, xxi,
        199–200, 261
    Zeckendorf building on East 60th
        Street, 190
Despont, Thierry, 200
Deutsche Bank
    Drake Hotel project and, 37,
        44–45
    Trump and, 278
developers. *See* real estate industry in
    New York
Diamond, Bob, 252
Diamond, Joel, 121–22, 123–24
Dias Griffin, Anne, 241
Diaz, Cameron, 166
Dilek, Emel, 125
Dime Savings Bank of Brooklyn,
    345–47
*Discipline and Punish: The Birth of the
    Prison* (Foucault), xiii
Doronin, Vladislav, 191
Douglas Elliman, 107, 234, 261
Drager, Laura, 285, 286, 287, 289
Drake Hotel project. *See also* 432 Park
    Avenue
    Children's Investment Fund and,
        80–81
    CIM and, 73–78

Citigroup Inc.'s private bank
    and, 79
CMZ Ventures and, 39–41, 43–46
Macklowes and, 13–14, 34, 35,
    37–38, 44–45
Dubai, 49, 346
Dyson, James, 266

East 60th Street between Park and
    Madison avenues, 190
EB-5 visa program, 89, 270
Ecclestone, Petra, 263, 264
Edward Durell Stone & Associates, 3
Ehrsam, Fred, 336
Eichner, Ian Bruce, 37, 314
80/20 program, 152
800 Park Avenue, 21–22
834 Fifth Avenue, 20
11 Madison Avenue, 78
Emaar Properties, 38
Emery Roth & Sons, 3, 101
Empire State Building, xxvii,
    xxviii–xxx, 48
Ethereum, 336
Extell Management and Investment
    Company
    basic facts about, 56
    Calvary Baptist Church and, 65
    Central Park Tower and, 271–72
    Andrew Cuomo and, 151–52, 153,
        154–55
    financial status of, 83, 335
    hundredth birthday of Iris Apfel,
        334–35
    One57 and, 100–101, 138–40, 142,
        150, 152–53
    Vornado and, 134, 136–37
    Zuckerman and, 154

façades
    Carnegie Hall, 24, 30
    53 West 53rd Street, 190
    One57, 83, 143
    111 West 57th Street, xxi, 212
    Steinway Hall, 30
fair housing laws, 205, 251
Fascitelli, Mike, 129

Fayed, Ali, 35, 75
Fegel, Gary, 290
Feldman, Ziel, 57, 62, 170
Fertitta, Frank, 266
Field, Nikki, 65, 101–3, 260
15 Central Park West
    Blackmon and, 88–89
    design, 142
    history of, 31–32
    marketing of, 94, 117
    projected sales of units at, 210
    purchase prices, 242, 252
    residents, 32, 86–87, 88–89, 90–91,
        209, 242
    residents moving to 220 Central
        Park South from, 208–9
    restaurant at, 31, 110
    Sukenik and, 130–31
53 West 53rd Street, 147–48, 190,
    266
financial crisis of 2008
    American housing market and, 52
    Barnett's plans for One57 and,
        82–83
    Extell and, 83
    Macklowe and, 3, 5
    traditional commercial banks and, 42
Financial District, high-rise condos
    in, 262
Finkelstein-LeBow, Jacqueline, 322
Firtash, Dmytro, 43–44, 45–46
Fiscal Policy Institute, 307
520 Park Avenue
    marketing of, 237
    residents and prices, 266
    sales of units at, 301
550 Madison Avenue, 191
Flaunt, 259
floor area ratios (FARs), 59, 60–61
Florida
    income sources of wealthy residents
        in, 205
    mansion listings, 240, 263
    Mink allegations against Stern and
        JDS in, 333
    supertalls in, 346
    ultra-wealthy in, 233, 315

Floyd, George, 314
Forbes, 89
Forrell & Thomas, 62
Fortress Investment Group, 343
Foster, Norman, 296
Foucault, Michel, xiii
421-A tax abatements, 150–55
432 Park Avenue. See also Drake
        Hotel project
    amenities and furnishings, 110
    basic facts about, xx
    competition with One57, 116,
        119
    construction defects at, 289–90,
        319–20, 323–24
    cost per square foot of, 201
    design, xx, 104, 105–13
    engineering challenges of, 107–9
    exodus of residents from, 326–27
    financing of, 288–89
    height of, 189, 194
    increase in cost of living at,
        324–25
    location of, **xxii**
    Harry Macklowe marriage to
        Landeau at, 283
    Harry Macklowe's lack of equity in
        residential portion, 288–89
    marketing of, 111–15, 116–20
    profitability of, 349
    purchase prices, 118, 119, 120, 252,
        321, 322
    residential board, 321–22
    residents, 118–20, 242–43, 321
    residents' lawsuit against CIM and
        Harry Macklowe, 322–26
    restaurant at, 110, 324–25, 327
    retail space at base of, 228
    sales of units at, 215, 260–61, 321
    shadows in Central Park from,
        144–45
    vacant floors, 148
    value of Macklowe apartments at,
        286–87
    Viñoly and privacy of residents,
        xiii–xiv
Frazier, Joe, 27

Frers, German, 226
Fries, Richard, 42–43
Fuller Building, 92

Galleria, 21
Gamma Real Estate, 296
Gates, Rick, 46
Geffen, David, 188
General Motors building, 3–4, 11
Giacometti, Alberto, 286, 341–43
Gigliotti, Michael, 203
Gilbert, Bradford Lee, 47
Gilder, Warren, 281
Gill, Gordon, 193, 195
Glasgall, Donald, 124
Glick, Deborah, 307
Global Inequality Lab, 337
"the Godfather of Bling," 34–36, 119, 346
Goldberger, Paul, 25–26
Goldfarb, Alex, 136, 206
Goldman Sachs Group, 190, 256, 266
Goldstein, Elizabeth, 148
Gong, Tim, 336
Goodman, Wendy, 115
Gough, Christabel, 176
Graves, Michael, 235
Grebin, Jason, 230
Greenland Group, 279
Griffin, Ken, xxi, 238–42, 302, 303, 315
Gross, Mich, 139
Grubb & Ellis, 40
Guardian, 85
Gwathmey, Charles, 4

Hackett, Veronica, 124, 128–29. See also 220 Central Park South
Haji-Ioannou, Polys, 290
Hakkasan, 186
Hardenbergh, Henry J., 194
Hard Rock Cafe, 26, 27
Harley-Davidson Cafe, 26
Harter, Ryan, 322
Hearst, estate of William Randolph, 263
Hefner, Hugh, 263

height
of Central Park Tower, xxi, 189, 192–93
of 432 Park Avenue, 189, 194
of One57, 189
of 111 West 57th Street, xxi, 194
of 220 Central Park South, xxi, 189
Heller, Woody
basic facts about, 66
CIM and, 68
Drake Hotel project and, 74, 75–77, 78
Harry Macklowe and, 66–68
Helmsley, Harry, 101
Helmsley, Leona, 101
Hergatt, Shaun, 110
Herjavec, Robert, 339
Herskovitz, Karen, 98
Herzog & de Meuron, 192
High Line, high-rise condos in, 262
high-rise buildings. See also individual structures
basic facts about, 47–49
financial structure of, 70–73
setback regulations, 59
Hilfiger, Dee Ocleppo, 315, 334
Hilfiger, Tommy, 315, 334
Hines, 147, 190, 266
Hirsh, Yael, 168
Hirtenstein, Michael, 97
HNA Group Co., 93, 339
Hoffmann, Josef, 105, 112
Hofstaedter, Viktoria, 114–15
Hohn, Christopher, 80
homelessness, 9, 29, 144, 304
"hope certificates," 75, 228, 294
"Horrifying Hellhole." See 432 Park Avenue
Hotel Macklowe, 10
Hoylman, Brad, 303, 307, 309
Hurricane Sandy, 138–40, 328

Il Palmetto (Palm Beach, Florida), 263
Ingrao, Anthony, 97, 98
Inovalis, 40–41

International Petroleum Investment Company (IPIC), 50, 51
Israeli bond market, 271–72
Izadpanah, Sheri, 253

Jacob & Co., 35, 346
Jacob K. Javits Convention Center, 28
Jacob the Jeweler, 34–36, 119, 346
Jahn, Helmut, 24
JDS, 161
 Bianco lawsuit and, 280
 construction accidents and, 329, 330
 Largo lawsuit and, 332
 Miami project, 333
 111 West 57th Street and, 293
 Parkside and, 330
Jeddah Tower (Saudi Arabia), 346
Jekyll & Hyde Club, 26
The Jewish Daily Forward, 34
Joel, Billy, 20
Jones, Mary Mason, 15–16
Joseph, Elliott, 163–64, 171
Joyce Manor, 62–63
J.P. Morgan, 295
JSF Capital, 322
Julis, Joleen, 118
Julis, Mitch, 118, 326–27
Juracich, David "Wavey Dave"
 basic facts about, 159–61
 lawsuit against, for method of financing 111 West 57th Street, 331
 Maloney and, 170–71
 Stern and, 161–66, 281
Juul-Hansen, Thomas, 82–83, 84

Karadus, Jason, 296
Keinan, Shahar, 271
Keller, Thomas, 31
Kern, Deborah, 207
Khashoggi, Adnan, 17–18
Kim, John, 261
Kim, Roy, 83, 84
Kimmelman, Michael, 143, 193
Kin-man, Yeung, 266
Klar, Steven, 99
Klarfeld, Neil, 129

Klarman, Seth, 273–76
Korangy, Amir, 168–69, 309
Korein, Sarah (née Rabinowitz), 123
Kreuther, Gabriel, 300
Krutoy, Igor, 90
Kuala Lumpur, 49
Kuba, Shaul. *See also* CIM
 basic facts about, 68, 69
 Macklowes and Drake project, 70, 73, 76, 77

LaBarbera, Gary, 217–19, 330
Lampley, Brooke, 341
Landeau, Patricia, 227–28, 282–84, 285, 313
Largo Investments, 332
Lasry, Marc, 296
LeBow, Bennett, 322
Lechtinger, Jim, 239
Led Zeppelin, 13–14
Lee's art Shop, 31
Lendlease, 137, 139
Le Nez (*The Nose,* by Giacometti), 286, 341–43
Lentelli, Leo, 30
Levy, Leon, 28
Levy, Lionel, 28
Lewis, Brent, 64–65
LeWitt, Sol, 112
"the Liar's Ball," 306–7
Liebman, Pam, 99, 207, 222, 241–42, 292–93
limited liability companies (LLCs), 181, 249–50, 260
Litwin, Leonard, 37–38
Lo, Karen, 209
"loan-to-own," 42
Lombardi, Thomas, 123
London real estate market, 85
Lopez, Jennifer, 119
Lorber, Howard M., 119–20, 192, 234, 241–42, 321
Los Angeles Times, 69, 181
Low, Jho
 basic facts about, 192
 Park Lane Hotel and, 191–92, 254, 255–56, 258

Lowy, David, 253
Lowy, Frank, 260

Mack, Kelly Kennedy, 92, 155, 311, 337
Macklowe, Billy. *See also* Drake Hotel project
  ascension as chairman of Macklowe Properties, 12
  birth of, 7
  characteristics of, 11
  departure from Macklowe Properties and founding of William Macklowe Company by, 78, 230
  description of Harry as peak bagger, 12–13
  Harry's Blackstone deal and, 5
  Harry's lawsuit against, 230–31
  Macklowe Properties's 57th Street assemblage and, 35
  negotiations with CIM, 73–78
  relationship with Harry, 11, 74, 78, 285
  transformation of Macklowe Properties by, 10–11
Macklowe, Charlotte, 7
Macklowe, Elizabeth, 7
Macklowe, Harry
  art investments, 7, 8–9, 228, 286, 341–43
  basic facts about, xviii, xxvii–xxix, 4, 6–7
  as buyer of two units at 432 Park Avenue, 120
  characteristics, 284
  COVID-19 and, 312–13
  Empire State Building and, xxvii, xxix, xxx
  financial crisis (2008)and, 3, 5
  image of, 9
  Landeau and, 227–28, 282–84, 285
  opinion of Sarina Abramovich, 325
  relationship with Billy, 11, 74, 78, 285

separation and divorce from Linda, 227–30, 284–89, 341–43
  Trump and, 312–13
  World Superyacht Awards, 226–27
Macklowe, Harry in real estate. *See also* 432 Park Avenue
  Billy's description of, 12–13
  characteristics of, 12–13, 40, 74, 77, 105, 107, 116–18
    instinctive decision making of, 10
  demolition of buildings without permits by, 9
  Drake Hotel project and, 13–14, 34, 35, 37–38, 39, 40, 44–45
  early prestigious projects, 9–10
  early ventures, 8
  432 Park Avenue's residents' lawsuit against, 322–26
  General Motors building and, 3–4
  Heller and, 66–68
  lawsuit against Billy, 230–31
  as marketer, 10
  negotiations with CIM, 73–78
  on One57, 116
  One Wall Street condominium conversion, 349
  Park Lane Hotel investment, 192
  profitability of 432 Park Avenue, 349
  purchase of office buildings from Blackstone by, 5, 11–12
  Vornado and, 127
Macklowe, Linda
  art investments, 7, 8–9, 228, 286, 341–43
  art training of, 9
  Drake Hotel project and, 45
  Harry's Blackstone deal and, 5, 12
  marriage of, 7
  separation and divorce from Harry, 227–30, 284–89, 341–43
  World Superyacht Awards, 226–27
Macklowe, Lloyd, xxvii
Macklowe Management, 230–31

Macklowe Properties. *See also* Drake Hotel project; Macklowe, Harry, in real estate
  Billy's ascension as chairman of, 12
  Billy's departure from, and founding of William Macklowe Company, 78, 230
  Billy's transformation of, 10–11
  57th Streeet assemblage, 35
  transformed by Billy, 10–11
Madison Realty Capital, 294–95, 330
Makowsky, Bruce, 264
Maloney, Kevin. *See also* 111 West 57th Street
  Barnett and, 169
  basic facts about, 169–70
  Bianco's lawsuit against, 223–25, 275, 278–80, 332, 349, 350
  New York Telephone building, 163–64
  111 West 57th Street characterized as failure by, 350
  Perlmutter and, 177
  regrets about building 111 West 57th Street, 333
  sales at 111 West 57th Street and, 222
  Saudi billionaires and, 183–87
  Spruce's "strict foreclosure" and, 277–78
  Steinway Hall and, 172
  Stern and, 170–72, 220–21
  Stern-union fight, 216, 219
  supertall project in Miami, 349
  Walker Tower and, 170
Manafort, Paul, 38, 39–41, 43–46
Manhattan Special Midtown District, 145
Mansion Tax, 269, 309
Mansour Bin Zayed al Nahyan, 50
Marble Row, 15–16
Marcos, Ferdinand, 191
Marcos, Imelda, 191
Marcus, Silvian, 109
Marks, Howard, 188
Marshall, Cathy, 122, 132, 133
Mayflower Hotel, 130–31

McCourt, Jamie, 118–19
Mechanic, Jonathan, 11
Meister, Stephen, 278–79
Mendelsohn, Nicole, 336
Mercier, Laura, 166
Mermel, Myers, xiv, 73
Mermelstein, Edward, 89, 90, 267, 297
Meta, 336
Metropolitan Life Insurance Company Tower, 9, 10, 24–25, 48
Meyer, Jane, 24
"mezzanine financing," 72
Michael Feinstein, 334
Michaels, Howard, 279
Middle East, supertalls in, 48–49
Miller, Jonathan
  anti-billionaire sentiment, 304
  "aspirational pricing," 99
  building of ultra-luxury condominiums outside of Billionaires' Row, 262–63
  developers' mentality, 348
  dilapidated condition of New York Coliseum, 29
  financing of One57 (2009), 52
  Macklowe divorce appraisal by, 286
  market slowdown, 262
  new market category of Billionaires' Row, 189, 190
  penthouse owned by Adnan Khashoggi and, 17–18
  prices and "greater fools' theory," 267
  risk-awareness of post 2008 lenders, 43
Mills, Donna, 136
Mindel, Lee, 209
Mink Development, 333
Moelis, Ken, 266
Mogilevich, Semion Yudkovich, 45
Molyneux, Juan Pablo, 25
Mosdot Shuva Israel, 34
Moses, Robert, 28
Motown Cafe, 26, 27
Mott, Charles Stewart, 21
Mott, Stewart R., 21–23

Mubadala (Abu Dhabi sovereign wealth fund), 258
Mueller, Robert, 46
Muller, Evelyn, 55, 56
Municipal Arts Society (MAS), 146, 148
Muschamp, Herbert, 26–27

Naftali, Miki, 316–17
Nahmad, Hillel "Helly," 119
Newman, Margaret, 149
New Valley, 192
New York (magazine), 291
New York Coliseum, 28–29, 31
New Yorker, 24
"New York is dead" narrative, 316
The New York Observer, 91
New York Post, 125, 131, 253, 283, 284, 285
New York Telephone Company building, 162, 163–65
The New York Times, 10, 16, 17, 22, 23, 25–26, 27–28, 31, 38, 44, 58, 97, 123, 139, 144, 147–48, 198, 205, 237, 250, 252, 283, 303, 309, 316, 320
New York Times tower, 57
New York World Building, 48
NFT art pieces, 335–36, 343
Niami, Nile, 264
Nippon Club, 53
NoMad, high-rise condos in, 262
Nordstrom, 14, 75, 155, 270, 279
Nouvel, Jean, 147, 190, 266
NYC Crane Hoist & Rigging, 329

Observer, 39
Ocasio-Cortez, Alexandria, 305–6
Och, Dan, 208, 340
Olayan America, 254
Olshan Realty, 338
Olympic Tower, 18–19, 20–21
Onassis, Aristotle, 18, 20
Onassis, Jacqueline Kennedy, 146
1MDB (Malaysia's sovereign wealth fund), 255
1 Park Lane. See Park Lane Hotel

1 World Trade Center, 193
One57
  amenities and furnishings, 82–83, 84, 92, 142
  assemblage process for, 61–65
  basic facts about, xx
  as brand, 93
  Chinese billionaires and, 93, 100–101
  competition with 432 Park Avenue, 116, 119
  construction defects at, 290
  cost per square foot of, 134, 209, 271
  design, 83, 142–43
  financing of, 51–53, 54, 256
  as first supertall, xi
  foreclosures of units at, 248–49, 251, 253–54
  421-A tax abatement and, 150–55
  height of, 189
  Hurricane Sandy crane incident, 138–40, 328
  location, **xxiii**
  marketing of, 91–92, 94–98, 100–101, 142, 292
  materials for, 84
  nickname of, xii
  purchase prices, 91, 92, 93, 98, 99, 235, 242, 248, 253, 260
  resales' prices, 338–39
  residents, xx, 53, 84, 92–93, 99, 144, 248, 315–16
  sale of rental units, 260
  sales of units after four years, 210
  sales slowdown, 215
  Saudis and, xii
  Winter Garden unit, 97–98
102 Prince Street, 233
111 West 57th Street. See also Steinway Hall
  amenities and furnishings, 214
  basic facts about, xxi
  construction mishaps, 328–29
  Corcoran Sunshine agreement, 236
  cost of first three years of project, 294

cost per square foot, 215
design, 212–14, 313
dimensions, 177
financing of, 179–82, 183, 184–87, 215, 223–25, 273–77, 294, 295, 330
height of, xxi, 194
Landmarks Preservation Commission and, 175–77
lawsuits arising from, 223–25, 275, 278–80, 331–32, 349, 350
location, **xxiii**
marketing of, 292
number of units, 214
pricing of units, 224
purchase prices, 336
reputation of, 277
residents, 336
sales of units at, 293, 330–31, 336, 350
sales on hold, 221–23
Spruce's "strict foreclosure," 277–78
use of nonunion construction workers, 217–19, 329–30
vacant floors, 213
as "win" for Stern, 350
Witkoff and, 330
One Beacon Court, 94, 128
One Hyde Park (London), 85
One Wall Street, condo conversion at, 349
One World Trade Center, 108
"open shop" construction, 216
Orenstein, Frank, 39–40
Osborne (apartment tower), 30–31
Ouroussoff, Nicolai, 147–48
"Outlaw Instagrammers," xii
Oxman, Neri, 315–16

"palace corners," 16–17
panopticons, design of, xiii
Park Imperial, 233
Park Lane Hotel, 191–92, 254, 255–56, 258, 330
Park Savoy Hotel as shelter, 304
Parkside Construction, 329–30
Pasquarelli, Gregg, 176, 212

Patel, Amit, 326
Patel, Meeta, 326, 327
the Peak, Hong Kong, 265–66
Pecunies, Ronald, 125
Pelli, César, 24
Pericles, 46
Perlmutter, Margery, 176–77
Petit, Philippe, 113–14
Petronas Towers (Kuala Lumpur), 49
Pfizer, 337
Piano, Renzo, 104–5
pied-à-terre tax, 307–9
Piketty, Thomas, 337
Pinto, Yoshiyahu, 33–34, 36
Planet Hollywood, 26
Platt, Michael, 296
Playboy Mansion, 263
Plaza, 90, 238, 286
Pontiac Land Group, 190, 266
Portale, Alfred, 300
Portzamparc, Christian de, xx, 83, 143
Posen, Zac, 198
"preferred equity," 72
Princess Tower (Dubai), 49
privacy, design of supertalls and, xiii–xiv
"the promote," 73, 288–89
Property Markets Group (PMG), 163–66, 280. *See also* Maloney, Kevin
Prudential, 129
Pugliese, Francesco, 330
Pugliese, Salvatore, 330
Putin, Vladimir, 89
Putman, Andrée, 25
"put" options, 274

Ratner, Bruce, 57
The Real Deal, 167, 172, 181, 208, 220, 251, 254, 271, 287–88, 309
real estate industry in New York
air rights and, 59–60, 62–65, 148
"aspirational pricing," 99–100
aspirational pricing phenomenon spread across US, 263–66

real estate industry in New York
(cont'd):
  assemblage process, 35, 58–59, 60,
    61–62, 75
  average price of land south of 96th
    Street, 263
  under Bloomberg, 53–54
  Brooklyn's first supertall, 345–47
  building code, 108
  building of ultra-luxury
    condominiums outside of
    Billionaires' Row, 262–63, 349
  characteristics of, xv–xvi
  Chinese billionaires and, 93,
    100–101, 102
  COVID-19 and, 312, 313–17, 335,
    337–38
  days to sell unit, 211
  decline in luxury market, 260–62,
    266–67, 301
  Democratic lawmakers and control
    of state government and, 305–9
  developers' mentality, xv–xvi, 348
  dominant families in, 57–58
  EB-5 visa program and, 89, 270
  80/20 program, 152
  financial structure of skyscrapers,
    70–73
  financing of, and money
    laundering, 45–46, 248–49,
    256–57
  financing of commercial, 41–43
  Floyd murder and, 314
  421-A tax abatements and, 150–55
  homeless and, 9, 29, 144, 304
  identification of true buyers of
    luxury units, 252–53
  income sources of wealthy residents,
    205, 253
  increase in average price per square
    foot for luxury, 263
  justification for ultra-high prices,
    264–65
  Landmarks Preservation
    Commission and, 175–77,
    194–96, 345–46
  LLCs as purchasers of, 249–50

  Mansion tax, 269, 309
  market conditions (2009), 52
  New York City taxation, 303
  "opportunity funds," 70
  panel on Asian investment in, 201
  pied-à-terre tax, 307–9
  presidential elections and, 314–15
  public input and, 145, 146–47
  record price for condominium
    (2011), 86
  record prices for sales of luxury
    units, 188–89
  record sales of condominiums
    (2021), 338
  regulation of, 41–42, 59–60, 145
  rent-controlled/stabilized
    apartments, 122–23, 125, 129,
    130
  resale brokers compared to onsite
    brokers, 235–37
  sales of luxury units down, 222
  SALT (state and local tax)
    deduction, 268
  skyscraper construction boom
    pinnacle, xxix
  "sponsors" in, 72–73
  unoccupied, owned luxury units,
    250
  US tax code overhaul and,
    267–68
Reichl, Ruth, 115
Related Companies, 31, 205
resale brokers, 235–37, 259
residents
  of Central Park Tower, 336
  Chinese billionaires, 93, 100–101,
    102
  cooperative boards and, 19–20, 21
  exodus of, from 432 Park Avenue,
    326–27
  failure to occupy units on
    Billionaires' Row, 250
  15 Central Park West, 32, 86–87,
    88–89, 90–91, 209, 242
  520 Park Avenue, 266
  432 Park Avenue, 118–20, 242–43,
    321, 326–27

history and reputation of 57th
  Street and, 26–29
One57, xx, 53, 84, 92–93, 99, 144,
  248, 315–16
111 West 57th Street, 336
Osborne, 31
Russian billionaires, 86–87, 88–91,
  204–5
Saudi billionaires, xii, 183, 184–87
Time Warner Center, 90, 102, 205
of Trump Tower, 23–24
220 Central Park South, 199,
  203–6, 208–9, 302
types of, appealed to by
  condominiums, 20–21
Walker Tower, 165–66, 184–86,
  257
Ressler, Debra, 68
Ressler, Richard
  basic facts about, 68–69
  Drake project, 74
  432 Park Avenue lawsuit and, 323
  Viñoly and, 104
Ressler, Tony, 68
Richards, Keith, 262
Richardson-Ruhan, Tania, 281
Riverside Boulevard building and
  Barnett, 145
River Tower, 67
Rizzoli bookstore, 30
Rockefeller, David, 343
Rockefeller, Peggy, 343
Rodriguez, Alex, 119
Rosenblatt, Gary (Champion
  Parking), 133–37
Rosenblatt, Kenneth (Champion
  Parking), 133–37
Rosenthal, Linda B., 150
Ross, Leonard, 263
Ross, Wilbur, 262
Roth, Daryl, 128
Roth, Jordan, 128
Roth, Steve. See also 220 Central
  Park South; Vornado Realty
  Trust
  Barnett and, 133–37, 201, 209, 210
  basic facts about, xix

characteristics of, 126–28, 199, 203
fair housing laws and, 205, 251
Harry Macklowe and, 127
office portfolio, 348
sales of units and, 203–6, 208, 261
success of 220 Central Park South,
  348
Rothstein, Stuart, 350
Rowland, Spotty, 249
Rozenholc, David "the barracuda,"
  129–33, 134–35
Rubenstein, David, 303
Ruddy, Cetra, 165
Rudin Center for Transportation
  Policy and Management, 58
Ruhan, Andy
  basic facts about, 180–81
  divorce, 280–81
  Klarman offer and, 275
  Saudi billionaires and, 187
  Steinway Hall and, 181
Russian billionaires
  attraction of Billionaires' Row to,
    89–90
  EB-5 visa program and, 89
  15 Central Park West, 86–87,
    88–89, 90–91
  Putin and, 89
  Time Warner Center and, 90, 205
  220 Central Park South and, 204–5
  US sanctions and, 267
Russian Tea Room, 25, 30
Ryan, Paul, 268
Rybolovlev, Dmitry, 86–87, 88–89,
  90–91
Rybolovlev, Ekaterina, 87
Rybolovleva, Elena, 90

S. Muller & Sons, 55–56
Sail Harbor Capital, 317
SALT (state and local tax) deduction,
  268
Sanders, Bernie, 303
Schleider, Steven, 286
Schuman, Lichtenstein, Claman &
  Efron (SLCE), 25
Schumer, Chuck, 306

Schwab, Charles R., 315
Sears Tower (Chicago), 49
Seinfeld, Jerry, 316–17
"senior loans," 72
Serezhin, Maxim, 332
Serhant, Ryan, 93, 259, 326, 348
Sertic, Emily, 94–95, 141, 142–43
740 Park Avenue, 17
Severance, H. Craig, xxix, xxx
Shanghai Chengtou, 279
Shanghai Tower, 279
Shatz, Brian, 294
Shemesh, Avi, 68, 69
Sherry Netherland, 119
Shimotake, Jean E., 125
Shleifer, Scott, 315
SHoP Architects, xxi
Shulman, Sophie, 211
Silver, Sheldon, 306
Silverstein, Larry, 127
Simpson, Nicole Brown, 27
Simpson, O.J., 27
Sinatra, Nancy, 27
Singer Building, 48
single-room-occupancy properties
    (SROs), 9
Sitt, Joe, 118, 322
Skelos, Dean, 306
skyscrapers. See also supertalls;
        individual structures
    basic facts about, 47–49
    construction boom pinnacle, xxix
    financial structure of, 70–73
    setback regulations, 59
SL Green, 58
Slinin, Eduard, 322
Smith, Adrian, 193
SMI USA, 270, 271, 279, 296
Sofield, William, 214, 313
Sokoloff, Jonathan, 118
Solomon, Mary, 262
Solow Building, 30
Sony Building, 191, 254
Sotheby, 341, 342–43
Specter, David Kenneth, 22
Spelling Manor, 263, 264
Spitzer, Eliot, 38

Spruce Capital Partners, 277–78, 279,
    280
St. John, Warren, 144–45, 149–50
Stacom, Darcy, 3, 6, 175
Starwood Capital Group, 164–65,
    172. See also Walker Tower
steel frame construction, 47
Stein, Joshua, 42–43
Steinberg, Leonard, 234
Steinway Hall. See also 111 West 57th
    Street
    basic facts about, 173–74, 175
    Becker and, 181
    Bianco (AmBase) and, 179
    design, 30, 173–74
    Maloney and, 172
    Ruhan and, 181
    small lot next to, 172–73
    Stern and, 172–73, 175
Steinweg, Heinrich Engelhard, 173
Stern, Michael Zev. See also 111 West
    57th Street
    Alexander brothers and, 233
    basic facts about, xix, 161,
        167–69
    Bianco's lawsuit against, 223–25,
        275, 278–79, 332, 349–50
    Brooklyn's first supertall, 345–47,
        349
    building trades unions and, 216,
        218–19
    Corcoran Sunshine and, 292–93
    COVID-19 and, 313
    Juracich and, 161–66, 281
    lawsuits against
        for method of financing 111
            West 57th Street, 331–32
        relating to Park Slope
            condominium, 332–33
    Maloney and, 164, 170–72,
        220–21
    Mink allegations against, 333
    Spruce's "strict foreclosure" and,
        277–78
    Steinway Hall and, 172–73, 175
    as on Titanic, 295
    Witkoff and, 330

Stern, Robert A. M.
    classic design of 220 Central Park
        South, xxi
    53 West 53rd Street, 190
    550 Madison Avenue, 191
    220 Central Park South, 199
    Weill and, 87
Stern, Sandra Feagan, 87–88
Sternlicht, Barry, 172
Sting, 209
Stroll, Lawrence, 93
Studley, Julian, 8, 66
Styler, Trudie, 209
Sugarman, Jay, 74
Sugimoto, Hiroshi, 118, 200
Sukenik, Herb, 130
Sun, Justin, 343
Sunshine, Louise, 208, 238
supertalls
    "air rights" for, 148
    in Asia and Middle East, 48–49
    Brooklyn's first, 345–47
    building of ultra-luxury outside of
        Billionaires' Row, 262
    first, xi
    forum panel about issues
        surrounding, 149–50
    number of (2010-2015), 189
    planned beyond New York metro
        area, 346, 349
    privacy and design of, xiii–xiv
    public input and, 145, 146–47
    scaling of, xii
    vacant rate of, xiv
    wind and base-to-height ratios of,
        107–9, 213
"supervisory goodwill," 178–79
Swiatycki, Chaim, 55
Swiatycki, Gershon. See Barnett, Gary

Taipei 101 (Taiwan), 49
Talos Capital, 81
Tasameem, 50, 54
tax code overhaul, 267–68
3 Sutton Place, 296
Tiffany & Co., 30
Times (London), 181

Times Union, 153
Time Warner Center
    basic facts about, 31
    Chinese billionaires and, 102
    Low unit seized by government,
        254
    marketing of units at, 94
    Russian billionaires and, 90, 205
Tonacchio, Domenick, 333
Tourondel, Laurent, 300
Tower Building, 47
"Tower of Power," 239
"Towers of Secrecy" (The New York
        Times), 205
"Towers of Secrecy" investigation, 252
transfer tax, 269, 309
Tron, 343
Trump, Donald
    Barnett and, 57
    design of One57, 143
    Deutsche Bank and, 37
    General Motors building and, 4
    Harry Macklowe and, 312–13
    Meister and, 278
    presidential election (2020), 315,
        337
    Roth and, 126–27
    Shleifer and, 315
    Trump Tower, 23–24
    uncertainty of foreign buyers and,
        267
Trump, Ivanka, 27
Trump International Hotel and
        Tower, 94
Trump Soho, 78
Trump Tower, 23–24
Tsai, Joseph, 340
Tubb, Dan, 94, 95, 96, 115–16
Turnbull & Asser, 35, 75
Turrell, James, 113
Tuthill, William Burnet, 30
217 West 57th Street, 133
220 Central Park South
    after death of Korein, 123–24
    amenities and furnishings, 198–99,
        200–201
    Barnett and, 133–37

220 Central Park South (cont'd):
  basic facts about, xxi
  Central Park Tower and, 194, 210,
    211
  cost per square foot of, 201, 209–10
  design, 199–200, 261
  financing of, 202
  height of, xxi, 189
  location, **xxiii**
  marketing of, 203–8, 292
  purchase prices, 242, 261, 302
  as rent-controlled/stabilized
    building, 121–22
  resales' prices, 339–40
  residents, 199, 203–6, 208–9, 302
  restaurant at, 200
  sale of original building, 124–26,
    129, 131–33
  sales of units at, 203–6, 208, 210,
    261, 301, 318, 348
  "villa" component, 209
Two Guys (department store chain),
  126
Tymoshenko, Yulia, 45

Uncle Sam Umbrellas and Cane, 62
Unfurled (Macklowe yacht), 226–27
unions, 216–19
United Arab Emirates, 50
United States
  California, 205, 253, 263–64
  EB-5 visa program, 89, 270
  Florida, 205, 233, 240, 263, 315,
    333, 346
  sanctions and Russian billionaires,
    267
  spread of aspirational pricing
    phenomenon across, 263–66
  tax code overhaul, 267–68
Upper West Side, high-rise condos
  in, 262
US Crane & Rigging, 329

Vaccaro, Jon, 14
Valdés, Manolo, 200
Van Alen, William, xxix–xxx
Vance, Cyrus R., Jr., 329–30

Van Cleef & Arpels, 30
Vanderbilt, Alfred Gwynne, 16
Vanderbilt, Cornelius, II, 16
Vanity Fair, 85
Vavilov, Andrei, 90
Velasco, Julian, 118
Verizon, 162, 163–65
Vida, Juan Beckmann, 289–90
Villalobos, Alfred J. R., 69–70
Vinder, Ron, 257
Viñoly, Rafael
  basic facts about, 105, 107
  425 Park's privacy and, xiii–xiv
  432 Park Avenue design, xx, 104,
    105–9
  Richard Ressler and, 104
Viola, Vin, 188
Vongerichten, Jean-Georges, 31, 201
Vornado Realty Trust. *See also* Roth,
    Steve
  basic facts about, 124, 126, 127–29,
    203
  220 Central Park South's art, 200
  220 Central Park South's marketing,
    206, 261
  220 Central Park South's original
    tenants, 131–32
  220 Central Park South's parking
    garage, 133–37
  value of, 58, 202, 210, 318, 348

Wagner, Robert F., 28
Walker, Ralph, 162
Walker Tower
  financing of, 220–21
  Maloney and, 170
  New York Telephone Company
    building, 162, 163–65
  price per square foot, 165
  residents, 165–66, 184–86, 257
Wallgren, Richard, 115–16, 117
The Wall Street Journal, 11, 12, 54, 69,
    91, 153, 189, 252, 257, 301,
    314, 325, 339
Wang Jian, 339
Warren & Wetmore, 30, 173–74, 191
"waterfalls," 72

Weill, Sanford I., 87–88
Wharton, Edith, 15, 16
Whitman, Tyler, 254
Willis, Bruce, 262
Willkie, Hall, 88–89
Winklevoss twins, 336
Witkoff, Steve
    111 West 57th Street and, 330
    Park Lane Hotel and, 191–92, 254,
        255–56
Wolf, Mel, 8
Wood, Gavin, 336
Woodbrey, Jeannie, 94, 237
Woolworth Building, 48
World Superyacht Awards, 226–27
Wright, Frank Lloyd, 28
Wynn, Steve, 38, 95, 188

Yardeni, Ofer, 196, 209
Ye Jianming, 252

Yota, 182
Young, Greg, 260

Zackson, Brad, 38–41, 43–46
Zackson, Stephen, 39
Zeckendorf, Arthur. See also 15
        Central Park West
    building at East 60th Street between
        Park and Madison, 190
    520 Park Avenue and, 237, 266,
        301
Zeckendorf, William. See also 15
        Central Park West
    building at East 60th Street between
        Park and Madison, 190
    520 Park Avenue and, 237, 266,
        301
Zegen, Josh, 294
Zell, Sam, 127
Zuckerman, Mort, 11, 153–54

ABOUT THE AUTHOR

KATHERINE CLARKE is a reporter at *The Wall Street Journal,* where she covers the high-end real estate market across the United States. Previously, she wrote for the New York *Daily News* and *The Real Deal.* A native of Northern Ireland, she studied at Trinity College Dublin and at the Columbia University Graduate School of Journalism.

TWITTER: @KATHYCLARKENYC

ABOUT THE TYPE

This book was set in Bembo, a typeface based on an old-style
Roman face that was used for Cardinal Pietro Bembo's tract *De
Aetna* in 1495. Bembo was cut by Francesco Griffo (1450–1518)
in the early sixteenth century for Italian Renaissance printer and
publisher Aldus Manutius (1449–1515). The Lanston Monotype
Company of Philadelphia brought the well-proportioned letter-
forms of Bembo to the United States in the 1930s.